Ian Williams was foreign corresponde  in Russia (1992–1995) and then Asia NBC News as Asia Correspondent (2C in Bangkok and Beijing. As well as rep 25 years, he has also covered conflicts and Ukraine. He won an Emmy and BAFTA awards for his discovery and reporting on the Serb detention camps during the war in Bosnia. He has a keen interest in the darker corners of the online world, more recently studying cyber security at Royal Holloway, University of London and King's College, London. He has written two novels, the cyber thrillers *Beijing Smog* and *Zero Days*.

EVERY BREATH YOU TAKE

CHINA'S NEW TYRANNY

IAN WILLIAMS

BIRLINN

First published in 2021 by
Birlinn Limited
West Newington House
10 Newington Road
Edinburgh
EH9 1QS

www.birlinn.co.uk

ISBN: 978 1 78027 711 0

British Library Cataloguing-in-Publication Data
A catalogue record for this book is available from the British Library

Typeset by Initial Typesetting Services, Edinburgh

Printed and bound by Bell & Bain Ltd, Glasgow

Contents

Acknowledgements

This book is the culmination of many years' travelling and reporting from China, and I am very grateful to friends, colleagues and contacts for their help and insights along the way. They are too numerous to name individually, and many – especially those still working or living in the People's Republic – prefer anonymity. It is safer that way. Xi Jinping's China is an increasingly dangerous place for those who express critical opinions. This book is dedicated to those who still try.

I am indebted to the Information Security Group at Royal Holloway, University of London and the Department of War Studies at King's College, London, where my studies after returning to the UK enabled me to better understand the surveillance technologies that sustain Xi's rule. I am also grateful to the British diplomat I met on one of my first visits to Beijing. 'Anybody who claims to understand China is misinformed,' he gruffly announced between large gulps of beer. That spurred me on. Yes, China is complex, but understanding the reality of Xi's China and the threat it poses is more important than ever.

Thanks are also due to Hugh Andrew of Birlinn, who immediately recognised the importance of this book; to my editor, Andrew Simmons, for his deft touch and expertise; and to my agent, Andrew Lownie, for his enthusiasm and encouragement throughout. Lastly, I am grateful for the support of my family, and their no-nonsense feedback.

Ian Williams
March 2021

Introduction:
'Love the Party, Protect the Party'

When a novel coronavirus first emerged in the Chinese city of Wuhan in December 2019, the Communist Party covered up the outbreak and persecuted those who sought to tell the truth. Not until 20 January 2020 did officials admit publicly what doctors had suspected for weeks – that Covid-19 was spreading from person to person. Three days after that admission, the authorities quarantined Wuhan, sealing off and shutting down the city. But even then, they continued to drag their feet on sharing crucial information with the international community; it was not until mid-February that a full World Health Organization delegation with international experts was allowed to visit Wuhan. The delays and a seemingly wilful lack of transparency cost the world time, and countless lives.

China's initial response was depressingly familiar; what followed was less so. As the lockdown spread to other Chinese cities and regions, the Communist Party put on a chilling demonstration of a new sort of power. It deployed the full force of a surveillance state that Xi Jinping has been constructing since he became Party leader in 2012, tapping into a trove of data on the movements and behaviour of China's 1.4 billion people – all complemented by a casual brutality towards those who resisted quarantine after being flagged by the Party's hungry algorithms.

The surveillance tools ranged from a vast network of facial recognition and thermal imaging cameras calibrated for face coverings, to smartphone tracking, as well as fine-grained analyses of social media behaviour, and the monitoring of social interactions. Freedom of movement was determined by a colour-coded smartphone app – the 'traffic light' app, as it became known. The program crunched the data and awarded its user a red, amber or green code according to its determination of infection risk. If you were green you could move around; red meant immediate quarantine. The code had to be presented at checkpoints that blanketed the country – even in taxis, and at the entrances to shops and apartment blocks – where automated readers checked the code and sucked data from the smartphone. Drones swooped down on those not wearing masks or who lingered for too long outside, ordering them to obey the rules. Covid-19 gave this Orwellian system its day in the sun; with more than 500 million people in China under travel restrictions by mid-February, it could be field-tested on a massive scale – and all in the name of tackling a health emergency.

By mid-March, the Party claimed to have largely brought the virus under control, though by then it was rapidly spreading internationally. The early weeks of the outbreak in China had seen a rare outbreak of open criticism on social media and the emergence of a brave band of citizen journalists, determined to discover what was really happening. But now the Party moved to silence its critics, rounding up and jailing the more outspoken, stepping up censorship and closing social-media accounts. Party propaganda outlets proclaimed Xi Jinping the hero of the hour.

Anybody who thought China would emerge from the pandemic with humility was sorely disappointed. With Western democracies distracted and stumbling in their response to the virus, the Party went on the offensive, claiming its resolute action had bought the world time. It used a multitude of fake Twitter and Facebook accounts to spread disinformation worldwide about the origin of the virus and to highlight the missteps of others – actual and invented. For a regime that bans most Western social media in its own country, the Party and associated organisations have become prolific users to spread disinformation internationally.

It threatened and insulted countries which called for an independent international investigation into the origins of the coronavirus. Australia, which led those calls, was hit by an economic boycott and sweeping cyberattacks. Personal protective equipment, of which there was a dire shortage worldwide, was leveraged as a propaganda tool. China is the world's biggest producer, and shipments were accompanied by demands for public displays of gratitude from desperate recipients, usually in front of the assembled cameras of Chinese state media.

Beijing stepped up its belligerence in other ways – further cracking down on Hong Kong's democracy movement and imposing a draconian national security law on the territory. This not only rips up the 'one country two systems' formula of semi-autonomy under which the territory has been governed since returning to Chinese rule in 1997, but is a clear breach of the Sino-British Joint Declaration, a legally binding international treaty. China also staged aggressive military manoeuvres around disputed islands in the South China Sea, intensified its sabre rattling towards Taiwan and scuffled with India along a disputed Himalayan border.

This accelerated a reassessment by Western democracies of their relationship with Beijing – and with it a growing, if belated, recognition that Xi Jinping could not be trusted. The United States, already taking a harder line before the coronavirus pandemic, stepped up sanctions amid talk of a new Cold War. Washington's rhetoric was no doubt turbo-charged by President Donald Trump's calculation that bashing China would help his faltering campaign for re-election. Whatever his motives, a tough new realism is spreading. China scepticism is a bipartisan sentiment in America.

Dominic Raab, the British foreign secretary, was articulating a commonly held feeling among US allies when he told a Downing Street press conference at the height of the pandemic, 'There is no doubt we can't have business as usual after this crisis.'[1] Within a few short weeks Britain had excluded Huawei, the Chinese telecoms giant, from its 5G networks on national security grounds and was trading barbs with Beijing over Hong Kong. The relationship had seemingly gone from 'golden era' with Britain as China's 'best partner in the West' (as articulated by the David Cameron government), to the deep freeze.

Many China-watchers were puzzled by Xi's actions; upsetting so many people on so many fronts seemed guaranteed to accelerate the global push-back. But that is to assume that Xi any longer cares what the world thinks. He has particular disdain for criticism from Western democracies, which he regards as weak, divided and in decline. By this reasoning, there could not be a better moment for China to assert itself.

John Sawers, a former head of MI6, wrote in the *Financial Times* in early July 2020, 'The last six months have revealed more about China under Xi Jinping than the previous six years.'[2] Which does rather beg the question of what he and his former employer were doing for all that time. Xi's behaviour has certainly been a wake-up call, opening the eyes of the world to the reality of his China. But the world – and Britain in particular – should really have been paying more attention to his

accumulation of power, his increasingly repressive rule, and his paranoid and combative world view. Had it done so, then China's actions
during the pandemic would surely have come as no surprise at all.

Xi Jinping became Communist Party leader on 15 November 2012 –
and he was almost an hour late for his first public appointment. I was
among journalists invited to an ornate room of the Great Hall of the
People on Tiananmen Square for what was billed as a presentation of
China's new leadership to the world's media. It came at the end of the
Party's 18th National Congress, an event held every five years, and the
culmination of a secretive selection process. As we waited alongside
banks of cameras, the delay provoked all kinds of speculation. Had
there been some sort of glitch – some last-minute manoeuvring within
the Party's notoriously opaque and, at times, brutal system of power?

Then Xi entered the room, leading the new seven-strong standing
committee of the Politburo, the most powerful men in China – and they
were all men, all with dyed black hair, and all wearing dark suits and
red ties, with the exception of Wang Qishin. His tie was blue, a hint,
perhaps, of what was to come – of the special status that Wang would
occupy as Xi's personal enforcer, his anti-corruption tsar, cleansing the
Party of Xi's enemies in the name of fighting graft.

Xi seemed remarkably relaxed, his manner informal. It wasn't what
we'd come to expect from usually stiff Chinese leaders. The men stood
in front of a huge landscape painting, which stretched the full length
of the wall behind them and waited to be introduced by Xi. He looked
towards the madly clicking cameras, the faintest of smiles. 'Sorry to
have kept you waiting,' he said – an apology, another first.

Xi's elevation to Party leader had been well flagged, but that didn't
dampen speculation about a vicious behind-the-scenes power struggle.
Just months before the congress, Bo Xilai, the charismatic Party chief
in the south-western province of Chongqing and a man considered a
principal rival to Xi, was removed from his post and eventually given
life imprisonment for corruption and abuse of power. Bo's wife, Gu
Kailai, was convicted of the murder by cyanide poisoning of a British
businessman called Neil Heywood, who fronted deals for the Bo family.
He was allegedly shifting money out of the country on Gu's behalf at
the time of his death, which was originally declared accidental and
blamed on alcohol poisoning. Chongqing's police chief was convicted
of covering up the murder; he sought asylum in the US consulate in the

city, but the Americans handed him back – presumably after their own detailed debriefing.

Bo and Xi had much in common. They were both 'princelings', the sons of revolutionary founders of the People's Republic of China; both of their fathers were companions of Mao Zedong, and both were purged during the Cultural Revolution and subsequently rehabilitated. That gave their sons enormous status in the Party. Bo Xilai was the more flamboyant of the two. He created a powerbase in Chongqing, where he pioneered a noisy populism, driven by Maoist nostalgia and a ruthless crackdown on 'lawlessness' – a populism that Xi Jinping would later emulate. Bo made little secret of his leadership ambitions. His trial was unusual because he contested the charges and mounted a spirited defence. The case presented an unusually detailed window on thuggery and corruption at the highest levels of the Party, but in spite of all the lurid details, many remain convinced that it was not his actions, but his challenge to Xi and his lack of contrition that led to his very public downfall. It was an early lesson in what lay ahead in Xi's China.

But the questions we struggled to answer on that November day were: who is Xi Jinping, and what does he stand for? His bare-bones Party résumé gave very little away. He was born in 1953, making him fifty-nine when he became general secretary of the Party. From 1975 until 1979, he studied chemical engineering as a 'worker-peasant-soldier-student' at Beijing's prestigious Tsinghua University. That was followed by a course in Marxist theory and ideological education, before working his way up through the Party ranks in four provinces – first in Hebei, and then in three of China's more prosperous coastal areas, culminating in the top Party job in Shanghai. He became a member of the Politburo's standing committee in 2007, and a year later was appointed vice-president and presumed heir-apparent to then Party leader Hu Jintao.

He appeared to have kept his head well down; he was well-connected, but had toed the Party line and avoided making enemies. That made him the perfect apparatchik, though in policy terms, the man who stood before us was a blank piece of paper. It was impossible to know what his priorities would be, though he appeared to grasp the crisis of legitimacy facing a Party riven with graft. 'There are also many pressing problems within the Party that need to be resolved, particularly corruption, being divorced from the people, going through formalities and bureaucratism caused by some Party officials. We must make every effort to solve these problems. The whole Party must stay on full alert. To address these problems, we must first of all conduct ourselves honourably,' he said.

Many China-watchers were quick to declare him a liberal and a reformer, largely on the basis of his family history. Not only had his father been persecuted during the Cultural Revolution, but Xi Zhongxun later become a leading economic reformer under paramount leader Deng Xiaoping, only to be sidelined again after opposing the military crackdown in Tiananmen Square in 1989. A sister of Xi Jinping died during the mayhem of the Cultural Revolution, during which Xi was sent to work in a remote farming village for seven years – an experience that has subsequently been much mythologised as the Party has sought to present him as a 'man of the people'. He has been married twice, and at the time of his selection as leader, his second wife, a famous folk singer called Peng Liyuan, was better known among Chinese people than her husband. Their daughter studied at Harvard University under an assumed name. And he'd once visited the United States, an educational study tour in 1985, during which he had stayed with an American family.

These biographical nuggets were assembled into a narrative that led some China-watchers to describe Xi as 'China's Gorbachev', likening him to Mikhail Gorbachev, who brought glasnost (transparency/openness) and perestroika (restructuring) to the Soviet Union. It was the wildest of wishful thinking. Gorbachev also brought the collapse of the Soviet Union, and while Xi Jinping did obsess about him, it was not as somebody to emulate, but as personifying a nightmare future the Chinese Communist Party had to avoid at all costs. Gorbachev was an object of disdain for Xi. Through a lack of discipline and ideological rigour Gorbachev had recklessly destroyed the Soviet Communist Party, and with it the Soviet Union and its socialist allies. With hindsight, a more appropriate comparison for Xi would be 'China's Putin'. Xi's experience of the Cultural Revolution did not turn him against Mao, but instilled in him an almost pathological obsession with order, discipline and stability – to be achieved via the primacy of a powerful Communist Party, which under him would extend its reach into all walks of life.

Xi Jinping's China contains many of the familiar repressive trappings of dictatorship. Opponents are purged, often under the pretext of fighting corruption. Critics are silenced – the crackdown on dissidents, their lawyers and civil society in general has been unrelenting. Censorship becomes progressively tighter – Xi setting the tone early in his tenure, telling journalists during a tour of state media newsrooms that they must 'love the Party, protect the Party, and closely align themselves with the Party leadership in thought, politics and action'.[3] They needed little encouragement, fuelling a growing personality cult, slavishly portraying Xi as a wise and strong leader.

'If you want to marry, marry someone like Xi Dada, a man full of heroism with an unyielding spirit,' urges a song that went viral on the internet. 'Dada' means 'uncle' or 'big daddy', and the title and the image of Xi as a man of the people was heavily promoted. Online videos instructed people how to dance to the song. To older Chinese this provokes uncomfortable memories of the personality cult that surrounded Mao, and of the Cultural Revolution when a 'loyalty dance' to Mao was sometimes mandatory.[4]

Xi dramatically stepped up the role of the Party in all walks of life. Party members are urged to study his words, branded 'Xi Jinping Thought', which has been written into the constitution, alongside that of Mao Zedong. At the same time, Xi's crackdown on civil society and dissent has been described as 'arguably the most severe since the crushing of the student demonstrations in Tiananmen Square in 1989'.[5] According to official figures, spending on domestic security now exceeds that of the defence budget by around 20 per cent.[6]

'Xi Jinping Thought' nods towards Marxism – or 'socialism with Chinese characteristics' – even though there is little that is socialist or Marxist about contemporary China. The Chinese Communist Party is communist in name only, and now represents itself as the inheritor of 5,000 years of continuous history. Xi's ideology (as far as one can be identified) is a hotchpotch that draws selectively from that history and from classical Chinese philosophy. There is a touch of Maoist nostalgia mixed in there too, all overlaid with an aggressive and at times paranoid nationalism, bordering on xenophobia. The Party routinely denounces Western ideas and influence in schools and universities, and blames the 'dark hand' of foreign powers for unrest in Xinjiang and Hong Kong. Victimhood is a constant theme, and Xi's much-promoted 'Chinese Dream' is a nationalistic vision of the rejuvenation of the country after a century of humiliation at the hands of rapacious foreign powers. Though this anti-colonialist narrative is somewhat undermined by the colonial nature of China's signature foreign investment programme, the Belt and Road Initiative, and by the way it subjugates its own ethnic minorities.

This has been accompanied by a growing assertiveness abroad. China has aggressively pushed its territorial claims in the South China Sea, snatched dissidents from the streets of Hong Kong and Thailand, and has generally been far more willing to use its growing economic clout to push its global interests. Xi has abandoned the famous dictum of paramount leader Deng Xiaoping: 'Hide your strength, bide your time.' Under Donald Trump, America abandoned global leadership, accelerating a retreat of liberal democracy. China is challenging the West militarily, economically and politically. The heavily used slogan of 'China's peaceful rise' was always more myth than reality, but Beijing no longer tries to hide its ambition to replace America as the world's pre-eminent power. Chinese diplomats have abandoned diplomacy for threats and abuse against those who criticise Beijing. Critics are branded as enemies out to 'thwart China's rise' and to deny Beijing its rightful role as a world power.

It is remarkable how many China scholars in the West still echo these slogans and deny the reality of Xi's China; others have been blinded by their hostility to America, particularly in its Trumpian form. Against all the evidence, they cling to the notion that China's rise is benign and it is the West, and the United States in particular, that is intent on turning China into an enemy. There are scholars and business people who argued until very recently that Xi is poorly misunderstood, that there is a method behind his repression, and that once he has cleared out his stubborn opponents, the real reformer will emerge and all will be sweetness and light. This is mostly self-serving nonsense. Business and academia have compromised principles for access (and for money), wilfully ignoring the obvious. If China is becoming an enemy – or at least an adversary – it is almost entirely of its own doing. Western democracies have shown remarkable forbearance, together with a greed and naïvety that is encapsulated by Britain's muddled China policy – if indeed it can be characterised as policy at all.

The desire to reset relations with Beijing, to push back, is no longer just the preserve of China hawks; it is increasingly mainstream. The biggest surprise is that is has taken so long to reach that point, that Beijing was given the benefit of the doubt for so long while it gamed the international economic system so effectively that Xi now believes he no longer needs it and can forge his own way. The exasperation in Washington is captured by former president Barack Obama, who tried very hard to engage China. He writes in his memoir, *A Promised Land*, that China's economic rise has seen Beijing 'evading, bending, or breaking just about every agreed-about rule of international commerce'. There is now a realisation that a richer China does not mean a more liberal and open China, and that engagement (and tolerance of China's repression, cyber espionage, predatory business practices and influence operations) has been a failure. This realisation has been slowest in Britain.

The centralisation of power around Xi was formalised in early 2018 when China's rubber-stamp parliament approved the removal of the two-term limit on the country's presidency, one of the trinity of top posts he holds alongside Party boss and head of the military. While the Party role is the most powerful, the move was seen as opening the door to Xi remaining in power for life. The time limit, along with a more collective leadership, had been introduced after the violence and chaos of the Mao era, and was designed to prevent the concentration of power in one person's hands. That safety net no longer exists.

The harshness of Communist Party rule in China since the Cultural Revolution has ebbed and flowed – periods of opening and then tightening that China scholars refer to as the *fang-shou cycle*. This reflected the relative strength of those favouring economic reform and a degree of political liberalism against those advocating more repressive controls and a bigger role for the state in the economy. The mid to late 1980s, until the Tiananmen Square protests and massacre, when hundreds, perhaps thousands, died at the hands of the People's Liberation Army (PLA), and the decade from 1998 to 2008, are generally considered more liberal periods. The latter is associated with the early days of the internet, which was hailed at the time as a tool for democratic change and accountability – even in China, where for a while it became a lively forum for discussion and criticism. When Xi Jinping came to power, it was one of his first targets, a tool of 'Western hostile forces', as his generals described it. China must 'resolutely protect ideological and political security on the invisible battlefield of the internet', thundered the *People's Liberation Army Daily*.[7] The harshest period in the *fang-shou cycle* is usually judged to be the three years after Tiananmen Square, but the repression of that period is now more than matched by that of Xi Jinping.[8]

Party rule has often been described as a sort of 'deal' with the Chinese people, the Party providing economic progress and stability, together with greater economic and social freedom, in exchange for political docility and compliance. This 'deal' in as far as it ever was true is now under severe strain. China's economic model is no longer sustainable; it is far more fragile than commonly appreciated, and the accelerating decoupling with America – and Western democracies more generally – will be an enormous challenge. It is partly with that in mind, that the Party is bolstering its repressive toolkit.

Xi has turned himself into the most powerful leader since Mao. His is a totalitarianism tailored for the twenty-first century, and at its heart are tools of surveillance and social control that Mao could never have dreamed of. It has been characterised as a surveillance state, although in many ways communist China always has been. It is the tools that have been upgraded, enabling a 'Chinese Dream' that puts Orwell's *Nineteen Eighty-Four* to shame. Xi Jinping's repressive rule is *defined* by technology. It is what increasingly underpins and sustains a Communist Party which now answers to him alone, harnessing the unrestrained power of surveillance and other repressive technologies. It is a system the likes of which the world has not seen before. Xi is building a digital totalitarian state – where Big Brother meets big data.

It has become a popular pastime to ask which of the great dystopian novels of the twentieth century 'got it right'. Was it George Orwell's *Nineteen Eighty-Four*, or possibly Aldous Huxley's *Brave New World*? Maybe even Yevgeny Zamyatin's *We*?

Nineteen Eighty-Four had the telescreen, the two-way television-like device that watches and listens. The truth is whatever the Party says it is. Winston Smith, the main character in the novel, works in the Ministry of Truth, rewriting history for a living, expunging people from the records, turning them into 'unpersons'. Wearing an improper expression that betrays anti-Party beliefs is a 'facecrime'. And, of course, there is Big Brother.

The people who inhabit Huxley's *Brave New World*, are part of a genetically engineered caste system. They are not so much cowering before Big Brother, as watching it – or a similar mindless soap – on television, kept in line by crass entertainment, hypnotism and mind-bending drugs. In *We*, the people of Zamyatin's OneState are given numbers, not names. There is no privacy, since everybody lives in buildings with glass walls, constantly watched by a secret police he calls 'the Guardians'. The blinds only come down during a state-mandated 'sex hour'.

There are echoes of all of these in Xi Jinping's China, though the technology imagined by Orwell, Huxley and Zamyatin seems quaint and clunky in comparison with the surveillance state being built in China. In *Nineteen Eighty-Four*, Winston Smith expresses relief that at least the telescreens don't know what you're thinking. Today's algorithms increasingly do. For all the idealism of the early techno-libertarians, the internet has opened possibilities for social control that Orwell never imagined. So have advances in surveillance and machine learning that give the ability to harvest and rapidly analyse vast amounts of personal data about every facet of behaviour offline and online. Xi's China is embracing these technologies with unrestrained enthusiasm.

This book is the story of Xi Jinping's surveillance state. It begins in Xinjiang, the country's remote western province, as big as Britain, Germany, Spain and France combined – and the scene of one of the greatest abuses of human rights of the twenty-first century. In a moving letter to the Chinese ambassador to London, the president of the Board of Deputies of British Jews, noted the 'similarities between what is alleged to be happening in the People's Republic of China today and what happened in Nazi Germany 75 years ago: People being forcibly loaded onto trains; beards of religious men being trimmed; women being sterilised; and the grim spectre of concentration camps.'[9]

Xinjiang, which the ethnic Uighurs refer to as East Turkistan, is ground zero for the surveillance state, a proving ground for a terrifying array of repressive technologies. In the name of fighting terrorism, China has turned Xinjiang into a police state like no other.

Many aspects of repression are familiar – the fear, the paranoia, the checkpoints, the late-night knock on the door. But it is repression powered by algorithms. It is a place where every move, every conversation, every action, online and offline, is monitored. It is a place where facial recognition cameras are not only able to identify faces, but the emotions they are wearing. It is a place where, by law, everyone must have spyware pre-installed on their phone. ID cards carry DNA information and 'reliability status', and any deviation in what the algorithms consider 'normal' behaviour or attitudes can lead to arrest. And, as a direct result, China has incarcerated civilians on a scale not seen since the Nazi concentration camps of the Second World War. As many as

1.5 million, one in six of the province's Turkic-speaking Muslim population, are being forcibly held in 're-education' camps.

In Xinjiang, China has gone faster and further in implementing a system of total surveillance and control, but its component parts are being rapidly adopted across the country. Chapters 2–5 examine the components in more detail. China is the world leader in marrying surveillance to artificial intelligence and facial recognition – systems able to recognise expressions and supposedly moods, as well as the way an individual walks. With a network of 600 million surveillance cameras (almost one for every two people), the government is hoovering up vast amounts of data. It is working with nominally private tech companies on systems able to reference rapidly millions of pieces of data, right down to micro-expression technology able to identify fifty-four brief, involuntary expressions, which the face often creates before the brain has a chance to control facial movements. China leads the world in electric vehicles, every one of which must, every thirty seconds, send data to the Chinese government, including the car's position, direction and speed, enabling its location to be pinpointed to within a metre.

Then there is the internet. The Communist Party has not just tamed it, cutting it off from the rest of the world, but has weaponised it as an instrument of social control. The internet was supposed to be liberating. For early pioneers, it was beyond the law and would challenge authoritarian rulers. There were early hopes in China that it could hold the Communist Party accountable. That now seems terribly naïve. Phase one was the Great Firewall, the most comprehensive system of censorship on the planet, employing hundreds of thousands of censors, blocking objectionable websites and keywords. Phase two is 'social credit', a system that will enable the authorities to track every detail of online behaviour and rate citizens according to their loyalty. It is already being used to limit access to goods and services, as well as travel, loans, education and jobs.

Orwell famously wrote, 'Who controls the past controls the future. Who controls the present controls the past.' History has always been manipulated by the Communist Party for its own purposes. Writing and rewriting, snipping opponents from the picture, in order to justify events and leaders of the present. Events such as the 1989 Tiananmen Square massacre are excluded from books and from the media, and have been scrubbed from the internet. Now, digital technology is being used in the service of the Party, taking censorship and the rewriting of history a step further. China is digitising its historic archives and, in the process, systematically deleting and rewriting Chinese journal and textbook articles that challenge the views of Xi Jinping. For academics who rely on databases for research, it suggests a much deeper rewriting of history. In the past it required the physical removal of articles in magazines. Now it is being done at the click of a mouse.

None of this would be possible without the close collaboration of China's nominally private technology companies. Many people were surprised when Jack Ma, the creator of China's e-commerce giant Alibaba, was identified as a Communist Party member. They should not have been. The surveillance state is a joint venture between the Communist Party and China's Big Tech companies, who control the digital infrastructure (mobile phones, networks) and the data. These companies are closely bound to the Party and to the goal of 'national security', and this marriage is crucial to the system of mass surveillance and control.

Chapters 6–9 look at the implications for the rest of the world. Western companies and institutions have aided and abetted the construction of the surveillance state. Some unwittingly, where technology is stolen; others grudgingly – feeling obliged to hand over technology or to censor their products as a condition for market access; some willingly. Tech companies are the worst offenders. For example, Apple fights FBI demands to access data in the US, but without protest censors apps in its China app store on behalf of the Communist Party. Facebook has cosied up to Beijing in an effort to regain entry (it is currently banned); Google has explored a China-friendly search engine (i.e. heavily censored). Western companies are investors in the private Chinese firms at the heart of the surveillance state. Western universities and elite schools have set up campuses in China, where they are subject to Party oversight, and Western academics collaborate with companies and research servicing the surveillance state.

Every state seeks influence in international relations, but a belligerent new China has crossed the line into interference, combining largesse with threats and bullying, while perfecting the art of righteous indignation when called out. We are used to reading about Russia's influence operations, its attempts to undermine democratic elections in the West and to spread disinformation. Beijing's influence operations are more extensive and smarter. They range from pressuring and co-opting Western academics to weaponising trade and investment – even big-spending tourists – in an effort to curb criticism and punish those who question its policies. The Communist Party is exercising ever greater control over the army of Chinese students studying in the West (and on whose fees Western academic institutions are heavily reliant – especially in the UK), disrupting talks given by dissidents, and shaping academic curriculums and research though carefully directed grants and investment.

China is aggressively exporting its model of state capitalism with tight social and political control, together with the technology to enforce it – an inspiration to dictators (and would-be dictators) everywhere, and aided by the retreat of Western liberal democracy. A multi-billion-dollar scheme with the clunky title 'Belt and Road Initiative', offers massive infrastructure loans along a new Asian 'Silk Road' and beyond. It is an exercise in neo-colonialism, generating vassal states. It is riddled with corruption and creating debt bondage, but with a clear ambition: to snatch global leadership away from the United States and remake the world economic order in Beijing's image.

Huawei in particular has become a corporate standard-bearer of the surveillance state and a lightning rod for China's critics in the growing US–China showdown. Its technology is cheap, widely used in the latest 5G telecommunications networks, but deeply suspect in the eyes of Western intelligence officials. Policy towards the company has split Western allies. After much agonising and intense pressure from Washington, Britain is phasing out Huawei from 5G networks, but the company will retain its role in earlier 3G and 4G systems. Britain allowed itself to become highly dependent on Huawei, and now faces delays and extra expense. Huawei has splashed money on research facilities and has courted leading universities. It has also controversially bought a stake in the company that commercialises research at Oxford University, giving it access to a treasure trove of early-stage science developed by British academics.

China's behaviour towards dissidents overseas has become more aggressive, as has its assertion of dubious territorial rights, notably in the South China Sea. Dissidents have been snatched from Thailand, as well as Hong Kong and Macau (which supposedly had separate legal systems). Others have been intimidated (including in the US), their families in China threatened.

Beijing uses cyber espionage to plunder industrial and economic secrets from Western companies, a theft that has aided China's technological rise and which former US intelligence officials have described as 'the biggest transfer of wealth in history'.[10] State-sponsored hackers also target dissidents and other critics – the use of cyber weapons against the Hong Kong democracy movement is the biggest and most extensive ever seen against a dissident group. President Obama thought he'd done a deal to curb China's wholesale plunder of American industrial and economic secrets. His cyber 'non-aggression' pact was widely applauded, and Beijing's cyber espionage did appear to fall for a while. In reality it was wishful thinking on Obama's part. China never accepted the American distinction between hacking for political reasons and hacking for economic gain. Beijing has reorganised and refocused its cyber forces, and their level of activity and expertise is now higher than ever. During the Covid-19 pandemic, it was accused by Western intelligence agencies of hacking into British and American research facilities to steal data about vaccine development. Beijing has identified the twenty-first century technologies with which it wants to lead the world, and the list closely corresponds to the targets of China's latest round of cyber snooping.

Chapter 10 looks at the push-back from Western democracies – a reaction that was hesitant, lacklustre and complacent at first, particularly in the UK, is now gaining momentum. Xi Jinping's plan to lead the world in futuristic technologies has been a wake-up call in America. His 'Made in China 2025' plan, pouring billions of dollars into research in fields ranging from biotechnology to artificial intelligence and robotics, has triggered what has been described as a technological arms race. Others have warned of a new Cold War, though the analogy is not accurate, since Western and Chinese economies are far more intertwined than were the Soviet Union and the West, and the world is a far more complicated place than it was in the days of the two rival blocs. What is happening now is better described as a decoupling, as the West looks to lessen its economic dependence on an increasingly capricious and aggressive China. It is also a competition about values and ideas, as embedded in rival systems of innovation and oversight.

Donald Trump penalised Chinese companies and launched a trade war. His motives were mercantilist, and he cared little about human rights issues. Although Joe Biden has a record of engagement with China, a more robust stance towards China is one of the few policies that commands bipartisan support in America, as well as the growing backing of allies. Even the innately cautious EU is re-examining the way it does business with China and is looking to restrict access to technology, and scrutinise the purchase by China of strategic assets. Western companies, for so long at the beck and call of Beijing, are beginning to look more closely their supply chains and broader relations with China. Beijing has miscalculated the degree of pent-up anger at its behaviour. Trump's erratic and unilateral 'America first' foreign policy played into the hands of China. He alienated allies, pushing some countries into the arms of an unloved Beijing. Biden seems intent on re-building alliances and restoring trust in America. Beijing believes it can face him down and divide the EU. A post-Brexit Britain, searching for allies and markets, is particularly vulnerable. The UK is dangerously dependent on Chinese money and technology, as evidenced by the agonising over Huawei's role in next generation telecoms. British politicians have been especially short-sighted in their dealings with Beijing.

The uprising in Hong Kong, and Beijing's attempt to stifle it, is a particular flashpoint between the West and China. While the draconian national security law imposed on the territory may dampen protest, it will only deepen the festering discontent. Though the protests were driven primarily by the demand for democracy, there is also a deep fear of the surveillance state. For the moment, this remains the only part of China able to read about the horrors of Xinjiang. The democracy movement has been targeted by state-sponsored hackers on an unprecedented scale. Amid the street battles and protests, Hong Kong became a testing ground for *anti*-surveillance technologies. The self-governing democratic island of Taiwan, which Beijing claims as its own and has threatened to invade, watches warily, determined to protect its freedoms. Together, Hong Kong and Taiwan represent an arch of resistance to Xi's digitally driven totalitarianism.

Inside China, support for Xi may not be as solid as often portrayed. When internal Party documents about the Xinjiang camps were leaked to Western journalists in 2019, they revealed new details about the organisation of the camps, but also suggested something else: internal Party dissent. The Communist Party is an opaque and secretive organisation. There are rarely leaks. Yet somebody wanted the world to know about Xi's culpability.

China is often compared to a pressure cooker. Arguably, in the early years of the internet, the online world acted like a vent for pent-up anger and frustration. In closing the vents, and just about every other avenue for dissent, Xi Jinping may be setting the scene for an even larger explosion. His anti-corruption campaign has certainly made him many enemies. In the absence of any meaningful ideology, the Party falls back on nationalism and a growing economy as a means of legitimation. That is a potentially dangerous tactic; nationalism, once inflamed, is an unpredictable emotion, difficult to contain. And growth is slowing, the economy far more fragile than is commonly appreciated.

The surveillance state is a threat, but it is also a warning to us all. It is not some distant dystopian nightmare. It is happening now, and is a frightening demonstration of what can happen when repressive new technologies are imposed without debate, restraint or oversight, and in an environment of large-scale indifference.

There are other reasons for vigilance. In the new high-tech 'arms race', China has one big advantage: lots of data, and data has been called the new oil, the raw material that fuels the hungry algorithms of artificial intelligence. Beijing faces no constraints on the way it is gathered or used, since no serious notion of privacy exists in China. Internet users are often described as 'running naked' online.

The final chapter examines in more detail China's response to Covid-19. That response graphically brought together many of the themes examined in this book – from the frightening array of surveillance technologies deployed and the casual brutality and repression of criticism, to the bullying and threatening of those countries outside China who questioned its handling of the coronavirus. But if Covid-19 was a watershed moment, when the world woke up to the reality of Xi Jinping's China, it also illustrated the strengths and weaknesses of the surveillance state. It was the moment when Xi Jinping's 'Chinese Dream' of a rejuvenated nation was exposed as a dystopian nightmare. It also begs the question: Are his actions those of a strong and confident leader or those of a paranoid dictator at the helm of a regime far more brittle than commonly understood?

Throughout this book, I will refer to Xi Jinping's two volumes of speeches and written works – *The Governance of China I* and *II*. For a man who claims to be widely read, a master of Western and Chinese classical literature, according to Party propaganda, these books are mind-numbingly dull. They are for the most part written in Party jargon; if there is a contemporary version of Orwell's newspeak – the fictional language of Oceania, his totalitarian superstate, with a deliberately restricted and convoluted vocabulary and grammar designed to limit freedom of thought – then this is surely it. Nevertheless, the books do provide some pointers towards what drives him, his thinking and his priorities.

Many recent studies of China refer to the 'Party-state', as shorthand for the one-party state and in recognition of the overwhelming power of the Communist Party in Xi Jinping's China, where any notion of the 'state' or 'government', or 'the authorities' are subordinate to the interests of the Party. I share that view, which is clear in the narrative that follows, but have chosen to mix up the references, finding it stylistically easier than constant reference to the clunkier 'Party-state'.

The Dutch historian Frank Dikötter knows a thing or two about dictators. He is the author of 'The People's Trilogy', three books which examine the impact of communism on ordinary lives in China. The first in the series, *Mao's Great Famine: The History of China's Most Devastating Catastrophe, 1958–1962*, estimates that during those four years, 45 million people were worked, starved or beaten to death during the madness of the Great Leap Forward, Mao's attempt to catch up with the West. More recently he has written a biography of eight of the twentieth century's most prominent dictators.[11] In the introduction he says, 'naked power has an expiry date'. That may be so, but Xi Jinping believes he can push back that date, if not eradicate it completely. That is a chilling ambition. Can a surveillance state entrench and empower dictatorship in a manner not seen before, or will it all come tumbling down, buried under a beeping and flashing pile of SIM cards, chips and surveillance cameras? That is the question at the core of this book. It might also be the defining question of our generation.

I have Sting to thank for inspiration for the title of this book. When in 1982 the then frontman for the band The Police wrote the hit single 'Every Breath You Take', it was seen by some as being about a stalker; others misinterpreted it as a love song, and it became popular at weddings. He clarified the meaning in a 1983 interview with the *New Musical Express*, saying: 'It's a nasty little song. Really rather evil. It's about jealousy and surveillance and ownership.'[12] It could not be a more appropriate title for a book about Xi Jinping's China.

CHAPTER 1

Xinjiang – Ground Zero

Zharkent is a small desert town in Kazakhstan with a rich history and a hopeful future. The name of its main street, which translates as Silk Road, is an expression of both. The border with China is just under twenty miles away, and the promise of Chinese investment to reinvigorate the old trade route is bringing a fresh buzz to a town with the distinction of being one of the furthest places on earth from an ocean.

Ordinarily there'd be little reason to stop there, yet in July 2018, the town's three-story pastel green courthouse was packed as Sayragul Sauytbay, a forty-one-year-old kindergarten teacher, was led into the room. A guard removed her shackles and placed her in a glass-fronted pen. The eyes of her family and supporters followed her in, as did those of three Chinese diplomats, who sat impassively at the rear of the courthouse.

Sauytbay, a Chinese citizen and an ethnic Kazakh, had been arrested at the behest of China, who demanded she be sent back after she crossed illegally into Kazakhstan. She sat facing the judge, wearing a white T-shirt and a look of steely determination, her dark hair swept back, a sheet of paper in front of her. The courtroom fell silent as the judge asked her to deliver her statement.

'In China, they call it a political camp, but in reality it's a prison in the mountains,' she said. 'They took me there in 2018.'

Her emotional testimony provided the first public evidence of what China was strenuously denying – a network of detention centres across the country's Xinjiang province in which as many as 1.5 million Uighurs, Kazakhs, Kyrgyz and other Muslim minority groups were being incarcerated. Her testimony was all the more powerful because Sauytbay had worked in one of them. She said she had no choice, that she'd been ordered to teach at a camp in the mountains close to the border because she could speak fluently both Mandarin and Kazakh.

She said that in her camp alone there were 2,500 people. She spent four months there before being allowed to return to her kindergarten. She was horrified by what she witnessed and desperate to join her husband and two small children in Kazakhstan. Her passport had been confiscated, so she crept across the border. She told the judge that because she was disclosing state secrets to the court, she feared for her life if she was deported. Her lawyer was more explicit. 'A death penalty is all that awaits her if she returns,' he said.

Kazakhstan was in a bind. Beijing wields enormous and growing economic clout in the region and was applying intense pressure to hand her back. But Kazakhstan could not ignore popular anger at the treatment of ethnic Kazakhs in neighbouring Xinjiang. The court found her guilty of illegal border crossing, but refused to deport her. Instead, it ordered her released with a six-month suspended sentence, a verdict that was greeted with cheers and applause by her supporters in the court. A video news report from Radio Azattyq (part of the Radio Free Europe/Radio Liberty network) showed the Chinese diplomats striding quickly and angrily away across the court compound.[1]

In an interview with Canada's *Globe and Mail* shortly after the verdict, Sauytbay said the camp was surrounded by high walls and barbed wire. It was 'very, very scary. Just one glimpse would frighten you.' She said she taught Mandarin, but also how to sing the Chinese national anthem and other propaganda songs, and that if a person refused to learn they would be threatened. She said there was never enough to eat. 'People didn't dare to speak even a single word out loud. Everyone was silent, endlessly mute.'[2]

Seven thousand miles away, in the Australian capital of Canberra, twenty-two-year old Nathan Ruser was beginning work as an analyst at the Australian Strategic Policy Institute's International Cyber Policy Centre. He has a fascination with satellite imagery and mapping, and an extraordinary ability to ferret out information from high-resolution images, cross-referencing with other open-source data. As a student, he'd already made a name for himself – and embarrassed security agencies – by highlighting how running routes used by US troops at their Syria base were exposed by data from an exercise app. He'd also used imagery to highlight the abuse of the Rohingyas in Myanmar. Now he turned his attention to Xinjiang.

There appeared to be a construction frenzy in the Chinese province, images showing hundreds of large and rapidly expanding compounds, with high walls, watchtowers and barbed-wire fencing clearly visible. He and his colleagues closely examined twenty-eight of the facilities that covered the 'equivalent of 43 Melbourne Cricket Ground stadiums'. They matched the images with building tender documents and other open-source data they found on the internet that pointed to the rapid recruitment of police and other security personnel. One tender document sought bids for building what it called a 'transformation through education' facility. Gathering the online documents became a race, since China's censors were deleting them from the internet almost as quickly as researchers were finding them. But the censors were not fast enough, and Ruser came to one inescapable conclusion: China was constructing a sprawling gulag of fortified facilities – a vast system for extra-legal detention and forced indoctrination. 'Moreover, the structures being built appear intended for permanent use. Chillingly, stories of detainees being released from these camps are few and far between.'[3]

Information continued to seep out of Xinjiang. Exiled Uighurs and other Turkic Muslim minorities reported they were no longer able to contact family members in the province. *The Washington Post* interviewed three former detainees who had escaped to Kazakhstan, and described days spent singing propaganda songs, such as 'Without the Communist Party, there would be no new China'. They described nights locked in crowded cells; one man claimed to have been waterboarded.[4] Singers, artists, academics, civil servants – even a well-known comedian – were among those to have disappeared into the camp system.

A month after Sauytbay's testimony, UN human rights experts in Geneva said they had received 'credible reports' that China had detained a million or more ethnic Uighurs. Gay McDougall, a member of the United Nations Committee on the Elimination of Racial Discrimination, said that in the name of combatting religious extremism, China had turned Xinjiang into 'something resembling a massive internment camp, shrouded in secrecy, a sort of no rights zone'. She said that accounts from the region pointed to Muslims 'being treated as enemies of the state, solely on the basis of their ethno-religious identity'.[5]

Beijing reacted furiously, flatly denying that camps existed and accusing the West of stirring up trouble. Hu Lianhe, a senior Chinese Communist Party official, told a UN human rights panel: 'There is no such thing as re-education centres.' Allegations that 1 million Uighurs had been forcibly detained were 'completely untrue'.[6]

But it was a fiction increasingly difficult to sustain in the face of mounting evidence, and two months later, in October 2018, China admitted for the first time to the existence of what Xinjiang governor, Shohrat Zakir described as 'a vocational education and training program in Xinjiang', established to combat the 'three evil forces' of terrorism, extremism and separatism. 'The purpose is to fundamentally eliminate the environment and soil that breeds terrorism and religious extremism,' the governor said. He attacked what he called 'scandalous lies' about the camps, and denied any mistreatment. He said the 'trainees' were learning new skills, including Mandarin, in order to 'accept modern science and enhance their understanding of Chinese history and culture'.[7]

The authorities organised tightly controlled visits to three of the facilities for a small group of foreign journalists and diplomats. In a report, the Reuters news agency described inmates sitting at desks, staring blankly at a book entitled 'Our motherland is so vast'; others glanced awkwardly at the reporters. In another classroom the inmates gave a lively rendition in English of the song 'If You're Happy and You Know It Clap your Hands,' which appeared to have been arranged specially for the visit. Inmates allowed to speak to reporters praised China and parroted Beijing's line about 're-radicalisation'. Visible security was kept to a minimum during the visit.[8]

Human rights groups and Uighur exiles came to their own conclusion: that China's purpose was nothing less than the destruction of Uighur identity and that of other Turkic Muslim minorities. 'The Chinese government is conducting human rights abuses in Xinjiang unseen in the country in decades,' said Sophie Richardson, China director at Human Rights Watch, which accused Beijing of mass arbitrary detention without any due process.[9]

Researchers increased their estimates of the number of detainees to 1.5 million spread over hundreds of facilities, an astonishing one in six of the adult Turkic-speaking population of Xinjiang. The figure is twice the daily peak reached in Nazi concentration camps in January 1945, and creeping towards the 2 million level of the Soviet gulag system.[10] Poring over the satellite imagery and official documents, researchers also identified factories built close to or inside camps, suggesting the authorities were eager to put their 'trainees' to work.[11]

Boarding schools were also constructed to accommodate the large numbers of children separated from their parents. At first this looked like a tragic side-effect of such a vast system of detention. But official documents suggest that while the issue of 'double detained' children was a headache for the authorities, it was also seen as an opportunity for indoctrination, as the 'left-behind children' could now study 'under the loving care of the Party and the government'.[12]

As more details emerged, Britain was among Western democracies calling for the release of those detained and for the UN to be given access. But mostly the world shrugged, and the shrug was biggest from those countries which have received Chinese largesse. Most Muslim-majority nations remained silent. The human rights commission of the fifty-seven-member Organisation of Islamic Cooperation issued a report 'commending the efforts of the People's Republic of China in providing care for its Muslim citizens'. Although Kazakhstan resisted the deportation of Sayragul Sauytbay, not wanting to inflame Kazakh nationalism, it avoided openly criticising the camps, while in interviews with the *Financial Times*, the leaders of Pakistan and Indonesia claimed they knew nothing about what was happening in Xinjiang.[13]

The *New York Times* quoted from a critical private account of a Malaysian diplomat who had been taken to visit the area, in which he said he could sense the fear and frustration of those in the camps, and referred to the usually bustling Xinjiang cities of Hotan and Kashgar as 'zombie towns'. The diplomat suggested China was 'using the threat of terrorism as an excuse to "sanitise" Uighur Muslims until they become acceptable Chinese citizens'. The Malaysian Foreign Ministry expressed 'serious displeasure', not at China, but at the publication of the report.[14] Turkey, which has cultural and linguistic ties with the Uighurs, did break the silence. Its foreign minister described the camps as 'a shame on humanity'. But he was quickly slapped down by Beijing, whose ambassador in Ankara warned in a Reuters interview, 'If you choose a non-constructive path, it will negatively affect mutual trust and understanding and will be reflected in commercial and economic relations.'[15]

Beijing could scarcely conceal its glee when fifty-four UN member states took that to heart and dutifully issued a statement in support of China. In a commentary, the state-run *Xinhua* news agency declared, 'There is no so-called "human-rights issue" in Xinjiang.' It questioned America's 'sinister intentions' and declared its counter-terrorism and de-radicalisation measures a great success. 'In the past three years, no terrorist attack has happened in the region, and the whole society remains peaceful and stable.'[16]

The policeman stubbed out his cigarette in a plastic lunch box, which was filling fast with butts and ash amid the soggy residue of his noodles. He wiped his brow with the sleeve of his stained blue shirt and then barked another question. I didn't really need the translation, since it was the same question he'd been repeating on and off for hours, but the translator dutifully turned his words into English. 'He wants to know who told you about Happiness Garden. He asks who else was part of the conspiracy.' I repeated that my source was none other than Wang Lequan, Xinjiang's top Communist Party official at the time, and that if he didn't believe me he should ring Wang's office. He lit another cigarette.

It was June 2008, two months before the Beijing Olympics, and I was getting my first lesson in terrorism with Chinese characteristics. China claimed to have thwarted a terrorist plot against the Games,[17] and Wang had given an interview to state media in which he described a raid on a terror cell during which police were met with a hail of grenades. Seven officers were injured before they eventually overcame the fifteen militants, killing two of them. The way Wang told it, the 'terrorists' had been holed up in a fourth-floor flat at Happiness Garden, and it had been one hell of a firefight. I had travelled with a film crew to Urumqi, the capital of what China calls the Xinjiang Uighur Autonomous Region, but which many Uighurs prefer to call East Turkistan, and located the apartment complex in the north-west of the city. On the fourth floor where the shoot-out supposedly took place, we were invited in for tea by a rather bemused young Chinese woman who laughed heartily and told me, 'There was nothing like that at all.'

We were arrested shortly after we left the apartment block. The surveillance state was in its infancy back then, but every complex had informers, and news of our presence had quickly reached the police. We were taken to a shabby neighbourhood police station, where they too had no knowledge of the fierce firefight described by Wang. When we were released late in the evening, I detected the faintest of smiles on the face of the interrogating officer, who'd become more amiable as the hours ticked by. I felt sure that he and the young woman in the apartment were laughing at me as much as they were at the claims I was investigating. If they had one thing in common, it was astonishment that anybody could possibly believe the words of a top Party official.

'Terrorism' and 'terrorist' are very elastic terms in China, routinely used to taint political opponents engaged in activities that would be regarded as perfectly legitimate in the West. More recently, the Chinese authorities have used the terms against pro-democracy protesters in Hong Kong.[18] In Xinjiang, 'terrorism' has become a staple of Party propaganda, though it has not always been that way.

There has been sporadic unrest in Xinjiang ever since the People's Liberation Army in 1949 marched in and put an end to a short-lived East Turkistan Republic. Until 2001 most violent incidents of resistance went unreported or else were referred to as 'hooliganism', 'accidents' or 'sabotage'. It was only after the 9/11 attacks on the World Trade Center in New York that Beijing re-branded previous unrest as 'terrorism' and from then on 'terrorism' has been the lens through which all opposition to Chinese rule is viewed.

China has faced sporadic Uighur violence against civilians: in October 2013, an SUV was driven into a crowd and burst into flames beneath the portrait of Mao Zedong in Tiananmen Square, killing two tourists, as well as the occupants of the vehicle. Five months later a knife-wielding attacker killed thirty-one people at Kunming railway station; a similar attack the following month at Urumqi railway station, killed three. In May 2014, explosives thrown from the window of two SUVs killed forty-three people in an Urumqi market street. But, as horrific as these individual incidents were, most experts agree that the threat is exaggerated and the response excessive. Xinjiang is not awash with bombs and extremists. Furthermore, much of the unrest is localised and rooted in deep-seated grievances against heavy-handed Chinese rule. Christian Tyler's words in his 2003 history of Xinjiang are as pertinent today:

> The Han discriminate partly because their history has taught them to, partly because they live in fear of the people they are colonizing. They are afraid to travel on Uighur buses, to walk alone in Uighur areas. Many Chinese in the east are under the impression that Xinjiang is a no-go area, that some kind of war is being fought there. Fear leads the Han to take extreme measures. By clamping down on all expressions of difference or dissent, under the cloak of fighting 'splittism', 'nationalism',

'fundamentalism' or 'terrorism' – depending on the season – they have turned a minority of Uighurs to violence, and reduced the majority to an impotent and resentful silence.[19]

In July 2009, eleven months after the Beijing Olympic Games, Urumqi was rocked by ethnic rioting. An initially peaceful protest at the killing of Uighur migrant workers by Han Chinese at a factory in southern China exploded into violence. Uighur attacks on Han Chinese and their property were followed by two days of revenge attacks and killings. The authorities said 200 people died; the true figure is thought to be much higher.

I arrived in the city to find streets strewn with debris and lined with smouldering gutted shops and charred cars. Trucks full of armed police cruised the streets. The city was tense, the mostly poor Uighur districts seethed with anger and resentment. After heavy Chinese migration, Uighurs were now a minority in this, the main city in Xinjiang. 'Our situation is too tragic,' one woman told me. 'It would be better to shoot and kill us than live like this.' Police watched as hundreds crowded into the courtyard of the city's main mosque, where another man said: 'This is our land, but we can't survive in our own land.' Another woman wept as she showed me a photograph of her fifteen-year-old daughter, missing since a security clampdown on the area. Tracing loved ones was all the more difficult because the authorities cut the mobile phone lines and the internet. It would be another nine months before they were fully restored.

When the People's Liberation Army marched into Xinjiang in 1949, Han Chinese comprised 6 per cent of the population; the latest figure is around 40 per cent of the province's 22 million people. Uighurs now comprise around 45 per cent, with the rest made up of ethnic Kazakhs like Sayragul Sauytbay, and other Turkic-speaking Muslim minorities. The mineral-rich region is China's biggest oil and gas producer. China claims it has brought prosperity, but the settlers have been the biggest beneficiaries of Xinjiang's 'development'. There are huge disparities of wealth. Around one in six of the population, most of them Han, live in separate communities run by an organisation called the Xinjiang Production and Construction Corps, or *Bingtuan*. It is an apartheid-like system in which many Han Chinese behave like colonial overlords, making little effort to interact with Uighurs, who have been made to feel like third-class citizens in their ancestral land. As Tyler writes in his history, China has always regarded the far west with a mixture of fascination and fear. 'For the Han Chinese, the Uighur's way of life is a problem. On the one hand, they have been taught to see Uighurs as primitive, superstitious, reactionary, treacherous – and dangerous. On the other, they find them exotic, amusing and attractive.'[20]

The Uighurs have faced an extraordinary blend of repression and humiliation. Where culture has not been assaulted it has been turned into a kitschy song and dance show for tourists. Fine for entertainment, but an obstacle to development and to assimilation. Arbitrary detention and mistreatment at the hands of the police has been routine, even before the camps were established. The Uighur language has been marginalised, Mandarin replacing it as the main language of instruction from kindergarten to university. Little is now published in the Uighur language. Religious activity has been curtailed, including a ban on veils and 'abnormal' beards that could 'whip up religious fanaticism', and on naming babies with names that 'exaggerate religious fervor'.[21] Fasting during Ramadan has been banned, with restaurants forced to stay open and officials checking people's homes to see they are not secretly observing the practice.[22]

Never one for historical accuracy, the Communist Party claims the region has been an 'inseparable part of China' since 206 BC,[23] though few serious independent scholars give this much credence.[24] [25] The Alaska-size region contains vast tracts of mountain and desert, including the Taklamakan, 'the worst desert on earth' in the view of Charles Blackmore, who led a 1993 expedition across that inhospitable expanse of sand.[26] It was where China tested its nuclear weapons. More recently it has become crucial to the success of Beijing's Belt and Road Initiative, a vast programme of investment in trade and infrastructure that's touted as a new Silk Road. 'Stability', always an obsession of the Communist Party, has become even more important in Xinjiang, even if that means turning the area into a vast prison camp. It is partly the promise of billions of dollars of investment that has enabled China to gag its Central Asian neighbours over the camps.

Sayragul Sauytbay's court testimony at first emboldened the exiled Uighur community in Kazakhstan, but the authorities, under Chinese pressure, told them not to speak out. Anti-Chinese protesters were arrested, as was Serikhan Bilash, a campaigner who had collected testimony from former camp inmates. He was eventually released, but only after agreeing to end his activism.[27] Sauytbay feared that Chinese agents might simply snatch her, as they have done with dissidents elsewhere in the world. Kazakh authorities did not want her to remain in the country, and after ten months her family was granted political asylum by Sweden.

Their new home is a sparsely furnished apartment in the port city of Trelleborg in southern Sweden. It was a grey, rainy day when I arrived to meet her, a bitter wind blowing from the Baltic Sea. The town's most popular sculpture in the main shopping street is of a group huddled under umbrellas. It could not be further removed from the deserts of Xinjiang, but there was little disguising Sauytbay's enormous sense of relief. 'It's been a long time since we've felt safe,' she told me, before adding cautiously, 'But China has a very long reach.'

Her memories of arriving at the camp are still raw. 'I was mortified, filled with dread. The fear in that place was paralysing. It was more scary than any prison that exists.' Even though she was taken there to teach, she was hooded for the journey, the camps still at that time shrouded in secrecy. The guards were heavily armed and aggressive. 'I was told that my main duty was to teach the inmates Chinese, but if there were other tasks I would carry them out without question. This included teaching the culture of everyday Han Chinese people, the songs they play, what a Chinese wedding looks like, their burial rituals, and the ideas as well as the principles of the Communist Party and Xi Jinping.'

As a teacher, Sauytbay was given separate accommodation, but the inmates slept twenty to a small room. They ranged in age from thirteen to eighty-four, were shaven-headed and shackled. Everywhere was monitored by cameras. 'They had cameras in every room, in every corner, in the hallways. There was no corner left unseen. There was no form of privacy, even when going to the toilet.' There was one exception to this blanket surveillance: the 'Black Room', so-called because what took place there was never recorded. It was the punishment room.

Sauytbay is not a tall woman, but she has a powerful presence. She spoke clearly and confidently, pausing only to adjust her floral head-scarf. It was easy to imagine her commanding the attention of a class of school children, but her voice cracked, and she wiped away a tear as she described what happened in the 'Black Room'.

'The main purpose of this room was torture and punishment for not paying attention to the rules,' she said. This might include low grades in language and propaganda tests, or not demonstrating sufficient enthusiasm for the 'lessons'. Sometimes there seemed to be no real reason at all for an individual to be singled out. 'You could hear the bloodcurdling screams of these people pleading for their lives, pleading for mercy.'

She was once taken to the 'Black Room' herself after comforting an eighty-four-year-old woman who had been sent to the camp after being accused of 'conspiracies using her phone'. The woman said she didn't own a phone. Sauytbay was beaten with batons and starved for two days. 'There were so many tools and weapons in that room that I could hardly see the wall. There was a chair with nails embedded in it . . . and an electric chair, police batons and stun sticks. Many of the things I could not recognise, things I'd never seen in my life before.'

Listening to Sauytbay talk, my mind went to George Orwell's *Nineteen Eighty-Four* and its Room 101. In the novel, Room 101 is the punishment room that contains a person's ultimate phobia or nightmare. The mere thought of it generates almost paralysing fear. 'The thing that is in Room 101 is the worst thing in the world,' says O'Brien, the novel's dark Party official.

'We were not seen as human beings, more like cattle,' Sauytbay told me, hinting also at sexual abuse at the hands of the guards. 'The young girls, the more beautiful women, they felt the least safe.' It is impossible to verify such allegations, which are strenuously denied by Beijing, but they are consistent with other claims of torture, medical experimentation, beatings and even rape made by former inmates.[28] [29] [30]

When Sauytbay eventually left the camp and was returned to her school she felt like she had lost all feeling. 'I felt so hopeless I could hardly think. I was like an empty shell. A human without a soul.' She soon came under suspicion herself because her family were in Kazakhstan, and she feared that she would be returned to the camp – this time as an inmate. She made her plans to escape.

She knew that would not be easy. The camps are not some standalone monstrosity, but at the pinnacle of a wider system of surveillance and control, the likes of which has not been seen before. 'There is no respect for life anymore. We are just numbers. The whole of Xinjiang is like a prison,' Sauytbay said. Beijing has turned Xinjiang into a technology-driven police state, in which every aspect of life – every movement, every conversation, every relationship – is monitored and evaluated for signs of disloyalty. It has become a place with the familiar trappings of a police state, but where repression is increasingly driven by an algorithm.

Sauytbay remembers the building blocks of this digital cage being put in place. The explosion of police checkpoints, surveillance cameras sprouting around lamp posts and rooftops like clusters of invasive plants until it was impossible to move without being followed by their prying eyes. And she remembers the sudden official concern for the health of the non-Chinese people of Xinjiang. 'There was a new law that everyone had to come in for a physical examination once a year.' The programme was called 'Physicals for All', and presented as a benevolent and caring government inviting its minority citizens to come for a free health check. Some invitations were sent by text message; in other areas officials went from door to door. It was an offer they couldn't refuse.

'There were all kinds of tests. They swabbed around my eyes, then I had to do different facial expressions, from crying to laughing, while they took photographs. They recorded my voice, then made me wear a device to check my eyes.' They also took blood and fingerprints. It was like no health check that she had been through before.

The 'health checks' began in September 2016, and *Xinhua*, the state news agency, reported that over a two-year period 36 million were carried out in Xinjiang, bringing great 'benefits' to public health.[31] Similar collections were made when residents were required to upgrade their IDs to 'third generation' digital cards.

It was a vast scheme to harvest biometric data, feeding photographs, DNA samples, fingerprints, iris scans and blood types of all residents between the age of twelve and sixty-five into a central searchable database. Official guidelines for the programme, obtained by Human Rights Watch, say the collection of biometric data has to be comprehensive, that officials must 'ensure that (information from) every household in every village, every person in every household, every item for every person' is collected.[32]

At the same time, teams of officials conducted home visits, which they called *fanghuiju*. They went door to door, asking a broad array of personal questions, the information from which was used to compile dossiers and identify what they deemed undesirable attitudes or behaviour.[33] It wasn't a random operation, but one guided by an app. The authorities were looking for thirty-six 'person types', which included those who engaged in religious activities – donating to mosques or preaching the Koran – and those who'd been abroad or had relatives overseas. There was also a category for persons who had switched from a smartphone to an analogue one (presumably a sign they were trying to evade eavesdropping), and a type who 'does not socialise with neighbours, seldom uses front door and acts suspiciously'. Another cause for suspicion was failing to appreciate the Communist Party, a person who 'for no apparent reason, [is] unwilling to enjoy the policies that benefit the people or fails to participate in activities organised by the local government or the Party'. They also asked whether people owned exercise equipment, suggesting that keeping fit was also potentially subversive. The use of network tools, such as WhatsApp, Viber and VPNs was also regarded as suspicious.

These details were obtained by Human Rights Watch, who reverse-engineered a copy of the police app.[34] They had experts disassemble it, looking at the data and the app interface. The app requires the user to log in and submit a range of information about a person. As well as the 'person types' page, it requires information about personal appearance, such as hair colour and height. The app had facial recognition and search functions.

The app feeds into what is called the Integrated Joint Operations Platform (IJOP), the 'brain' of the system, to which all the data is uploaded. The IJOP's 'algorithms of repression' are hungry, they have a voracious appetite for data. As well as the information fed into it from the *fanguiju* home visits, the platform is able to track people by the GPS location data on their smartphones, and also harvest other information from those phones. Every person in Xinjiang is required by law to have spyware installed on their mobile phones, enabling the authorities not only to track them, but to monitor calls and messages, and other online and social media activity.

Information also comes from tracking vehicles and scanning ID cards at police checkpoints, which blanket the province, particularly in Uighur-majority towns and cities. These checkpoints also have data extraction cradles for smartphones, able to suck the data for upload to the IJOP – just in case there is anything they have missed. It is an offence to refuse to hand over a password, an act that in itself would be seen as evidence of malign intentions. There are smaller checkpoints at the entrance of banks, parks, petrol stations, schools, apartment blocks and mosques. These will frequently have facial recognition cameras and iris scanners. Doorplates of apartment blocks have been fitted with

QR codes, readable by handheld devices and giving the police instant access to the personal information of those living in the building

Then there are the ubiquitous surveillance cameras, able to recognise people from their faces or the way they walk. On a visit to Hotan, a predominantly Uighur city in the south-west of Xinjiang, *The Economist* reported seeing poles with clusters of cameras at intervals of 100 to 200 metres along every street.[35] Around 80 per cent of Uighurs live in the south-west of Xinjiang, and consequently this is the area with the most intense surveillance. There have been reports of the testing in Xinjiang of cameras able to identify not only faces, but the emotions on those faces. At a tech show in the southern city of Shenzhen, a Party official from Altay City in Xinjiang told the *Financial Times* he was already using it. 'Using video footage, emotion recognition technology can rapidly identify criminal suspects by analysing their mental state . . . to prevent illegal acts including terrorism and smuggling,' he boasted.[36]

More data is gathered by WiFi 'sniffers', typically located at airports, stations and checkpoints. These are able to penetrate local networks and monitor the traffic both for content and for IP addresses of computers, smartphones and other devices using the network, and from which the owner can be identified. There have been reports of tourists and traders having an app able to extract emails, texts and contacts installed on their phones upon entry into Xinjiang.[37]

The IJOP algorithms crunch the data, looking for any deviations from what is considered 'normal' behaviour. This might include leaving your village without permission, obtaining a new phone number, or contacting friends or relatives abroad. It 'aggregates data about people and flags to officials those it deems potentially threatening; some of those targeted are detained and sent to political education camps and other facilities,' according to Human Rights Watch.[38] Others are kept under house arrest, confined to their village, or subject to extra surveillance. The police are sent on additional 'investigative missions' via the app. The authorities themselves have described the system as a series of 'sieves' or 'filters' to sift out undesirable elements. Others describe it as a 'virtual cage' with a simple purpose: 'To transform them [the Uighurs] into secular citizens who will never challenge the ruling Communist Party.'[39]

To further that cultural assimilation, local families are required to 'adopt' officials. These Han 'relatives', as official media describes them, pay regular visits to Uighur households, even moving in for short periods of time in order to demonstrate their superior ways to the backward Uighurs – a 'pairing and assistance program between officials and the ethnic minority citizens to promote communication and interaction', with the aim of 'bringing advanced technology and views to rural districts', as the programme is officially described. In the two years up to September 2018, 1.1 million civil servants were 'paired up' with 1.69 million 'ethnic minority citizens' to 'improve unity', according to the *Global Times*, a Party newspaper.[40] Sayragul Sauytbay shakes her head as she recalls the humiliation of having to live with her government-assigned minder. 'I was forced to share everything with my Chinese "relative". Some days I would live with him, or he would live with me, and I would have to live the way he lives. I had to adapt to his way of life.'

At local level, the surveillance operation has been described as a 'grid management system', dividing towns into units, each containing several hundred people. Every unit has a 'convenience police station', which, in spite of their cuddly name, are typically grey, windowless concrete bunker-like structures. In bigger towns they can be seen every few hundred metres. Each unit of the grid operates like a cell in the surveillance system.

Leaked Communist Party documents, obtained by the International Consortium of Investigative Journalists, underline the enormous scale of the security dragnet and call for 'strict secrecy' about the camps. They contain detailed instructions about how the camps should be built and run, describing a system of complete physical and mental control in which inmates could be kept indefinitely and where 'preventing escape' is a top priority. The documents say that during just one week in June 2017, the IJOP flagged more than 24,000 'suspicious persons' in the four southern districts of Xinjiang alone, two-thirds of whom were sent to the camps.[41]

A leaked spreadsheet from the south-western district of Karakax contains the names and ID numbers of 300 local residents sent to the camps, and confirms that religious activity was the main reason for detention, including praying, giving up alcohol, attending a mosque and growing a beard. It designates households as 'trustworthy' or 'not trustworthy', their attitudes graded as 'ordinary' or 'good'. It divides families by their 'light' or 'heavy' religious atmosphere.[42]

One irony of this vast surveillance operation is that the authorities (and the companies supplying the technology) have not always been very careful about protecting the mass of data they are harvesting. In early 2019, Victor Gevers, a Dutch cybersecurity investigator found online an unsecured database containing real-time data on 2.5 million people from Xinjiang. As well as basic information such as names, birthdates, home addresses and places of employment, there were notes on where they had most recently visited – including hotels, mosques and restaurants. SenseNets, a Chinese facial recognition company, had left the database unsecured for months. The real-time data appeared to come from facial recognition cameras and was being constantly updated with GPS coordinates.[43]

In the Turkic language Sayragul translates as 'Singing Flower'. Aziz Isa Elkun was so moved by the courage of the kindergarten teacher that he wrote a poem to her:

> You are a voice for the voiceless – sing, Sayragul
> You are a freedom fighter – sing, Sayragul
> You are an envoy for freedom – sing, Sayragul
> You hover like an eagle – sing, Sayragul!

Aziz is a Uighur activist, poet and scholar who now lives in Britain, where he was given political asylum in 2001. He has watched in mounting horror as China not only built a cage around his homeland, but reached out through the bars and targeted exiles like him in an effort to silence them. 'There's no room anymore to express dissent. Nothing. I don't know what will be next,' he told me.

When I met Aziz in north London, home to most of Britain's small Uighur community, he had not been able to speak with his seventy-eight-year-old mother or any other family member in Xinjiang for two years. The last time he spoke to his mother was shortly after his father died in November 2017. The Chinese embassy refused him a visa to visit his father in his final days. He remembers the uncertain, nervous tone of his mother on that last call, as if she knew the call was being monitored. Perhaps there were police in the room with her. The call ended abruptly. 'It's a bit difficult to talk at the moment,' were her final words. 'Since then I have had no news about my mother or other relatives from our village. I hope for the best that my mother is still alive,' Aziz said.

China has effectively cut communication between Uighurs at home and those abroad. Where it allows contact, it is using relatives to pressure activists overseas. Many exiled Uighurs have reported receiving calls or text messages from loved ones that are stilted and awkward, as if being read or at least guided. The content was remarkably similar in each case, praising the Communist Party for improving their lives, and urging the overseas activists to think of their family's safety. The *Guardian* interviewed Uighurs living across Europe and the United States. 'Tales of threats are the rule, not the exception,' the paper reported.[44]

Up to 1.6 million Uighurs live outside China, and Chinese embassies have been tasked with tracking them down, collecting information and recruiting informants, according to an Amnesty International report. 'Individuals reported being warned that family members would be detained if they did not return to Xinjiang or that they would not be able to see their family again if they refused to provide information about other Uighurs living in their communities,' the report says. Often the only way of communicating with friends and relatives in Xinjiang is via the Chinese messaging app WeChat, which is heavily monitored. Amnesty reported widespread threats, including intimidating calls and messages. 'The result of these measures is that Uyghurs in diaspora communities often live in fear and refrain from speaking about the situation in Xinjiang.'[45]

Aziz learned from friends that his sister had been detained in an internment camp for one and a half years and that his mother was still alive. There was no news of other relatives. Then he saw his mother, and heard her voice again – but the context was chilling. She was used as a prop in a video shown on CGTN, China's international propaganda channel, in which she is compelled to condemn her son and refute allegations that the authorities are destroying Uighur graveyards. Her words are stilted, as if they are being dictated, and for the first time that Aziz could ever remember she is not wearing a hijab. Aziz was appalled, 'Let her be united with her son, to give her a chance to live in peace in her late years,' he said.

The crude video appeared to be a response to Aziz speaking out about the plight of his family and the razing of his father's grave. Blocked from travelling to Xinjiang, the last he'd seen of his father before he passed away was in a video, sent by a relative and showing a frail but dignified old man walking slowly with the aid of a stick. When he died, his body was placed in a family tomb close to his home. Over the months that followed, Aziz 'visited' the grave regularly but remotely via Google Earth – until one day it was no longer there. It had been destroyed, the area replaced by a flattened empty field.

It appears to have been part of a wider campaign in which the authorities have destroyed hundreds of burial grounds, shrines and even mosques on a scale not seen since the Cultural Revolution, according to evidence collected from satellite photography.[46] [47] The *Global Times*, a Communist Party mouthpiece, denied the destruction, claiming the authorities were merely 'relocating graves to public cemeteries'.[48] Others saw it as a further assault on Uighur culture and religion.

The Communist Party identifies fifty-five different ethnic minorities, or *minzu*, living within the People's Republic. They number around 120 million people, some 8.5 per cent of the population, with half living in the country's more remote western provinces and borderlands. The remainder are identified as Han Chinese. The Uighurs are only the fourth largest minority, after the Zhuang, Hui and Manchu. But together with the Tibetans (number eight), they have presented the biggest challenge to Party leaders, who have grappled with the '*minzu* question' ever since seizing power in 1949.

Aside from the madness of the Cultural Revolution, when all expressions of ethnic identity were brutally supressed, the Party has tried to strike a balance between recognising and respecting diversity and promoting national unity. At times this provoked fierce debate within a Party that was, after all, nominally communist and supposedly concerned with helping disadvantaged groups. Navigating the line between ethnic diversity and dignity on the one hand and national integration and social cohesion on the other was a constant challenge. One man remembered for his softer, more tolerant line on ethnic policy is Xi Zhongxun – Xi Jinping's father.

After the communists came to power, Xi senior ran the Northwest Bureau, which included Xinjiang. For much of the 1950s and early 1960s, he was vice-premier with responsibility for religious issues. In the 1980s, after being purged during the Cultural Revolution and then rehabilitated, he continued to take a close interest in Tibet and Xinjiang. He instructed local officials to resolve protests by peaceful means and to address local grievances. In 1985, he wrote: 'Looking back upon history, countless facts prove that, with regards to dealing with religious issues, the more our policies are tight and inflexible, the more that in practical terms religion is supressed, things run counter to one's wishes, [and] the exact opposite results occur.'[49]

In the early 1980s, Xi Zhongxun led an informal dialogue with the exiled Tibetan community. The Dalai Lama, Tibet's spiritual leader, remembers him as 'very friendly, comparatively more open-minded, very nice'.[50] The two men had known each other since the 1950s, when the Dalai Lama gave Xi senior an expensive watch, which he continued to wear years later. Xi senior died in 2002; if the watch was passed to his more hardline son, it's unlikely to be an heirloom he will flaunt.

The Party established 155 ethnic autonomous areas, including five autonomous regions (Tibet and Xinjiang being two of them). In practice, any meaningful notion of 'autonomy' is severely constrained, and real power lies with the local Party apparatus, which is Han Chinese controlled. In most cases the local Party boss is a Han. Even at its most liberal, ethnic policy was built on a foundation of Han chauvinism, albeit a pragmatic version, which accepted that different groups could be allowed to progress at different speeds towards the shared goal of socialism and harmony. As China scholar James Leibold describes the policy: 'In China, the advanced Han majority must lead the way, but also assist their minority "brothers and sisters" in catching up. In response, revolutionary parties like the CCP (Chinese Communist Party) should provide breathing space and preferential development assistance to build up the trust and mutual understanding required for national integration.'[51]

Deng Xiaoping, who was China's most powerful leader from the late 1970s until his death in 1997, argued that the 'withering away' of ethnic diversity, though desirable, was a long-term process. In the meantime, it would be a mistake to ignore 'differences and peculiarities'. Under a series of affirmative action programmes, ethnic groups were exempted from China's one-child policy, given tax breaks and allowed to enter university with lower education scores. The years between the mid to late 1980s were relatively liberal across China, and that was reflected in a more relaxed attitude towards religion, as reform-minded Party leaders sought to make amends for the way ethnic minorities were treated during the Cultural Revolution.

As Deng saw it, national unity was best achieved by the economic development of 'backward' regions, which he believed would reduce conflict and hasten assimilation. To that end, the Party sunk billions of dollars into frontier regions. However, as we have seen in the case of Xinjiang, this was accompanied by a mass influx of Han Chinese, which marginalised the Uighurs, exacerbated inequalities and stoked resentment. At the same time, the 'tolerance' of diversity frequently amounted to little more than turning minority cultures into objects of entertainment for the Han.

Ethnic policy during this period has been characterised as a sort of Confucian paternalism, treating ethnic groups as one large family under Han Chinese leadership, interspersed with periods of severe repression, especially of the Uighurs and Tibetans. Still, ethnic groups regard this era as one of relative cultural freedom compared with what was to come.

Even before Xi Jinping took power in 2012, Party hardliners were pushing back. To them, the breakup of the Soviet Union into independent republics based on broad ethnic lines, and a spate of ethnic conflicts and 'colour revolutions' that followed, served as a warning of the dangers of pandering to diversity and of liberal policies in general. They were emboldened by unrest in Tibet in 2008, and then rioting in Urumqi the following year. They saw this as evidence of a failure of an ethnic policy that allowed the development of separate cultures and identities. They articulated a growing resentment among Han Chinese at the perceived advantages of the minorities, and at their lack of gratitude for the help they were being given.

Unlike his father, Xi has very little experience of ethnic issues. His rise through the Party ranks was mainly in more wealthy coastal regions. Neither volume of his book, *The Governance of China*, contains anything substantial on ethnic policy. But there is plenty on national unity, national rejuvenation and the leadership of the Party – all central to his notion of the 'Chinese Dream'. Faced with further resistance in Xinjiang, Xi quickly embraced the view of the hardliners, making clear that minorities should be required to conform to Han norms. Although repression in Xinjiang has been justified by Xi as a response to 'terrorism', he has presided over a fundamental sea change in ethnic policy that goes well beyond the Uighurs. Other provinces with significant minority populations are being urged to 'learn from Xinjiang'. To that end, affirmative action programmes are being rolled back, and cultural and religious symbols outlawed, including Arabic signage in public places.[52] Under Xi's policy, diverse ethnic cultures, religions and identities, in all but their most anodyne and kitschy form, are being subsumed by a virulent cultural nationalism.

National unity is Xi's overriding goal, achieved by repressing minority cultures. 'Patriotic education' is now at the forefront of ethnic work – in order to 'guide the people in establishing and persisting with the correct view of the fatherland, nation, culture and history, and constantly enhance the sense of belonging, identity, dignity and honor of the *Zhonghua* (Chinese) nation,' according to a Party directive.[53] Xi's ethnic policy is one of sinicisation of ethnic groups. He sees diversity as a threat to nation and to Party – and as such his strategy is a repudiation of the previous policies so closely associated with his father.

During the 2017 session of the National People's Congress, China's rubber-stamp parliament, Xi called for the building of a 'great wall of iron' to safeguard national unity, ethnic solidarity and social stability in Xinjiang.[54] Internal Communist Party documents leaked to the *New York Times* include secret speeches in which Xi called for an all-out 'struggle against terrorism, infiltration and separatism', using the tools of 'dictatorship'. He said the Party should show 'absolutely no mercy'.[55]

For 2,000 years, the oasis city of Kashgar has been an important trading post on the Silk Road. It is also a proud centre of Uighur culture and religion. Much of the old town has been razed, centuries-old architecture replaced by an artificial version, better equipped for surveillance. Today it is a place where people don't dare to speak the traditional Islamic greeting, *as-salaam alaikum*, where mosques are strung with banners to 'Love the Party, Love the People', alongside facial recognition cameras and metal detectors. It is a place where billboards proclaim that Xi Jinping is 'linked heart to heart with Xinjiang minorities', and where homes are colour-coded to denote 'virtuous households'.[56]

At the Id Kah mosque in Kashgar, the oldest and most important in China, every worshipper is watched, their identity recorded. The mosque sits on the corner of the city's main square, where a large clock tower shows the time – Beijing time. Kashgar is more than 2,000 miles west of the Chinese capital, meaning it should be two or three hours behind, but in China everywhere is officially on Beijing time. Unofficially, the lanes of teeming shops, cafes and market stalls that surround the square ignore Beijing's clock and follow their own rules, opening and closing according to 'Kashgar time'. Locals simply turn their own clocks back two hours. It started as a very practical thing to do, following the natural flow of the day, but now has an added edge, a gesture of defiance.

There's also a big screen overlooking the square, broadcasting propaganda, the world according to Xi Jinping and his Xinjiang Party boss, Chen Quanguo. Since Chen took over as Party secretary in 2016, his extreme security measures, reducing or even eliminating the ability to move around, have hit the economy hard, particularly in Uighur-majority areas.[57] The exception is the security industry. In a single year, between August 2016 and July 2017, Xinjiang advertised 90,866 security-related positions.[58] The hard-nosed former soldier was previously Party secretary in Tibet, where he was credited with crushing dissent through a policy of blanket policing. He was sent to Xinjiang with instructions to 'strike hard' in a region now regarded by Beijing as a far more serious security threat.

China has continued to insist that reports of forced detention are 'pure fabrication'. The Xinjiang governor claimed in December 2019 that the 'trainees' had all completed their studies and 'returned to society', without presenting any evidence.[59] Five months later the *South China Morning Post* reported that a 'job placement scheme', delayed by the Covid-19 outbreak, had been resumed. Tens of thousands of 'graduates' from the camps were being sent to work in factories around the country, where they were to be kept under close supervision, barred from leaving their dormitories without permission.[60] A report from the Canberra-based Australian Strategic Policy Institute described the scheme as, 'a new phase in China's social engineering campaign'. It identified twenty-seven factories in nine provinces, some of them part of the supply chains of leading global brands, that had taken 'batches' of Uighurs. The conditions, including constant surveillance, ideological training outside working hours and a ban on religious observance, 'strongly suggest forced labour'.[61]

A coalition of 180 human rights groups issued a 'call for action' over forced labour, pointing out that some 84 per cent of China's cotton production comes from the Uighur region, and that this fabric is used in factories across the country and across the world. 'Almost every major apparel brand and retailer selling cotton products is potentially implicated,' they state.[62]

Uighur and human rights groups and scholars have characterised China's behaviour in Xinjiang as 'cultural genocide', an attempt to 're-engineer' minorities to make them more like the Han Chinese, to forcibly assimilate them and eliminate their cultural differences.[63] That's not a defined crime in international law, but as a description of Beijing's assault on Uighur cultural identity – their language, religious institutions, cultural activities and practices, the forced separation of children from their parents – it is surely accurate.

Adrian Zenz, a China scholar who helped expose repression in Xinjiang, believes Beijing may have crossed the line to physical genocide by 'imposing measures intended to prevent births within the (targeted) group'. Zenz obtained local government documents that set 'performance targets' for mass sterilisations and the fitting of intrauterine devices (IUDs) in Uighur majority districts of southern Xinjiang. Hotan City alone set a sterilisation target of more than a third of married women between eighteen and forty-nine in a single year. In 2018, 80 per cent of all newly placed IUDs in China were fitted in Xinjiang, and the province performed at least seven times more sterilisations than the national average. By 2019, the authorities planned to subject four out of five married women of childbearing age in the rural southern prefectures to what they described as 'birth control measures with long-term effectiveness'.[64]

Forced contraception, sterilisation and abortions were once a feature of China's now abandoned 'one-child policy' – though that policy never applied to minorities, who were allowed two or even three children. Now it seems a version of that policy has returned, this time with the specific aim of reducing the birth rate among minorities, part of what Zenz describes as 'a systematic state campaign of suppressing minority births, while simultaneously encouraging a mass influx of new Han Chinese workers and settlers'.

Zenz also suggests that the internment camps are used to threaten and punish those who do not comply with population control measures. Having too many children is a leading reason given for detention in leaked reports, and detainees have described women in the camps being forcibly fitted with IUDs, or being subjected to sterilisation surgery. Others report being given injections that coincided with changes or cessation with their menstrual cycle. During 'anti-terror' lessons, inmates chanted, 'If we have too many children, we are religious extremists.'

Xinjiang is an algorithm-powered police state, but it would be wrong to describe this as simply a piece of predictive policing using artificial intelligence and big data. The algorithms being used against the

Uighurs serve a very specific purpose of social engineering and the repression of a targeted minority. Xinjiang is a laboratory for a new sort of totalitarianism. A test bed. A playground, almost. And while these chilling technologies are being used to bring Xinjiang to heel and eradicate Uighur culture, they are being primed and adapted for use against dissent elsewhere in China, while being packaged for export to autocrats across the world.

CHAPTER 2

Mass Surveillance

It was an unusual garden party, but that was to be expected of Ai Weiwei. The artist was easy to spot. A heavily set man dressed that day in neon pink, he moved through a crowd of supporters, signing T-shirts and posing for photographs. He was trailed by a group of foreign journalists who had made the journey to the small restaurant in Beijing's Caochangdi art district for what turned into a day-long party.

I was with a film crew, but it was not an easy event to cover. T-shirts, banners and badges were all emblazoned with the words 'Fuck Green Dam', and the American news network I was working for at the time was squeamish about broadcasting that sort of language in prime time. It was a challenge to my cameraman to capture the colour and senti-ment of the party, without bringing the dreaded f-word into the homes of Middle America.

The Green Dam Youth Escort, to give its full name, was a piece of censorship software that the government had ordered to be pre-installed on all personal computers sold in China. The authorities claimed it was to restrict online pornography, but its functions went well beyond that, automatically blocking access to banned websites and collecting pri-vate data. We all knew the garden party was being closely monitored by the police, but this was 2009. There was still some latitude for dissent, which Ai Weiwei exploited to the full.

He revelled in the role of thorn in the side of the Communist Party. His art was challenging and provocative. His 'Study of Perspective' was a series of photographs of his middle finger raised in front of well-known monuments, including Tiananmen Gate and its portrait of Mao Zedong.

Unlike many other dissidents, Ai had a degree of protection – at least for a while. He had a high international profile, and his father was a renowned poet, persecuted during the Cultural Revolution. Ai had also helped design the Bird's Nest stadium, which was the centre-point of the Beijing Olympic Games just a year before his Caochangdi garden party. But the Communist Party's patience was wearing thin, and in April 2011 he was grabbed by police at Beijing Capital airport as he was about to board a flight to Hong Kong. His studio was raided. He was held without charge for almost three months and then put under house arrest, amid vague allegations of 'economic crimes'.

The authorities installed fifteen surveillance cameras on a 100-metre stretch of road outside his house to monitor his movements and his visitors. Ai decorated them with red lanterns. 'I asked them why they needed so many,' he recalls. 'They told me they were owned by different departments. Some are civil, some are police, some are secret police. They don't trust each other.'

He then installed four live webcams *inside* his home, a live feed that could be viewed by anyone online. One was over his bed, one above his desk, one in his studio and one overlooking his yard. He described it as a favour to the police, just in case there was anything they'd missed. He told them he didn't have any secrets. Over the next two days his feed was viewed 5.2 million times. Then the police ordered him to shut it down. He complied, since he'd made his point, highlighting the way he was being watched – and also the irony and absurdity that while the Communist Party put him under surveillance it objected to him surveilling himself. When house arrest was eased, he was followed and photographed everywhere he went – to the park, to restaurants, walking his young son, meeting his girlfriend. 'They even photographed my driver's shoes. What for?'

When he discovered listening devices hidden in his studio, including one behind an electric socket, he shared pictures of them on social media. In a video post, he sets off firecrackers in a bin next to one device. A caption alongside reads, 'Can you hear this?' He laughs now looking back at that period. 'The Communist Party is probably the funniest thing that exists – but it doesn't have a sense of humour.' He knows that humour and ridicule can be powerful weapons against totalitarianism, but his experience from childhood – from watching the persecution of his father to his own struggle today as a dissident artist – has also opened his eyes to what he calls the 'toxic' reality of Party rule. 'I have been facing surveillance all my life,' he says. 'Surveillance is not about just monitoring you, rather it's to create fear and insecurity. It's the knife that never really cuts your skin, but is just next to your skin. Any moment blood can come out.'

The 'bunch of bedbugs', as Ai described the listening devices he found in his studio, seem rather retro compared with the surveillance tools Xi Jinping is now assembling. In 2015, as soon as he was allowed to travel, Ai left China. He moved first to Berlin, where he has a studio, and then to Cambridge, England, from where he spoke to me by Skype during the coronavirus lockdown.

'Today is beyond any science fiction,' he said. 'You have to see your power extend to the last door in the most remote village, and to know exactly what they are thinking behind that door.' The cameras that were once trained on his Beijing door had a specific purpose – to watch a single troublesome dissident and his visitors. Today's cameras are not only far more sophisticated, but part of a vast system of mass surveillance. Ai described Xi Jinping's China as a new type of state, a prototype. 'Now they know everybody, everywhere, if they want to, so there's no piece of land which is not infected. It's just like the coronavirus, it's the best metaphor for today's surveillance,' he said. 'It can get you anywhere, as long as the air is there and you can breathe, then you can get it.'

It is of little surprise that the police state and surveillance in general play a large role in Ai Weiwei's art. In an elaborate 2017 installation in New York called 'Hansel & Gretel', scores of overhead cameras and drones film each visitor, tracking them around the dimly lit hall. The images are displayed in red boxes on the floor beside them as they move around leaving a ghostly digital trail. One of Ai's most famous works is entitled 'Surveillance Camera', and consists of a camera on a plinth, carved out of a single block of white marble. It is simple and powerful, and there could not be a more fitting symbol for Xi Jinping's China.

'The people have sharp eyes' was a slogan used during the Cultural Revolution, the decade-long period of political frenzy launched by Mao Zedong in 1966 and ending when he died ten years later. Friends, family and neighbours were urged to spy on each other for signs of disloyalty to the leader. Estimates of those who died during those years of madness vary enormously, but it is certainly in the millions, many of them denounced as 'class enemies' and beaten to death.

'At that time they had perfect surveillance by asking everybody to examine themselves and to criticise others. This is so toxic, because the whole society was required to report husbands, report fathers – and students would report their teachers,' Ai Weiwei said. It was an experience his family shared with that of Xi Jinping. Both Xi and Ai were children of the Cultural Revolution; both of their fathers were persecuted. Yet they drew very different lessons. Ai became a rebel, a fierce critic of communist dictatorship and surveillance in general; in Xi, the experience instilled a deep fear of chaos and disorder and an obsession with stability, which in his view can only be achieved through an all-powerful Communist Party – even if that means borrowing techniques from the man responsible for the Cultural Revolution, Mao Zedong. Ai Weiwei has incorporated surveillance into his work; Xi Jinping is using it on an unprecedented scale to underwrite his power.

Surveillance has deep roots in communist China. For decades, life revolved around work units called *danwei*, with movement monitored and controlled by internal passports linked to a system of household registration called *Hukou*. In addition, there were secret political files called *dang'an* kept on every individual, and linked to their national identification cards. More than a dozen government agencies collected and updated personal information ranging from political views to birth control. The files were secret and couldn't be examined or challenged, but they affected every aspect of life, determining careers, education and mobility. After 1979, when Deng Xiaoping began to open up the economy, one impact was mass migration to coastal special economic zones, and the system came under growing pressure. Xi Jinping's surveillance state can be seen as a rebooting of these old practices for the modern era – but it is much more than that.

Cameras have long been an indispensable tool of the police state, though in the past they have been used primarily for targeted surveillance, as with those outside Ai Weiwei's house. A museum at the former Berlin headquarters of the Stasi, the East German secret police, who excelled at covert surveillance, provides a flavour of that world with its display of secret cameras hidden in belts, ties, watering cans and tree trunks. These days they seem almost quaint, but not the quote from Erich Mielke, the former head of the Stasi: 'Comrades, we have to know everything,' in large letters on the museum wall. It could easily be a leitmotiv of Xi's China.

According to a July 2020 report by Comparitech, a British technology website, 18 of the world's 20 most monitored cities and over half the surveillance cameras in use globally are in China.[1] The most surveilled city in the world was Taiyuan, the capital of Shanxi province, with Beijing taking the number five slot. Facial recognition cameras are now the norm, and Comparitech reports that at the current frantic rate of growth, China's camera count could rise to 540 million in 2021. Others estimate the 2020 count was already more than 600 million – that's almost one camera for every two people.

The Cultural Revolution slogan 'Sharp Eyes' faded away after Mao's death, but has been resurrected by Xi Jinping as the name of one of the newer components of his surveillance system – the extension of video surveillance, already all-pervasive in cities, to the most distant corners of rural China. According to government documents published by *China Digital Times*, the purpose was to have the system fully installed in rural regions by 2020, with 'full coverage, network sharing, real-time availability, and full control'. The documents mandate the installation of the latest cameras in order to provide blanket coverage of public areas and major industries, including transport systems, and with the ability to share the data widely across security agencies.[2]

There are cameras and there are cameras. Early surveillance cameras were 'dumb'. They monitored and recorded the scene in front of them, but needed people to interpret what was going on. In most cases the video was only accessed after an event, perhaps an accident or a crime, when the police were spooling through the video looking for evidence. The new cameras are smart, very smart. And China is leading the world, not only in unfettered mass surveillance, but in marrying those cameras to facial recognition and artificial intelligence.

The Shenzhen Convention and Exhibition Centre claims to be the largest single building in the southern city of Shenzhen, a booming metropolis of 13 million people, located right next to Hong Kong. The centre, a sprawling, glistening metal monster of a place, more than half a kilometre long, sits at the heart of the city. Its exhibition space is spread over nine halls with a combined area roughly the size of fifteen Wembley football pitches.

Over the last weekend of October 2019, the cavernous halls of the city's exhibition centre played host to the world's biggest surveillance technology show, the China Public Security Expo. The show's website modestly described it as 'the most influential exhibition in the world'.[3] Walls were festooned with prying cameras of every shape and size, from tiny dome-type devices – 'more discrete', as the sales literature describes them – to chunkier bullet or box-like cameras, their lenses moving eerily as they tracked passers-by. Scantily clad models wandered the aisles with wearable cameras pinned to their outfits, while the occasional drone buzzed overhead. They all fed big screens flickering with the high-resolution images. An army of sharp-suited and fast-speaking salespeople swarmed around the closely packed booths, which resembled a flickering and beeping high-tech shanty town.

In packed conference rooms their bosses preached the brave new surveillance world with evangelical zeal. 'We believe, over the next 20 to 30 years human society will enter a smart era with omnipresent sensing, all connectivity and pan-intelligence,' gushed Huawei executive director Wang Tao to an audience of hundreds.[4]

The faces on the screens around the hall looked as if they were enmeshed in cages, crisscrossed with lines and dots – illustrating the algorithms doing their work. They were reading the geometry of each face – examining the eyes, the nose, the mouth, and the distances between them, measuring the length from forehead to chin, and searching for other defining features. The more advanced systems search for dozens of facial landmarks, or 'nodal points', as the salespeople describe them, from which they construct a unique 'facial signature'. Little windows alongside each face on the giant screens displayed the algorithms' conclusions about the gender, estimated age and even the mood of each passer-by.

Companies claim their latest cameras can not only identify a face, but read its emotional state. Grumpy or happy, anxious or sad. Sales staff called this a sure-fire crime stopper, a way to read *intent*. Grab them before they do something bad. Think *Minority Report*, the science-fiction movie starring Tom Cruise in which a specialised police department nabs would-be criminals based on foreknowledge provided by psychics called 'precogs' – except in China's brave new world the precogs are mood-reading cameras.

'Using video footage, emotion recognition technology can rapidly identify criminal suspects by analysing their mental state . . . to prevent illegal acts including terrorism and smuggling,' Li Xiaoyu, a policing expert and Party official from the Public Security Bureau in Altay City in Xinjiang, told the *Financial Times*. He said the system had been deployed at customs posts to identity signs of aggressiveness and nervousness, as well as stress levels.[5]

Other cameras come with night vision, thermal imaging and directional microphones. Then there is motion tracking, cameras that are able to recognise people by the way they walk – their gait. The same grid-like lines and dots that had earlier encaged faces, now followed the movements of legs, the shuffling of feet, the swaying of bodies, the angle of heads. Every single movement analysed and digitised. They made passers-by look like cartoon characters – and to the algorithms I suppose that's what they are, not humans at all, but a series of data points that, crunched together, are unique identifiers.

'These cameras actually know the way the agent walks, how he talks, the way he moves, right down to his facial tics,' says Ilsa Faust (Rebecca Ferguson) in the movie *Mission Impossible – Rogue Nation*, as she briefs Benji Dunn (Simon Pegg) about gait analysis at a closely guarded power plant the team wants to break into. Images from the movie were used in promotional material by the Beijing-based start-up Watrix, which claims to be able to identify a person from fifty metres away by examining thousands of different metrics in the way they walk, even if they have their backs to the camera or head covered.[6] Gait recognition has the advantage that it doesn't require people to look at the camera, and can be done at considerable distance. Watrix claims to be able to recognise people in poor light and from any angle, and to have the world's largest gait database. 'Our accuracy at the laboratory level exceeds 96 per cent,' the company's co-founder Huang Yongzhen boasted to the *South China Morning Post*.[7]

The organisers of the Shenzhen show claimed it was the largest ever, with 1,500 exhibitors. They included most of the big names of the Chinese surveillance industry – the likes of Hikvision, the world's biggest manufacturer of surveillance cameras, and Dahua, a rapidly growing rival. A Dahua handout invited buyers to witness its new 'intelligent network camera', incorporating 'multiple lenses that can be remotely and independently adjusted, suitable for panoramic and detailed monitoring' for more efficient 'target tracking'. SenseTime, Ping An, Yitu and of course Huawei were also there. None of them, apart from possibly Huawei, are household names in Britain. But they are all rapidly growing companies – the nominally private contractors building China's surveillance state, with whom we shall become more familiar as this book progresses.

Buyers came from 150 different countries, though those who mattered most were Chinese – government and Party officials and the police, to whom the industry is beholden. The estimated global spend on surveillance equipment in 2019 was almost $20 billion, almost half of that by China.[8] China's internal security budget, the money earmarked by the government for surveilling its own people, reached $196 billion in 2017, exceeding the total for the military by 20 per cent.[9]

You didn't need an emotion-reading camera to detect that the assembled companies were extremely happy. But to prevent them getting too carried away with their booming businesses, there was one stall designed to keep them grounded – to remind the assembled companies who they are ultimately beholden to. This stall didn't display gadgets, but books – one book, to be precise. It was Xi Jinping's *The Governance of China* volumes I and II. The second volume has a message for entrepreneurs: 'You should always love the motherland, the people and the Party; practice the core values of socialism.' And, as for the younger generation of private sector leaders, 'They should be encouraged to carry forward the . . . great tradition of answering the call of and following the Party.'[10]

Shenzhen was where China's economic reforms began, a laboratory for paramount leader Deng Xiaoping's 'reform and opening' policy. It was China's first Special Economic Zone, established by Deng in 1980, and offering a degree of economic freedom to investors – reforms that were supervised by Xi Jinping's father, Xi Zhongxun. The city was initially fenced off from the rest of China, and ordinary Chinese citizens needed special permits to travel there. At that time it was a sleepy rural backwater with a population of barely 300,000; now it is the fifth most populous city in China, a sea of glistening skyscrapers.

As the reforms were extended, Guangdong, the region around Shenzhen, attracted massive investment. It became known as the 'factory of the world' because of the density of manufacturing facilities – tens of thousands of factories, churning out everything from toys to shoes, buttons, clothes and consumer electronics.

Shenzhen has at times been treated with suspicion by Party hardliners, for whom it is just a little too freewheeling and too heavily influenced by neighbouring Hong Kong – though economically useful all the same. These days, the city is applauded for leading the economy away from its dependence on low-cost, low-wage manufacturing to more 'value-added' businesses, in the jargon of economists. The tech sector now accounts for some 40 per cent of the city's economy, according to the local authorities. Yue Hai district is the high-tech hub, boasting dozens of home-grown start-ups, nurtured with generous government support. It is also home to Tencent, a social media giant; ZTE, a telecoms company; and DJI, the world's biggest manufacturer of drones. Even its highways have a tech theme – including Science and Research Road and High Tech Road. The corporate headquarters of Huawei Technologies is about a half-hour drive away. The area has frequently been described as China's Silicon Valley.

Shenzhen also has thirteen golf courses, the largest number of any city in China, with individual memberships typically costing more than $100,000 a year. Among them is Mission Hills, the biggest golf course in the world by number of holes. It's not surprising, perhaps, that a game so closely associated with wealth and deal-making should thrive in an entrepreneurial city, especially when big exhibitions come to town. Yet, in China, golf is not quite what it seems; it occupies a legal twilight zone, which the Party has exploited to the full. It is a metaphor for many of the ills and challenges of modern China – and a warning to those tech giants of Yue Hai.

When he came to power in 1949, Mao Zedong described golf as a bourgeois sport and had all golf courses dug up, turning many into zoos or communal farms. He banned government officials from playing the game, a ban that has never been officially lifted. In the early 1980s, as reforms began, the game crept back, farmers were forced from their land and unlicensed golf courses started sprouting across the country. They were banned again in 2004, ostensibly for consuming too much land and water, but they increased threefold *after* the ban. Hundreds were constructed, more than anywhere else in the world, though usually described as something different – typically a resort, country club or leisure facility, after the necessary arrangements were made with the local authorities.

Author Dan Washburn describes golf as China's 'Forbidden Game'[11] – it is banned, but booming, while at the same time it is a symbol of China's vast inequalities of wealth and of systemic corruption. When Xi came to power he too banned Party officials from playing and ordered the closure of more than 100 of China's 600-odd courses. It's impossible to know how those were chosen, since technically all golf courses are illegal; after lying low for a while, some quietly reopened. It seemed arbitrary, but that was probably intended. As I shall examine later in this book, the Party has a number of ways to ensure compliance from nominally private entrepreneurs, especially in the tech sector – legal, organisational and through old-fashioned fear and intimidation. But the Party also thrives in an atmosphere where rules are often opaque and arbitrarily enforced. By firing a shot across the fairways, Xi was demonstrating the power of the Party over those waiting to tee off below.

The practical application of the cameras on display in Shenzhen has spread rapidly across China. Some of the early uses of facial recognition were quirky, but with chilling undertones. In June 2017, the state-owned *Xinhua* news agency reported that facial recognition technology had been installed in several cities in order to shame jaywalkers.[12] In Jinan, the capital of Shandong province in the east of China, cameras were installed at fifty major junctions, taking several still images and a fifteen-second video of each offender crossing on a red light. The images were then displayed on a large video screen and matched with provincial police databases. 'Within 20 minutes the offender's photograph and personal information such as their ID number and home address are displayed on the screen at the crossroad,' Xinhua reported.

The Jinan police claimed to have nabbed 6,000 pedestrians in a little over a month. As well as shaming the offenders with the big screens, the police posted the images on social media, and said they'd be reported to their employers and residential communities. Offenders were contacted directly and given a choice between a fine of 20 yuan (just over £2), a half-hour course in traffic rules or twenty minutes assisting police in controlling traffic. The news agency quoted Jinan police saying the system had cut jaywalking from 200 cases a day to 20.

More than thirty major hospitals in Beijing installed facial recognition cameras to combat appointment scalping. Appointments can be tough to get in China, especially at the capital's more prestigious hospitals, and the system of making bookings online, known as *guahao*, is widely abused. Scalpers use the online system to make multiple appointments and then sell the appointment tickets to patients desperate to get to see a doctor. The medical authorities created a database of more than 2,000 of what they described as known 'scalpers', who were ejected from hospitals as soon as they were spotted by the cameras.[13]

Then there's toilet paper. The Beijing authorities turned to facial recognition to combat the rampant theft of paper from the toilets in public parks. The *New York Times* reported that before visitors are allowed to enter a public toilet at the city's Temple of Heaven Park, a top tourist attraction, they must 'stare into a computer mounted on the wall for three seconds before a machine dispenses a sheet of toilet paper, precisely two feet in length. If visitors require more, they are out of luck. The machine will not dispense a second roll to the same person for nine minutes.' The newspaper reported the approving comments of a nineteen-year-old customer called He Zhiqiang: 'Toilet paper is a public resource. We need to prevent waste.' Others though became frustrated at the short length of the paper dispensed and resorted to hammering the machines with their fists.[14]

In 2018, Ping An, a Chinese financial services conglomerate began to use micro-expression technology as a lie detector in order to assess applications for loans. The company claimed its technology could identify fifty-four brief and involuntary expressions created by the face before the brain takes full control. These include otherwise imperceptible movements of eyeballs and rapid blinking, each taking just a fraction of a second, providing pointers about whether a person is telling the truth, the bank claimed. 'It captures subtle changes in customers' facial expressions which help to identify and warn against fraud risks,' said Lee Yuansiong, one of Ping An's deputy chief executives.[15] The technology did not take the final decision, but flagged an applicant for further investigation. 'We've reduced credit losses by 60 per cent using this technology,' boasted Lee.

Facial recognition cameras are being used for access control, notably at housing complexes and schools. School children are required to look into screens mounted on automated gates, which swing open once a child's identity has been verified with a student database containing facial 'signatures'. The housing complex cameras restrict automatic entry to those registered as residents. Both claim to provide greater safety and security for those studying and living beyond the cameras, but also demonstrate how the ambitions of the surveillance state rapidly snowball.

Zhejiang Hangzhou No. 11 High School, in the eastern Chinese city of Hangzhou, has taken facial recognition well beyond the gates. It tracks not only the attendance record of each of the school's 1,010 students, but also their behaviour in class. The 'intelligent classroom behaviour management system', to give the system its full and creepy name, scans the classroom every thirty seconds. In a glowing report, the People's Daily, a Party newspaper, said: 'The camera is designed to log six types of behaviours by the students: reading, writing, hand raising, standing up, listening to the teacher, and leaning on the desk.

It also records the facial expressions of the students and logs whether they look happy, upset, angry, fearful or disgusted.'[16]

The *Global Times*, another Party newspaper, reported that more than ten schools in Guizhou province are keeping tabs on students by requiring them to wear 'intelligent uniforms', consisting of two microchips inserted in the shoulders. An alarm sounds if a student walks out of school without permission. And the uniforms are washable, says the paper, approvingly, and 'can endure temperatures of up to 150°C and 500 washes.'[17]

The effectiveness of facial or gait recognition cameras depends on the quality and size of the databases to which they are linked. The cameras are only part of the package, since the signatures must be matched speedily and accurately. The salespeople roaming the aisles at the Shenzhen show call this 'artificial intelligence' (AI), which has become a standard part of technology sales patter in East and West. It's a vague term, often heavier on the 'artificial' than the 'intelligence'. In the case of the cameras it can be better described as machine learning – algorithms able to process vast amounts of data, looking for patterns and matches, and cross-referencing with other available data sets.

As I shall examine in more detail later, China has a big advantage in building and linking these databases, since companies are unrestrained by any meaningful notion of data protection or privacy. AI platforms, containing the algorithms and databases, are increasingly part of the surveillance package offered by the tech companies, the databases often assembled in close cooperation with the police.

'Our machines can very easily recognise you from at least 2 billion people in a matter of seconds,' said Zhu Long, of his facial recognition algorithms. Zhu is the fresh-faced, bespectacled co-founder of Yitu Technologies, whose booming business occupies three floors of a new Shanghai skyscraper. Yitu, which roughly translates as 'according to the picture', was set up in 2012 when Zhu returned from the United States, where he worked for ten years. He has a PhD in statistics from the University of California in Los Angeles, and later became a postdoctoral fellow at the Massachusetts Institute of Technology.

In other words, Mr Zhu is a very smart man, with considerable experience of working in the West. His company does not make the physical cameras, but the AI systems that make them smart. In a futuristic meeting room exuding Silicon Valley 'cool' – dim lights and floor to ceiling windows overlooking the city – he tells a visiting journalist from the *South China Morning Post* that his technology will make the world a safer place, that 'AI is a revolution that will eventually surpass the scale and pace of the industrial one.'[18]

His first big break came with car number-plate recognition systems. His algorithms have also been tested in the ATM machines of one of China's leading banks, customers withdrawing money by showing their face to a camera built into the machine. Yitu is also working on diagnostic systems for hospitals.

Mostly, however, Yitu works with China's Ministry of Public Security, the police, for whom he has developed a system called 'Dragonfly Eye'. The police supply photographs for its vast database, while Yitu provides the algorithms and navigation tools to search and match. Zhu is vague about the precise source of all the photographs, but they are likely to be from the digital (machine-readable) IDs that all Chinese are required to carry, as well as from China's borders, where everyone, foreigner and Chinese, is photographed upon arrival and departure. He boasts that his system is being used in 150 municipal public security systems across the country, and is already making China a safer place.

Zhu claims that in its first three months in operation in the Shanghai metro system, 567 suspected lawbreakers were caught, while elsewhere some twenty-two 'wanted people' were arrested during the Qingdao International Beer Festival, and pickpocketing on Xiamen's city buses fell by 30 per cent. The company has won a Science and Technology Progress Award from the grateful Ministry of Public Security.

When asked about the speed at which such systems are being implemented in China, he falls back on euphemism. The Chinese people are 'very open to new stuff', he says. For which read, they have no choice. The government is also keen on it, and as a result 'opportunities for business abound'. No arguing with that. He points out that, like him, many of China's new tech elite studied abroad. And China has a lot of people, 1.4 billion of them, and people are data – and data is what feeds the hungry algorithms of AI. 'The idiosyncrasies of China make research in these fields more meaningful and practical than other countries,' he tells the *Post*.

Yitu is not unusual. Comments such as those from Zhu are routinely heard at tech conferences and shows in China. One Chinese technology executive I met, described the use of data in China as 'Privacy with Chinese characteristics.' Whenever the term 'Chinese characteristics' is used as part of a description it should always set alarm bells ringing. Usually it completely negates the words it follows. There is no privacy in China, which is why it is such an attractive laboratory for return- ing AI techies like Zhu (and quite a few of his Western counterparts). For all intents and purposes, the surveillance state is a joint venture between the Communist Party and China's nominally privately owned tech firms, something I shall examine in more detail later in this book.

Nabbing 'criminals' and preventing 'anti-social behaviour' are frequently cited as a reason for the proliferation of surveillance cameras, and as justification for the increasingly intrusive system. But the Communist Party has an extremely broad and ever-growing definition of what con- stitutes a 'criminal' and what is 'anti-social'.

As long ago as 2007, the government began compiling electronic databases of what were officially referred to as 'key individuals'. A set of 'Key Population Management Guidelines', defined these individuals as those 'suspected of threatening national security or public order' or providing a vague threat to 'stability'. Specific categories include religious believers, drug addicts, foreigners, paroled criminals and peti- tioners. The last category refers to those following a tradition dating back to Imperial times of directly petitioning the country's leaders for justice where citizens believe they are victims of the abuse of power.

It is reasonable to assume that under Xi Jinping these categories have been deepened and broadened. In practice the police can desig- nate almost anybody as a 'threat' and therefore a target of surveillance. *Foreign Policy* magazine has reported that building databases on key individuals has become a lucrative part of China's surveillance tech- nology sector, with at least thirteen tenders for such projects issued by public security bureaus across the country between 2015 and 2019. The systems are able to provide the police with automatic alerts about the movements of targeted individuals.[19]

Initially, the burgeoning surveillance systems were mostly under the control of the local police. But the government is now knitting together these disparate systems into one centrally managed national network of blanket video surveillance. The 'sharp eyes' programme is the rural component of this. The urban end was known as 'Skynet'. Perhaps somebody pointed out to Xi Jinping the Arnold Schwarzenegger con- nection – 'Skynet' was the AI system in the *Terminator* movies that became self-aware and triggered nuclear mayhem and much more

– because it has now been renamed *Pingan Chengshi*, or 'safe cities', which sounds a whole lot more cuddly.

'Safe cities' is another project of the Ministry of Public Security, a 'National Video Surveillance Networking Platform', in the jargon of its creators. The aim is to create what the National Development and Reform Commission in 2015 described as an 'omnipresent, fully networked, always working and fully controllable' system, incorporating facial recognition technology. The initial target was to provide '100 percent' coverage in public and residential spaces by 2020, when the number of cameras was expected to reach 626 million. This would give the police the ability to cross-reference images from cameras all over China, matching facial 'signatures' with those in the rapidly expanding databases.[20]

But the ambition of the Ministry of Public Security does not stop there. It also wants the ability to match the camera data with vast and growing sets of other personal data – a programme that has become known as the 'Police Cloud'. Human rights groups have gathered details from tender documents posted online by police bureaus, as well as academic and press reports. The system aims to integrate 63 types of police data and 115 types of data from dozens of other government departments and industries. These include basic data about family relations, address, birth control methods and religious affiliations, as well as travel details gleaned from flight, hotel, and vehicle number-plate records. Other data include biometrics and location information from mobile phones.

The purpose of bringing together these vast and multiple data sources is to 'improve social stability' and 'strengthen the ability to issue early warning about abnormal behaviour of key personnel', according to directives from the Ministry of Public Security. The system aims to track where individuals have been, who they have been with, what they have been doing, and to make predictions about their future activities. 'It is frightening that Chinese authorities are collecting and centralizing ever more information about hundreds of millions of ordinary people, identifying persons who deviate from what they determine to be "normal thought," and then surveilling them,' said Sophie Richardson, China director at Human Rights Watch.[21]

It is a massively scaled-up version of what has been built in Xinjiang. Whereas the Xinjiang system is designed to track around 10 million Uighurs and other Muslim minority groups, the 'Police Cloud' has 1.4 *billion* targets. As in Xinjiang, it is designed to aggregate and mine the data, searching for patterns of activities or associations that might prove threatening to the Party now or in the future. Human Rights Watch quotes Meng Jianzhu, the secretary of the Communist Party Political and Legal Committee, who said in 2015 that big data is important to 'find order . . . in fragmented information' and 'to pinpoint a person's identity'.

There was further insight from an article about new policing techniques published in the *Shandong Legal Daily*. In a report, highlighted by Human Rights Watch, it quotes a local policeman as saying: 'Every day at eight o'clock . . . based on our location and subscription options, the system sends us targeted messages; in particular, it alerts us to individuals who are involved in terrorism and in [undermining] social stability who've entered our jurisdictions.'

Xinjiang's version of the 'Police Cloud', the 'Integrated Joint Operations Platform', which aggregates all the data collected on the Uighur population and identifies those requiring further investigation and internment, is developed and sold by the China Electronics Technology Corporation, a state-run defence manufacturer with roots in China's nuclear weapons research programme. It is now marketing it aggressively elsewhere in China and abroad. It has been tested in the wealthy coastal provinces of Zhejiang and Guangdong, and the company has signed a deal with the police in Shenzhen, China's high-tech hub. At a demonstration of the system at an industry fair, a slogan on the screen read, 'If someone exists, there will be traces, and if there are connections, there will be information.' It treats a city like a battlefield, and is designed to 'apply the ideas of military cyber systems to civilian public security', according to a company blog post promoting the system.[22]

In Britain and other Western democracies, where a version of what's been called predictive policing has been used to analyse past patterns of crime to predict future criminal activities, it has been criticised for reinforcing racial and social profiling, and other discrimination. Not only is there no sign that this is a concern in China, but profiling minorities and targeting behaviour deemed a threat to the Communist Party is the very point of the system.

There have been questions about the accuracy of facial recognition – systems trialled controversially by the UK police had high failure rates.[23] Others have cited bureaucratic inefficiencies and questioned the ability of China to crunch such vast amounts of data. It may be that the Chinese system is not yet as accurate as it is often portrayed, but the technology is fast improving, and its implementation is racing ahead, unrestrained by any concerns for privacy or other political rights. And in any case, debating the technical shortcomings misses the point. The *perception* of mass surveillance, the fear this instils, and the way this fear can change behaviour is as important in a totalitarian state as the accuracy of the physical technology. In Orwell's *Nineteen Eighty-Four*, Winston Smith had to assume that 'every sound you made was overheard, and, except in the darkness, every movement scrutinised'. He didn't know for certain that was the case, but he modified his behaviour and self-censored accordingly.

This was also the central concept of Jeremy Bentham's panopticon penitentiary. The eighteenth-century British philosopher envisaged a circular building with a tower at its centre, from where all the inmates could be watched. They would never know for sure if they were being monitored at any particular time, but that didn't matter, it was the *fear* of being watched that was the most powerful tool. Bentham described his panopticon as 'a new mode of obtaining power of mind over mind'.

It's not clear how detailed a grasp Xi Jinping has over the nitty-gritty of the technology that increasingly underpins his rule, but he understands its power. Xi has a three-stage plan for AI: the first stage was to match the world's best by 2020, the second is to lead in certain areas by 2025, and finally to dominate the field by 2030. In October 2018, he convened a 'study group' during which AI experts briefed the Party's twenty-five-strong Politburo. Xi told them that China should 'ensure that critical and core AI technologies are firmly grasped in our own hands ... (and) fully give rein to our country's advantages of vast quantities of data and its huge scale for market application'. He added that it was necessary to 'promote the deep application of AI in the field of public security'.[24]

That same month, during a visit to an appliance-maker in Guangdong province, he said China should become 'self-reliant' in technology, a term that in China is closely associated with Mao.[25] Policies to support and protect indigenous technology and tech companies run though Xi's vision for the future, and, as I shall examine, is one of the key sources of tensions with the United States, compounded by China's theft of intellectual property.

Xi, dubbed the 'chairman of everything' for his accumulation of power, has taken personal control over aspects of technology and innovation policy, through the workings of 'leading small groups' and 'central commissions' within the Party. These have become key instruments of his rule.

Power in China has been likened to a Russian matryoshka nesting doll, where the bigger outer layers (like China's rubber-stamp parliament) are essentially powerless; it's the often obscure hidden layers that matter. In theory, the most powerful Party institutions are the Politburo and its seven-member standing committee. In practice, power lies with the small groups and commissions. These have always existed; Jiang Qing, Mao's wife, directed the early years of the Cultural Revolution through such a group. After the Cultural Revolution and before Xi Jinping came to power, they primarily served a coordination role, but he has expanded their use and turned them into powerful policy-making bodies, arranged around himself as self-proclaimed 'core' leader. This has enabled Xi to put himself in control of multiple areas of policy, personally overseeing central commissions on national security, cybersecurity and the integration of civil and military technologies. Seen through the prism of this decision-making system, technology and innovation are first and foremost issues of security.

Mao Zedong had his Little Red Book; Xi Jinping has an app. It is called 'Study the Great Nation' and contains videos and articles about 'Xi Jinping Thought', as well as his activities. Users can take part in competitions and quizzes, testing their knowledge about Xi, and earning points and prizes if they answer correctly. A leader board shows how well they've done and compares the score with other users.

The app, launched amid much fanfare in early 2019, was developed by the Communist Party propaganda department in collaboration with the Chinese tech giant Alibaba. The authorities claim that in its first three months it was the most downloaded app in China and had 100 million registered users – though not necessarily by choice. Not only was Xi's 'little red app' heavily promoted by schools, universities and the state media, but its use is mandatory among civil servants and Party officials. In order to obtain a press card and do their job, Chinese journalists have to pass a test on the life of Xi, delivered via the app.

It was not the first time that Xi had ventured into the world of social media; a year earlier, the Party launched an app called 'Learn from Xi', which was a collection of quotes and speeches from the first volume of his book, *The Governance of China*. It also contained a map of the country, showing where each speech had been made, and a series of academic papers analysing his views in glowing terms.

The new 'Study the Great Nation' app had an extra feature – a sting in the tail: it spied on users. The Open Technology Fund, a US-based internet freedom advocacy group, commissioned a technical exami- nation of the app, which found the version for the Android operating system, widely used on smartphones in China, had a backdoor which enabled the authorities to get access to the messages and photos on users' phones, snoop on their contacts and browsing history, scan the other apps on the phone, and activate microphones and audio record- ers.[26] It was what the cybersecurity community called spyware, and it had an enormous appetite. 'What's clear is that while the CCP (Chinese Communist Party) advertises "Study the Great Nation" as a way for citizens to prove their loyalty and study their country, the app's main- tainers are studying them right back,' said the Open Technology Fund in a summary of the report.[27]

The proliferation of facial recognition surveillance across China, and its linking to a growing number of other databases, is not the only security system developed and then adapted from Xinjiang. In the Chinese city of Baishan, DNA samples have been taken under the guise of 'health checks', while across the country saliva swabs or blood samples are routinely gathered from those arrested for minor misdemeanours. These include failing to carry identity cards or writing blogs critical of the state, accord- ing to documents presented to a national police DNA conference. 'We're transforming DNA technology from simply a criminal investigation tool into an important initiative for social control and safety keeping,' accord- ing to a conference paper from the police in the province of Ningxia.[28]

The aim is to build the world's largest DNA database; the initial target was 100 million genetic samples by 2020. Scientists are also looking at ways of using a DNA sample to create an image of a person's face. The process, called DNA phenotyping, analyses genes for traits like skin colour, eye colour and ancestry. Perhaps unsurprisingly, this research is also being carried out in Xinjiang, and if successful could considerably enhance facial recognition and surveillance systems.[29]

The illicit and wholesale harvesting of data from mobile phones is another surveillance technique field-tested in Xinjiang and now being deployed across China. French security researcher Baptiste Robert identified an app called MFSocket, which police are installing on smartphones during routine security checks. The app gives the police access to image and audio files, location data, call logs, messages, calendars and contacts.[30] Also fast spreading to police forces across the country are portable or desktop mobile-phone scanners, able to extract and analyse contact lists, photos, videos, social media posts and email, and feeding into a central repository of extracted data.[31]

There have also been reports of increased use of IMSI catchers in order to improve the accuracy of face recognition. The International Mobile Subscriber Identity (IMSI) is a number that uniquely identifies each user of a cellular network. The catchers are small white boxes, frequently installed alongside the cameras, which read the codes from passing mobile phones, which are then matched with faces. They can also trigger a virtual alarm when a person listed as suspect approaches a particular location.[32]

In its hunger for data, to track and to watch, China has turned to 'surveillance by design'. Take for example the boom in electric vehicle sales, a technology where China has vowed to become world leader. By law, all such cars sold and driven in China, must 'check-in' every thirty seconds, sending to the authorities a stream of data, including the car's location, speed and direction. Drivers are not made aware of how or why this data is harvested, but under a regulation of the Ministry of Industry and Information Technology, a mandatory 'monitoring platform' must be installed on every car and linked to local and national government databases.[33]

Entire cities are being redesigned and built for surveillance. These are usually referred to as 'smart cities', and are not just a Chinese phenomenon; there's nothing more guaranteed to quicken the pulse of techies worldwide than talk of intelligent, futuristic cities. By one account, half of an estimated 1,000 smart cities under construction worldwide are in China.[34] They generate a lot of techno-babble about a wired, networked future, but as *Scientific American* reported, 'The current reality of smart cities is that there aren't any. At the end of the day, most so-called smart cities are just cities with a few or several standout smart projects.'[35]

In Western democracies, smart cities have generated considerable controversy. A partnership between the city of Toronto and Google's Sidewalk Labs is supposed to transform a twelve-acre stretch of derelict waterfront into an urban shrine to information technology. It will bristle with sensors, using the data – on traffic, air quality, noise, energy use, even the amount of trash in its bins – to guide its operation and to manage services. But ever since the deal was struck in 2017, it has been bedevilled with concerns over privacy and distrust about how Google will use the data.[36]

There is no such anxiety in China, where many smart cities are being built from scratch. In spite of the vast number of pilots claimed by Beijing, it has provided very little detail about their operation, or the supposed benefits they are bringing to urban populations. We do know from reports that in Yinchuan, buses have facial recognition cameras that identify and automatically charge commuters, and there are wired trash bins that alert a central server when they are full.[37] In Hangzhou, the traffic lights are managed by something called the 'city brain', linked to a network of cameras and easing the flow of emergency vehicles through the traffic. It is no accident that in the Chinese context the term 'smart cities' is often used interchangeably with 'safe cities', since the emphasis is overwhelmingly on security and surveillance. As Rogier Creemers, an expert in Chinese law and technology at Leiden University in the Netherlands, told the *Financial Times*, 'It is very clear that surveillance is a significant element in China's conception of smart cities.'[38]

Shortly before Christmas 2019, China rolled out anther use for facial recognition. A law came into operation requiring everyone signing up for new mobile phone services to have their faces scanned.[39] For years Beijing has been trying to eliminate online anonymity, and force internet users to register with their real names. It had become a game of cat and mouse, users often hiding behind assumed identities to criticise the government. The Party was now attempting to close down any remaining loopholes, checking that faces match IDs.

It served as a reminder that while the surveillance state has been watching and tracking, dramatically extending its reach, the Communist Party has also been tightening its grip on the online world. The internet and social media, which once held so much promise in China have been weaponised by the Party and turned into instruments of social control. While the cameras watch behaviour, the internet and social media are being used to control, and even modify, it.

CHAPTER 3

Big Brother Logs On

The smog was so bad you could taste it. Buildings were fuzzy outlines in the gloom, hundreds of flights were cancelled or delayed, while cars, their headlights on throughout the day, crept gingerly along Beijing's darkened and eerie streets. 'It looks like the end of the world,' said one blogger, while another asked whether she would ever see the sun again. Beijing's foreign residents dubbed it 'The Airpocalypse'.

But the Beijing Municipal Environmental Protection Bureau had a different view. The filthy air had nothing to do with pollution. Indeed, said Du Shaozhong, the Bureau's vice-president, it is an 'indisputable fact' that air pollution in Beijing has improved in recent years.[1] It was 2011 and the miasma would descend on Beijing for days on end, but the authorities were in denial. If they acknowledged the smog at all, they called it 'fog' or 'mist', or they blamed the prevailing wind or some other weather-related phenomenon. Or else it was a scurrilous internet rumour, even a foreign conspiracy on account of the air quality monitor on the roof of the US embassy, which tweeted hourly readings.

The levels of fine particles in the air, the most dangerous, frequently went beyond index, which the embassy on one particularly grim day described as 'crazy bad'. The pollution levels were routinely multiples of what is deemed safe by the World Health Organization. The government responded by demanding the embassy shut down the monitor, claiming it violated Chinese sovereignty. The embassy refused, and China's army of bloggers reproduced and spread the figures, fuelling growing online anger and ridicule.

This was the height of Weibo power, when China's Twitter-like micro-blogging platform was at its most popular, influential and irreverent, giving Chinese netizens a platform to vent. And they did, with gusto – 'Beijing is dangerous!', 'How will our children cope?', 'The haze is back again, again, again, again!'. They accused the authorities of treating people like idiots and demanded action. They posted doctored photographs of monsters lurking in the gloom, selfies flaunting their anti-pollution masks, and before and after images of well-known landmarks. A micro-brewery advertised a new beer, the Airpocalypse, the price of which was based on the air quality index. If the pollution went off index, the beer would be free. Online sales of masks and air purifiers exploded.

For a while, the Communist Party responded in time-honoured fashion – it deleted posts. It blocked from websites a documentary about the pollution, *Under the Dome*, that had been made by a former journalist with the state broadcaster, CCTV, but only after it had been viewed 100 million times. But not even the Party, for all its well-practiced ability to deny reality, could continue to reject the blindingly obvious. It finally conceded there was a problem. Traffic restrictions were introduced on smoggy days and efforts made to reduce coal-burning and to cut emissions from the belching factories in the province surrounding Beijing. In 2012, the authorities began nationwide monitoring of the most dangerous particles, which they had not tracked before. Researchers analysing that data estimated that air pollution contributed to 1.6 million deaths a year in China.[2] The prime minister would later declare a 'war' on pollution and vow to 'make our skies blue again'.[3]

Air quality apps proliferated online, as did scepticism – the authorities were accused of paying lip-service to the pollution, or merely shifting the problem (with the polluting factories) to elsewhere in China. But the government had responded to the pressure; it was a victory for China's netizens, which they savoured and built upon.

The word netizen (citizen of the internet) originated in the West, where internet pioneer and author Michael Hauben is credited with inventing the term. It became popular in the mid 1990s, especially among internet libertarians who saw cyberspace as a kind of separate realm. That was very much in the spirit of John Perry Barlow, the joint founder of the Electronic Frontier Foundation who, in early 1996, issued a declaration of the independence of cyberspace, a libertarian challenge, in which he claimed the internet was beyond the sovereignty of nation states, a place where real-world laws have no legitimacy and cannot be applied.[4]

Not that there were many Chinese internet users around to read it.

That was the year when CHINANET, China's first commercial internet was launched. China's online population was tiny, but quickly exploded. A decade later it had reached 111 million and US President Bill Clinton was likening attempts to control the internet to 'trying to nail Jell-O to the wall'.[5] Pretty futile, in other words. By 2012, the year the Chinese authorities conceded that the country did indeed have a pollution problem, there were more than half a billion Chinese internet users.[6] By then the term netizen was going out of fashion in the West, but it resonated in China, where it was also a direct translation of the word *wangmin*. This breaks down as *wang* (net) and *min* (citizen), and arguably the symbolism was far greater in a society where to physically engage with politics was so much more dangerous. To Chinese netizens at that time, the internet really did feel like something new and liberating, where you could do and say things that could get you into serious trouble in the real world.

They targeted corrupt and double-speaking officials. The 'naked official' who syphoned public funds and sent them to relatives abroad; the 'watch brother' with a taste for luxury watches; the 'great, glorious and correct' Communist Party officials who insisted they were always right.

When two of China's high-speed trains collided on a viaduct near Wenzhou, killing forty people, the authorities reacted in familiar fashion – they tried to muzzle the media, a leaked propaganda directive ordered reporters to concentrate on heroic rescue efforts and not to link the crash to any failings in the country's prestigious high-speed rail programme. Netizens had other ideas, and accused officials of quite literally burying the evidence – images went viral of the authorities burying damaged carriages. There was outrage online, forcing Prime Minister Wen Jiabao to order a 'serious investigation'.

As a journalist working in Beijing at that time, it was refreshing to watch. We felt there really was something in China called public opinion, and it was being channelled via social media, notably Weibo. It was also a game of cat and mouse. The Chinese internet had a language of its own, a language of code, satire and metaphor. The netizens used images, acronyms, and other often bizarre abbreviations which evolved and mutated in order to keep one step ahead of the clunky government censors. As one reference was blocked, another would emerge. An entire dictionary was published by overseas Chinese dissidents to help journalists like me keep up with the language.[7]

The dictionary was called *The Grass-Mud Horse Lexicon*. The Grass-Mud Horse was a creature that emerged in 2009 in an online music video which went viral. In Mandarin, 'grass-mud horse' sounds the same as 'fuck your mother'. It was originally coined to poke fun at and get around censorship of vulgar content, but within weeks it became the mascot of Chinese internet users fighting for free expression. It inspired poetry, photos, clothing and artwork. Some bloggers had huge followings; anonymous accounts were frequently used. The risks seemed low. Netizens felt part of a huge community, which gave them a feeling of power and immunity.

The fourth of June is always a busy time for China's netizens and censors. The Party has attempted to write the 1989 Tiananmen Square massacre out of official history, and the anniversary is always a time when the Party's censors are working overtime, attempting to block any reference to the event or the date – even to words such as 'democracy', 'freedom' and 'protest', and just about any variation on that theme or that date. Type any of these into a search engine in China and a message will pop up telling you that according to relevant laws, statutes and policies, the results of your search could not be shown.

In 2013, a Dutch artist named Florentijn Hofman created a fifty-three-foot-tall sculpture of a yellow rubber duck and took it on tour to China, floating it on rivers and lakes in a number of Chinese cities. It was immensely popular. So much so, that as the Tiananmen anniversary approached, one imaginative netizen doctored the famous photograph of a protester facing down tanks, replacing the tanks with a row of ducks. It went viral before it was deleted by censors, who then added the phrase 'big yellow duck' to those that were blocked.[8]

In the office of NBC News, where I was correspondent, we employed a team of young interns to trawl through the chat rooms and micro-blogs of the internet. That was always more productive than flicking through the predictable news stories in dreary Party newspapers. It became our biggest source of original stories. An environmental protest in Guangdong? Check the chat rooms. Giant killer hornets creating mayhem in Hunan? A chemical explosion in Tianjin? A food scandal? Shoddily constructed schools collapsing in an earthquake? The best information and images were always online, as was the raw anger and frustration of the Chinese people.

When alleged Xinjiang separatists crashed and set fire to a jeep beneath the portrait of Mao Zedong at Tiananmen Gate in October

2013, it was possible to create an entire chronology from photographs and videos posted online. Of course, the photographs were quickly deleted by censors, but not before our intrepid interns were able to download them. The jeep was still smouldering beneath the portrait of Mao when I arrived in Tiananmen Square with a film crew. It was surrounded by police, who angrily pushed us away. When a public bus stopped nearby, the police immediately ignored my team and piled onto the bus like a deranged SWAT team, yelling and shouting. They set about angrily snatching smartphones, which had been lined up all along the bus window, desperate to prevent further images being uploaded to social media.

Mobile phones had yet to become the instruments of ubiquitous tracking they are today; instead they were wielded like weapons, a symbol of power, capturing and posting not just images of dramatic events, but everyday scenes of injustice – or just the arrogance and absurdity of petty officialdom. The yawning bureaucrat, the sleeping security guard, the lazy baggage handlers throwing bags towards a conveyor belt to an aircraft (and mostly missing), an abusive aircraft attendant, a traffic cop soliciting a bribe. If there was a confrontation with police in the street, it wasn't unusual to see people lined up like gunslingers in an old western, but instead of hands on holsters, they were preparing to draw their phones.

Social media was the pulse of young China. It provided space for discussion and criticism, and it gave hope that things were changing for the better. Yes, there was a system of online censorship, dubbed the Great Firewall, which was built largely around blocking websites and keywords, but it was slow and clunky. It was like a Swiss cheese. There were lots of holes in it, and a determined netizen could always find a way to access banned content or express how he or she felt without too much fear of reprisal.

It really did feel like the Communist Party had met its match with the internet, that the online world was introducing a form of accountability to an authoritarian system and changing China for the better. We even speculated that more liberal elements in the Party saw the internet as a good way of allowing people to let off steam, especially when anger was aimed at local officials. It enabled the government to identify and tackle grievances before they developed further.

Of course, we saw what had happened in Xinjiang, where, following the 2009 riots in Urumqi, the authorities shut down the internet.

It would be a year before it was fully restored, with once thriving Uighur-language websites permanently closed, bloggers and webmasters imprisoned. It was a heavy-handed and crude response, almost an act of desperation. It seemed inconceivable that the government would do that elsewhere in China; it was committed to expanding cyberspace and reaping the internet's economic benefits. The internet felt simply too big, complex and anarchic to tame. Looking back now, that view was breathtakingly naïve and completely wrong.

The internet and social media played an important – though probably exaggerated – role in popular uprisings across the Middle East and former Soviet republics between 2009 and 2014. These were variously described as 'Twitter Revolutions' or 'Facebook Revolutions' because of the way these platforms were used to coordinate the protests, communicate between those who took part and generally spread unfiltered information. Lengthy articles and books have analysed the arrival of what was termed 'network protest'.[9] With hindsight, these uprisings were less about the power of social networks and the internet, and more about the sluggishness with which authoritarian governments responded to a new media they didn't understand, and didn't immediately see as a threat. They have fast been playing catch-up, and no more so than in China.

Facebook, Twitter and YouTube are blocked in mainland China, but the Communist Party was still shaken by the so-called 'colour revolutions'. They played to its deep sense of paranoia, and when pro-democracy protest first engulfed Hong Kong in 2014, it seemed like the techniques of those revolutions had arrived smack on its own doorstep.

Xi Jinping assumed power in 2012 determined to snuff out the brief era of online openness and dissent, and to re-take the internet. Online public opinion should be 'healthy and sound', he told a specially created Central Leading Group for Cyberspace Affairs, over which he personally presided. The internet should 'advocate things wholesome and positive, and disseminate and put into practice the core socialist values'.[10]

'The Internet has grown into an ideological battlefield, and whoever controls the tool will win the war,' thundered the *People's Liberation Army Daily* in an editorial. 'Western hostile forces along with a small number of Chinese "ideological traitors", have maliciously attacked the Communist Party of China, and smeared our founding leaders and heroes, with the help of the Internet,' according to the paper, which vowed to 'protect ideological and political security on the invisible battlefield of the internet'.[11]

Xi was determined to isolate China's internet from the outside world and assert what he called 'internet sovereignty'. He set about reinforcing and raising the Great Firewall. His ultimate goal: to curtail the power of the internet and social media as instruments of dissent and turn them into powerful weapons of social control.

Under Xi, the Great Firewall has grown into the world's most extensive and sophisticated system of internet censorship. It works on two levels: filtering and blocking traffic entering the country from the global internet, and monitoring and censoring the flow of traffic internally. It blocks entire websites, including those of Western news organisations. *The Economist*, BBC and *New York Times* are blocked as a matter of routine, as are those of international human rights organisations and others deemed hostile. It also searches for keywords, such as 'Tiananmen Square', 'Tibetan independence' or the 'Dalai Lama', or variations on those themes. The lists change according to events or circumstances. The system has the ability to conduct rapidly what computer scientists call 'deep packet inspection'. This involves delving inside the individual packets of data that make up internet traffic, searching for words or phrases. These packets can be messages, emails or documents.

The system has become far smarter since the Grass-Mud Horse came galloping onto the scene in 2009. Images and drawings were always a popular and relatively safe way of escaping the dragnet. For example, the symbol of the 2014 Hong Kong protests was an umbrella. Chinese netizens showed their support by sharing photographs of umbrellas. Some went further, and posted images of Chinese leaders, umbrellas in hand. They were hard to block by automatic filtering. But no longer. Citizen Lab, a University of Toronto-based group studying internet censorship, has found evidence of images blocked in mid-transit during chats on WeChat, a popular Chinese platform. A report describes this as, 'the first time we see image filtering in one-on-one chats, in addition to image filtering in group chats and WeChat moments'.[12] More recently, the system has been used against Winnie-the-Pooh. China's thin-skinned president has been likened online to the portly cartoon character. The image became a way of ridiculing him, and the authorities reacted by banning any references to the rotund bear.

The system also has the capability to backward search, so that not only is a post with an offending word or topic deleted on the day that it is discovered, but associated and earlier posts are also taken out. This is particularly the case when a new word or phrase is added to the censorship list. 'In essence, those earlier posts are removed from the records so that no search would detect them,' according to Dean Cheng, in his study of China's cyber operations.[13]

China employs an army of internet police – it has been estimated at between 50,000 and 100,000. Nobody knows for sure, although there is wide agreement that it has risen sharply under Xi Jinping. Their primary task is to catch the undesirable material that manages to get through the automated filters. Although they are usually described as a police force, most are employed by the internet service providers or social networks themselves. They are supplemented by animated police characters, which pop up from time to time and wander across your screen – as a not-so-subtle reminder that your online activities are being monitored. The Ministry of Public Security has also set up what it calls 'cybersecurity police stations' inside internet firms, presumably to monitor the monitors.[14]

Here too, the system has become more sophisticated. It employs up to 2 million additional monitors whose job it is not to block, but to join and steer conversations and debate, or simply change the subject. The Party's propagandists seem to have concluded that this can be more effective than simply blocking content. The monitors are not necessarily all Party loyalists; it is reported to be quite a popular and reasonably well-paid graduate job.

In Wisdom Mountain Twin Towers, a glass tower in a trendy part of the eastern port city of Tianjin, hundreds of young men and women sit in front of screens scouring the internet for videos and messages that run against Party doctrine. They are on the lookout for references to Xi and nicknames poking fun at state leaders. It is described by those who work there as an 'audit' centre and a 'cool place to work'. The number of employees rose from forty to nearly a thousand in just two years. An advertisement posted on the Tianjin Foreign Studies University's careers page sought 100 graduates to work in 'content audit', earning up to 6,000 yuan (£700) per month. Candidates needed to be 'politically savvy' and to 'love news and current affairs'.[15]

The system was analysed in groundbreaking research by American academics who estimate that the Chinese government 'fabricates and posts about 448 million social media comments a year'.[16] They say the operation is massive and secretive, the goal being to 'distract the public and change the subject'. The Communist Party describes this work as 'public opinion guidance'. Chinese netizens have dubbed the propaganda workers *wumaodang*, the '50-cent-army', because this is how much they are rumoured to be paid for each pro-government post.

A rare insight into the working of the system came in December 2015 when Pu Zhiqiang, a human rights lawyer, was given a three-year suspended sentence for 'picking quarrels and provoking trouble'. A leaked government document instructed 'internet commentators' to 'post three comments, including 1–2 pieces of quality content. Please everyone follow news reports to arrange posts with the following content: Pu always pled guilty, offered a sincere apology to the community and victims, and recognized the criminal charges of the prosecution.'[17]

The Cyberspace Administration of China has 'encouraged' online content providers to produce material 'publicizing Xi Jinping Thought', 'publicizing the Party's theoretical path, directives and policies', 'publicizing exceptional moral culture and zeitgeist, fully presenting the uplifting spirit of the Chinese people' and to turn out content 'that helps increase the international influence of Chinese culture'.[18]

The Party has also sought to recruit 'citizen sensors', asking internet users themselves to report 'inappropriate' content, and often rewarding them for doing so. They are asked to report 'pornographic', 'political' or 'terrorist' postings, with Shanghai's cyber administration going as far as organising a 'propaganda month' for volunteers to combat online 'disorder'.[19]

Sometimes, the efforts to achieve what Xi Jinping has called a 'wholesome and positive' internet can be surreal. *Douyin*, a short-video sharing platform, banned Peppa Pig and removed 30,000 video clips under the hashtag #peppapig. The pink cartoon pig had attracted a big following among Chinese children, but had also become a counter-cultural icon among young adults, dubbed *shehuiren*. 'They are unruly slackers roaming around and the antithesis of the young generation the Party tries to cultivate,' said the *Global Times*, a Party newspaper, explaining the Peppa Pig ban.[20]

It was about this time that I heard about a young Chinese stand-up comedian who had studied for several years in New York, where he learned his routine, and had recently returned to Beijing. He had started to perform in a small city venue, but I heard that he was struggling to get people to laugh. I wondered whether this was because stand-up comedy didn't really travel, or perhaps the need to tone down the politics in China had stripped it of its comic bite. He shook his head when I met him over a beer near Beijing's picturesque Houhai Lake. 'It's modern China,' he said. 'It's beyond parody.'

In the early days of the internet in China, it was easy to hide online. The ability to complain anonymously, and to poke fun at officials behind assumed identities, emboldened and enlivened discussion. It gave confidence to those seeking to expose corruption and other injustice. Rules against anonymity were not rigorously enforced, but have been progressively tightened. Anybody signing up for China's most popular micro-blogging sites, Weibo and WeChat, or using other online communities or discussion forums are supposed to use their real names, which the sites have to verify. The rules, issued by the Cyberspace Administration of China (CAC) cover any platform that has what the authorities call a 'news feature' or which 'mobilize society'. A further blow against anonymity came in late 2019 when it was announced that all mobile phone users must submit to facial recognition scans when registering new SIM cards.

The Party has also targeted virtual private networks (VPNs) and other tools that are used to circumvent censorship and access banned websites. It ordered the country's three telecommunications companies to block access to them, and has sought to eliminate them from app stores.[21]

Every computer has an identity called an IP address. A VPN allows an internet user to assume an IP address in a different country. Think of it as an encrypted tunnel for burrowing under the Great Firewall. In the UK they are commonly used by avid sports fans to circumvent geographic limitations on sports apps so they can watch their favourite games while on a foreign holiday. They have been widely used by millions of ordinary Chinese internet users as well as being an important tool for foreign businesses in China and for academics.

In a letter to US senators, Apple admitted that it removed 674 VPNs from its China app store at the request of the Chinese government.[22] Amnesty International described this as a 'deplorable decision'. While ExpressVPN, one of the biggest providers, said, 'It represents the most drastic measure the Chinese government has taken to block the use of VPNs to date, and we are troubled to see Apple aiding China's censorship effort.'[23] I will examine the role of Apple and other Western companies more closely later in this book; suffice to say at this point that Apple claimed it was merely obeying the law, while a spokesman for China's Ministry of Industry and Information Technology said its new rules were for 'cleaning and standardising' internet access.

The authorities also moved aggressively against a home-grown cottage industry supplying VPNs. One of the first victims in December 2017 was a software developer named Wu Xiangyang who was sentenced to five and a half years in jail for selling through his website an 'unauthorized' VPN and collecting 'illegal revenues'.[24]

China had until then grudgingly tolerated the use of VPNs. This is largely because of their widespread adoption by business and in academia, where there is a need for secure communications and access to unfiltered information from outside China. Both have now been subordinated to the Communist Party's desire for greater control. Beijing has offered to provide 'official' VPNs, though unsurprisingly, there have been few takers.

Tighter censorship has patched up the holes in the Great Firewall; the crackdown on VPNs has heightened the wall. The result has been to further disconnect the Chinese internet from the rest of the world, turning it into something more closely resembling one big tightly monitored and patrolled *intranet*.

The local tourist authorities describe Wuzhen as a 'National AAAAA Tourist Attraction'. That's a lot of As, awarded on account of it being one of China's 'Top Ten Charming Towns'. It's located just south of the Yangtze River in Zhejiang province and crisscrossed with canals, traversed via old stone bridges, and lined with traditional buildings. More recently it has become the focus of Xi Jinping's obsession with control of the internet.

Every year since 2014, usually in November or December, the throngs of tourists are joined by earnest techies, policymakers and other corporate types, in town for China's annual World Internet Conference, during which Communist Party leaders promote their vision of internet (or cyber) sovereignty. Broadly speaking, this is a belief that the global governance of the internet should be based on the right of individual governments to control what goes on in their own cyberspace – that virtual borders be as impermeable and sacrosanct as physical ones. 'We should respect the right of individual countries to independently choose their own path of cyber development and model of cyber regulation and participate in international cyberspace governance on an equal footing,' Xi told the 2015 conference,[25] a mantra he has repeated at numerous forums since.

China has also pushed the idea of new international norms and standards at the United Nations, demanding the UN's International Telecommunications Union (ITU), which is headed by a Chinese official, set the rules. The ITU is named as one of the sponsors of the Wuzhen event, and Beijing has won support from the ranks of autocrats, including Russia, Iran, Venezuela, Zimbabwe and Saudi Arabia. However, so far Western democracies have successfully defended the current, more open, decentralised and freewheeling system where management of the global internet architecture rests in the hands of a cluster of industry, academic and non-governmental actors.

Apple's CEO Tim Cook and Google's Sundar Pichai are among emissaries from Silicon Valley who have attended the Wuzhen conference and listened to the turgid speeches from Party leaders who preside over the most un-free internet on the planet. For many companies with business interests in China, or looking for a foothold in the Chinese market, it was an invitation they couldn't refuse. For the most part they are treated by the Party as supplicants, useful idiots to give the event a greater legitimacy. In the early years, the most sought-after private meeting was with Lu Wei, China's censor-in-chief. He was the head of the Cyberspace Administration of China – China's internet tsar, as he was known. Unfortunately, efforts to court Lu were somewhat set back when he was sacked from his post in 2016, accused of 'arbitrary and tyrannical' abuse of power, and subsequently jailed for corruption. Other alleged misconduct included building personal fame, making false and anonymous accusations against others, deceiving the top Communist leadership, extreme disloyalty, duplicity, trading power for sex, improper discussion of the Party and a lack of self-control.[26] It was quite a rap sheet for a man who accompanied Xi Jinping on a visit to Silicon Valley heavyweights, including Facebook, in 2014, and was assumed to be a conduit to Xi. For American tech entrepreneurs, Lu's downfall was a brutal lesson in Chinese politics in the Xi era.

The Wuzhen conference is a curious event since China has already asserted internet sovereignty by effectively walling off its internet from the rest of the world. But the conference is important in understanding how the internet fits into Xi's world view. He sees it as a vital economic tool, but also a potential existential threat. It originated in America, after all, as did most of the protocols that make it function; US tech companies built its early architecture. It has been used as a tool for protest and uprisings; Edward Snowden, the NSA whistle-blower, showed how control over digital pipes and technologies enabled global US eavesdropping.

The Wuzhen conference is an effort to project to the world the Party's model of censorship and surveillance, and to showcase China's growing technological prowess. It is a window on an alternative, authoritarian, digital future. The concept of cyber sovereignty has been expanded to include the control of digital technologies and data, and the companies that supply them, whether they be foreign or Chinese. It underlines Xi's view of the internet as an ideological battleground, where hostile forces lurk at every turn – and not even Winnie-the-Pooh or Peppa Pig are innocent. The internet must be tamed – and no longer just at home. Xi's China feels strong enough to project its vision globally. Under Xi, the Party fears whatever it cannot control, and 'charming' Wuzhen has become a symbol of that dark and paranoid vision.

The Communist Party has criminalised any online information that it regards as 'endangering national security, divulging state secrets, sub-verting the national regime, and destroying national unity', as well as anything deemed to be 'harming the nation's honor and interests' or 'promoting cults and superstitions'. The Party has also outlawed the 'dissemination of rumors, disrupting economic or social order' and 'any other content prohibited by laws or administrative regulations'.[27] In other words, 'illegal content' is just about anything the Party says it is.

Xi Jinping is determined that the Party be the sole arbiter of what is 'true' or 'real'. 'Rumour-mongering' is a particular catch-all, used by the Party to describe just about any online news that has not been sourced from an official Party mouthpiece. Bloggers face up to seven years in jail for spreading 'false information' that is shared more than 500 times or viewed by more than 5,000 people. Rumours 'can cause serious ideological confusion and affect people's confidence in China's reform and development process,' thundered the *People's Daily*, a Communist Party mouthpiece. 'Society should remain on high alert against the exponential growth of online rumors as the harm could be huge.

Online rumors are usually created to defame someone or to spread false information about public events. These rumors not only infringe upon others' interests, but also pose a threat to social stability.'[28]

Bloggers initially responded to the crackdown with the sort of disdain that typified the early years of social media in China. In one exchange, a Weibo user asked, 'So anything the government denies is categorized as rumor, right?' To which another responded, 'What about CCTV [China's state television] and *People's Daily*? How much false information have they spread?'[29] Others looked to the nineteenth-century German leader Otto von Bismarck for inspiration: 'Never believe anything until it has been officially denied,' the 'Iron Chancellor' once declared. That was a widespread view among Chinese netizens at the time, but the walls were rapidly closing in on them.

The Party targeted the most popular and most influential bloggers – the Big Vs, so-called for their status as 'verified accounts' on Weibo, some of them with tens of millions of followers, their thoughts widely shared. They were at the forefront of the online campaign against air pollution and corruption, and the most prominent bloggers pushed for greater openness and transparency.

Influential bloggers were summoned to a meeting at a state-run Beijing hotel for what was described as a seminar on 'domestic current affairs'. Those who attended described the atmosphere as cordial enough, but the message was blunt: they should stop writing about politics or anything else that went against the Party's official narrative. They were promised protection and other benefits if they cooperated.[30] For those who didn't cooperate, retribution was swift. Thousands of accounts were deleted for spreading 'rumours', while prominent bloggers were arrested and humiliated.

The crackdown had a chilling effect on online discussion and debate. The daily number of posts on Weibo fell by as much as 70 per cent, as prominent bloggers deserted it.[31] Many relocated to WeChat, which in character is closer to WhatsApp. It is not so public facing, allowing users to interact with friends either directly or in smaller groups. It seemed safer, though it was still subject to surveillance and censorship. For the Communist Party it was an ideal outcome. WeChat could be more easily managed; there was less chance of 'rumours' going viral. Or so the Party hoped. But the reinforced Great Firewall was to face one of is sternest tests when disaster hit the port city of Tianjin in August 2015.

**

Dan Van Duren and his girlfriend Ying were on the roof of her thirty-four-storey apartment building in Tianjin watching for an expected meteor shower when the sky exploded. The first explosion was small, 'maybe a gas station or something,' speculates Ying. Then seconds later another, far bigger, and then a third. 'Oh my God. Holy shit,' says Van Duren, surprise and curiosity quickly turning to fear and panic as the apartment block shakes and the night sky is filled with billowing burning clouds. 'Let's go, let's go down,' he yells, as they race for the dark stairs, the power in the building now out, debris beginning to rain down.

'I thought it was a small nuclear bomb,' he told me, still visibly shaken when I tracked him down days later. What he and Ying had witnessed on 12 August 2015 was the explosion of a chemical storage facility within the Tianjin port, less than a mile from Ying's apartment. Van Duren, an American aircraft mechanic from Washington state had been visiting Ying at the time and captured the explosions on his mobile phone, uploading the video (and its expletive-filled soundtrack) to the internet. It was viewed 623,000 times in the next five days.[32]

In the immediate aftermath of the explosion, the area around the port resembled a post-apocalyptic wasteland of twisted and charred debris. It was littered with the remains of smashed and smouldering shipping containers, which had been tossed around like pieces of Lego by the power of the explosion. Cars were scattered and crushed; it seemed as if a giant had tramped through the enormous parking areas full of vehicles waiting to be shipped. The windows had been blown out of surrounding apartment buildings. The official death toll was 165; hundreds more were injured.

As Van Duren's video and other images circulated on social media, so did the questions: What was in the deadly cocktail of chemicals that had exploded so violently? Why had it been located so close to residential areas? And who owned the company whose website had been quickly taken down? The company was accused of having no licence for handling dangerous chemicals and having corrupt links with local officials. The explosion was by far the biggest topic on Weibo and WeChat, China's leading social media platforms.

Netizens sneered when Prime Minister Li Keqiang visited and promised 'transparency'. In spite of his pledges, the government could not or would not provide answers, which created the perfect conditions for speculation. But it had been priming its censorship tools for just such an occasion. Censorship rates on Weibo soared tenfold in the wake of the disaster, according to censorship-tracking sites.[33] Among the deleted postings were those critical of the government's response, calling for accountability or which discussed the chemicals inside the warehouse. 'Tianjin' and 'explosion' were the most censored words.

A directive from the Cyberspace Administration of China (CAC) ordered that online news sources only use official despatches from the Party's *Xinhua* news agency and banned personal comments, opinions and live video feeds. Online news outlets were ordered to scrub photographs of the disaster from their homepages and to celebrate the heroism of firefighters.[34] The latter proved tricky, since scores of firefighters died and their relatives were among those in Tianjin angrily demanding answers. The respected business magazine *Caijing* interviewed one firefighter who claimed they had not been told that the warehouse contained chemicals that would react badly with water. The post was deleted, but only after it had been shared 10,000 times.[35]

The CAC announced that it would have 'zero tolerance' towards 'rumours' on WeChat and Weibo. The Ministry of Public Security said it had closed 165 accounts for 'relevant violations', and a *Xinhua* news agency despatch announced that 197 people had been punished for spreading 'online rumours' relating to the Tianjin blast and China's stock market meltdown. A common charge was 'picking quarrels and provoking trouble'. The report stated with some satisfaction that those punished had expressed 'repentance over their conduct' and called on internet operators to 'strengthen management to ensure cyberspace order'.[36]

The authorities seemed pleased with the result. They thought they'd contained the online rage, but, not for the first time, they forfeited trust. The city was fearful and angry. Rumour abounded. Nobody believed the woolly assurances coming from the authorities about what had happened, and what might still happen. Was the air even safe to breathe? As a foreign journalist covering the story it wasn't unusual to be stopped in the streets by distraught residents asking what we had heard.

Dan Van Duren prepared to return to America, having helped Ying salvage what she could from her devastated apartment. They were very much a couple of the digital generation – and not just because it was his video that went viral. They met online, an internet romance – he in west coast America, she in east coast China – and his visit to Tianjin was the first time they'd met in person. Which showed that at least in one respect the Great Firewall was not entirely impenetrable.

In volatile situations like Tianjin, the internet controls also serve a wider purpose. According to James Griffiths, who has written a book about the Great Firewall, it is not simply aimed at blocking content and stifling the flow of information. Instead its priority is blocking solidarity, preventing any sort of organisation outside the Party structure – and especially that aimed at the Party. 'When the internet came to China in the 1990s, it did not threaten the country's rulers because it risked undermining their control over information, but because it threatened to create a platform for organising against them,' he writes.[37]

By the middle of 2019, China had 854 million internet users, most of them now accessing the internet via mobile devices. That is the highest number in the world – more than India and the United States combined.[38] That year, for the fourth year running, Freedom House, a US-based NGO, designated China the world's worst abuser of internet freedom.[39] Reporters Without Borders, an international organisation advocating press freedom, described China as 'The world's biggest prison for journalists and citizen-journalists.' At that time, more than 100 Chinese journalists, citizen journalists and bloggers were behind bars.[40] Xi Jinping had neutralised the internet as a platform for political debate and criticism, tightening Party control over the flow and content of information, but his ambitions go well beyond censorship – he is attempting to turn the internet into a powerful instrument of social control.

Liu Hu's muck-raking blog once had nearly 750,000 followers, but he quickly learned the dangers of trying to hold corrupt officials to account in China. He was first arrested in 2013 and detained for a year for 'fabricating and spreading rumours' after accusing a local Party secretary of dereliction of duty; three years later, he was forced to publish an apology and pay a fine after being convicted of defamation. When the court demanded an additional fee, he disputed it and refused to pay.

Liu was lucky – at that time critical bloggers were facing lengthy jail sentences for far lesser offences. But unbeknown to him, he was facing other sanctions. When he tried to buy a plane ticket, the booking system rejected him, saying he was 'not qualified' to travel. He soon discovered that he was also barred from high-speed train travel, taking out a loan and buying property. 'There was no file, no police warrant, no official advance notification. They just cut me off from the things I was once entitled to,' he told Canada's *Globe and Mail*. 'What's really scary is there's nothing you can do about it. You can report to no one. You are stuck in the middle of nowhere.'[41]

Months later Liu discovered that he had been blacklisted, placed on a digital register of 'Dishonest Persons Subject to Enforcement'. The blacklist was run by China's Supreme People's Court and contained the names of those who had allegedly failed to comply with court judgements by not paying fines or not adequately apologising. Liu wasn't the only one. In 2018 alone, would-be travellers were blocked from buying flights 15.5 million times, and from buying train tickets 5.5 million times, according to a government report, which described the operation of the blacklist as, 'once discredited, limited everywhere'.[42] It was then expanded to include those who spread false information about terrorism, caused trouble on flights, used expired tickets or smoked on trains.[43]

The travel bans were an early component of what China calls its 'social credit' system, which aims to rate every person by their loyalty as a citizen, with the goal of creating what the Communist Party calls a 'trustworthy' society. That rating will determine life chances, including access to jobs, healthcare and education – and of course travel.

The system was first outlined in a 2014 document produced by the State Council, China's cabinet, which stated that the scheme should 'allow the trustworthy to roam everywhere under heaven while making it hard for the discredited to take a single step'. It was to encompass both individuals and companies, collecting and analysing a range of data in order to build what the government called a culture of 'sincerity' where 'keeping trust is glorious'. The document states that, 'It will strengthen sincerity in government affairs, commercial sincerity, social sincerity and the construction of judicial credibility.'[44]

The State Council set a target date of 2020 for it to be fully operational nationally, but for the moment it consists of dozens of pilot programmes, run by cities, provinces, government organisations and tech companies, all with the purpose of rewarding behaviour deemed to be 'good', while punishing the 'bad'.

In Rongcheng, in China's eastern Shandong province, each of the city's 750,000 people are assigned 1,000 starting points. Points are deducted for 'anti-social behaviour', ranging from breaking traffic rules and evading tax, to illegally spreading religion and defaming others online.[45] One man was deducted 950 points for serial complaining. He submitted more than 1,000 online letters appealing to officials for help with his mother's two-decade old medical dispute, and thereby broke a rule against 'using the online petition to repeatedly complain in spite'. Points are gained for good deeds, such as donating to charity or becoming a volunteer in one of the city's social programmes. Residents are graded from AAA to D, with top grades rewarded with treats such as cut-price bicycle rental or reduced fuel bills. Those who hit a D lose access to government jobs and loans, among other punishments.[46]

A system set up by the government of Ningbo, Zhejiang province, delivers what it calls a *wu dian* (stain) to personal records for such transgressions as dodging fares on public transport or failing to pay utility bills on time. A *wu dian* can affect an individual's chances of promotion at work or getting a mortgage. In Suzhou, negative behaviour that can hit credit scores includes cheating in online video games and not showing up for restaurant or hotel reservations. In the small city of Qinhuangdao, 'good' behaviour is rewarded with a 'model citizen' certificate and a free annual medical check-up.

The most ambitious schemes have been trialled by the companies with the most data – China's tech giants. Eight companies developed social credit schemes, with Alibaba and Tencent leading the way. Tencent owns WeChat, which is frequently described as the 'app for everything'. For many of its 1 billion users, it *is* the internet, an essential tool for organising their lives. It's a social network, but also a platform through which just about anything can be bought, sold and arranged. Or, as the *Financial Times* put it, 'The Chinese super-app is so sewn into the lives of the people of China – who use it to work, play, pay and everything in between – it is hard to last a day without it.'[47] This makes it the perfect tool for surveillance and misinformation. Furthermore, it is integrated with WeChat Pay, its mobile payments system. WeChat Pay, together with Alibaba's Alipay, dominate the mobile payment market in China, and China leads the world by light years in its march towards a cashless society. In April 2020, the People's Bank of China launched a central bank digital currency, to be tested in four cities as a prelude to converting the entire country.[48] Cashless is convenient, but it also generates a mountain of data; it enables close monitoring of everything a user does, everywhere they go. Cash can be a pain, but it's a last bastion of anonymity. It should come as no surprise that China has gone further and faster towards doing away with it.

The Alibaba social credit system, built by its affiliate Ant Financial (since renamed Ant Group), is called Sesame Credit, and is the bigger of the two. After crunching data about online behaviour, such as buying and browsing habits and contacts, it assigns a person a number between 350 and 950. That's the social credit score. Those with the highest scores can enjoy benefits including getting a credit card, shopping, applying for a loan, booking a hotel, or renting a car or house. Hospitals allow high scorers to pay later for treatment; low scorers pay in advance. For a while, high scorers could access priority lanes at Beijing airport and jump queues for online visas for Singapore and the Schengen Area of the European Union. Prospective employers frequently demand to see the scores of applicants for jobs; colleges and universities are doing likewise. It has become an important factor used by dating agencies.[49] [50]

Alibaba refuses to divulge precisely how it calculates the credit score, merely that it involves a 'complex algorithm'. The tech companies have also assisted in setting up local and city-based schemes. The links between the companies and the government are rarely explicit. They do not need to be. As I shall explain more fully later, they have always worked hand in glove. As a spokesman for Ant explained to the *New Scientist*, 'Sesame Credit works closely with the Ministry of Public Security, the Supreme People's Court, the Ministry of Education and the State Administration for Industry and Commerce to collect data.'[51]

Tencent's social credit pilot, Tencent Credit, rated users according to five broad metrics: honour, security, wealth, consumption and social. It accessed data on assets and loans from WeChat Pay, as well as data on the quality of a person's social network and information from telecom operators, financial institutions and government departments.[52] The government is now encouraging users of WeChat to link their ID card to the app. Users scan their faces to obtain a digital ID to register for a variety of services – giving Tencent and the Communist Party access to a vast store of integrated data.

A scheme piloted by Weibo, the micro-blogging platform, and dubbed 'Sunshine Credit', encouraged users to report one another for activities ranging from harassment to spreading 'untrue information'. Informers could boost their rating, while those they reported lost points, with persistent offending leading to their being labelled a 'low credit user' or even having their accounts deleted.[53] WeChat carried an app for the high court in Hebei province called 'a map of deadbeat debtors'. It alerts users if there are any debtors within 500 metres and invites them to inform the authorities if they believe the debtor can afford to repay debts. The aim is to enforce court rulings and 'create a socially creditable environment'.[54]

The schemes have not been without criticism in China. The *Beijing Times*, a state-run newspaper, compared social credit ratings with the 'good citizen' certificates issued by Japan during its wartime occupation of China.[55]

The authorities have portrayed the system as just an everyday tool of legal and economic management, an effort to overcome a chronic lack of trust. Zhu Hexin, the governor of the People's Bank of China has likened it to one giant credit rating agency. Social credit is 'irreplaceable in forestalling financial risks and ensuring financial stability', he said. He claimed that as of summer 2019, the system had information on 990 million individuals and more than 25 million enterprises, giving it the largest amount of data and widest coverage of any credit scoring system in the world.[56]

It is true that trust is in short supply in China – a legacy of the Cultural Revolution, which pitted friends and family against each other, but also of more recent and seemingly endless scams from food safety to pyramid schemes. Zhang Lifan, a prominent historian, told *Foreign Affairs* that trust is in such short supply in China that people often expect to be cheated or to get into trouble without having done anything wrong.[57] Yet the source of much of the distrust is the Party itself, which is why a fully fledged social credit system in its hands is such a chilling prospect.

Privacy and data protection are supposedly protected by law in China, most recently in a 2017 cybersecurity law, though like most laws, it is subordinated to the will of the Communist Party. This same legislation requires tech companies to hand over data on demand to the authorities on vague 'national security' grounds. There is a saying in China, that internet users are 'running naked online', since in practice there is virtually no limit to the harvesting and use of personal data for commercial, political or 'security' purposes. Tracking is a free-for-all.

At the time of writing the social credit system is a hotchpotch of schemes with varying degrees of sophistication and reach – and very little transparency. There is as yet no single, all-powerful social credit score, though that remains the Communist Party's ambition. Its 2020 target for bringing them all together into a national scheme has slipped, though it remains committed to creating a unified system in which each person is rated not only as a consumer, but by their loyalty to the Party. By tying a person's rating to their life chances, from education to work and healthcare, the goal is political conformity and compliance – modifying the behaviour of those with suspect loyalty, while incentivising others to act as enforcers.

The Party says a person's score should take into account vaguely defined sins such as 'assembling to disrupt social order' and 'conduct that seriously undermines . . . the normal social order'. Other vague categories of 'bad' behaviour that will influence ratings are dissent, expressing opinions and posing a threat to security.[58] Even apparently technical infringements that hit a person's rating, such as penalising blogger Liu Hu's failure to comply with court judgements, can be highly political. The judgements themselves are frequently designed to stifle dissent. There is no rule of law in China in any meaningful sense. The law and the courts serve the Party and dissent has been criminalised, offline and online; what the Party defines as 'deadbeat' debtors are frequently victims of political repression, convicted of 'crimes' that would not be recognised as such in a functioning democracy.

Speaking at the World Economic Forum at Davos in January 2019, the philanthropist George Soros said, 'The social credit system is not yet fully operational, but it's clear where it's heading. It will subordinate the fate of the individual to the interests of the one-Party state in ways unprecedented in history. I find the social credit system frightening and abhorrent.'[59]

The social credit scheme is troubling enough on its own, but it should be seen as one more tool of a digital totalitarian state. Taken alongside the systems of mass surveillance and blanket censorship it will provide an unprecedented level of control. It is a chilling vision of the future, but the Party also knows that to truly control that future, it must also control the past.

CHAPTER 4

He Who Controls the Past

'How tall was Mao?' I asked my guide. She looked at the massive painting, then at me, then back at the painting, studying it, taking her time, before telling me that, yes, Mao Zedong was tall, he was a *big* man. 'But *how* tall?' I insisted. She looked again at the painting, and then into the middle distance, towards the door. 'The exhibition continues this way,' she said awkwardly, as if I was trying to extract from her a state secret.

We were standing in a gallery at the National Museum of China in Tiananmen Square. The painting that towered above us was called 'Birth of New China', and stretched down one entire wall, nearly five metres in height and seventeen metres long. It depicted the 1949 founding ceremony of the People's Republic of China, sixty-three of the country's top leaders lined up along a Tiananmen Square rostrum. Mao was in the middle, reading a declaration, and he was the tallest. Earlier, upon entering the museum's vast mausoleum-like concourse, I'd been greeted by statues of Mao and his revolutionary generals lined up on a plinth. 'The Generals in the Great March of the Red Army,' read the caption. Mao was in the middle and even taller this time.

I know Mao was tall, but surely not the tallest man in China? But there he was, in every artistic rendition, towering over those around him. Chinese artist and scholar Yan Shanchun calls this the 'height problem', since it was a considerable challenge to those charged with painting or sculpting his image.[1] Dictators have to dominate the canvas, and as their megalomania grows, so must their physical presence in any works of art. Shanchun, in his study of Mao in contemporary art, describes a 1958 meeting in which Mao complained that Chinese artists in the early 1950s always depicted him as being shorter than Stalin, the Soviet leader, because that reflected the international communist pecking-order at the time. As the Sino-Soviet split grew, so did Mao, with the Cultural Revolution adding a few more inches. Mao's height in paintings had nothing to do with physiology and everything to do with politics. At the height of Mao's cult of personality, artists were required to depict him as the tallest, biggest and most prominent figure in the picture, and woe betide anybody who failed to do so.

My furtive guide ushered me into a permanent exhibition called 'The Road to Rejuvenation', the theme of which is the triumph of the Communist Party, leading China into a bright and powerful future after a century of humiliation at the hands of rapacious foreigners, who split and plundered the country prior to 'liberation'. One sculpture of toiling peasants is labelled, 'The Chinese people mired in misery.' A nearby information board explains: 'After Britain started the First Opium War in 1840, the imperial powers descended on China like a swarm of bees, looting our treasures and killing our people.' The turning point, as the exhibition tells it, came in 1949 with the liberation of the country by Mao and the generals I'd met in the entrance hall.

Much of this was repeated robotically by my guide, as we studied exhibits that included a white cowboy hat that Deng Xiaoping, China's then paramount leader (who rose to power after Mao died), had worn during a visit to America and a chair in which he had sat during an inspection tour of southern China. A plain Mao-style jacket was hung in the same display cabinet beside the chair. My guide explained this was the jacket Deng had worn while seated in the chair. 'Deng Xiaoping was the architect of China's reform and opening,' she said. Another cabinet contained a bullhorn used by a later Communist Party leader marshalling relief efforts after an earthquake in Sichuan.

'Today, China is facing a brilliant future of great rejuvenation,' said my guide, fixing me with a penetrating stare. 'The exhibition clearly demonstrates the historic course of the Chinese people of choosing Marxism, the Communist Party of China, the socialist road and the reform and opening up policy.'

It was Deng who in 1989 sent the People's Liberation Army to crush the Tiananmen Square protests, killing hundreds – perhaps thousands – in and around the square. The only reference in the museum to that period is a photograph of Deng meeting Mikhail Gorbachev, the then Soviet leader, who was visiting Beijing. It was the first Sino-Soviet summit for thirty years, and was supposed to signify the normalising of relations between the two Communist giants. The agenda had to be constantly amended because of the protests, but the meeting with Deng finally took place on 16 May, less than three weeks before the massacre, in the Great Hall of the People. Just outside, tens of thousands occupied the square, some holding placards hailing the Soviet leader as 'The Ambassador of Democracy' because of the reforms he was introducing in the Soviet Union.

The Tiananmen Square protests have been eradicated from official history. You will also find little mention in the National Museum, China's leading showcase of history, of the two other most disastrous periods of Communist Party rule – the Great Leap Forward and the Cultural Revolution, during which tens of millions of people died of starvation or abuse. The Great Leap, a campaign from 1958 to 1962 to transform the country's economy, which resulted in the most severe famine in recorded history, merits in the museum only the briefest of mentions: 'The project of constructing socialism suffered severe complications.' The Cultural Revolution, a decade-long campaign of political persecution and turmoil, is marked by a single photograph.

Many of those who protested in Tiananmen Square in 1989 were inspired by an earlier student uprising – the May 4th Movement, which was then marking its seventieth anniversary. The movement had its roots in protests that began on that day in 1919, also in Tiananmen Square. The protests were in response to the Chinese government's weak response to China's treatment at the end of the First World War, notably provisions in the Treaty of Versailles that allowed Japan to retain territories in China, and the protests soon spread nationwide.

The meaning of the movement is hotly contested. It had a strong nationalist and anti-imperialist tinge to it, but liberals also see it as a backlash against autocracy and a conservative culture, a call for China to learn more from the West. Before the Communist Party seized power in 1949, the movement was widely associated with the ideas of democracy and science;[2] the Party, which designates 4 May as Youth Day, stresses patriotism and resistance to foreign influence. It claims the movement was a revolutionary step towards the formation of the Party two years later, and has been determined that its version of history prevails. As an information board in the National Museum puts it, 'The May 4th Movement furthered the spread of Marxism, and the working class appeared on the stage of history as an independent political force. The integration of Marxism with the workers' movement gave birth to the CPC. The founding of the CPC was an earth-shattering event that brought new vitality to the Chinese revolution.'

As with the Tiananmen Square massacre, anniversaries of the May

4th Movement are always sensitive, and the centenary in 2019 (a month before the thirtieth anniversary of the massacre) was accompanied by a fierce crackdown on university campuses. Xi Jinping, who has made the enforcement of 'correct' history a cornerstone of his rule, told a gathering in the Great Hall of the People to strive for the spirit of 4 May. 'The new era of Chinese youth should listen to the Party and follow the Party,' he said.[3]

Neither is there any mention in the National Museum of the violent – often nihilistic – rebel movements worldwide, from Cambodia's murderous Khmer Rouge to Peru's Shining Path, to which Mao provided material support and inspiration. That history does not fit with contemporary China's propaganda about 'non-interference' and 'peaceful rise'. As Julia Lovell explains in her comprehensive study of the worldwide impact of Mao's ideology, 'Deng Xiaoping told the world that China would "never seek hegemony" and almost every foreign policy PR campaign since then has been devoted to arguing China's status as a victim, not activist or aggressor, in international politics.'[4]

The reality is somewhat different. To take the Khmer Rouge as one example, it is unlikely Pol Pot's genocidal regime, which killed an estimated 2 million people between 1975 and 1979, would have been possible without Chinese support. As Lovell writes: 'It [Maoist China] schooled Pol Pot and gave him over $1 billion in aid, free military assistance and medical check-ups. On the brink of committing genocide, Pol lounged by Mao's swimming pool as the moribund chairman lauded the Cambodian's emptying of the country's cities into forced labour projects and killing fields: "Your experience is better than ours . . . You are basically right."'[5]

The Cambodian genocide killed around a quarter of that country's population; per capita that is truly horrifying, though the absolute number – 2 million – is dwarfed by the number of Chinese murdered by Mao or who died as a result of his disastrous policies, where credible estimates range from 40 to 70 million.

As we moved on from the 'Road to Rejuvenation' my guide gushed about China's '5,000 years of history'. There is no doubt that China has a rich past, but the claim to 5,000 years of continuous history is more propaganda than history. It has become a mantra of Communist Party leaders, trotted out at receptions and banquets to bolster their nationalist credentials as the natural inheritors of an ancient unified nation. It is especially pernicious when used to justify Han Chinese occupation of areas such as Xinjiang and Tibet, which have their own distinct culture and history. Another permanent exhibition tells of how the country's disparate ethnic groups pulled together to create what it calls 'brilliant achievements'. Try telling that to imprisoned Tibetans or Uighurs.

This is not a history book, but suffice to say that the notion that Chinese civilisation is either unified, continuous or the longest is challenged by respected scholars. It is a twentieth-century fiction. As Julia Lovell writes:

> Capitalising on a long held, though hazy, Chinese public pride in the antiquity of their state, the Communist patriotic education campaign transformed the idea that the Chinese nation leapt, fully formed, into existence thousands of years ago into a cliché spouted tirelessly by agents of the Chinese Politburo, by a number of opportunistic academics and by lazy tour guides, to bludgeon anyone listening – Chinese or foreign – into believing that this is how China always was; and ever more shall be (until the Communists say differently).[6]

Neither do serious China scholars give too much credence to the 'century of humiliation'. The Qing Dynasty was certainly ravaged by outsiders, but as history it is incomplete, ignoring the role of domestic rebellions and corruption in weakening the empire. Yet it is central to the Communist Party's myth of victimhood and its own redemptive power.

The museum itself has a complicated history of its own, having spent almost as much time closed as it has open, with Communist Party leaders frequently bickering over what constitutes 'correct history'. It formally opened in 1961, two years later than planned, because Prime Minister Zhou Enlai complained that Mao's thoughts were not sufficiently emphasised. It then closed again in 1966 at the onset of the Cultural Revolution, remaining shuttered until 1979, presumably to protect the antiquities from the ravages of Mao's Red Guards. The present incarnation opened in 2011 after a ten-year renovation, and combined the Museum of Chinese History and the Museum of the Chinese Revolution. It sprawls down the eastern side of Tiananmen Square, looking out towards Mao's mausoleum, where the Great Helmsman lies embalmed.

The *New York Times* reported that curators argued the museum should confront at least in part the country's more troubled recent history.[7] They suggested a section called '10 years of tortuous development' which would include the Great Leap Forward, arguing that the Party was strong enough to withstand criticism, but the suggestion was rejected.

The renovation cost $400 million and was aimed at creating the world's largest museum under one roof. China's leaders wanted not only to showcase the country's history and culture but to be right up there in the global museum stakes alongside the likes of the Louvre, the Uffizi and the British Museum. It was to be a monument to China's rising power and prestige. Instead it is a monument to the distortion of history, a symbol of the way the Communist Party uses history as a means of justifying its rule and the way it suppresses any alternative points of view or events that would challenge its own narrative.

Two weeks after he was installed as general secretary of the Communist Party, Xi Jinping visited the Road to Rejuvenation exhibition at the National Museum. He was flanked by the six other members of the standing committee of the Politburo. They were all wearing dark jackets without ties, a contrived and awkward attempt to look casual, and they listened attentively as Xi introduced for the first time a populist slogan that has become a leitmotiv of his rule – the 'Chinese Dream'.

The setting was deliberate; Xi's 'Chinese Dream' was supposed to encapsulate the sentiments of the exhibition – the restoration of China's power and prestige under the leadership of the Party. 'In the future, the Chinese nation will "forge ahead like a gigantic ship breaking through the strong winds and heavy waves",' Xi said, quoting the Tang Dynasty poet Li Bai. 'In my opinion, achieving the rejuvenation of the Chinese nation has been the greatest dream of the Chinese people since the advent of modern times.'[8]

The slogan was essentially vacuous, but it quickly became a staple of Party propaganda, acclaimed by Party newspapers and studied in schools. Academics were asked to come up with 'Chinese Dream' research proposals. A folk singer called Chen Sisi, leader of a song-and-dance group run by China's nuclear missile corps, recorded a 'Chinese Dream' ballad, which topped the charts. Sometimes Xi used the slogan to describe people's aspiration for a better life; on other occasions it was used to underscore chest-thumping nationalism. Some commentators likened it to the idealism of the 'American Dream'. But while the American version is an assertion of individualism, the 'Chinese Dream' is not only collectivist, it places the Communist Party firmly at the helm of a powerful and united China. And as if to emphasise that, Xi took his standing committee to another building maintained as a museum, this one in Shanghai – the two-storey Shikumen building, site of the first congress of the Chinese Communist Party in 1921. Here, Xi led the seven men as, fists raised, they retook the Communist Party oath.

Xi peppers many of his speeches with quotes from the poems of Mao Zedong, but he also rehabilitated a man Mao loathed: Confucius. A year after becoming Party leader he travelled to Qufu, the birthplace of the great sage, who had been despised by revolutionary Marxists. While there, he declared the Communist Party to be 'the loyal inheritor and promoter of China's outstanding traditional culture'.[9] Confucius lived during the sixth and fifth centuries BC, and Confucianism was the backbone of the imperial system, although its legacy is contested. On the one hand, his philosophy is seen as one of social harmony and obedience to authority, whether that be within the family or to the emperor. On the other hand, those in authority – the sovereign – must earn that obedience by behaving in exemplary fashion. Some even see this as justifying a challenge to unjust authority. 'Obedience on the one hand, resistance on the other – Confucius' legacy has and will continue to be exploited, subverted and caricatured,' according to François Bougon, in his study of Xi's thinking.[10] Needless to say, in Xi's selective reading of Confucius, it is the obedient part that is emphasised.

Xi has also quoted philosopher Han Fei, who lived from 280 to 233 BC and served the emperor Qin Shi Huang, who unified China. Xi used Han's words to justify his anti-corruption clampdown – 'When those who uphold the law are strong, the state is strong. When they are weak, the state is weak.' Han Fei has been described as 'China's Machiavelli', and he was also a big favourite of Mao, who used him to justify the Cultural Revolution. He comes from what is called the Legalist tradition, where fear of the ruler, together with force and control are regarded as essential attributes of good governance.[11] Again, Xi's pickings are selective, though there are echoes of the Legalists in his intolerance of dissent, and his notion of the 'rule of law', which has nothing to do with the independence of the judiciary in the Western sense, but is better described as rule *by* law – the law in question being whatever the party says it is. Or, as Xi himself described it, 'In keeping to the path of the socialist rule of law, the most important thing is that we uphold the leadership of the Party.'[12]

'Xi Jinping Thought' – or 'Xi Jinping Thought on Socialism with Chinese Characteristics for a New Era', to give its full title – is a set of banalities inspired by this hotchpotch of half-baked ideas. It has been written into the constitution, become the subject of university courses and of compulsory study by Party members. Party propagandists even summoned more than 100 of the nation's top actors, film-makers and pop stars to a special cultural forum in order to study Xi's 'Thought' as a way of raising 'cultural-ethical standards'.[13]

As an ideology, 'Xi Jinping Thought' lacks any real coherence. Even the anti-colonial currents that underpin the 'Road to Rejuvenation' exhibition ring increasingly hollow in the light of Xi's repressive and chauvinistic behaviour towards China's own minorities, and the practices of his signature Belt and Road Initiative of international investment, which I shall examine later in this book. 'Xi Jinping Thought' suggests weakness rather than strength; the Communist Party no longer has any meaningful ideology, so the emperor casts around for new clothes, searching for a new traditionalist basis for his rule.

There are, however, three underlying themes. One is a nationalism, bordering at times on xenophobia, and an associated culture of grievance. The Party *needs* to exaggerate the pain of the past to justify its dominance of the present. It has become essential to its legitimacy. A glimpse of the darker side of this world view came in a film called *Silent Contest*, produced by the army and the National Defence University around a year after Xi came to power. To a soundtrack of ominous marshal music, it laments the collapse of the Soviet Union, which it puts down to ideological weakness. The conspiracy-laden film accuses Britain and America of undermining China's rightful rise through the infiltration of pernicious Western values. The cast of villains promoting 'subversion' in China include NGOs, diplomats, journalists and scholars. Educational exchanges are depicted as instruments of 'cultural invasion'. Only the Party can repel these hostile forces.

The second underlying theme of Xi's 'Thought' is to position the Party as the natural inheritor and embodiment of Chinese tradition and history. The third theme is Xi himself. The ideology, if indeed it can even be called that, is self-serving – selectively drawing from Mao, Marx and Chinese classical philosophers to justify Xi's accumulation of personal power. And in doing so, Xi, perhaps more than any recent dictator since Mao and Stalin, has shown that he understands the importance of controlling the past – manipulating history in order to justify and dictate the present.

The photographs appeared on the website of a library in Zhenyuan, a picturesque town in Guizhou province in south-west China. The town has a stunning location, astride a bend in the Wuyang River and surrounded by tall mountain peaks, but it wasn't the natural beauty that attracted attention in late 2019, but images of two women burning a pile of 'illegal' and 'improper' books outside the county library.[14] An article on the website said the library was following government instructions to remove and destroy illegal, improper or outdated books. A Ministry of Education directive had ordered school libraries to 'firmly cleanse' their libraries in order to create a 'healthy and safe environment for education'. It targeted books deemed to threaten national honour, security or stability, or which promoted 'incorrect global outlook or values'.

The images of the bonfire spread on social media, alongside comparisons with the Qin Dynasty practice of burning books (along with the scholars who wrote them) and Nazi Germany's book burnings of the 1930s. 'Ignorance is power,' said one post. Even the Party-owned *Beijing News* suggested Zhenyuan had taken the Communist Party's instructions a little too literally. The Party responded by deleting the photographs from the library website and censoring the critical articles and posts.

The librarians of Zhenyuan could justifiably feel a little aggrieved at having the photographs of their handiwork deleted. They were after all complying with the Party's increasingly strident efforts to control what is taught to Chinese children, efforts that have been stepped up under Xi Jinping. 'Patriotic education', and the study of China's 'century of humiliation' is a cornerstone of the country's education system. Under Xi it has been taken to almost hysterical levels, with the narrative of historic grievance and victimhood ingrained in every student and used to legitimise rule by an increasingly xenophobic Party that is now without any meaningful ideology.

The Party has an expression for viewpoints that challenge its version of history: 'historical nihilism'. And weeding it out has become an obsession for Xi Jinping. In March 2019 he summoned teachers from across the country to a seminar in Beijing, telling them that starting with toddlers, China must 'nurture generation after generation [of young people] to support Chinese Communist Party rule and China's socialist system'.[15] Their role, he told the assembled educators, was to instil patriotism and reject 'wrong ideas and ideology'. A directive from the Ministry of Education ordered the inspection of all textbooks used in elementary and middle schools to remove what it called 'foreign teaching materials'. Teachers were required to justify their use of textbooks and those failing to comply would be 'severely dealt with'. The *Financial Times* reported that for the first time the inspections would apply also to international schools, which enrol only students holding foreign passports, and had hitherto escaped the more draconian measures.[16]

The elimination of 'foreign ideas' has become a particular obsession. Turning his attention to the country's higher education, Xi ordered that the Party's 'leadership and guidance' be stepped up in universities. A Party document ordered educators to 'firmly resist infiltration by foreign forces'.[17] Party newspapers attacked academics for 'smearing' the state by discussing the Party's failures and promoting 'Western' ideas, such as the separation of powers and the rule of law. Universities were ordered to expand classes in Marxism and ideology.[18] Renmin University and Peking University are among dozens of higher education institutions to set up new departments on 'Xi Jinping Thought'.

Education minister Yuan Guiran declared that China should 'never let textbooks promoting western values enter into our classes . . . Any views that attack and defame the leadership of the Party or smear socialism must never be allowed to appear in our universities.'[19]

The Party stepped up its vetting of applicants for teaching jobs in universities, and teachers were sacked or demoted for breaching 'teaching ethics'. Among the most high profile victims was Xu Zhangrun, a constitutional law professor at the prestigious Tsinghua University, which is also Xi Jinping's alma mater.[20] He was stripped of his positions and stopped from teaching after writing a series of articles critical of political and social issues in China, including the personality cult surrounding Xi and the suspension of a two-term limit on the presidency that effectively gives Xi a job for life. Xu was far from being an outright dissident, choosing his words carefully. In the past he had enjoyed a degree of official tolerance, but it was always a treacherous balancing act, and there is no longer any space in Xi's China for academics deemed ideologically impure. In a text message to the *New York Times*, sent shortly after his suspension, Professor Xu likened his treatment to Mao's Cultural Revolution, when 'special case teams' hounded intellectuals. 'Yesterday the investigation team told me that I was suspended from research. But thinking is in our blood,' he messaged. 'Unless you liquidate me, how could you ever stop me doing my research?'[21]

The teaching of Xu's subject, constitutional law, has come in for particularly close scrutiny. 'Constitutionality' has been branded a dangerous Western idea, and the authorities are particularly sensitive to criticism that their practices fall far short of the guarantees in China's own constitution of freedom of speech, association and assembly. In Xi's China, everything is subordinate to the Party – including the law.

The authorities in the south-western province of Guizhou went as far as ordering universities to install surveillance cameras in classrooms to monitor lectures and tutorials. A document, published online, said the purpose was to 'build an all-round system of teaching quality control' that would help improve the system of appraising teachers.[22]

In late 2019, it was revealed that Fudan University in Shanghai, usually regarded as one of the country's more liberal institutions, had made changes to its charter. It dropped the phrase 'freedom of thought' and inserted a pledge to follow the Communist Party leadership. The revisions state that the 'Party committee is the core of the university', and that Fudan would 'weaponise the minds of teachers and students using Xi Jinping's socialism ideology with characteristics of China in the new era'. Two other universities made similar changes. There was a brief flurry of critical social media posts, which were quickly deleted by the censors.[23] In reality, the changes were a formality, merely confirming the suffocating reality of China's campuses under Xi Jinping.

China has a problem with Mao Zedong. By any objective criteria, the man was a tyrant, responsible for the deaths of more Chinese people than was Japan, whose brutal occupation of parts of China is laid out in gruesome detail in every Chinese classroom. But Mao was also the founder of the People's Republic and the Party draws its legitimacy from him. After his death, and following tortuous debate and numerous drafts, paramount leader Deng Xiaoping delivered in 1981 the official verdict on the Great Helmsman – that in spite of serious errors, Mao was a great man. Some had wanted a tougher line, but the whole exercise had nothing to do with historical justice.[24] It was (and remains) about the survival of the Party. Mao's portrait still has pride of place above Tiananmen Gate, his body lies embalmed in a mausoleum in the centre of the square (in spite of his wish to be cremated) and in the National Museum, Mao's 'mistakes' have been airbrushed from the historical picture.

Early hopes that Xi Jinping might turn out to be a liberal were based at least in part on his family's experience of the Cultural Revolution. Yet in power he has drawn heavily from the Mao playbook, from the cult of personality to his use of language, and of campaigns like the 'mass line', Maoist jargon for supposedly consulting the people and then enforcing the results, as interpreted by the Party. He has hailed 'Mao Zedong Thought', while seeking to elevate is own alongside it. But while Mao was impulsive and restless, an often crude outlier who glorified chaos and violence, Xi has always been a Party insider, obsessed with stability and control. Mao immersed himself in classical Chinese literature and wrote poetry; Xi likes to appear well-read, peppering his speeches with literary references.

The Party has sought to depict Xi as a literary genius – and not only in his knowledge of classical Chinese texts. During a visit to the United States in 2015, he claimed to have read the works of Thomas Paine, Henry David Thoreau, Walt Whitman, Mark Twain and Ernest Hemingway. Though that was nothing compared with his grasp of Russian literature: Pushkin, Gogol, Dostoyevsky, Turgenev and Chekhov, were among Russian writers on a list he gave when visiting Sochi for the Winter Olympics in 2014. Visits to France, Germany and the UK have generated similar bibliographic torrents.[25] During a speech to the UK parliament as part of a 2015 state visit, he quoted Shakespeare's *The Tempest*, telling lawmakers, 'What's past is prologue.'

The claims have attracted ridicule. 'He is doubtless the most well-read Chinese leader since the birth of China. But really, does he have time to read?' the dissident writer Murong Xuecun told French journalist François Bougon, with more than a hint of irony.[26] And if Xi is widely read, it has not rubbed off on his own literary efforts, which are for the most part formulaic and jargon-ridden. *The Governance of China*, stretches to two volumes of turgid speeches, which have been translated into twenty-six languages and distributed in 160 countries.[27] More than 6 million copies of the first volume have been published, meaning it has been handed out in greater quantity abroad than works by any leader since Mao.[28] In spite of China's rich literary tradition, they are often the only books to be found on the stands of the Party-controlled China International Publishing Group at book fairs worldwide – albeit in numerous translations.

It was notable that during the crackdowns on university campuses, a group of avowedly 'Marxist' students were not spared. Several were detained. They were part of a neo-Maoist left that combines an almost cult-like following of Mao with at times extreme nationalism, and Xi had until then been far more tolerant of these 'patriotic' groups. They and their websites have been given far more leeway than have liberals. After all, much of what they are arguing for is supposedly what the Party (rhetorically) represents. The tipping point seems to have come with their ability to organise – always seen by the Party as the biggest threat – and their not unreasonable observation that in practice China's economy and society today bear little resemblance to anything that could be remotely described as socialist.

When Mao complained to aides that paintings in the early 1950s always depicted him as being shorter than Stalin, it is a fair bet that a similar (though inverted) conversation had already taken place in the Kremlin, where the Soviet dictator's cult of personality pre-dated Mao's. Though such was Stalin's addiction to violent purges of perceived rivals and critics, that no errant artist lived to tell the tale.

Stalin's solution to troublesome history was to falsify art and photographs on an epic scale. An entire industry grew around him, armed with brush and scalpel. As rivals were physically eliminated, so were their pictorial images, cropped or airbrushed from official photographs as if they had never existed. David King's *The Commissar Vanishes* contains a classic collection of before and after images of these disappearing cadres.[29] One print, dating from 1915, two years before the revolution. shows a meeting in a Siberian village of fourteen Bolshevik exiles, including Stalin. By 1939, when the photograph appeared in a portfolio called 'Stalin' to celebrate the tyrant's sixtieth birthday, only eight were left, the remainder replaced by vegetation, a fence and a log cabin. When the censors weren't snipping former comrades from pictures, they were placing Stalin in all manner of locations, where he was usually feted by bulging and adoring crowds – 'painting Stalin into places where he had never been, glorifying him, mythologizing him,' King explains.

During my time as a correspondent in Moscow in the early 1990s, one of my most heart-warming stories came from the archive of

Gosteleradio. The USSR State Committee for Television and Radio Broadcasting, to give it its full name, owned an anonymous warehouse in a grim suburb of the Russian capital, inside which row upon row of shelves strained under the weight of 400,000 classical music recordings. It dwarfed anything comparable, and we reported at the time that it was bigger than the combined lists of the world's five top recording companies. Aside from its sheer size, it was a musical history of the Soviet Union, but also a story of repression and resistance. As leading artists – Dmitri Shostakovich, Mstislav Rostropovich and Kirill Kondrashin among them – fell out of favour or defected, so their recordings disappeared from the airways. Keepers of the state archive were instructed to remove their names from recordings and in many cases to destroy the physical recordings altogether. They couldn't bring themselves to do so, and at great risk to themselves, replaced names with numbers or other codes and hid them away, dusting them off and restoring the names years later when it became safe to do so.

So China is not the only country to manipulate history, and there are plenty of museums other than the National Museum in Beijing that to some extent massage the historical record. But what makes China so unique is the almost pathological zeal with which the Communist Party goes about its mission to completely supress versions of history that do not agree with its own. In Xi Jinping's playbook, history is black and white. There is no room for shades of grey.

The story of the Moscow music archive is a story of resistance – but it is resistance in the analogue age. Record companies were soon lining up to do deals to digitise and commercialise the recordings, to bring them to a bigger and wider audience. It was the early days of the digital revolution, which promised access to information on a scale never seen before. It promised a gilded future. But it is also proving to be a great opportunity for dictators. No more physically searching through dusty old files and photos, or manually removing articles from magazines. Not when history can be manipulated and rewritten at the click of a mouse – and here too China is leading the way.

Aziz Isa Elkun has seen the promise of digitisation – and he's also seen the curse. He has seen how it has been used as a tool by China's Uighur minority, but also how quickly it can be shut down and the digital record erased by the Communist Party.

We met Aziz, a London-based Uighur scholar and poet, in Chapter

1, where he described losing touch with his Xinjiang-based family and the destruction of his family grave as China turned his homeland into one vast prison camp. He has worked tirelessly to draw attention to those abuses. He has also set himself a broader mission – to preserve Uighur culture and the integrity of historical records, online and offline, analogue and digital, which are under threat like never before.

He has clocked up thousands of miles of travel across Central Asia, collecting Uighur-language books, magazines and other documents that languished in dusty archives across the region. He sees little hope for those that remain in China itself. The Communist Party has destroyed books and archives, arresting scholars and academics, as part of its assault on Uighur culture. He has now collected so many publications that he is running out of storage space for the dozens of bulging packing cases. He lifts the lid on one and reads from a stirring poem of love, and then he tells me, 'What's happening in East Turkistan [Xinjiang], it's not about race or religion, it's a human tragedy.'

Hard though it is to imagine today, there was once a thriving thing called the Uighur internet. The first Uighur language website within Xinjiang was established in 1998. It then grew rapidly, especially after software became available to support Uighur Arabic script. This was the heyday of the internet all across China; censorship was strict, but sites were not as consistently monitored or blocked as they are today. By 2009, the Uighur internet was a large and vibrant community of more than 4,000 websites, the heaviest concentration registered in Urumqi, the provincial capital. They were filled with news, blogs, music, bulletin boards and chatrooms, and the content ranged from social issues to history, culture and literature, including contemporary poetry. They were cautious about politics, they had to be, but bulletin boards frequently carried anonymous postings on corruption and police abuse, and poems were often a vehicle for oblique criticism, as was humour and irony. They were the most developed of all minority language sites in China, and were particularly popular among students and intellectuals.[30]

Aziz believes the authorities were alarmed by the popularity of the Uighur internet well before the riots of July 2009, which provided the pretext to shut it down. It would be almost a year before full internet connectivity was restored, but not the Uighur internet as it had existed before. Websites were deleted, webmasters arrested or simply disappeared, their fate unknown. The Xinjiang authorities warned that the internet would no longer be used by 'criminals as a tool of communication'.[31] To Aziz this was not just an act of censorship, but another example of cultural vandalism. 'So much history was online,' he despaired, believing it had all been lost. Then he discovered the Wayback Machine.

The Wayback Machine is a web archiving tool developed by The Internet Archive, a US-based non-profit organisation, dedicated to archiving the entire internet. Since 1996, it has archived more than 330 billion web pages, and provides free access to scholars, historians and researchers, as well as the general public, searching for sites that have been 'deleted' or simply taken offline. Aziz and a team of young Uighurs based in the US and Japan went to work. 'We have to recover these websites. All this valuable data, valuable information. News, culture, history, community. Politics with a small p,' he said. It can be a slow and painstaking task, but the aim is to create their own Uighur web archive. Aziz hopes also to digitise the physical documents he has been collecting and to make them part of a searchable archive.

Theirs is a bold vision and the reality for the moment is that few in Xinjiang will be able to access their work, such is the repression in their homeland. In some ways Aziz is a contemporary version of the Soviet music archivists, determined to preserve cultural heritage from destructive totalitarianism, keeping it safe for the day it can be fully restored. The Soviet archivists had to wait until communism was disintegrating, while for the moment Xi Jinping is tightening his grip and determined to take his rewriting of history to a whole new level.

Glenn Tiffert, an historian of modern China, who specialises in the country's legal history, made his discovery almost by accident. He was going through his files of old photocopies of articles published in China during the 1950s, which reflected an often fierce debate at that time over the shape of the new socialist legal system. The articles had been published in the country's two most prominent legal journals, *Political-Legal Research* and *Law Science*, between 1956 and 1958 – a period which saw a brief political thaw – and they examined such issues as judicial independence and presumption of innocence.

The journals had been digitised and made available on new online platforms in China, and Tiffert saw little point in keeping his old dog-eared paper copies. First, though, he wanted to confirm their availability as a download. Several appeared to be missing. He pulled out more of his old paper copies, looking for discrepancies, and immediately saw a pattern. The two principal online archives had uniform gaps in their records; exactly the same articles were missing in both. He discovered that over a three-year period, more than 8 per cent of the articles, comprising 11 per cent of the page count, had been erased from the online version of the journals. The fiercest cuts have been to critiques of the practical defects of the emerging socialist legal system.

As we have seen, lawyers have been a particular target of President Xi Jinping, as have scholars advocating (or merely studying) constitutionality and the rule of law. Erasing or distorting the historical record fits Xi's agenda and Communist Party orthodoxy, but to historians such as Glenn Tiffert it goes further – striking at the very heart of academic research, which depends on the reliability and integrity of archives as a source base. The historical record was being amended during the *process* of digitisation. Tiffert reached a chilling conclusion, that 'the practice of history, to say nothing of other empirical disciplines, may never be the same again.'[32] Search engines are blind to the censorship, 'returning only sanitised results'. Academic researchers could no longer assume that the keepers of archives were some sort of neutral third parties: 'For censors, the possibilities are mouthwatering. Digital platforms offer them dynamic, fine-grained mastery over memory and identity, and in the case of China, they are capitalizing on this to engineer a pliable version of the past that can be tuned algorithmically to always serve the CCP's present. Dazzled by the abundance of sources on these platforms, we have failed to grasp these Potemkin-like possibilities, much less their historiographical implications.'[33]

Tiffert notes that many other Chinese state archives are transitioning to digital document delivery, and that artificial intelligence opens the possibility not only of censorship of what the archive contains, but of screening requests for material – surveilling what a researcher is interested in and tailoring the response, a far more subtle piece of manipulation.

He also criticises Western publishers who make common cause with Communist Party censors. He cites the 2017 case of Cambridge University Press, which at the request of its Chinese importer removed 315 articles and book reviews from the online edition of its respected academic journal *The China Quarterly*. It did so without consulting editors or authors. 'For subscribers in China, the items simply disappeared,' Tiffert writes. There was an outcry when the censorship was exposed, and CUP reversed itself, refusing further Chinese requests to censor dozens of articles from the online edition of the *Journal of Asian Studies*, the main publication of the US-based Association for Asian Studies. Tiffert accuses those Western publishers who comply with Chinese censorship of little less than complicity in the misrepresentation of history by 'contaminating research based on their holdings and violating the trust of their users. By tendentiously distorting consciousness of China's past, they are prejudicing its possible futures.'[34]

CUP is not the only Western publisher to cooperate with Chinese censorship. Springer Nature, which bills itself as the world's largest academic book publisher, blocked access in China to at least 1,000 articles containing references to such keywords as 'Tibet', 'Taiwan' and 'Cultural Revolution'. The company defended its censorship as necessary to comply with 'local distribution laws'.[35]

Tiffert suggests that very *process* of digitisation provides mouth-watering opportunities for censorship and the rewriting of the historical record – creating a digital dependence on a distorted version of history. His nightmare is of the process becoming fully automated by artificial intelligence. No more manually snipping the uncomfortable truth from hard copies of magazines, journals and newspapers, but creating 'bespoke versions of the historical record on demand, each exquisitely tuned to the shifting ideological or political requirements of the present'.[36]

Rewriting history was what Winston Smith did for a living. The main character in Orwell's *Nineteen Eighty-Four*, is a clerk in the records department of the Ministry of Truth, where he revises newspaper articles and doctors photographs so that they reflect the current party line. But one of the most powerful dystopian novels of historical manipulation has come out of China itself – *The Fat Years*, by Chan Koonchung.[37] Not surprisingly, it was banned in his home country.

The book is set in a booming and increasingly prosperous China, where an entire month in the recent past has gone missing, seemingly erased from the official record and collectively forgotten about in an act that one of the key protagonists describes as 'complete collective amnesia'. In search of the truth, Koonchung's central characters kidnap a senior Party official and demand he tell them what exactly happened during the lost month. The official reveals a month of chaos and repression, and how the leadership ordered that all newspapers in all public libraries be in digital form only in order to facilitate the rewriting of history. 'Very soon the new version of things became the only available version,' he says. He also reveals that the authorities put an ecstasy-style drug in the water supply, so that people felt nothing but great love, but he says it still came as a surprise to the leadership how quickly and easily people forgot. 'If the Chinese people themselves had not already wanted to forget, we could not have forced them to do so. The Chinese people voluntarily gave themselves a large dose of amnesia medicine.'

Though banned in China, the book attracted a considerable underground audience, and its central tenet of an entire nation gripped by collective amnesia was seen by many as analogous to the suppression of the memory of the Tiananmen Square massacre. Journalist Louisa Lim titled her book on the events of 1989 and their aftermath *The People's Republic of Amnesia*, and in it she looks at how modern perceptions (and misperceptions), especially among young people, have been shaped by censorship and official propaganda, but also fear of openly discussing the events. Many of those who do know something about Tiananmen, especially among the emerging middle class, claim the crackdown was justified by the stability and prosperity that followed. They want an easy life and to simply move on.

In his 'biography' of Orwell's *Nineteen Eighty-Four*, Dorian Lynskey says 'Totalitarian states depend on Julias.'[38] He is referring to Winston Smith's lover who doesn't remember the past, doesn't particularly care about the future and is generally incurious about society. She falls asleep while Smith is reading aloud a blasphemous book supposedly written by Emmanuel Goldstein, principle enemy of the state, which is said to contain the secrets of the party and how to overthrow it. Julia lives for the moment and for the physical. 'She has said things she doesn't really believe so many times that she doesn't really believe in anything she can't touch,' says Lynskey. He quotes Hannah Arendt on how mass propaganda erodes all truth and morality: 'Mass propaganda discovered that its audience was ready at all times to believe the worst, no matter how absurd, and did not particularly object at being deceived because it held every statement to be a lie anyway.'[39]

Is this an accurate portrayal of modern China? I will return to this question later when I look at the fragility of the Chinese system and the way it can be, and is being, challenged. Suffice to say here that history matters. Our knowledge and understanding of the past shapes our understanding, provides context, and informs our actions in the present. In an interview with the *Financial Times*, Zhang Lifan, a Beijing-based historian, who has been blocked from using social media because of his criticism of Mao Zedong, predicted that curbing historical research and manipulating the archives will backfire on China's leaders. 'If government officials don't know the real history, it will lead to stupid decisions and stupid policies,' he said.[40] At the same time an entire generation is growing up in China with a frightening ignorance of modern history and a world view that can best be described as an alternative reality.

When as many as 2 million Hong Kongers – more than a quarter of the population – from all walks of life took to the streets in 2019 to demand the scrapping of a bill that would have allowed criminal suspects in the territory to be tried in mainland courts, China's censors at first worked overtime. They attempted to eliminate any reference to the protests from mainland social media. Then they changed tack, and flooded the airways in China with images that exaggerated the violence, together with vitriol blaming 'terrorists' and foreign 'black hands' for stirring up trouble. Conspirators – usually from the CIA or the old British colonial power – were seemingly everywhere, organising and of course funding the protests. Even by the standards of Chinese propaganda, it reached almost hysterical proportions. *The Economist* called it a depressing lesson in the power of disinformation to see decent patriotic Chinese sharing such tales, 'For the claim is both nonsensical and, in the mainland, widely believed . . . There is something positively alarming about signs that, at some level, Communist Party bosses believe the black-hands story. Neither evidence nor common sense supports the tale's central charge that outsiders tricked or provoked as many as 2m[illion] Hong Kongers into joining marches.'[41]

A Hong Kong-based friend, a mainlander, described to me how she was flooded with calls and messages from family and friends back home, who not only believed the propaganda, but were now so fearful for her safety in the city, that they were convinced she would be lynched at any moment by a crazed mob egged on by the CIA. When foreign companies or celebrities have made even the mildest of statements in support of the protests – or have been insufficiently 'patriotic' in their condemnation of them – they have faced not only the wrath of the authorities, but online mob anger as an army of aggressive and xenophobic trolls have at times heaped violent abuse on them.

***

On 3 September 2015, China held a massive military parade to mark the seventieth anniversary of the defeat of Japan in the Second World War. It was an unprecedented display of military might and at the same time an unashamed distortion of history.

Security was extremely tight; the city was locked down and it took hours to reach our seats in a viewing stand beside Tiananmen Gate, where the media were seated alongside wizened veterans in military uniforms dripping with medals. The weather was unbearably hot, the skies blue after thousands of factories in the surrounding province were closed to ensure the air was smog-free for the event. First, we heard the rumble, sending a vibration through the stand, then the distant sound of stamping boots on concrete. The veterans gasped as they came into view – the goose-stepping troops, tanks and latest ballistic missiles paraded in front of us along Beijing's Chang'an Avenue, the city's main ten-lane east–west thoroughfare. Fighter jets streaked overhead. Xi Jinping inspected lines of camouflage-clad troops, his upper body emerging from the roof of a black limousine, a bank of microphones affixed in front of him. 'Hello comrades!' he said repeatedly, while the soldiers shouted back their support – as did the veterans.

The Victory Day holiday was new – introduced by Xi shortly after he came to power in order to claim the victory over Japan for the Communist Party. The parade was planned for months. 'The victory of the Chinese People's War of Resistance Against Japanese Aggression is the first complete victory won by China in its resistance against foreign aggression in modern times,' Xi said in a speech that conflated that victory with praise for the Party and the People's Liberation Army. In fact, the Communist Party played only a marginal role in the fight against the Japanese. Most of the key battles were fought by the Party's civil war rivals, the Nationalists, led by Chiang Kai-shek, whom Mao would go on to defeat in 1949.

One of the abiding Party myths of that period is the 'five heroes of Langya Mountain', where five communist soldiers, fighting off Japanese invaders, supposedly leapt to their death shouting 'Long live the Chinese Communist Party', rather than surrender. An historian who questioned the story was convicted of defaming the heroes and forced to apologise.[42]

Russian President Vladimir Putin topped the guest list at the Victory Day parade; the most prominent African leader to attend was the president of Sudan, Omar al-Bashir, indicted by the International

Criminal Court on genocide charges. Most Western leaders stayed away, not wanting to be seen to endorse China's growing military might and uncomfortable with the glorification of the Party's dubious role in the fight against Japan. It also came amid rising concerns about China's aggressive actions in the South China Sea, where it was building and militarising artificial islands in disputed waters. To many Western diplomats, the parade was the clearest and most ominous sign yet that they were dealing with a new kind of Chinese leader, that the Deng Xiaoping mantra of a low-key, peaceful rise was a thing of the past. Yet that message continued to be ignored by most Western political leaders, and for the West's corporate bosses it continued to be business as usual.

The term 'doublespeak', referring to language that deliberately distorts or reverses the meaning of words, disguising or distorting the truth, is often attributed to Orwell's *Nineteen Eighty-Four*. In fact, the term is not used in the book, though he does use two close relatives – 'doublethink', referring to the ability simultaneously to accept two contradictory beliefs as correct, and 'newspeak', an increasingly restricted and controlled language, meant to limit the freedom of thought. Both to some extent describe the vocabulary of Xi Jinping's Communist Party, and are indeed necessary tools for the Party's vast falsification of history. Perhaps the most frequent example is the use of the term 'Chinese characteristics', a favourite of Xi and his fellow leaders. As a general rule of the thumb its use negates the very words that come before it, such as 'socialism with Chinese characteristics', or the 'rule of law with Chinese characteristics', or 'human rights with Chinese characteristics'. It has also been used to follow the words Marxism, globalisation, diplomacy and democracy.

Sometimes its use can be close to surreal. Shortly before Christmas 2018, the *Global Times* reported that organisations representing China's Christian communities had vowed to 'explore blending church activities with Chinese characteristics'. The newspaper said the aim was to make Christians patriotic and conduct religious activities in line with socialist society. Churches 'should respect Chinese traditional culture and explore new forms of religious activities with Chinese characteristics'.[43] The report suggested rewriting the Bible to emphasise the bits that are in line with 'core socialist values'.

More details can no doubt be found on the 'Study the Great Nation' app. That's the Xi Jinping app – his Little Red Book – that supposedly has 100 million regular users, who can win credits by the their knowl-edge of 'Xi Jinping Thought'. It's the app that doubled up as spyware so that the Party could monitor users and their phones. It is the app that was developed by the Party's propaganda department, together with a company called Alibaba.

CHAPTER 5

Not So Corporate China

When a former English teacher named Jack Ma was revealed to be a member of the Communist Party there was consternation among Western business people and financiers because, as the creator of the business group Alibaba, Ma was the pin-up boy of Chinese private enterprise. Even his British biographer was taken aback.[1]

Ma was China's richest man at the time, with an estimated fortune of $35 billion. His rags to riches story was repeated in numerous glowing profiles, which portrayed him as the very personification of Chinese enterprise. 'Jack, more than any other, is the face of the new China,' Duncan Clarke said in his 'insider's account' of how Ma revolutionised the way Chinese people shop, and how he built an e-commerce giant rivalling Walmart and Amazon. He is 'the standard-bearer for China's consumer and entrepreneurial revolution,' Clarke stated.[2]

Ma graced the World Economic Forum in Davos, dining with business and political leaders, as well as celebrities such as Leonardo DiCaprio, Kevin Spacey and Bono. Former US president Bill Clinton shared platforms with him. He was welcomed to Downing Street by then Prime Minister David Cameron, who appointed Ma to his business advisory group.[3] Ma and Tom Cruise lavished praise on each other at the Shanghai premiere of *Mission Impossible – Rogue Nation*, which was financed in part by Alibaba. The company's 2014 initial public offering on the New York Stock Exchange was the world's biggest ever, raising $25 billion.

He was outed as a Party member by one of their own mouthpieces, the *People's Daily*, in November 2018. The newspaper made the disclosure in an article in which he was listed among business leaders who had contributed to China's modernisation.[4] It was also revealed that Ma had visited Yan'an, a city often described as the birthplace of the revolution and a place of pilgrimage for ardent Party members.

China's constitution requires Party members to place Communist Party principles and interests above all else, to implement its policies and to observe Party discipline. It also requires them to consciously study Marxism, Leninism and the thoughts of Mao and Xi – an odd reading list for the country's leading entrepreneur, but an increasingly necessary one for those who wish to survive in business.

In reality, Jack Ma's Party membership should have come as no surprise. There is no such thing in China as a private company in any meaningful sense, and certainly not in the Western understanding of the term. Ultimately, all Chinese companies are beholden to the Party; they exist at its pleasure. That is particularly the case for Chinese technology companies. The Party will never sanction private control of information – and data more generally. Moreover, the surveillance state is a joint venture between the Communist Party and China's nominally private tech companies. Whatever the motive for outing Jack Ma as a member of the Party, the *People's Daily* was merely stating the reality of doing business in China. In Xi Jinping's country, when the Party comes knocking, turning it away is simply not an option, not if you value the continuation of your business – and even your liberty.

We have seen how Alibaba developed with the Communist Party propaganda department the 'Study the Great Nation' app, Xi Jinping's digital version of Mao's Little Red Book, which also doubles up as spyware. Alibaba has declined to comment on the revelations about the app harvesting information. We have also seen how Alibaba's Sesame Credit system, capitalising on its vast troves of user data, is the most highly developed of the pilot social credit systems that the Party wants to combine into a national system of social control. The company is also a big investor in facial recognition software companies that have been accused of facilitating repression in Xinjiang, and in the construction more broadly of the surveillance state. I will examine these companies more fully later in this chapter.

On one level it is easy to understand why the story of Jack Ma is so compelling. He is self-made and he has transformed the way China shops and does business. But like so much of China's nominally private sector, the structure of his business is complex and opaque. At the time of Alibaba's record-breaking US listing, the comedian Jon Stewart pointed out that what investors were buying was not a stake in Alibaba China, but a holding company incorporated in the Cayman Islands. In *The Daily Show*, he pretends to telephone Alibaba, and demands, 'So I paid for a share for something on an island, and I don't own it? You're selling us a time share, is that what it is? A time share in a company – without giving us a free vacation to sit through your pitch?'[5]

Alibaba had originally wanted to list its shares in Hong Kong, but was turned down because the Hong Kong Stock Exchange was concerned about the ownership structure and governance. 'Oh I see,' Stewart quips. 'The company's trading in the US to escape the more stringent regulatory environment of China. *China.*' The former British colony of Hong Kong does not sanction multi-tier stock structures, which allow a small core of insiders to control a company. In Alibaba's case, Jack Ma and other founding executives – the 'Alibaba Partnership' – were able to nominate most board members in spite of their minority stake.

The Cayman Island holding company, in which shares were being sold, was known as a 'variable interest entity' (VIE), which did not actually own any assets in China itself. Instead, it owned a contract to share in Alibaba's profits. 'A VIE is essentially designed to allow you to own an asset the Communist Party specifically prohibit you from owning,' says Gillem Tulloch, who runs GMT Research, an accountancy research firm based in Hong Kong. Mark Mobius, an emerging markets fund manager, warned at the time that it was a 'dangerous' corporate structure, which left shareholders with little legal recourse if problems emerged.[6] A headline in *Foreign Affairs* posed the question, 'Son of Enron?' likening Alibaba's structural complexity to that of the collapsed energy giant.[7]

Jack Ma had already taken ownership of Alipay, the company's online payments system and arguably its most valuable asset, out of Alibaba and into a new company controlled by him. The company said this was to comply with Chinese laws, which required payments systems to be domestically owned, although this – and the manner of the transfer – was hotly disputed and triggered a dispute with Yahoo and SoftBank, two of Alibaba's biggest shareholders at the time.[8]

Initially, investors were unfazed by the warnings, and scrambled for a share in Chinese tech. For fund managers it was all about exposure to that vast market, however tangential, and they willingly held their noses when it came to the complexities of precisely what they were buying.

In September 2019, Jack Ma stood down as chairman of Alibaba, saying that he wanted to concentrate on philanthropy. By that time his net worth was estimated at a little under $40 billion, and the company had a market capitalisation of $460 billion. But it was testament to the opaque nature of the company structure that it was unclear what his stepping down actually meant, and how much influence he would retain. He remains a member of the now thirty-eight-strong Alibaba Partnership, which exercises ultimate control, and he still controls Alipay, since renamed Ant Financial and now Ant Group, and itself with an estimated value of more than $300 billion. There has even been speculation that he was forced out by the Communist Party, which required a less flamboyant, more pliable, figure at the helm of one of the country's most important companies.

Whatever the reason for his departure, he has fared better than some of his contemporaries. One of Jack Ma's early competitors was an e-commerce company called 8848, also established in 1999. It modelled itself closely on Amazon and was backed by Chinese-American venture capitalist Charles Xue. Xue would go on to invest in hundreds of internet start-ups and soon join the growing club of Chinese billionaires. He also became an influential blogger, with an online following of 12 million people for posts that covered social and political issues. In 2013, he was detained by Beijing police for allegedly hiring a prostitute. Three weeks later, state broadcaster CCTV aired his 'confession', which confirmed that the real reason for his detention was not his alleged late-night activities, but his blogging. Wearing handcuffs and dressed in a green prison uniform, he renounced his web posts and urged greater government control of the internet. 'I got used to my influence online and the power of my personal opinions,' he said. 'It gratified my vanity greatly.'[9]

Guo Guangchang was another of Ma's contemporaries, and Clarke, in his biography, describes them as friends. Guo is chairman of Fosun International, an investment group, and he's worth an estimated $8 billion. He's often described as the 'Warren Buffet of China', but in December 2015 he went missing. At first neither his company nor his family could explain his abrupt disappearance. Eventually it emerged that he was 'assisting authorities with an investigation'. He was released three days later, and to this day his detention has never been fully explained.[10]

Guo was one of a string of business people who temporarily went missing around that time, a stark reminder of the arbitrary exercise of Communist Party power. When once asked about his relationship with the government, Jack Ma quipped, 'As always, be in love with them, but don't marry them.'[11] Xi Jinping has demonstrated that he requires far more commitment than that, and Ma's Communist Party membership suggests they are at least cohabiting. Relations with government were characterised in a far starker way by Feng Lun, the chairman of one of China's largest real estate companies. In a blog post at the time of Guo's disappearance he wrote, 'A private tycoon once said, "In the eyes of a government official, we are nothing but cockroaches. If he wants to kill you, he kills you. If he wants to let you live, he lets you live".' The post was quickly deleted.[12]

Alibaba is a picture of transparency compared with many Chinese companies; it had to provide a certain amount of information for its New York listing. Within China itself it can be extremely difficult to obtain even the most basic of information about nominally private companies – including who ultimately owns and controls them and where precisely the funding comes from. This is often part of a defence tactic. It wasn't until 1988 that private enterprise in China was fully legalised; ambiguity was seen by entrepreneurs as a useful tactic against the often capricious and arbitrary actions of the Party. Another tactic was to bring in as shareholders and senior executives the sons and daughters of powerful Communist Party figures, a tactic designed to give them greater influence and protection (and mimicked by many Western companies working in China). However, employing these 'princelings' is not the surefire winner it once might have been. As Xi Jinping has stepped up his purge against opponents, it has become increasingly difficult to judge who is going to be targeted next, and a 'princeling' asset can quickly become a liability.

The Economist once described the Chinese stock market as 'a crazy casino'[13], but that is really a disservice to casinos. Michael Pettis, a senior fellow at the Carnegie–Tsinghua Center in Beijing and finance professor at Peking University, says the markets are driven by speculation and detached from economic fundamentals because it is impossible to know what those fundamentals are. Writing in the Financial Times, he described the Chinese stock market as one 'in which macroeconomic data is questionable, financial statements are not credible, corporate governance is unclear, government intervention is unpredictable, and interest rates are repressed'.[14] The newspaper described China as 'a country where corporate governance is stuck somewhere back in the Qing Dynasty'.[15]

A Western financial analyst based in Shanghai once described Chinese statistics to me as 'one of the greatest works of contemporary Chinese fiction'. Claims about the rate of economic growth were about as real as the handbags and DVDs in the once notorious Silk Street market in Beijing. They were political first and foremost. Analysts employed an array of esoteric techniques to try and ascertain what was really going on with the economy. They looked at diesel and electricity demand, the fluctuating levels of the country's chronic air pollution, car sales and congestion. One enterprising analyst regularly sent spies to ports to count the ships and throughput of trucks. No less an authority than Prime Minister Li Keqiang reportedly developed his own way of measuring economic performance that became known as the 'Li Keqiang index'. When he was head of Liaoning province, he ignored GDP and focused instead on rail cargo volumes, electricity consumption and loans as a proxy.[16] More recently analysts have pored over satellite images, looking for clues in traffic flows or the number of empty parking spaces at shopping malls or other commercial facilities.

There was much amusement among analysts when Wang Baoan, director of China's National Bureau of Statistics, angrily criticised those with a more bearish view of the Chinese economy. That was 'just one school of thought', he said. 'Facts speak louder than words.'[17] A few days later he was arrested for 'serious disciplinary violations' – the usual euphemism for corruption.

The extraordinary nature of China's markets was well illustrated in summer 2015. The stock markets had risen by 150 per cent in just over a year, egged on by the government in an effort in part to divert hot money away from the property market. In attempting to deflate one bubble it inflated another. Inevitably it popped, and during a few wild weeks that summer the stock market fell by 50 per cent. The stock-buying party was over and the Communist Party panicked, fearing social disorder from the legions of angry and mostly small investors. It ploughed an estimated $200 billion into the market in a failed effort to stabilise prices. Then it resorted to what the Party always resorts to: diktat. Trading in more than half the quoted companies was halted, large shareholders were banned from selling and any reporting about the market meltdown was restricted. The public security apparatus was mobilised to track down what were described as 'malicious short-sellers'.[18] An official directive ordered state media to avoid stoking panic. 'Do not conduct in-depth analysis, and do not speculate on or assess the direction of the market. Do not exaggerate panic or sadness. Do not use emotionally charged words such as "slump", "spike" or "collapse",' the directive said.[19]

Wang Xiaolu, a reporter for *Caijing,* China's top financial publication, quickly fell foul of the new regulations. He had done what financial reporters throughout the world do on a routine basis – picked up some gossip in the market. He then wrote a story speculating that the authorities would soon end their costly intervention. He was promptly arrested, and paraded on state television to 'confess' to causing market chaos through his reporting. He said he had used 'abnormal channels' to gather his information (the substance of which was never denied). 'I shouldn't have published the report at such a sensitive time, especially when it could have great adverse impact on the market,' he said, looking tired and drawn. 'I shouldn't have caused our country and shareholders such great losses just for the sake of sensationalism and eye-catchiness.'[20] He was jailed for 'spreading false information'.

The witch-hunt continued throughout the summer. The *China Daily*, another Communist Party mouthpiece, proudly proclaimed that the authorities had launched twenty-two cases involving 'suspected market manipulation, insider trading, false information fabrication and dissemination'. Four executives at the country's largest broker had apparently been arrested and placed under what the paper called 'criminal compulsory measures'.[21] It truly was a market with Chinese characteristics.

China's top nine tech companies have a combined market value of around $1.5 trillion. While America has the FAANGs, China has BATs – both are horrible acronyms, invented by financial commentators to describe the highest-flying technology companies. In America's case it's Facebook, Amazon, Apple, Netflix and Google; China has Baidu, Alibaba and Tencent. They are all giants. Alibaba dominates e-commerce in China. Baidu is China's biggest search engine by far, the Google of China, though it is also investing heavily in artificial intelligence and autonomous cars. Tencent owns WeChat, the 'app for everything', but is also heavily into gaming (its biggest money-spinner), and its fast-growing online payments system is second to that of Alipay. All of which make the BATs key components of China's surveillance state.

The Chinese government facilitated the rise of the BATs by banning foreign competitors, such as Facebook and Twitter. Baidu rose to prominence after Google withdrew from the country in 2010 over censorship and hacking concerns. The rapid rise to e-commerce dominance of Alibaba was aided by the retreat of eBay – usually blamed on the American giant's misreading of the Chinese market, but the company was also a victim of the Great Firewall, China's internet filtering and censorship system, which slowed down and often blocked traffic to eBay's US-based servers.[22]

Although the authorities have begun to install 'police stations' within internet companies, much day-to-day internet censorship is outsourced to the companies themselves, which monitor content in line with an evolving list of banned subjects and words provided by the authorities and delete offending accounts. Security researchers have raised concerns more broadly about the privacy standards of both Baidu and WeChat. Alibaba and Tencent are among tech companies that have piloted their own 'social credit' systems.

Tencent is Asia's most valuable company. The company's founder and chief executive, Ma Huateng, who also goes by the name Pony Ma, is not known to be a member of the Communist Party, although has been a member of the Chinese People's Political Consultative Conference, an advisory body. He vies with Jack Ma for the title of China's richest man, but compared with the Alibaba founder, he keeps a low profile. In public, he chooses his words carefully, telling one tech conference, 'We really are a great supporter of government in terms of information security. We try to have a better management, a better control of the internet.'[23]

Robin Li, the CEO and co-founder of Baidu, provoked a social media backlash when he suggested that his users didn't care about privacy. 'I think the Chinese people are more open or are less sensitive about the privacy issue,' he said during a panel discussion at the 2018 China Development Forum. 'If they are able to trade privacy for convenience, for safety, for efficiency, in a lot of cases they are willing to do that.'[24] It is a sentiment (or a hope) shared by Big Tech in China and the West, but rarely stated so baldly. 'The truth is that most of us have no clue how our personal information gets misused, leaked and sold for profit,' was one typical reaction on Chinese social media, suggesting that at least some users had not totally abandoned hope for greater privacy.

In 2018 Baidu entered an artificial intelligence partnership with military researchers – described as a 'joint lab for intelligent command and control technology'. The company's partner was China Electronics

Technology Group Corporation (CETC), which develops electronic warfare technology for the People's Liberation Army. Yin Shiming, Baidu's vice-president of cloud computing, said the partners should 'work hand in hand to link up computing, data and logic resources to further advance the application of new generation AI technologies in the area of defence'.[25]

Also that year, in what was described as the '40th anniversary of reform and opening up', Robin Li, Pony Ma and Jack Ma (as well as Ren Zhengfei, president of Huawei Technologies, whom we shall meet later in this chapter) were all included on a Communist Party list of 100 private business people whose 'entrepreneurial style' had contributed to building 'socialism with Chinese characteristics'. Fan Youshan, vice-chairman of the All-China Federation of Industry and Commerce, said that they each 'firmly support the leadership of the Communist Party of China'.[26] In reality, they have no choice. Chinese law requires that they give the Party unfettered access to their networks and to their data. As Human Rights Watch describes it:

> The government . . . has a number of laws that empower state agencies and private companies to collect and use information concerning citizens, and government departments as well as local governments have issued numerous directives, rules, and regulations to collect and use miscellaneous information. State security-related legislation, such as the State Security Law, invests police and other state security agents with the broad power 'to collect intelligence involving state security.' The Cybersecurity Law, while imposing requirements on network operators to keep user data confidential and to get consent before collecting it, also compels internet companies to store user data in China and provide undefined 'technical support' to security agencies to aid in investigations.[27]

The text of China's National Intelligence Law is explicit (my emphasis): '*All organizations and citizens* shall, in accordance with the law, support, cooperate with, and collaborate in national intelligence work, and guard the secrecy of national intelligence work they are aware of. The state will protect individuals and organizations that support, cooperate with, and collaborate in national intelligence work.'[28]

Another article in the law states that national intelligence agencies may 'establish cooperative relationships with relevant individuals and organizations, and entrust them to undertake relevant work'. It is vague as to the scope and bounds of what 'intelligence work' means. Ambiguity is frequently a feature of Chinese law, giving the Party plenty of leeway to interpret as it sees fit.

Cybersecurity (or information security) is defined very differently in China than in Britain and other Western democracies. In the West it usually refers to defending networks and computer systems, and it begins with what the cybersecurity industry calls the CIA triad – defending the confidentiality, integrity and availability of these systems. When China refers to information security, it means controlling the content of, and access to, information. It is seen as a function of national security, and its primary purpose is censorship and control. It is closely related to Xi Jinping's notion of 'cyber sovereignty' – reinforcing the country's virtual borders and policing what goes on in its cyberspace as tightly as it does its physical borders. Taken together, the national intelligence and cybersecurity laws bind Chinese technology companies into the Party's public security system, making them vital cogs in the surveillance state.

Xi Jinping has also heavily promoted what he calls 'civil–military integration' – under which technologies developed by private sector researchers and companies, as well as academics, must be shared with the military. In 2017 he had it written into the constitution, and has described integration as a 'key measure to deal with complex security threats and gain national strategic advantage'.[29] He heads a commission overseeing these efforts, and as the Party's *China Daily* reported in 2018, 'civil–military integration has become a national strategy and a priority on the leadership's agenda since Xi was elected top Party leader in late 2012.'[30] The Baidu tie-up with CETC is one component of this. A key focus is on artificial intelligence, which is at the heart of the surveillance state, and where the aim is to fuse the commercial and security economies.

Shoshana Zuboff's book, *The Age of Surveillance Capitalism*, focuses primarily on American tech companies, but she does reflect on China, and the nightmare marriage of surveillance capitalism with the totalitarian state, where data is exploited simultaneously for profit and for political control. She points out that until the mid 1990s the most common word for privacy, *yinsi*, didn't even appear in popular Chinese dictionaries. She writes:

In the Chinese context, the state will run the show and own it, not as a market project but as a political one, a machine solution that shapes a new society of automated behaviour for guaranteed political and social outcomes: certainty without terror. All pipes from all supply chains will carry behavioural surplus to this new, complex means of behavioural modification. The state will assume the role of behaviourist god, owning the shadow text and determining the schedule of reinforcements and behavioural routines that it will shape. Freedom will be forfeit to knowledge, but it will be the state's knowledge that it exercises, not for the sake of revenue, but for the sake of its own perpetuation.[31]

This is presented as a prediction, but it is already becoming a reality, as nominally private Chinese tech companies are integrated into the Party's surveillance system. Like their American counterparts, these Chinese companies are driven by an insatiable appetite for data to monetise, even as the Party leverages it for control, and the focus of computer power shifts from *learning* about behaviour to seeking to *shape* it.

China is the world's biggest market for, and largest producer of, surveillance equipment. The internal security apparatus has an insatiable appetite, and has spawned a vast industry – most of it nominally private – to service its needs. The China Public Security Expo, which we visited in Chapter 2, is its shop window. The show attracts buyers from around the world, and China is aggressively marketing the latest tools of repression, which I shall examine in more detail later. For now, though, the industry's single-most important customer is the public security apparatus of the Communist Party, to which it is closely bound.

Hong Kong's *South China Morning Post* reported in February 2019: 'Big brother in China is watching you, and there is a good chance that it is watching through a camera made by Hangzhou Hikvision Digital Technology.'[32] Hikvision is the world's largest manufacturer of surveillance cameras, and it supplies equipment to hundreds of surveillance projects in cities across China. According to a report by the Australian Strategic Policy Institute, it has taken on hundreds of millions of dollars of security-related contracts to facilitate the crackdown in Xinjiang, including facial recognition cameras at mosques, and has supplied surveillance equipment to the region's internment camps, where more than a million Uighurs and other Muslim minorities are being forcibly held for 're-education'.[33]

Hikvision is publicly listed on the Shenzhen stock exchange, but even the company itself has admitted that its ownership structure can be hard to grasp. In a 2015 statement that attempted to address accusations that it was a tool of the Communist Party, Jeffrey He, the president of its US and Canada division, conceded that the company has a 'complex ownership structure'.[34] It is 41 per cent owned by the China Electronics Technology Group Corporation and a related entity.[35] This is the state-run defence contractor that has a joint venture with Baidu and has been designated as a 'vanguard' of Xi's project for 'civil–military integration'. A company owned by CETC developed the police operating platform in Xinjiang that aggregates data and flags people for detention.[36] By one estimate, Hikvision and Dehua Technologies (the world's second-largest producer of surveillance cameras) won at least $1.2 billion in government contracts for eleven separate, large-scale surveillance projects across Xinjiang between 2016 and 2018.[37]

Hikvision was established in 2001, when it morphed out of a CETC research lab run by Chen Zongnian, now chairman of both Hikvision and CETC. He is a committed Communist Party member. At a 2018 event commemorating Karl Marx's 200th birthday, he said, '[Hikvision] must conscientiously implement the Party's line and principles and policies, ensure that the direction is not deviated, that the top level should strengthen strategic leadership, do a good job of coordination and supervision, and strengthen the Party organization.'[38]

In October 2019, Hikvision was among twenty-eight Chinese organisations blacklisted by the US government over human rights concerns, effectively barring the company from buying US products.[39] The Trump administration had already banned, on national security grounds, the use of Hikvision cameras by US government agencies. Britain has been far more welcoming of the Chinese company. An estimated 1.3 million Hikvision cameras are in use in the UK, where they are widely used by airports, councils and NHS Trusts.[40]

The US government also sanctioned artificial intelligence start-ups SenseTime, Megvii and iFlytek, which the Commerce Department said were 'implicated in human rights violations and abuses in the implementation of China's campaign of repression, mass arbitrary detention, and high-technology surveillance against Uighurs, Kazakhs, and other members of Muslim minority groups'.[41] SenseTime and Megvii are fast-growing leaders in facial recognition technology, closely involved in state surveillance systems across China. Alibaba has invested substantially in both. Speech recognition is the focus of technology being developed by iFlytek, which has been named a 'national champion' by the Chinese government, with which it works closely, and from which it has received substantial subsidies. Wang Shilei, a senior executive of the company, told the *Financial Times*, 'Chinese don't worry about freedom and privacy to the same extent as in the West. We have always had an emperor.'[42] That has become a fairly standard riposte from those involved in China's tech sector.

Huawei, one of the first Chinese tech giants to face US sanctions, is perhaps the best-known Chinese company internationally, where its role in next generation telecoms networks is highly controversial. I will examine those arguments in detail later. For now, it is important to understand its role and status within China.

Huawei is based near the southern city of Dongguan, where it employs 18,000 people on a sprawling campus made up of twelve replicas of European towns. These include Spanish mansions, German castles and Italian palazzi. A red antique-style train chugs between them; a herd of bronze rhinoceroses stands near a lake. *The Economist* characterised it as 'Impressive, mad and a bit tacky.'[43] The rhinos and European ramparts used to be strictly off-limits; until recently Huawei was one of the most secretive companies in China, and its founder and chairman Ren Zhengfei, a former military engineer, shunned publicity. More recently, the company has tried to be more open, inviting journalists to its campus, and presenting itself as a victim, poorly misunderstood and benign.

Ren founded the company in 1987, initially focusing on manufacturing phone switches for the rural Chinese market, though his real break seems to have come in the early 1990s with a contract to supply telecoms equipment to the People's Liberation Army, his former employer. In 1996 the company was given the status of 'national champion', which meant generous state support, including protection from foreign competition. Today, its businesses range from smartphones to building telecoms networks and it is now the largest telecommunications equipment manufacturer in the world, and a vital component of the surveillance state.

According to the Australian Strategic Policy Institute, Huawei has provided the Xinjiang Public Security Bureau with technical support and training.[44] This has included collaboration on video surveillance, data and cloud computing infrastructure, and a partnership with local television to 'maintain social stability and create positive public opinion'. The 'cloud' is a crucial component in surveillance, since it enables every security official, no matter where they are located, to access all the data they need from one place. In 2018, an Urumqi government website quoted a Huawei director as saying, 'Together with the Public Security Bureau, Huawei will unlock a new era of smart policing and help build a safer, smarter society.'[45] The Australian report prompted more than a dozen British parliamentarians to call on the British government to exclude the company from Britain's next generation 5G network until accusations of human rights allegations are comprehensibly dismissed.[46]

Huawei gets quite tetchy when critics accuse it of being subsidised, owned or controlled by the Chinese Communist Party, or of having close links with the army and intelligence services. It insists it is a privately run commercial company owned by its employees, and presents itself as a kind of glorified cooperative. In reality, as with most nominally private companies in China, it doesn't really matter what names appear on the share register. Special categories of shares and convoluted structures can mean that a minority of insiders control the company – as with Alibaba – but the main reason it doesn't matter is the law, as outlined earlier in this chapter, which subordinates all companies to the Party, and gives them no choice but to cooperate on security and intelligence on demand. At the same time, the Communist Party has tightened its grip over the day-to-day operations and decision-making of Chinese companies – and even foreign joint ventures operating in the country.

I met Gillem Tulloch at the Foreign Correspondents' Club in Hong Kong a day after an estimated 800,000 pro-democracy protesters had filled the streets of the semi-autonomous Chinese territory, a two-mile-long human snake winding its way between the towering skyscrapers. The protests had just entered their seventh month, and showed no sign of flagging, even though the Hong Kong government had now withdrawn the extradition bill that first ignited the protests. The bill would have allowed suspects to be sent to the mainland to be tried in Communist Party-controlled courts under China's opaque legal system.

'I could not have stayed in Hong Kong if the bill had become law. No way,' Tulloch told me. He is one of Hong Kong's most astute financial analysts. His company, GMT Research describes itself as an accounting research firm, and it examines company books looking for financial anomalies and other accounting shenanigans. There is much in the books of Chinese companies to keep him busy, and many that are upset by his forensic research. He feared that if the extradition bill had become law, he could have faced trumped-up charges on the mainland. 'They might have pursued a case against us which ended up in our being extradited to a mainland court for revealing state secrets,' he said. 'State secrets' are very broadly and arbitrarily defined in China.

The morning I met him, he had just endured two days of cyberattacks on his company's computer systems following a negative report on one major Chinese company – his systems bombarded with requests until they were overwhelmed, an attack known as a Distributed Denial of Service, or DDoS attack. He was able to laugh that off, and at the time we met, the Hong Kong legal system still gave him protection from the whims of mainland courts.

Tulloch handed me a new GMT report that analysed the thirty largest US-listed Chinese companies and evaluated their risk. 'Our analysts regarded over 70% of this sample as a high accounting risk, and found multiple examples of shenanigans,' the report states. Fraud was identified as the greatest risk facing investors, 'thereafter, it was profit manipulation, window dressing, off-balance sheet businesses and corporate governance'.[47] It identified the use of offshore tax havens, and complicated legal and ownership structures, stating: 'Arguably, this structure is being exploited to avoid regulatory oversight and lower disclosure.' It was not a pretty picture.

I first interviewed Tulloch in 2011 about China's 'ghost cities' – a string of new cities the country was building as part of a spending splurge that followed the 2008 global financial meltdown. They were vast, and he'd discovered them by studying Google Earth. They had all the trappings of urban life – except people. He'd described it as a gigantic bubble, and another symptom of what he believes to be an ultimately unsustainable economic system. 'Yes, the economy is growing, but the quality of growth is deteriorating,' he says. 'Empty property in the middle of nowhere, roads and railways to nowhere, airports serving nowhere.'

***

China's economy is 'unstable, unbalanced, uncoordinated and unsustainable'. That verdict did not come from a hawkish American, but from China's former premier, Wen Jiabao. Similar views have been expressed by his successor, Li Keqiang. That may seem surprising. After all, this is the world's fastest-growing economy, and the second largest after the US in nominal terms. It is the world's largest manufacturer and exporter. Its GDP per person has grown more than tenfold since 1990; some 850 million people have been lifted out of poverty, according to the World Bank.[48] These are impressive figures, but they hide an economic fragility that is not commonly appreciated.

Growth rates are falling. Until now, the economy has been powered on the one hand by low-cost, low-end manufacturing for export, and on the other by heavy public infrastructure investment. Both are in trouble; costs have been rising, making China's low-end assembly lines less competitive. And the splurge on shiny new airports, railways, highways – and those ghost cities – has left the public finances mired in red ink. There are an estimated 65 million apartments sitting empty, ghostly testament to the building binge. Rather like a drug addict, the economy is getting less and less from each successive hit.[49] China's total corporate, household and government debt is estimated at more than 300 per cent of GDP, but that's just a guestimate.[50] There is an enormous shadow banking sector, the size of which can only be guessed at. The finances of many local governments and banks are shaky at best. Property and stock market bubbles have inflated and burst and inflated again; there is massive over-capacity in heavy industries like steel and ship-building.

The Party's response has been twofold. Firstly, it has tried to encourage people to spend more and save less, to shift the system away from its addiction to wasteful investment and create a consumer-driven economy. This has shown some signs of progress, but is not easy because communist China has only a limited social welfare system, obliging people to save for ill-health or old age. The second response is to take the economy up-market, as it has with some success in Shenzhen. The idea is to shift away from low-end assembly and processing, towards high-tech industries that add more value.

It is often claimed that nominally private companies are now the main drivers of the economy, yet not only is ownership frequently murky, but these firms are increasingly hidebound by Party controls. China wants to create a modern innovation and knowledge-driven economy, but the Party thinks this can be achieved by diktat – or simply by creating and protecting 'national champions' and throwing money at research and development. Money helps, but innovation requires flexibility and openness; it rarely thrives in closed and repressive political systems, an issue I shall examine in more detail in Chapter 10.

There are other reasons for caution on China's economy. China may well get old before it gets rich. Demographics are working against it, a legacy of the now-abandoned one-child policy. The workforce is shrinking and the country is ageing faster than anywhere else in the world. The government estimates that by 2050, the workforce will have shrunk from a 2015 figure of 911 million to around 700 million.[51] It estimates that by 2050 some 487 million people – about a third of the population – will be over sixty years of age. A strategy paper published by the Party's central committee in late 2019, recognises that the country faces a serious challenge, but is notably short on detail, stating that China must 'find its own way out, and that means taking a path with Chinese characteristics'.[52]

China's growth model has also resulted in appalling environmental degradation, from unbreathable air to contaminated soil and undrinkable water, which are a big source of popular anger and discontent. In addition, communist China is now one of the most unequal societies on the planet, with the richest 1 per cent of households owning almost a third of China's wealth.[53] The country comes second after the US in the number of millionaires (4,447,000 of them in 2019)[54] and in billionaires (389 in 2020).[55]

As Gillem Tulloch sees it, the most salient feature of corporate governance in China is control by the Communist Party. All companies, whatever their formal ownership status, must have Party cells. 'The Party controls everything,' he said. 'They have to consult the Communist Party before they make major decisions. So effectively they're under state guidance.' And from the most powerful billionaire to the smallest of start-ups, there is one overriding reality to business in China: 'The Communist Party can take away your company immediately if they want to. There's no good legal means of redress.'

Party control was not always so tight, and in the years before Xi Jinping came to power, it appeared to be loosening – at least as far as business was concerned. Zhangjiagang was typical of that trend. There is today little to distinguish it from any other of the grey industrial cities that line the Yangtze River. But in the 1990s the Communist Party awarded it the title of 'National Civilisation City' for five years on the trot. Model workers or peasants who toil selflessly for the good of the nation have long been staples of Party propaganda; now it was naming Zhangjiagang as a model city for what the Party leader at the time, Jiang Zemin, described as 'spiritual civilisation'. It was one of his pet slogans, and as far as it contained any meaning at all it seemed to refer to order, civility and cleanliness, which the Party enforced through various carrots and sticks. It was a sort of modest offline version of the Orwellian social credit system it is now rolling out online to reward 'good' behaviour and punish the 'bad'.

I visited the city in 1997 and was taken to a factory that made vans and minibuses, and was described as a 'spirtually civilised enterprise'. Like many companies in those early days of reform, its ownership was ambiguous – sort of private, but with close links to the local government and the Party. The young general manager was bubbling with enthusiasm for his vans, reeled off plans for rapid growth and listed all the countries he intended to export to. He was an impressive advocate for what we all hoped was the new China, but he kept being interrupted by the factory's sullen Communist Party secretary. The secretary kept trying to steer the conversation to the Party's success in giving workers what he called a 'healthy character', which seemed to involve bombarding them with Party slogans while punishing bad habits like drinking and gambling. I watched the body language between the two of them. The general manager could barely disguise his disdain for the Party secretary, who was a couple of decades his senior. At one point he winced and rolled his eyes at a fresh barrage of slogans.

It was a performance I would remember over the following years as Party cells inside companies (and in higher education) seemed to become increasingly less relevant, especially with the growth of the private sector. They were becoming decorative, their powers waning, operating – if they operated at all – as sort of glorified social clubs. That has been reversed sharply under Xi Jinping, who has overseen a dramatic increase in the role and power of the Party in every aspect of life in China. Committees now operate in most nominally private companies, and even in foreign joint ventures. The Party's *Global Times* reported in late 2018 that, 'Party cells inside private firms can help guide and supervise enterprises to follow the country's laws and regulations and safeguard the legitimate interests of all parties.'[56] The newspaper reported that tech firms in particular have been strengthening their 'Party construction work'. Any organisation is required by law to set up a Party unit if it has at least three Party members. The report stated that shareholders have the same 'core interests' as the Party, and that Alibaba alone has nearly 200 Party branches and 7,000 members. The newspaper quotes Su Wei, a professor at a Party school in Chongqing, as saying, 'The board of shareholders is in charge of decision-making and daily operations, while Party cells are set up to make sure the company's operations are in line with the principles and policies of the CPC [Chinese Communist Party].' The *China Daily*, under the headline 'Private firms benefit from closer bonds with government', claimed that companies active in 'Party building activities' come up with better operational results and such activities 'help to develop an advanced corporate culture'.[57]

According to 2017 figures, Party units now exist in nearly 70 per cent of some 1.86 million privately owned companies. The law requiring Party organisations to be set up had been treated as largely symbolic, but companies, including foreign firms, have come under increasing pressure to not only embrace Party units, but allow the Party final say over business operations and investment decisions.[58] Many companies have now made their subordination to the Party more explicit: more than thirty Chinese companies listed on the Hong Kong stock exchange have written the Party into their articles of association, typically describing the Party as playing a core role in 'providing direction (and) managing the overall situation'.[59]

At Huawei, the Party secretary is reportedly Zhou Daiqi, a twenty-five-year veteran of the company, who also doubles up as the company's chief ethics and compliance officer.[60] Yet Ren Zhengfei is dismissive of the Party's influence. In an interview with the BBC, he claimed the Party committee 'serves only to educate employees. It is not involved in any business decisions.'[61] In reality even the smallest of tech start-ups in China now see a Party cell as important if their business is to prosper. 91Finance, a fintech start-up run by entrepreneur Xu Zewei, holds meetings to urge employees to join the Party. Strong Communist Party links mean that 'supervisory bodies and clients have more trust in our work', he told the *Financial Times*.[62]

Little surprise that the Party under Xi Jinping has come up with its own definition of 'entrepreneurship', which encapsulates patriotism and professionalism, as well as observing discipline and obeying laws. Xiao

Yaqing, who heads the State Assets Supervision and Administration Commission, said that 'excellent, well-managed, profitable companies have a good management team. That is surely because the Party leadership plays an important role in team-building and corporate governance.'[63]

The most feared institution in China among Communist Party members and those who associate and do business with them is housed in a grey twelve-storey building, beyond a seven-foot-high wall in downtown Beijing. It does not appear on maps and has no sign or logo to identify it. It operates entirely outside the official criminal justice system, yet its investigators can arrest, seize evidence and interrogate at will. It runs a network of secret prisons, where detainees can face prolonged solitary confinement, cut off from the outside world, with no access to family or lawyers.[64]

This is the Party's Central Commission for Discipline Inspection, its graft-busters. It is Xi's main instrument for controlling the Party and purging his enemies within it. Xi launched an anti-corruption campaign shortly after he came to power, vowing to target 'tigers and flies', the powerful as well as lower-level Party officials. It was a popular campaign with the public, for whom the Party was a bi-word for corruption, and in its first three years the commission claimed to have disciplined more than 750,000 officials, with 35,000 of them prosecuted.[65] There were reports that the clampdown had become so extensive that day-to-day government business was grinding to a halt, with officials no longer sure how to navigate the traditional paths of power.[66]

Those prosecuted included 146 'tigers'. Among these high-ranking officials were Zhou Yongkang, the country's former internal security chief, sentenced to life imprisonment after a secret trial, and Ling Jinua, the former personal aide to Xi's predecessor, Hu Jintao. Ling had tried to cover up a car crash in which his son smashed his Ferrari sports car, dying instantly. Two young women, one naked the other semi-naked, were in the car with him, and both were seriously injured. Senior military figures and provincial Party leaders have also been targeted in the purge. The Party had seen anti-corruption drives before, but never of this intensity and persistence, and never with such senior targets.

The commission is a Party organisation, and the Party has around 88 million members subject to its oversight. Yet, under Xi Jinping, the Party has vastly extended is influence into all walks of life – and with it the commission's extrajudicial reach. There is no doubt that graft had become endemic, and Xi's campaign is motivated at least in part by a desire to restore the standing of the Party. But it has been used to consolidate his power and to eliminate rivals – and also as a warning to those who might challenge him.

The danger for Xi is that it merely makes fresh enemies, and will ultimately fail in its stated aim of rooting out corruption. There are two reasons for this. The first is in the nature of the Chinese economy, which Minxin Pei, a Chinese-American political scientist who studies governance in China, describes as classic 'crony capitalism', characterised by looting, lawlessness and collusion at its upper reaches. A key feature of the system is intrinsic collusion between Party and business leaders. 'Collusive corruption, in theory as well as practice, is more destructive than individual corruption because such behaviour destroys the organisational and normative fabric of the state, increases the difficulty of detection, and produces greater financial gain for perpetrators,' he writes.[67] Ultimately, Pei believes China's crony capitalism is irreformable, since its institutions are 'the very foundations of the regime's monopoly of power'.[68]

The second reason the campaign will fail is a lack of transparency and an absence of any independent oversight or accountability. Endemic corruption is the natural outcome of a system where the police, the courts and the media are all controlled by the Party and criticism and scrutiny are criminalised. Corruption campaigns in effect become games of musical chairs, shifting one faction from money-making opportunities, only to be replaced by another more favoured faction.

In late 2019, the Chinese government gave state and public institutions three years to remove all foreign computer equipment and software from their offices and to switch to domestic suppliers. The directive was interpreted as the Party's response to efforts by the US to curb Chinese technology in the West. In fact, efforts to protect and bolster home-made tech, and shield domestic technology companies, pre-date the trade tensions with the Trump administration. China has a long and extensive record of protectionism. Western companies operating in China have been forced to hand over technology and Chinese companies have benefited from intellectual property theft and extensive cyber espionage. Too many companies have been prepared to go along with this as a price for doing business in China.

It is common for Western economic analysts, especially those with a stake in the Chinese market, to stress the size of China's private sector, often described in awestruck terms as the 'motor' of the new economy. Yet nominally private companies are so intertwined with the Party and state, that the distinction is blurry at best. Chinese law and the reality of Party power under Xi Jinping have bound them ever closer to the surveillance state. That is the reality of Xi's China. By contrast, Western companies operating in China do have a choice. Yet in too many cases Western business people, as well as politicians and academics, have allowed themselves to become willing accomplices to repression, handmaidens to the Party, as Xi strives to extend the tentacles of the surveillance state beyond China's borders.

CHAPTER 6

The West's (Often Willing) Enablers

The chairman of Cathay Pacific, a Hong Kong-based airline, sounded every bit the enlightened employer when, on 8 August 2019, he defended the freedom of expression of his staff. 'We certainly wouldn't dream of telling them how to think about something,' John Slosar told a press conference held against the background of mounting pro-democracy protests in the city in which Cathay staff had taken part and a pilot was arrested. 'They're all adults. They're all service professionals. We respect them greatly.'

Unfortunately, China didn't see it that way. Party-controlled media on the mainland shrilly denounced the company; nationalist anger was whipped up on social media. The *Global Times*, a tabloid frequently deployed as a Party attack dog, had already warned that Cathay would 'pay a painful price' for its 'actions'. Now, the Party moved to extract that price. China's aviation authority demanded that as a 'safety measure' Cathay submit identification documents of all crew flying into China or over Chinese airspace and remove those who had taken part in or supported protests. State-owned banks downgraded the company's shares, one putting a 'strong sell' recommendation on the airline's stock; state-owned companies ordered their employees not to fly Cathay. Merlin Swire, the chairman of Swire Pacific, Cathay's principal shareholder, was summoned to Beijing.[1]

Cathay quickly fell into line. Several employees, including two pilots, were sacked. Swire, with deep roots in colonial-era Hong Kong and substantial business interests on the mainland, issued a statement in which it said it 'resolutely supports the Hong Kong government' and condemns 'all illegal activities'.[2] The company said it would comply with China's new aviation regulations, which affected an estimated 70 per cent of its passenger and cargo flights. 'Cathay Pacific Group employees who support or take part in illegal protests, violent actions, or overly radical behavior shall be immediately suspended from any activity involving flights to the mainland,' Chief Executive Rupert Hogg wrote in a memo to staff. 'Cathay Pacific Group's operations in mainland China are key to our business.'[3] The memo was one of his last acts as a Cathay employee, as days later he was forced out of his job. At the beginning of September it was announced that Chairman John Slosar was also stepping down after working for Swire and related companies for thirty-nine years.

To add insult to injury, Hogg's departure was first reported by China's state broadcaster, CCTV, on its social media account – half an hour before it was announced by the Hong Kong stock exchange, where the company's shares are listed. A gloating CCTV paired the news with an internet meme, which translates roughly as, 'If you don't do stupid things, they won't come back to bite you.' Hong Kong-based analysts were shaken. David Webb, an activist investor, described the removal of Hogg as 'shameful appeasement' and the 'most appalling kowtow to Beijing'.[4] While Ivan Su, at Morningstar, a financial services firm, told the *Financial Times*, 'This is my first time seeing something like this happen . . . over my career here in Hong Kong. We are talking about a Hong Kong company, not a Chinese company. This happens with Chinese companies.'[5]

By humiliating Cathay, Beijing was sending a message to other international companies operating in Hong Kong: if you want to operate in China, do our bidding, toe the line. As such, it worked wonders. The big four global accountancy firms – PwC, Deloitte, KPMG and EY – issued statements distancing themselves from a full-page ad supporting the protests that had appeared in a local newspaper, apparently paid for and signed by employees of the firms. 'We will never fear or compromise with injustice and unfairness,' the ad read. The *Global Times* was again unleashed by the Party, urging the companies to fire their errant employees or risk 'becoming the next Cathay Pacific'. In its statement, PwC said the ad 'does not represent the firm's position', stressing that PwC, 'firmly oppose any action and statement that challenge national sovereignty'.[6]

HSBC was next to be embroiled in controversy, accused by protesters of helping the city's police to shut down one of the main sources of funding of the protest movement. Police officers made several arrests for money laundering and froze the Spark Alliance Fund, a crowdsourcing operation that had raised around HK$80 million (a little under US$10 million) to help protesters with living expenses, as well as legal and medical costs. A spokesman for HSBC rejected the accusation, saying the bank had closed the fund's account a month before the police action, purely for compliance reasons. It said the decision was 'unrelated to the current HK situation'.[7]

Then, in October 2019, Apple removed from its app store a crowd-sourcing app called HKmap.live, which enabled protesters to track the movements of police. The company had been targeted by the *People's Daily*, another Party newspaper, where an editorial accused Apple of aiding 'rioters' and said that 'letting poisonous software have its way is a betrayal of the Chinese people's feelings.' Charles Mok, a pro-democracy legislator, said the app was designed to help people avoid police brutality, and that Apple could 'uphold its commitment to free expression and other basic human rights, or become an accomplice for Chinese censorship and oppression'. In response, Tim Cook, Apple's chief executive, claimed in an email to employees that the app had been removed after receiving 'credible information' from the authorities that it was being used to target individual police offices for violence. It was not the first time Cook had made an awkward statement in defence of censorship in China.[8]

In 2017, I published my first novel, *Beijing Smog*, a satire on modern China in which the main character is an online image of a stick alien, which goes viral on the internet. The image is posted as a joke by Wang Chu, a young and rather naïve Chinese blogger, but soon becomes a symbol of opposition. It ends up challenging the Communist Party, which doesn't have a sense of humour. At one point in the novel, Wang creates an app, a game, in which little stick aliens emerge at ever greater speed from beneath the portrait of Mao Zedong in Tiananmen Square. The aim of the game is to gain points by swatting the aliens with a giant fly swatter as they run across the square. When the book was published I decided it might be fun to create the app for myself as a kind of marketing gimmick, and I commissioned *Whack an Alien*, a game that is remarkably true to Wang's original. I then submitted it to the Apple app store.

The Apple approval process is usually pretty quick, and essentially involves searching for technical glitches. I never anticipated any other problems. While the book is quite a biting satire on Communist Party corruption and repression, *Whack an Alien* was, after all, only a game.

After two weeks I had heard nothing, so re-submitted. Two weeks after that I received a message from Apple asking me to phone a member of their review team in San Jose, California. When I did, I was told that while my app was technically sound, it would be 'hidden' from Apple's China app store because its content is 'not appropriate and breaks local laws.' I asked what content was not appropriate? – 'I do not have that information.' Why was it not appropriate? – 'I do not have that information.' What local laws? – 'I do not have that information.' We went around in circles like this until eventually she suggested I consult a local lawyer if I did not understand the local laws they were refusing to tell me about. It took me back to my days in Beijing – it was like talking to a Party functionary. I then received this email:

> Hello,
>
> As discussed on the phone, we are writing to notify you that your application, Whack an Alien, will be removed from the China App Store because it includes content that is illegal in China, which is not in compliance with the App Store Review Guidelines:
>
> 5. Legal
>
> Apps must comply with all legal requirements in any location where you make them available (if you're not sure, check with a lawyer). We know this stuff is complicated, but it is your responsibility to understand and make sure your app conforms with all local laws, not just the guidelines below. And of course, apps that solicit, promote, or encourage criminal or clearly reckless behavior will be rejected.
>
> Specifically, your app contains content and features that are not appropriate on the China App Store.
>
> While your app has been removed from the China App Store, it is still available in the App Stores for the other territories you selected in iTunes Connect.
>
> Best regards,
>
> App Store Review

I appealed against the decision, and over the course of the following weeks I wrote to Apple three times, asking for clarification about which laws the app contravened, what content and features were not appropriate, and why they were not appropriate. I also asked Apple to explain the process of arriving at this decision. Apple did not respond to my appeal or to any of my questions.

They were evidently busy – this was the time the company was removing hundreds of the anti-censorship tools called VPNs from its China app store. In her 21 November 2017 letter to US Senators Ted Cruz and Patrick Leahy, Cynthia Hogan, Apple's Vice President for Public Policy Americas, said that the company had removed 674 VPNs from the app store in China 'at the request of the Chinese authorities' because they violated laws requiring VPNs to have a permit.[9] Cruz and Leahy had written to Tim Cook, telling the Apple CEO, 'we are concerned that Apple may be enabling the Chinese government's censorship and surveillance of the internet.'[10]

Also that month the New York Times reported that Skype was among a number of 'voice over internet' apps removed by Apple from its China app store on the grounds that they 'do not comply with local law'.[11] Earlier in the year, the Times's own news app, in Chinese and English, was removed, an Apple spokesperson saying, 'We have been informed that the app is in violation of local regulations.'[12] Tibetan activists accused the company of removing twenty-nine popular Tibetan-themed apps dealing with news, religious study, tourism, and even games.[13]

The message I received from Apple about Whack an Alien seems pretty pro forma – it is identical to that received by some VPN developers as was the company's reluctance to discuss the opaque process by which it censors apps for the China app store. Apple does publish what it calls a 'Transparency Report', updated every six months, stating the number of requests received from governments to hand over data or for the removal of apps. This shows, for instance, that between July and December 2019, 203 apps were taken down from the China app store at the request of the government, most relating to gambling or pornography. Apple portrays its role as purely reactive, responding to legal requests. But it provides little detail of the process, and my experience suggests Apple is more proactive in censorship, screening apps for content that might offend China. The review team member I spoke to described the censorship of Whack an Alien as 'Apple's decision'. This is supported by research from the Tech Transparency Project, part of the Campaign for Accountability, an advocacy group, which compared the availability of apps across app stores worldwide. It found that 3,200 were missing from the China store but were available in other countries, almost a third relating to human rights topics such as privacy tools, Tibetan Buddhism, Hong Kong protests and LGBTQ issues.

BuzzFeed News reported that in 2018 Apple gave guidance to creators of shows for its Apple TV+ service that they should avoid portraying China in a bad light. Apple declined to comment on the report.[14] Also that year, a US security researcher shed further light on the technical lengths (and intricacies) of Apple's censorship for China. Patrick Wardle was asked by a Taiwanese friend who lived in San Francisco to inspect his iPhone, which crashed every time the Taiwanese flag emoji appeared. Wardle, a former National Security Agency staffer, tracked the problem to an intentional censorship feature installed by Apple to apparently placate the Chinese government, which maintains that Taiwan is part of China. 'Basically, Apple added some code to iOS [the iPhone operating system] with the goal that phones in China wouldn't display a Taiwanese flag,' Wardle told *Wired* magazine, 'and there was a bug in that code.' Wardle said the censorship function was designed to click in when iPhone location settings were switched to China, but 'somehow the phone got confused about what region and locale it should be in.' Wardle warned Apple about the flaw, and the company released a patch, but would not comment further about the censorship or the nature of the bug. To Wardle it highlighted the power of hidden censorship code. 'They say "We're not going to spy on our users." But if China asks, they'll build censorship into their devices and not really talk about it,' he told *Wired*. 'Hypocrisy is the term I would use.'[15]

That same year, Apple began moving the iCloud accounts of its China-based customers to Chinese servers. This included the storage of encryption keys for those accounts. Until then, Apple had stored the codes for all global users in the US. The company's partner in China is Guizhou-Cloud, a company overseen by the local government of Guizhou province. Apple said it was complying with local laws that require data on Chinese users to be stored in China. The company said it will ensure that the keys are protected, though it didn't explain how. Apple's updated terms and conditions for China users say that Apple and Guizhou-Cloud 'will have access to all data' and 'the right to share, exchange and disclose all user data, including content, to and between each other under applicable law'. Matthew Green, a professor of cryptography at Johns Hopkins University, told the *Wall Street Journal*,

'Once the keys are there, they can't necessarily pull out and take those keys because the server could be seized by the Chinese government . . . Ultimately, it means that Apple can't say no.'[16]

Human rights groups saw it as tantamount to handing over data, including photos, messages, contacts and documents, to the Chinese government. 'Tim Cook preaches the importance of privacy but for Apple's Chinese customers these commitments are meaningless. It is pure doublethink,' said Nicholas Bequelin, East Asia Director at Amnesty International. An Amnesty International ad campaign declared that 'All Apple users are equal, but some are more equal than others,' a nod to Apple's iconic '1984' advert, when in that year it launched its first Macintosh computer. In that award-winning ad, which was directed by Ridley Scott, the director of the movie *Blade Runner*, scores of grey-clad clones watch a giant screen from which Big Brother is celebrating 'information purification directives'. A brightly clad and athletic woman then storms past the clones and throws a sledgehammer at the screen, which explodes, a voice over saying, 'On January 24th, Apple Computer will introduce Macintosh. And you'll see why 1984 won't be like "1984".'[17]

When pressed on its behaviour in China, Apple usually falls back on the well-worn argument that engagement is the best way to bring about positive change, that it will help in the further opening of China. Speaking at the Fortune Global Forum in Guangzhou, China, in December 2017, Cook said, 'Your choice is: do you participate, or do you stand on the sideline and yell at how things should be? And my own view very strongly is you show up and you participate, you get in the arena because nothing ever changes from the sideline.'[18]

Cook has certainly engaged with Beijing, becoming a regular at business forums in China. In October 2019 he was appointed chairman of the advisory board of the prestigious Tsinghua University School of Economics and Management in Beijing.[19] The appointment coincided with a growing crackdown on free speech on China's campuses. It came just months after Xu Zhangrun, a Tsinghua law professor, was stripped of his positions and stopped from teaching after criticising the personality cult surrounding Xi.[20]

The problem with the 'engagement' argument, variations of which are made by business leaders and Western politicians, it is that it hasn't worked. China under Xi Jinping has become significantly more repressive, and less market- and investment-friendly. 'Engagement' arguments are largely self-serving. Apple has a great deal at stake in China. The country accounts for around 20 per cent of its revenue,[21] and is also critical to its supply chain. The chain is complicated, but most Apple products, and nearly all the world's iPhones are assembled in China. One single factory complex alone in Zhengzhou, central China, dubbed iPhone City, reportedly employs 350,000 workers and produces 500,000 units per day.[22]

It is easy to see why Apple is reluctant to upset the Chinese government. But its willingness to kowtow to the Communist Party is in strong contrast to the way it has portrayed itself in the West as a champion of privacy, seeking to differentiate itself from the Facebook and Google business model, built around leveraging customer data for commercial gain: '. . . we're not going to traffic in your personal life. I think it's an invasion of privacy. I think it's — privacy to us is a human right, it's a civil liberty,' Tim Cook said to applause from a studio audience in a 2018 interview with the American cable network MSNBC.[23] In the US, the company strongly resisted demands from the FBI to help unlock the iPhone of the gunman in a 2015 terrorist attack in San Bernardino, California, in which fourteen people were killed. In an open letter to customers, explaining the company's refusal to comply, Tim Cook said, 'Compromising the security of our personal information can ultimately put our personal safety at risk. That is why encryption has become so important to all of us.'[24] Those fine sentiments, it seems, stop at the Chinese border.

There's a scene in my novel *Beijing Smog* in which an American businessman ends up in hospital after being hit by an electric buggy while walking through an airport in the Chinese city of Ningbo. It's clearly the fault of the driver of the golf cart-like vehicle, which is speeding towards a departure gate carrying a group of self-important local officials, but the police confiscate the businessman's passport and refuse to give it back until he pays $5,000 compensation for damage to the cart. A US diplomat tries to intervene, but the businessman rejects the help because he doesn't want to rock the boat. He's chasing a big deal with a local state-owned company and *wants* to pay the compensation.

The incident is fictional, but it was inspired by numerous conversations with business people based in China. I could more or less script those conversations in advance. There would be a litany of complaints about the way they were being treated. Forced technology transfer, whereby companies are obliged to hand over technology to a Chinese partner as part of a joint-venture deal, usually topped a list that also included arbitrary rules and regulations, piracy and the theft of intellectual property, and cyber espionage. By the time I left China it had become routine in many big foreign companies for visiting executives to use burner phones and throwaway laptops. You simply could not trust a device once it had been exposed to Chinese surveillance. But very few were prepared to go public with their complaints. They would complain to their chambers of commerce, just as long as the complaint wasn't attributed directly to them, and the conversations with me were inevitably off the record or non-attributable. Like my fictional business person in Ningbo, they did not want to rock the boat and were prepared to accept almost any indignity as the price of doing business in the Middle Kingdom. That reality was spelt out in one financial analyst's matter-of-fact guest post in the *Financial Times*:

> Simply put, if China doesn't feel it is learning from a business, or a business is just exploiting an advantage it has, it will gently or abruptly stop it (for example with import tariffs or corruption investigations, or more subtly with changes to joint venture ownerships, ease of doing business, or taxation).
>
> Businesses that are providing Chinese people with an opportunity to learn how to manufacture premium parts for the automotive or aerospace industries, for example, or gain knowledge of innovative technologies, will be more welcome and accommodated.
>
> Once this degree of market control is understood, Western businesses will realise that any business opportunity in China comes with strings and a time window attached – it may last five or ten years, or possibly longer, but it will be finite without evolution. If businesses become too big, they tend to be brought firmly under state control, or managed so as not to get too powerful or influential.[25]

Much of this is not new. In his book *One Billion Customers*, James McGregor describes an age-old vision of 'the teeming Chinese masses waiting to be turned into customers, the dream of staggering profits for those who get there first, the hype and hope that has mesmerised foreign merchants and traders for centuries'. If only 1 per cent of

China's 1.4 billion people could be tapped, so the argument goes, that's 14 million toothbrushes, razors, shoes – or even iPhones. McGregor chronicles the pitfalls as those peddling that vision have tripped on the heavily potholed road along the way.[26] McGregor's old newspaper, the *Wall Street Journal*, has accused US corporate chiefs in particular of being 'focussed on preserving short-term profits in China by trying to stay on the right side of a hard line – and increasingly antiforeign – regulatory regime'. The newspaper said foreign companies were the targets of a 'state directed heist' and that by remaining silent, they were suffering from a kind of Stockholm Syndrome, whereby hostages begin to identify with their captors.[27]

More recently, the Communist Party has moved to strengthen its organisational presence within foreign companies. All companies are required by law to establish Party cells, but foreign companies long regarded this rule as largely symbolic. Reuters reported that companies were coming under 'political pressure' to revise the terms of their joint ventures with state-owned partners to allow the Party the final say over business operations and investment decisions.[28]

Beijing is also introducing a corporate 'social credit' system, akin to the pilot schemes described in Chapter 3 for the surveillance and social control of individuals. The corporate system empowers tax inspectors and customs agents to rate companies in accordance with compliance with regulations and to share blacklists of those found in violation. The EU Chamber of Commerce in China highlighted plans to draw up a list of 'heavily distrusted entities' that could be sanctioned for 'endangering national security'. Jörg Wuttke, the chamber's president, told the *Financial Times* the measure could give Beijing more leverage over companies perceived to have violated China's stance on politically sensitive issues. 'It has the toolbox in the future to bring us into line politically,' he said.[29] At the same time new 'cybersecurity' regulations have raised fears that the computer systems of companies operating in China would be subject to local inspections in the name of 'securing the network'.[30]

China's actions are often justified by Beijing and its apologists overseas in terms of the country's understandable desire to foster a home-grown tech industry and not unreasonable fears of American snooping following the revelations from National Security Agency (NSA) whistle-blower Edward Snowden. Not only did the NSA spy on Chinese firms, notably Huawei, but it was also able to leverage the global dominance of US tech companies, obliging them to provide access to their data and systems.[31] The NSA also actively sought to weaken encryption and build backdoors into network equipment. I will examine these arguments in more detail later. Suffice to say for now that Beijing's actions against foreign companies pre-date Snowden and go much further than can be reasonably justified by 'national security'.

As Hong Kong illustrates, China's strategy towards foreign companies goes further than protectionism and acquiring technical know-how. It is also about how companies think. Self-censorship and ideological compliance are now requirements for doing business in China. Mercedes Benz abjectly apologised for 'hurting the feelings of the Chinese people' after facing attacks in state media for posting an anodyne quote from the Dalai Lama, Tibet's spiritual leader, on its Instagram account. The company promised 'no support, assistance, aid or help to anyone who intentionally subverts or attempts to subvert China's sovereignty and territorial integrity'.[32]

China demanded that thirty-six foreign airlines remove from their websites any language that implies that Taiwan, a democratically run, self-governing island, is not part of China, threatening that their operations would be disrupted if they did not comply. Marriott, the hotel chain, and the retailers Zara and Gap were among other companies pressured over how they refer to Taiwan. Marriott's Mandarin-language website was temporarily taken down by the authorities. Most companies targeted have apologised and amended their references to Taiwan, usually to read Taiwan, China.[33]

Publishers are avoiding putting any type of map – even historic maps – in books for China, since the censorship process is now so tortuous. The Party is rejecting any map that does not rigidly represent the world as it sees it, with particular sensitivity to Taiwan and the South China Sea, both of which China regards as its territory.[34]

Leica, the German camera company, disowned one of its own ads after criticism that it was 'insulting China'. The ad, which was not made for the China market, featured one of the world's most famous images – the 'tank man' clip of a protester confronting tanks during the Tiananmen Square massacre. Leica, for whom China is the biggest growth market, faced an orchestrated attack on Chinese social media and was blacklisted by internet censors. Any search for the company turned up instead a response saying, 'The content contains information that violates the relevant laws or Weibo's community guidelines.' A

Leica spokesperson claimed that the short film was not 'officially sanctioned'. She said: 'Leica Camera AG must therefore distance itself from the content shown in the video and regrets any misunderstandings or false conclusions that may have been drawn.'[35]

Nike cancelled the release in China of a line of limited-edition sports shoes after its Japanese designer expressed support for Hong Kong protesters in an Instagram post. Nike has marketed itself as a champion of social causes, and its action in China is in sharp contrast to the slogan of a 2018 ad campaign featuring the American footballer and anti-racism protester Colin Kaepernick, who angered President Donald Trump by refusing to stand during the US anthem – 'Believe in something. Even if it means sacrificing everything.'[36]

Not even basketball has been spared. The game is big in China, generating an estimated half a billion dollars in annual revenue for America's National Basketball Association (NBA), with deals ranging from streaming rights to merchandise sales. In October 2019, Daryl Morey, the general manager of the Houston Rockets, one of America's most popular teams, tweeted an image that read 'Fight for Freedom. Stand with Hong Kong'. Local sponsors, broadcasters and the Chinese Basketball Association immediately suspended ties with the Rockets. Morey quickly deleted the tweet, backtracked and apologised, saying, 'I was merely voicing one thought, based on one interpretation, of one complicated event.' The NBA tried to smooth things over saying it was 'regrettable' that Morey's comments had caused offence. There were reports that the owner of the Rockets considered sacking Morey to placate Beijing, but instead publicly rebuked him, saying the manager didn't speak for the team.[37] The contrast is striking with the NBA's more devil-may-care attitude at home, where basketball stars speak out on social and political issues. Superstar LeBron James, for example, regularly insulted President Trump.[38]

In late 2019, Mesut Özil, a midfielder for the London football club Arsenal, and a practicing Muslim of Turkish descent, criticised the repression of the Uighurs in Xinjiang. '[In China] Qurans are burned, mosques were closed down, Islamic theological schools, madrasas were banned, religious scholars were killed one by one. Despite all this, Muslims stay quiet,' he wrote on Twitter. He was attacked by Chinese state media, and the next Arsenal game was abruptly dropped from Chinese television. Arsenal quickly tried to distance itself from Özil's comments, tweeting that 'The content he expressed is entirely Özil's personal opinion. As a football club, Arsenal always adheres to the principle of not being involved in politics.' China is British football's most lucrative overseas market, a three-year deal for broadcasting rights is estimated to have netted the Premier League $700 million.[39]

There are numerous other such examples as Western companies scramble to protect their businesses in the face of Beijing's intolerance of criticism. Foreign companies have long argued that they have no choice, that submitting to censorship and complying with frequently arbitrary rules and regulations is the sometimes humiliating price of doing business in China. But there is often a fine line between compliance and complicity, and too many companies, especially Western tech firms, have been willing to cross that line and become enablers of repression.

Friday, 18 March 2016 was a grey, cold and smoggy day in Beijing. One of those mornings where the colour seemed to drain from everything; a smell of burning coal hung in the air and irritated the throat. At 9 a.m., the air quality monitor at the US embassy showed the level of PM2.5 particles, the most damaging to human health, at 305 micrograms per cubic metre, a level deemed hazardous under international health standards. It wasn't one of those mornings you'd want to spend too much time outside, certainly not without a mask – and definitely not jogging. Yet there was Mark Zuckerberg, the Facebook founder, running in front of the Forbidden City, with five other people in tow, none of them wearing masks. 'It's great to be back in Beijing! I kicked off with a run through Tiananmen Square,' he wrote in a Facebook post, alongside a photograph of the group.

Facebook has been blocked in China since 2009, while Instagram was shut out in 2014, yet Zuckerberg was desperate to get back in. The 'smog jog' was interpreted as a further effort to curry favour with the Chinese authorities, who have played down the impact of the filthy air, but it was ridiculed on social media. 'Kissing up?' said one posting, while another wrote. 'He climbed over the Great Fire Wall to breathe in smog. He's trying too hard.' One post drew a link between the staged photograph and the 1989 Tiananmen Square massacre. 'The floor you stepped on has been covered by blood from students who fought for democracy. But, enjoy your running in China, Mark.' One post carried a doctored version of the famous 'tank man' photo from that time, replacing the man facing down the tanks with a grinning, jogging Zuckerberg.[40]

Two days after the 'smog jog' Zuckerberg met with Liu Yunshan, China's propaganda chief, and a member of the Communist Party's Politburo standing committee, who reportedly explained to the Facebook CEO about China's notion of internet governance 'with Chinese characteristics'. Heavy censorship, in other words. Zuckerberg was undeterred. He made multiple visits to China around that time, becoming a member of the advisory board of China's Tsinghua University School of Economics and Management (which at the time of writing is chaired by Apple's Tim Cook). During a 2017 annual gathering of advisers, Zuckerberg (and Cook) were able to meet Xi Jinping to press their case. Zuckerberg has made much of his efforts to learn Mandarin, even attempting a faltering interview during one China visit. He hosted Lu Wei, then head of the Cyberspace Administration of China, at Facebook's Menlo Park, California, offices. During the 2014 visit, Xi Jinping's book, *The Governance of China*, was sitting conspicuously on Zuckerberg's desk.[41]

In late 2016, eight months after the 'smog jog' and Zuckerberg's meeting with the Party's propaganda head, the *New York Times* reported that Facebook was working on a censorship tool to help the company get back into China. The software under development would suppress posts from appearing in people's news feeds in specific geographic areas, and would be provided to a local partner. A Facebook spokesperson told the newspaper that the company had made no decisions on its approach to China. 'We have long said that we are interested in China, and are spending time understanding and learning more about the country,' she said. Zuckerberg, facing employee unease about the project, reportedly told a question-and-answer session with staff that his China plans were 'nascent'.[42]

The Facebook founder's oft-repeated mantra is that his company is on a mission to make the world more open and connected. 'You can't have a mission to want to connect everyone in the world and leave out the biggest country,' he once said. 'Over the long term that is a situation that we will need to try to figure out a way forward on.'[43] The problem is that China under Xi Jinping is *disconnecting* from the global internet, and the price for entry to its censored and surveilled version negates all the values Zuckerberg claims to have once stood for.

When Google pulled its search engine out of China in 2010 it was applauded by free speech advocates throughout the world. The company said it would no longer censor search results on its China service, a requirement for operating there. It was also angered by attempts to spy on dissidents using its Gmail service. The company appeared to be living up to its motto, 'Don't be evil' (since changed to 'Do the right thing').

But it seems that like Facebook, Google grew restless sitting on the sidelines as the number of internet users in China exploded, and decided that in commercial terms it had perhaps done the wrong thing. The Intercept, an online news service, revealed in 2018 that Google was working on a censored version of its search engine for China that would blacklist websites and search terms deemed unacceptable by the Communist Party. The Intercept, quoting from confidential internal documents, said the project was called Dragonfly and was accelerated following a December 2017 meeting between Google's CEO Sundar Pichai and top Chinese government officials.[44] According to one memo, the search system was being designed as an app for both Android and iOS (Apple) devices and would be linked to a user's telephone number. It would require users to log in to perform a search and would track their location. The information would be shared with an unnamed Chinese partner, who would have 'unilateral access' to the data.[45] The revelations triggered a backlash among Google staff, more than 1,000 of whom called for more transparency and a new code of ethics. Pichai tried to quell the discontent by claiming to staff that Google was 'not close' to launching the project.[46]

Google's culture of allowing its employees to speak up had already been tested that year in relation to artificial intelligence. More than 4,000 signed a letter arguing against a programme with the Pentagon that aimed to use AI to interpret video images to improve the targeting of drone strikes. 'We believe Google should not be in the business of war,' the letter said. It played into a fierce debate over the ethical use of AI, and, as a result, Google announced that it would not renew the Pentagon contract.[47] But it did not stop the company from opening an AI research centre in China, where companies are obliged by law to cooperate in 'national security' and share technology with the military. In a December 2018 blog post, Fei Fei Li, Google's Chief Scientist AI, who launched the centre, praised China's AI expertise, and said, 'I believe AI and its benefits have no borders.' She said the centre would focus on 'basic AI research' and that 'Google AI China Centre will also support the AI research community by funding and sponsoring

AI conferences and workshops, and working closely with the vibrant Chinese AI research community.'[48]

Peter Thiel, a tech entrepreneur, slammed Google in a column in the *New York Times*: 'How can Google use the rhetoric of "borderless" benefits to justify working with the country whose "Great Firewall" has imposed a border on the internet itself?' he asked. He described AI as a 'dual use' technology and said, 'All one need do is glance at the Communist Party of China's own constitution: Xi Jinping added the principle of "civil-military fusion," which mandates that all research done in China be shared with the People's Liberation Army, in 2017.'[49]

Google is widely acknowledged to be a world leader in AI, which some have predicted will transform warfare as much as nuclear weapons have.[50] Its British-based sister company, Deep Mind, developed AlphaGo, an AI programme that famously defeated Ke Jie the world's number one (human) player of Go, a strategy board game. It was considered a huge landmark for AI. The exhibition game was played in Wuzhen, China.[51]

Microsoft is also spending heavily on AI. It has had a research centre in Beijing since 1998, where 'our researchers and engineers push the boundaries of innovation by reaching into their imaginations and turning their ideas into reality,' according to the company website.[52] The *Financial Times* revealed the centre had been working with a Chinese military-run university on AI that could be used for surveillance and censorship. 'Three papers . . . were co-written by academics at Microsoft Research Asia in Beijing and researchers with affiliations to China's National University of Defense Technology, which is controlled by China's top military body, the Central Military Commission,' the newspaper reported. In response, Microsoft said it conducted research with scholars and experts from around the world. 'In each case, the research is guided by our principles, fully complies with US and local laws, and . . . is published to ensure transparency so that everyone can benefit from our work.'[53]

Microsoft has worked hard to cultivate relations at the highest level in China. Company founder Bill Gates reportedly has met three Chinese presidents, and Xi Jinping has visited the company's Redmond, Washington headquarters, where he praised Microsoft for 'driving forward the development of China's ICT [information and communications technology] industry'. In July 2020, Microsoft was the only US company invited to a televised entrepreneurs summit with Xi.[54]

When it comes to criticism of their China activities, America's high-tech giants have been there before. In a 2006 Congressional hearing, Representative Tom Lantos, a California Democrat, said of Google, Yahoo, Microsoft and Cisco Systems, 'I do not understand how your corporate leadership sleeps at night.' While Representative Christopher Smith, a Republican of New Jersey, accused them of 'sickening collaboration' with the Chinese government. The senators were angered by Cisco's sales of internet hardware for China's Great Firewall, while Yahoo had provided information about democracy activists, landing them in jail. Microsoft had shut down the blog of a prominent activist, while Google – yet to make its decision to leave – censored search results.[55]

Those transgressions seem almost quaint compared with the current extent of collaboration – and the stakes today are far higher. Xi Jinping has named AI as one of the defining technologies of the twenty-first century, in which he wants China to lead the world, to realise his 'Chinese Dream'. These ambitions are one of the triggers for a trade war with America – a burgeoning high-tech Cold War – which I will examine in more detail later. AI is a key technology driving mass surveillance in China. It is at the heart of the digital totalitarian state, though it's not the only technology that is enabling Xi's repression. As we have seen, that repression is at its most brutal in the western province of Xinjiang, but even here Western companies have seen an opportunity for business and investment.

The journal *Nature* is one of the world's most respected science and technology publications, with a dedicated global readership of research scientists. But an article by Yves Moreau, a Belgium-based geneticist, was not the kind of peer-reviewed research for which *Nature* is famous. It was an appeal. Under the headline 'Crack down on genomic surveillance', he called for tighter ethical rules in the field of DNA-profiling, and for geneticists to take greater care and responsibility for the way their work is applied. 'More academics working on biometric identification technology should reflect on the potential misuses of their inventions,' he wrote. 'In short, the scientific community in general – and publishers in particular – need to unequivocally affirm that the Declaration of Helsinki (a set of ethical principles regarding human experimentation, developed for the medical community) applies to all biometric identification research.'[56]

His immediate concern was China, and Xinjiang in particular, where DNA profiling is being integrated into the system of blanket surveillance and control of the Uighur population and other Muslim minorities. As we saw in Chapter 1, DNA samples have been taken under the guise of health checks – a programme called 'Physicals for All'. Moreau highlighted the purchase by Xinjiang of DNA-profiling equipment from America, and warned that Western academics and academic publications have been too willing to engage with Chinese academics and institutions who have obtained genetic materials unethically and who are aiding human rights abuses.

DNA profiling equipment was sold to Xinjiang by Thermo Fisher Scientific, an American company based in Waltham, Massachusetts. 'Thermo Fisher Scientific researchers have worked with China's Ministry of Justice, and with researchers at the People's Public Security University of China, which falls directly under the Ministry of Public Security, to tailor the technology specifically for use in Tibetan and Uyghur populations,' Moreau wrote.

The *New York Times* revealed that Thermo Fischer equipment was credited in patents filed by China's Ministry of Public Security. The equipment was said to 'have no equivalent in China' and was used to help fight 'terrorism' by differentiating between the DNA of Han, Uighur and Tibetan people. By one estimate, the Chinese market for gene-sequencing equipment and related technologies was worth a billion dollars in 2017, and could more than double in five years. China accounts for 10 per cent of Thermo Fisher's revenue, and the company employs nearly 5,000 people there, according to its 2017 annual report. 'Our greatest success story in emerging markets continues to be China,' the report said. Facing enormous pressure from human rights groups, Uighur activists and US senators, the company said in 2019 that it would no longer sell its equipment in Xinjiang. 'As the world leader in serving science, we recognize the importance of considering how our products and services are used – or may be used – by our customers,' the company said.[57] It is not clear what, if any, restrictions the company has imposed on sales elsewhere in China, where Xinjiang-type surveillance is rapidly being adopted, nor how it can control that equipment ending up back in the Uighur areas.

An investigation by *Foreign Policy* magazine identified a second US-based biotechnology company as a supplier to Xinjiang. Chinese government procurement documents show the authorities sought to purchase equipment from Madison-based Promega. Public security officials were after very specific equipment able to create records from small traces of DNA. A piece of Promega kit called a PowerPlex 21 is considered to be the only piece of equipment advanced enough for this type of work. Promega did not respond to questions from *Foreign Policy*.[58]

Building the surveillance state is a huge enterprise, and extremely lucrative for the companies selling every type of surveillance equipment. As we have seen, China's security apparatus is often highly specific in the shopping it does overseas, when kit cannot be sourced from a home-grown company. Those home-grown surveillance companies have not only prospered on the back of orders from the surveillance apparatus, but have benefited directly from Western investment. Hikvision has been particularly popular, a Bloomberg report in April 2018, was entitled, 'Foreigners Can't Get Enough of This Chinese Surveillance Stock'.[59] Vanguard, JPMorgan and Fidelity are among those whose institutional funds have invested in the company.[60] A *Wall Street Journal* investigation revealed that of thirty-seven Chinese companies praised by the Beijing-backed China Security and Protection Industry Association for their outstanding contribution to the surveillance industry, '17 have publicly disclosed financing, commercial or supply-chain relationships with U.S. technology companies.'[61] The *Journal* claimed that US companies, including Seagate Technology, Western Digital, Intel and Hewlett Packard, 'have nurtured, courted and profited from China's surveillance industry. Several have been involved since the industry's infancy.'

This chapter has looked at the role of Western companies inside China, and the role they are playing in the construction of the surveillance system. Sometimes they are bullied, often it's a kind of perverse pragmatism – justified as the price for doing business in China – but too often they are acting with their eyes open as willing enablers. They can always walk away, and under pressure some have done so – companies like Thermo Fisher, who have weighed up the commercial benefits against the reputational costs of being associated with human rights abuses. But China is becoming bolder and more assertive, and it is increasingly exporting the surveillance state beyond its own shores.

CHAPTER 7

From Influence to Interference

When panda twins were born at Berlin Zoo, a local newspaper asked its readers to suggest names. The most popular, according to *Der Tagesspiegel*, were 'Hong' and 'Kong', an apparent vote of support for Hong Kong's pro-democracy protests. The zoo, Germany's oldest and most respected, instead named them *Meng Xiang* and *Meng Yuan*, which translate roughly as 'long-awaited dream' and 'dream come true'. In reality, the zoo had little choice but to ignore the newspaper – not if it wanted to keep the pandas.

The twins were expected to be a magnet for visitors. Their parents were already the zoo's most popular attraction, presented to Germany by China in 2017. Xi Jinping and Germany's chancellor, Angela Merkel, were there for the handover, with Merkel calling the giant pandas special ambassadors between the two countries and speaking of a 'new beginning' in relations.[1]

There's something adorable, almost intoxicating, about pandas – and especially about panda cubs. Breakfast television presenters the world over drool and coo from their sofas at the sight of them; politicians and celebrities compete to be photographed alongside them. I was once told during a visit to a panda research station in China's Sichuan province (to shoot a report for a breakfast show!) that they trigger the same neural reaction in us as the sight of human babies. Perhaps, but giant pandas are also cold and calculating instruments of Chinese diplomacy. Beijing has long treated them as envoys to countries deemed to be friends or to those with whom it is seeking influence.

China has a monopoly on giant panda production. It is the only place in the world where they live in the wild. The pandas in Berlin Zoo, as with every other foreign zoo that hosts them, are rented from China. Berlin Zoo pays around a million dollars a year, and under the terms of the contract they must be handed back after fifteen years. Any offspring also belong to China, which can take them back whenever it sees fit. Since the 1950s, China has strategically placed scores of giant pandas in countries around the world. In 1972, a pair of giant pandas were famously loaned to the National Zoo in Washington as a symbol of rapprochement between Beijing and Richard Nixon's America. Xi Jinping is said to personally approve the placement of every panda.

There are thought to be a little under 2,000 giant pandas left in the wild, mostly in the mountainous areas of Sichuan province, in the country's south-west. Those which are lent overseas are bred at the Chengdu Research Base of Giant Panda Breeding, a sprawling facility outside the provincial capital. Critics have accused China of neglecting conservation and the panda's dwindling forest habitat, and instead breeding them solely for 'politics, prestige and profit'.[2] Either way, 'panda diplomacy' has been very successful. Arguably the giant panda, which China calls its 'national treasure', is the country's most successful export. Forget about smartphones, steel and toys, they cannot compete with those cuddly instruments of what diplomats call 'soft power'. That's usually defined as the ability of a country to attract and influence by persuasion, to get its way by example, projecting an attractive image and culture, rather than by coercion. Pandas are made for it – quite literally in the case of China's panda production system. Across the world, politicians as well as ordinary people have been wooed by what the *Wall Street Journal* called their 'weaponized adorability'.[3]

And why not? Influence is central to diplomacy; China is not alone in seeking to shape how the world sees it. That's what all counties do, or at least aspire to. Xi has vowed to strengthen China's soft power overseas. But diplomats will also tell you that there is a fine line between influence on the one hand and intimidation, manipulation and interference on the other. And those who work with pandas will remind you that behind that cuddly façade, they have sharp claws and can be extremely vicious.

'Emily' was studying in Britain when pro-democracy protests erupted in her home city of Hong Kong in 2019. The third-year undergraduate at Sheffield University wanted to show support and solidarity. She joined a Facebook group, Sheffield Stands for Hong Kong, which provided information and updates about the protests, she took part in rallies, and handed out leaflets explaining the goals of the protesters.

She watched with horror the escalating levels of violence and intimidation in Hong Kong, but never expected for one moment she would be targeted in Britain. 'We knew what friends in Hong Kong were facing. Now we have to be wary about our personal safety here too,' she told me on condition that I didn't use her real name. 'I stopped going to lectures. I had nightmares about being grabbed on the street. When I walk along the road, I keep away from the edge. I try not to walk alone.'

On 2 October 2019, she and a small group of Hong Kong students set up a stall and began to hand out leaflets in Sheffield High Street. They were surrounded by around 200 students from mainland China, chanting abuse and singing the Chinese national anthem; a banner was ripped from them, a bottle was thrown. 'It was terrifying,' Emily recalled. 'They were yelling at us, "What are you doing? Why are you doing that? If I see you criticise the Chinese government again, I'll kill you. We'll beat the shit out of you."'

One of the Hong Kong students telephoned Councillor Ben Miskell, who was at a meeting at the nearby town hall, and Miskell rushed to the High Street. He organised a police escort back to the safety of the council chamber. 'The scenes were very aggressive,' he told me. 'The Hong Kong students sat in our city debating chamber, traumatised by what had happened to them. What struck me that afternoon was how a large group of Chinese young people were subverting the democratic rights and freedoms available to them in the UK, in a bid to intimidate and close down the rights of others. What I saw that afternoon was deeply undemocratic and troubling.'

The bottle-thrower, a twenty-five-year-old student studying at Sheffield University's international college, was cautioned by police, and briefly suspended by the university, but the intimidation continued. Hong Kong student activists were photographed and videoed by Chinese students, the pictures published online. They faced online trolling and death threats against them and their families back in Hong Kong. One was forced to move apartments. 'When we set up a stall outside the students' union, they'd come over to us, taking videos, pushing us, shouting at us, telling us to leave,' Emily told me. 'They'd follow us in the street, calling us rioters, terrorists, cockroaches. These things happen all the time.'

Troubled by what he'd witnessed, Councillor Miskell organised a meeting with Sheffield University officials. 'The University of Sheffield was quite combative,' he told me. 'Whilst they met with me after the event, they weren't hugely interested in engaging. The feeling was that they were constantly trying to downplay the significance of what was happening and that they were effectively washing their hands of it. They didn't want to take our evidence and many of the Hong Kong students felt that the university didn't want to know.'

Mainland Chinese are by far the biggest group of international students at Sheffield University, numbering more than 1,000, according to the Complete University Guide.[4] The international officer of Sheffield University students' union, a Chinese national at the time, appeared to urge students to pass on information about Sheffield's Hong Kong activists to Chinese diplomats. In a posting to her WeChat account she urged students to 'actively report' to 'officials', with an emoji of the Chinese flag next to the word 'officials'.[5]

Rallies in support of Hong Kong's democracy movement took place on university campuses across Britain, and students at Aston, Cambridge, Exeter, Liverpool and Newcastle universities reportedly faced the same pattern of harassment from mainland Chinese students, threatening, photographing and videoing them. A member of Exeter University's Hong Kong society said that during their pro-democracy rally in the city centre they were 'stalked and followed'.[6] A Hong Kong student at Cambridge University said he no longer felt safe in the city after receiving emails containing 'graphic abuse' against him and his family.[7]

Hong Kong students at Newcastle University wanted to establish a 'Lennon Wall' on campus as a focal point for expressions of support. The idea originated in Prague in the 1980s, where a wall carried John Lennon lyrics about freedom and peace, as well as grievances against the regime. During Hong Kong's 2014 pro-democracy protests, a colourful Lennon Wall sprung up in the city's Central district. It was festooned with Post-it notes of support and other artwork, beside a big banner with the lyrics, 'You may say I'm a dreamer, but I'm not the only one', from Lennon's song 'Imagine'. The walls have now become a common feature of protests, both across Hong Kong and among supporters overseas wanting to show solidarity. But Newcastle University refused permission. At Warwick University students went ahead anyway, but their artwork was taken down by security after mainland Chinese students complained that they found it offensive.[8]

Universities issued boilerplate statements supporting students' right to peacefully protest and saying they do not tolerate harassment or intimidation. Sheffield University wrote to all its students to remind them of its code of conduct. It said it was working with the student union to address concerns and was 'committed to ensuring everyone feels safe and welcome on our campus and in our city'.

Councillor Miskell believes discussion and debate is being subverted by the desire to maximise income from fees. 'Chinese students are a big source of income and I don't think that UK universities want to rock the boat. My experience is that universities are not prepared to confront what is a fundamental threat to freedom of speech and democracy.' For her part, Emily felt increasingly unsafe and unwelcome. She felt abandoned by the university. 'The university doesn't really understand. They see it as an argument between Hong Kong and Chinese students. It's much deeper than that.'

There is something almost touching about mainland Chinese students exercising their right to protest on British university campuses, a right that does not exist in China, where any sort of critical student activism can result in expulsion, arrest or worse. Xi Jinping has cracked down on any semblance of free expression, promoted 'patriotic education', and generally turned the Chinese education system into a blinkered and heavily censored incubator of aggressive nationalism – of the sort displayed in the anti-Hong Kong protests at British universities. The Communist Party has issued explicit instructions about foreign students. 'Assemble the broad numbers of students abroad as a positive patriotic energy,' a 2015 directive says. 'Build a multidimensional contact network linking home and abroad – the motherland, embassies and consulates, overseas student groups, and the broad number of students abroad – so that they fully feel that the motherland cares.'[9]

The main instrument of that policy overseas is the Chinese Students and Scholars Association (CSSA), which has more than 100 subsidiary associations and 150,000 members throughout the UK, and depicts itself as a social, cultural and welfare organisation. Much of its work is no doubt of that nature, but it also works in tandem with, and is at least partly funded by, the Chinese embassy. It is the embassy's eyes and ears, keeping tabs on Chinese studying overseas, and mobilising them to hound perceived enemies and critics. In an entry on the King's College London students' union website, the organisation describes itself as being 'guided by the Embassy of the P. R. China'.[10]

In 2017 the CSSA worked with Chinese diplomats to try and bar a critic of China's religious and human rights record from speaking at

Durham University.[11] When the university refused, Chinese students tried to barricade the building where the debate was to take place. In 2019, the CSSA mobilised Chinese students at the London School of Economics to demand changes to an art installation, an upside down globe that showed Taiwan in a different colour to China.[12] The LSE added a disclaimer in the form of a plaque beneath the artwork reading, 'The designated borders, colours and place names do not imply endorsement by the LSE concerning the legal status of any territory or borders.' An asterisk was added beside Taiwan.

The organisational power of the CSSA was displayed when Xi Jinping visited Britain in 2015 – a visit hailed by the then chancellor, George Osborne, as marking the beginning of a 'golden era' for UK–China relations. The Association worked with the embassy to bus to London thousands of flag-waving Chinese students. Identical flags and banners were distributed from cardboard boxes that were marked 'diplomatic bag', with a postal label for the Chinese embassy.[13] They were directed to drown out Tibetan, Uighur and other human rights groups protesting against the visit.

In Sheffield, the CSSA was part of a closed WeChat group that coordinated protests and shared images of Hong Kong activists. A paper written by former diplomat Charles Parton for the Royal United Services Institute (RUSI) says of the Association: 'Its open aim is to look after Chinese students, but it also reports on them to the embassy and authorities, tries to stop discussion of topics sensitive to China (Taiwan, Tibet, Tiananmen), and takes more direct action under guidance of the embassy.'[14]

Despite growing evidence of CSSA interference and intimidation on British campuses, Britain has been slow to wake up to the threat – far slower than the US, Canada, Australia and New Zealand, where the Association's actions have encountered far closer scrutiny and it has faced campus sanctions. US Vice-President Mike Pence accused CSSA of being part of a Communist Party effort to foster a 'culture of censorship' in academia.[15]

Students from the People's Republic of China are now the single biggest group of overseas students studying in Britain, with a total of 120,385 enrolled in higher education institutions in 2018–19,[16] more than doubling in a decade. Universities these days act more like businesses, they are money-driven and overseas students are cash cows, paying as much as £40,000 a year to study in the UK. British universities are now highly dependent on fees from Chinese students. When students from China first began coming to study in Britain, it was frequently argued that their presence would help spread liberal values, and enhance the UK's influence. The free flow of information and ideas could only open the eyes of those coming from a repressive system, or so the argument went. That can happen – Emily in Sheffield was at pains to point out that her group did have support from some mainland Chinese students, but it was quiet support. Under the watchful eye of the CSSA, they were too afraid to speak up – for their own sakes, but also for that of their families back in China. As British universities fall over themselves to recruit overseas (and particularly Chinese) students, the argument about spreading liberal values is rarely heard, and the very group that was supposed to absorb those values is being allowed to actively undermine them.

At first sight it looked like a typical propaganda photograph from the front page of a Communist Party newspaper – officials, identical red shovels in hand, turning the soil for some new and gargantuan construction project. Except the photo was in a Cambridge University press release, and the grey-suited foreigner at the centre of the group, peering down into the hole in front of him was Professor Stephen J. Toope, the university's vice-chancellor. He was in China for the ground-breaking ceremony for a new Cambridge University–Nanjing Centre of Technology and Innovation, funded by the Nanjing Municipality. The press release described the project as Cambridge's 'first overseas enterprise of this scale' that 'will allow Cambridge-based academics to engage with specific, long-term projects in Nanjing'.

Standing beside Zhang Jinghua, Nanjing's Communist Party boss, the vice-chancellor of Britain's top-ranked university said: 'Here in Nanjing, an ancient city and former imperial capital, we are embarking on a unique enterprise . . . The innovations emerging from this Centre will enable the development of "smart" cities in which sensors can enable sustainable lifestyles, improve healthcare, limit pollution and make efficient use of energy.'[17]

As we have seen, those same sensors can also enable hitherto unseen levels of surveillance and repression. Perhaps smart cities will improve urban lifestyles in many different ways, as Toope suggests, but in the Chinese context, they are inextricably linked to surveillance and control. They are nodes in the Communist Party's surveillance state, facilitating repression. Nanjing boasts that it is leading the way towards building an all-seeing, all-listening, all-knowing city. Telecoms giant Huawei has been an important partner with the city in fulfilling those ambitions, building an extensive surveillance system for the 2013 Asia Youth Games in Nanjing. That worked so well that it has been vastly expanded, 'like a safety net across the city. It now enables sundry private communications, video surveillance and command and dispatch functions for all manner of public and private facilities,' the company boasts. 'Smart cities are, as a concept, safer cities,' where everything is digitally connected, 'to afford governments new tools to improve public services such as crime-fighting, and to keep an eye on what is going on generally.'[18]

The Jiangbei New Area of Nanjing, where the Cambridge project has its building, is not just a science and tech park, but an entire new city covering 788 square kilometres. It will take the 'smart city' concept to a new level – an urban lab for Huawei's brave new world. Sitting beside the Yangtze River, it will be a city of 'smart government affairs, smart industries and smart people's livelihood,' Relying on advanced technologies such as cloud computing, Internet of Things and data analysis, it will build an open new area with all things connected, perceived and intelligent,' according to its management committee.[19]

Astonishingly, the Cambridge ground-breaking ceremony in Nanjing took place in September 2019 at the height of the Communist Party's crackdown in Xinjiang. Blanket surveillance and incarceration of more than a million Uighur and other Muslim minorities was being widely reported, as were details of the suffocating surveillance system that facilitated it. If any of this discomforted Cambridge, that was not evident in reports of proceedings of the university's Board of Scrutiny, a governance body charged with 'ensuring transparency and accountability in all aspects of University operations'.[20] The Board appeared to view the tie-up as a fine example of the sort of relationships the university should be building now that Britain was leaving the European Union: 'Developing such activities outside the EU is part of our response to Brexit and the Board notes recent announcements of initiatives such as the strategic partnership with the Nanjing Municipal Government. China in particular is committed to substantial investment in research, which should be a priority for Cambridge given our existing strengths and international profile.'[21]

It did note that as overseas activities were scaled up, so was exposure to financial, and what it called 'other', risks, which would need to be managed. It did not elaborate on the nature of these risks nor how they would be addressed. A separate report from the university's 'General Board on the establishment of certain Professorships', accepted the academic case for a Nanjing Professorship of Technology and Innovation in the Department of Engineering, which would be paid from the funds from the China deal – from the Chinese government, in other words. It valued the deal at £10 million. 'The establishment of the Professorship will cement the flourishing academic links with commercial and academic research groups in the Nanjing area of China,' the report said.[22] The 'Nanjing Professor' would be expected to spend three months per year at the new innovation centre. A full job description, outlining responsibilities, says the new professor is also expected to join the Electrical Engineering Division of the Department of Engineering at Cambridge, which has six research themes, listed as: Functional Nano and Layered Materials; Multiscale Power and Energy Systems; Communications, Pervasive and Intelligent Systems; Photonic and Quantum Technologies; Smart Electronics and Surfaces; and Systems and Devices for Health.[23] Cambridge ranks number one in Britain for electrical engineering,[24] and these are cutting edge technologies with multiple uses – including in defence and security.

Officials from Nanjing were busy in the months leading up to the Cambridge ground-breaking, visiting Britain and striking a series of deals with UK universities, including Sheffield, which signed a memorandum of understanding with Nanjing University on teaching and research. 'I am deeply proud of the longstanding and ever-closer partnership between the University of Sheffield and China's leading universities,' said Sheffield's vice-chancellor, Sir Keith Burnett.[25]

East of Nanjing, halfway to Shanghai and a little inland from the Yangtze, sits the city of Wuxi, where Surrey University researchers have been busy at Jiangnan University, collaborating on facial recognition technology that is potentially able to identify masked protesters. The work is part of a programme called FACER2VM – standing for 'face matching for automatic identity retrieval, recognition, verification and management', and is described on the programme's website as 'a five-year research programme aimed at making face recognition ubiquitous by 2020'. The aim is to overcome current limitations of the technology and 'This will be achieved by addressing the challenging problem posed by *face appearance variations* introduced by a range of natural and image degradation phenomena such as *change of viewpoint, illumination, expression, resolution, blur and occlusion.*' (Emphases are in the original). Others involved with the project include Imperial College London and the University of Stirling.[26]

The programme's 'lead investigator' is Professor Josef Kittler, of Surrey's Centre for Vision, Speech and Signal Processing. In 2016, he was awarded the Chinese Government Friendship Award for his collaboration with Jiangnan University, which included the establishment of a Joint Laboratory of Pattern Recognition and Computational Intelligence.[27] In 2018, a jointly developed algorithm with far-reaching potential in surveillance won the annual Visual Object Tracking (VOT) competition at the European Conference on Computer Vision in Munich, Germany. The algorithm was described as 'one of the most advanced in the world' for tracking objects in video. 'This success is a result of our close and long-standing collaboration with Jiangnan University,' Professor Kittler said.[28]

On its website, Huddersfield University lists among 'our partners in China' the National University of Defense Technology (NUDT), which was founded as the People's Liberation Army (PLA) Military Academy of Engineering, and describes itself as being 'under the direct leadership of the Central Military Commission . . . heavily invested by the state and the military'.[29] Huddersfield has signed a research collaboration treaty with the NUDT, which 'will allow our two institutions to continue to work together on cutting edge research projects,' according to Vice-Chancellor Professor Bob Cryan.[30]

In reality, the examples outlined above only scratch the surface. There is a fast-expanding web of tie-ups between China and British universities. Research collaborations between the UK and China increased by 115.6 per cent between 2013 and 2019. There were 15,623 such tie-ups in 2019, making China Britain's biggest research partner after the US and Germany, and the fastest growing.[31] Boosting academic collaboration was a key plank of China policy under David Cameron's Conservative government, a policy that his chancellor, George Osborne, characterised as making Britain 'China's best partner in the West'.[32]

The extent to which China has been leveraging this relationship for the benefit of its military was highlighted by an Australian Strategic Policy Institute report documenting extensive links between British universities and Chinese defence companies. It identified collaborations with scientists from China's hypersonic missile programme and on research topics ranging from robots to smart materials.[33]

A *Sunday Times* investigation estimated that 500 Chinese military scientists have spent time in British universities in the last decade. 'They include some who have worked on technologies linked to jet air-craft, supercomputers, missiles and even microscopically thin film that could be used to disguise tanks and ships.' In response, a spokesperson for Universities UK, which represents British universities, said, 'We are unaware of any systematic attempt to interfere with the sector.'[34]

Academics frequently respond to scrutiny of their research rela-tionships by invoking the spirit of academic freedom and purity, not wishing to engage with the grubby details of how their innovations might be used in practice by their partners. They staunchly defend the ideal of the free exchange of ideas. Which is all very well, but extraordi-narily naïve in the context of China, where free exchange has a different meaning – the flow of tech to the military and security apparatus, as mandated by policy, law and the reality of a powerful Communist Party.

A parallel fear is that reliance on Chinese funding and favour is stifling academic debate on British campuses on subjects sensitive to Beijing, such as Taiwan, Tibet, Xinjiang, democracy in Hong Kong and human rights more generally. In some universities this is neutering critical China studies. 'There are real issues in terms of the Chinese govern-ment interfering with academic life in the UK, and using visas as a weapon as leverage against academics,' according to Professor Steve Tsang, who is originally from Hong Kong and is now director of the School of Oriental and African Studies China Institute at the University of London.[35] Being cut off from conferences, contacts and other China-based resources could be the kiss of death to an aspiring academic career.

Jesus College Cambridge boasts of having a long interaction with China, dating from the 1940s. The college hosts a China Centre, which aims to 'deepen mutual understanding between China and the West at the crossroads of civilisation'. It also has the UK–China Global Issues Dialogue Centre, which is 'committed to promoting active dialogue between academics, policy makers and business people around major issues we face in the world today and tomorrow.'[36] Until March 2020, parts of the China Centre website read like Communist Party prop-aganda, the sort of boilerplate Party language that appears in Party handouts or on information boards in the National Museum. Here's one section: 'Under the leadership of the Communist Party of China since 1978, [China] has experienced an extraordinary transformation under the policy of "Reform and Opening Up". China's national rejuvenation is returning the country to the position within the global political economy that it occupied before the nineteenth century.'[37]

As China came under growing criticism for its Covid-19 cover-up, the website was rewritten. This, and other phrases parroting Party propaganda, were removed and replaced with more neutral language about fostering 'a deeper appreciation of China today'. The website also lists a number of China-friendly events, but among the mostly anodyne listings for 2019 there are no programmes on the repression in Xinjiang, the Hong Kong protests, the democratic elections in Taiwan, Xi Jinping's ruthless clampdown on free speech (including on university campuses), or the construction of the surveillance state, arguably the most significant China-related developments of that year.

The director of the China Centre is Professor Peter Nolan. He was also the first Chong Hua Professor in Chinese Development, a chair sponsored by the China-based Chong Hua Foundation. The professorship was set up in 2012 with a £3.7 million endowment, Cambridge claiming at the time that Chong Hua was a private foundation with no links to the Chinese government. It was later revealed that the charity, registered in Bermuda, was run by Wen Ruchun, the daughter of former prime minister Wen Jiabao. She is a former student of Professor Nolan, who also co-authored a book with her husband, Liu Chunhang. The university refused to provide further details of the endowment since, 'the donors have requested complete anonymity'.[38] Nolan is also director of the Chinese Executive Leadership Programme, which 'each year brings CEOs from China's largest firms to the University of Cambridge for a three-week training programme, taught by a combination of academics and the leaders of international firms,' according to the University of Cambridge website.[39]

The UK–China Global Issues Dialogue Centre is a partnership between Jesus College, China's Tsinghua University and the National Development and Reform Commission (NDRC), the Chinese government's state planning agency. In October 2019 it hosted a 'digital governance dialogue'. A subsequent white paper, with a forward by Vice-Chancellor Professor Stephen J. Toope, declared that, 'A key feature of our discussion was the much more prominent role now taken by China, and Chinese companies, in global communications, and the need for new approaches that fully include them.'[40] The event was funded by a grant from Huawei, and two of the thirty-six listed participants were from the company.

As we have seen, internet governance (and the related concepts of internet and cyber sovereignty) are key mantras of Xi Jinping – shorthand for building digital walls, for draconian censorship and for harnessing the digital world for unseen levels of social control. This is the very antithesis of the free flow of information and ideas that Western academics – Cambridge dons among them, presumably – supposedly stand for. A Jesus College spokesperson told *Varsity*, a Cambridge University newspaper, 'Jesus College Cambridge and Huawei have a two-year research and innovation agreement, exploring global telecommunications and technology development. The China–UK Global Issues Dialogue Centre owns all research results; Huawei cannot veto the publication of views, research findings or conclusions.'[41] Jesus College, responding to a freedom of information request from *The Times*, said the Dialogue Centre had received £155,000 from Huawei, and £200,000 from an agency that is part of China's state council, a government body.[42]

Liverpool and Nottingham universities have taken their collaboration with China a step further and established branches in China. The campus of University of Nottingham Ningbo was established in the coastal city of Ningbo in Zhejiang province in 2004 and now has around 8,000 students and almost 900 staff. Xi'an Jiaotong–Liverpool University is in Xi'an, Shaanxi province and was established in 2006. It now has around 10,000 students and staff. In total, around 2,000 education joint ventures have been established in China since 2003. At first, they were promised academic freedom, but in 2017 Xi Jinping ordered them to install Communist Party units and to grant decision-making powers to a Party official. A directive from the Education Ministry (drafted by the Party's organisation department) stated that the Party secretaries at each joint venture should be given vice-chancellor status and a seat on the board of trustees – effectively handing them veto power, since many boards require unanimity in such decisions as senior hires and budget allocation.[43]

The following summer Nottingham Ningbo removed from its management board a British academic who had been critical of the Party. The Party objected to the renewal of Stephen Morgan's contract after he wrote an online article for a University of Nottingham magazine that was critical of the 19th Communist Party Congress. Morgan had been Nottingham Ningbo's associate provost since 2016.[44] It has also been reported that Nottingham University managers pressured academics on their UK campus to drop events linked to Tibet and Taiwan, though the university insists, 'Any reports of political influence at our campuses are very much wide of the mark.'[45]

Again, this is only scratching the surface. Funding from opaque China-related entities or individuals is too often accepted with little due-diligence and a lack of transparency. At the London School of Economics, a revolt by academics forced the university to 'put on hold' a China programme that was to be funded by a strongly pro-Beijing financier. Eric Li, who has justified the 1989 Tiananmen Square massacre and regularly praised Xi Jinping, offered millions of pounds to fund research and support new undergraduate and postgraduate courses on Chinese economics, politics and society. The scheme was to be overseen by an advisory group of 'distinguished individuals from China'. Chris Hughes, a professor of international relations at LSE, and one of those who objected, said in a letter to management that the project would compromise the school's values. He told the *Financial Times*, 'I'm really furious about this . . . it is an insult to our intelligence.'[46]

Professor Hughes contributed to an inquiry by the House of Commons Foreign Affairs Committee, which reported in 2019 that it had received 'alarming evidence about the extent of Chinese influence on the campuses of UK universities'. It said the government was not doing enough to protect academic freedom from 'financial, political or diplomatic pressure, with a view to shaping the research agenda or curricula . . . or attempts to limit the activities of UK university campuses'. It criticised the complacency of the Foreign Office. 'The FCO's role in advising universities on the potential threats to academia from autocracies is non-existent,' it said, recommending that the government *'provide up-to-date guidance to universities on the political, diplomatic and legal implications of accepting funding and pursuing collaboration with institutions based in non-democratic states'*. (Emphasis in the original report.) The report said that representatives of top British universities who gave evidence 'did not acknowledge the issue', and noted that 'the issue of Chinese influence has been the subject of remarkably little debate compared to Australia, New Zealand and the US.'[47]

***

'The level of threat we face from foreign espionage and interference activities is currently unprecedented,' an Australian spy chief has warned. 'It is higher now than it was at the height of the Cold War,'[48] he said after widespread evidence was revealed of Chinese meddling in Australian politics and on university campuses.[49] A new law on political funding was introduced after it was revealed that politicians and political parties received donations from businessmen linked to the Chinese government.[50] One senator, after accepting money, called on Australia to respect China's claims in the South China Sea.[51] Another package of new laws criminalise covert, deceptive or threatening actions that are intended to interfere with democratic processes or provide intelligence to overseas governments. Former prime minister Malcolm Turnbull acknowledged 'disturbing reports about Chinese influence', and said, 'Foreign powers are making unprecedented and increasingly sophisticated attempts to influence the political process both here and abroad.'[52]

Across the Tasman Sea, New Zealand has faced calls for similar laws, after attempts to buy political access were linked to China. Intelligence agents also investigated a China-born MP for the National Party who spent years teaching at a spy school in China, a detail he did not reveal when he applied for citizenship. Since moving to New Zealand, Jian Yang had been a big fundraiser among the Chinese diaspora. As an MP, he served on New Zealand's parliamentary select committee for foreign affairs, defence and trade, and has taken policy positions echoing those of China's Communist Party. Yang denied being a spy, but acknowledged he had been a 'civilian officer' who trained people who went on to be intelligence officers. He accused his critics of conducting a 'smear campaign' and suggested they were motivated by anti-Chinese racism.[53]

A New Zealand academic who investigated Chinese influence operations was the target of a campaign of intimidation she believes was directed by Beijing towards her and her family. Anne-Marie Brady, a China expert at the University of Canterbury in Christchurch, had her home burgled, her office broken into twice and her family car tampered with. She also received a threatening letter and phone calls in the middle of the night, despite having an unlisted number[54] – all after publishing a paper on Beijing's potential to 'undermine the sovereignty and integrity of the political system of targeted states'.[55]

Australia and New Zealand have been soft targets, described as 'guinea pigs for interference'.[56] Their economies are heavily dependent on China and they have tried hard to ingratiate themselves with Beijing to secure investment. Australia's mineral-dominated economy in particular is reliant on the Chinese market. China is New Zealand's second largest trading partner, a big market for dairy products. Beijing has courted their Chinese diasporas – much larger as a proportion of their populations than in Britain – through the backing of so-called 'patriotic' organisations. Australia and New Zealand are both members of the Five Eyes signals intelligence alliance (which also includes Britain, the US and Canada), and prising them away from their traditional allies would be a considerable coup for Beijing.

In the often obscure vocabulary of the Communist Party, influence operations are described as 'united front' work. As a concept it dates back to Lenin in the Soviet Union. In China, it is run by the Party's United Front Work Department from a large, nameless compound next to Party headquarters in Beijing. According to Anne-Marie Brady, the New Zealand academic, united front work has been a particular priority of Xi Jinping. 'Even more than his predecessors, Xi Jinping has led a massive expansion of efforts to shape foreign public opinion in order to influence the decision-making of foreign governments and societies,' she says.[57]

Broadly speaking, united front work involves the Party extending its influence over non-Party individuals, groups and organisations inside and outside China. Some of the work is overt, but some is clandestine and can range from ethnic minorities to professional and religious groups, academics and business people, as well as politicians. A particular international focus under Xi has been the overseas Chinese, including students. Although the original concept can be traced back to Lenin, it was Mao Zedong who, during the Chinese civil war, described it as one of his three 'magic weapons', alongside armed struggle and Party-building. Xi began to reinvigorate the system soon after coming to power. In a 2015 speech to the Central Conference on the United Front, he called on them to step up their befriending of non-Party individuals: 'We conduct the United Front work not for window dressing or good name, but for pragmatic reasons, because it plays a role, a big role, and an indispensable role. In the final analyses, the job of the United Front is to win over more people; we use the United Front to strengthen the forces for the common goal.'[58]

A United Front Work Department teaching manual obtained by the *Financial Times*, describes united front work as 'a big magic weapon which can rid us of 10,000 problems in order to seize victory'. It exhorts cadres to be gracious and inclusive as they attempt to 'unite all forces that can be united,' but to be ruthless against enemies: 'Enemy forces abroad do not want to see China rise and many of them see our country as a potential threat and rival, so they use a thousand ploys and a hundred strategies to frustrate and repress us,' the manual says.[59]

The term 'influence operations' has in recent years been more closely associated with Russia, as with Moscow's meddling in the 2016 US presidential election. But whereas Russian action is usually aimed at destroying trust and undermining Western political systems, China largely works within those systems. Beijing's operations are simply more clever and it is 'very good at it', according to John Garnaut, a former senior adviser on China to Australia's former prime minister, John Turnbull. 'The Chinese are strategic, patient, and they set down foundations of organizations and very consistent narratives over a long period of time,' he told the Armed Service Committee of the US House of Representatives.[60]

Compared with its allies, the UK has paid very little attention to the growing evidence of Chinese meddling. China has chosen Britain as the European production centre for its principle international propaganda outlet, China Global Television Network (CGTN). The broadcaster has established a 30,000-square-foot facility in Chiswick, West London. It is part of a vast worldwide expansion of China's state-owned media, which China's leaders have described as the 'eyes, ears, tongue and throat of the Communist Party',[61] and it comes as Western journalists in China come under increasing pressure.

CGTN has been banned from Twitter after being accused of spreading disinformation and propaganda about the Hong Kong pro-democracy protests, coverage which Ofcom, the regulator charged with upholding standards of fairness in British broadcasting, described as a 'serious failure of compliance'.[62] The regulator also received complaints that CGTN aired forced confessions. These included that from Peter Humphrey, a British corporate investigator who spent twenty-three months in a Chinese prison for 'illegally acquiring personal information'. He and his wife were paraded on state television wearing orange prison vests and handcuffs in order to 'confess' to their supposed crimes and apologise to the Chinese government.[63] Once released and safely out of China, Humphrey revealed the duress they were under, the brutality of their detention and the complicity of state television.

Forced and staged confessions have surged under Xi Jinping. A staple of the Cultural Revolution re-tooled for the information age, pumped out domestically and internationally via state propaganda channels, including television and social media. Victims include human rights lawyers, allegedly corrupt officials and even foreign nationals who had fallen foul of the Party, paraded in front of the cameras to confess and apologise for their alleged crimes. An analysis by Safeguard Defenders, a human rights NGO, of forty-five staged confessions between 2013 and 2018 found they were 'routinely forced and extracted through threats, torture, and fear; that police routinely dictate and direct the confessions'.[64]

Britain has also been welcoming to another key part of China's overseas propaganda: Confucius Institutes. These state-funded bodies officially teach Mandarin language and spread Chinese culture world-wide, but have been accused of peddling Party propaganda under the guise of teaching, interfering with free speech on campuses and spying on students.[65] Agreements with universities frequently allow the insti-tutes to determine course content, events and materials, and to evaluate teachers.[66] The House of Commons Foreign Affairs Committee heard evidence of Confucius Institute officials confiscating materials that mentioned Taiwan at an academic conference.[67]

They have faced a growing backlash worldwide; Australia, the United States, Germany, Sweden, France and Japan have all cancelled agreements or curbed their activities. In the UK, however, they are flourishing. Britain has the highest number in Europe and the second highest number in the world, with twenty-nine attached to universities including Edinburgh, Liverpool, Sheffield, Manchester, Newcastle, Nottingham, Cardiff and University College London. There are also 148 Confucius 'classrooms' in schools around the country.[68]

In Britain, the blind spot to Chinese influence has been shared by the political left and right. On the left, criticising China does not fit with an anti-imperialist mindset that prefers to demonise America. The right sees China primarily in terms of inward investment. As I shall examine in more detail in the next chapter, the Conservative government of David Cameron (and his China-friendly chancellor, George Osborne) embraced this approach with blind enthusiasm – and David Cameron now heads the UK–China Fund, a billion dollar fund to invest in 'innovative and sustainable growth opportunities in both the UK and China'.[69]

'The UK is in a battle and the country doesn't even know it,' according to Martin Thorley, who spent seven years in China, studying at Tianjin University and then running a business in Beijing helping Chinese and China-based groups recruit foreign experts. He interacted with a range of Chinese officials and industry leaders. He was a keen observer, and when he returned to the UK in 2015 he began research at Nottingham University into the elite relationships between the two countries. He told me that when it comes to Chinese strategies for currying favour and influence, Britain just doesn't understand what it is dealing with. 'It's about British weakness and naïvety as much as it is about Chinese strategy. The UK just don't get it – this is especially true of a number of British universities.'

Jerome Cohen, one of the world's foremost China scholars, despairs at the silence of most Western China-specialists in the face of appalling human rights abuses in Xinjiang. In an open letter to the *South China Morning Post*, a Hong Kong newspaper, the professor at New York University School of Law and director of its US–Asia Law Institute, appealed to fellow academics to speak out: 'The silence of most China specialists is disturbing, yet also unsurprising. Those of us who know China best have many reasons to rationalise not speaking out. Doing so risks the wrath of a rising power that is determinedly hostile to criticism, and that closely monitors what scholars say and write about sensitive topics. Yet, none of these reasons should be sufficient to warrant silence in the face of crimes against humanity.'[70]

During twenty years travelling and reporting from China, I learned to be extremely wary of the term 'Friend of China'. I was flattered when I was first referred to in that way, but soon learned that in China it is more than an innocent label or term of praise about your knowledge. It is more of a job description. In his book about doing business in China, James McGregor warns, 'As a "friend" you will be considered an enlightened foreigner who understands the complexities of China. But friendship in China carries heavy obligations. In China, it is considered almost immoral to turn down the request of a true friend.'

There is a fine line between influence and interference, and it could be argued that the examples above are merely good statecraft from a rising power seeking to play a bigger role in the world. After all, the US has historically thrown its weight around to achieve international outcomes in its favour. Beijing regularly accuses critics of its practices of having a 'Cold War mentality'. But as China's economic power grows, so it is increasingly stepping well over that line.

The Washington-based National Endowment for Democracy, a think tank, coined the term 'sharp power' to describe the way both China and Russia exercise influence. It's not really soft, but neither is it hard in the fully coercive sense.

> This authoritarian influence is not principally about attraction or even persuasion; instead it centres on distraction and manipulation. These ambitious authoritarian regimes, which systematically suppress political pluralism and free expression at home, are increasingly seeking to apply similar principles internationally to secure their interests. We are in need of a new vocabulary for this phenomenon. What we have to date understood as authoritarian 'soft power' is better categorized as 'sharp power' that pierces, penetrates, or perforates the political and information environments in the targeted countries.[71]

Yet, if the exercise of power is seen as a continuum from soft to hard, China under Xi Jinping is shifting inexorably towards the harder end. The surveillance state is being packaged for export, and Beijing is becoming increasingly assertive – and frequently aggressive – in its international dealings. As James McGregor goes on to advise, 'Your goal is to be friendly but not foolish.'[72] China has been taking the world – and Britain in particular – for a fool.

CHAPTER 8

Bulldozers Down the New Silk Road

Gui Minhai was at his holiday home overlooking the Gulf of Thailand on the day he disappeared. The view from his seventeenth-floor apartment in the Thai resort town of Pattaya seemed to inspire the Hong Kong publisher, and he had a raft of new ideas for lurid and gossipy books about China's leaders.

The man who came for him spoke only broken Thai, instead talking in Mandarin Chinese on a mobile phone as he waited at the apartment gates for Gui to return from buying groceries. When Gui got back, the two spoke for a while before Gui handed the groceries to an apartment manager, asking him to take them upstairs. Security-camera footage shows Gui and the unidentified man then climbing into Gui's car and driving off. Two weeks later, four unidentified men returned and collected a computer, files and other documents from Gui's apartment. They wrote Chinese names in the apartment logbook, almost certainly false.[1]

Three months later, on 17 January 2016, Gui reappeared – in China. In a video broadcast on Chinese state television, which stretched credulity even by the standards of China's staged confessions, Gui slumps forward, his face crumpled and tearful, and says he returned voluntarily to face justice for a fatal drunk-driving accident twelve years previously in his hometown of Ningbo. Or as the *China Daily*, the Communist Party mouthpiece, reported, 'He said he was prepared to shoulder the responsibility and willing to be penalized in whatever way he deserved, adding that he didn't want any organization to intervene or spread malicious rumors about the matter.'[2] The one-time poet had gone into exile after the Tiananmen Square massacre and became a Swedish citizen. He was, by most accounts, a gregarious man, portly and with thick dark hair, but now he looked frightened and broken. He renounced his Swedish citizenship, saying, 'I really feel that I am still Chinese and my roots are in China.'[3]

Gui's company, Mighty Current Media, owned a cramped book-store in Hong Kong's Causeway Bay which specialised in salacious stories about the private lives of Chinese leaders. The titles that lined its shelves included *The Mystery of Xi's Family Fortune* and *The Dark History of the Red Emperor*. Planned books included *The Pimps of the Chinese Communist Party* and *The Inside Story of the Chinese First Lady*. Gui was said by confidants to be planning another on Xi Jinping's female liaisons. The books were a racy mixture of rumour and reality, but were extremely popular in the former British colony – and were snapped up by visiting tourists from the mainland.

During the three months that Gui was missing, four others associated with his company also vanished. One of them, Lee Po, a British citizen, was snatched from outside the company's warehouse in Hong Kong; the others were detained on visits to mainland China. Over the following months, Gui's colleagues were freed on condition they stop their activities and say nothing about their ordeal. But Lam Wing-kee, the bookshop's manager, broke his silence when he returned to Hong Kong, describing how he had been snatched, blindfolded and handcuffed by a group of men at the Hong Kong border. He was kept in solitary confinement in a cramped cell and forced to confess on Chinese television to 'illegal trading', reading from a script prepared by his captors. Another condition to his release was that he provide further information on the bookshop's customers and authors, who mostly wrote under pseudonyms. One pro-democracy lawmaker in Hong Kong accused Beijing of political thuggery. 'They behave like some mob . . . They are like political thugs. They behave like gangsters,' said Claudia Mo.[4]

Gui Minhai remained in captivity, his ordeal far from over. In late 2017 he was released from detention and put under house arrest in Ningbo. In January 2018, escorted by Swedish diplomats, he took a bullet train for Beijing, where the Swedish embassy had arranged a medical examination. Around 400 kilometres short of their destination, a group of plain-clothes agents barged into their carriage and grabbed Gui from his seat, ignoring pleas from the diplomats. Two years later, in early 2020, and following yet another 'confession', he was jailed for ten years for 'illegally providing intelligence overseas'.[5]

The abduction of the booksellers sent shockwaves, not only through Hong Kong's publishing industry, but also among exiled dissidents worldwide. China had demonstrated its own version of 'extraordinary rendition', its agents snatching critics from beyond its borders (and from semi-autonomous Hong Kong, where they were supposed to enjoy legal protection). Even though two were Western citizens, the abductions attracted only timid criticism from Western governments. As one Swedish newspaper complained in an editorial, 'Is there anything China won't get away with?'[6]

And the booksellers were not the only ones. In January 2016, around the time that Gui was making his tearful 'confession', Li Xin, a former website editor for the *Southern Metropolis Daily*, a newspaper published in the southern Chinese city of Guangzhou, disappeared after boarding a train from the Thai capital Bangkok to Nong Khai on the Lao border. He had fled from China and published details of the way the Party propaganda machine directed China's newspapers. A month after his disappearance he resurfaced back in China, in detention, from where he was allowed to talk briefly to his wife. His fate is unknown.

Thai investigations into the disappearances of Li and Gui were perfunctory at best, even though there was security-camera footage of Gui's apparent abductors. Thailand's military rulers have been particularly accommodating to Beijing's demands, handing over to the Chinese authorities two other human rights activists, despite their having been recognised as refugees by the United Nations. Thailand also forcibly deported about 100 ethnic Uighur Muslims back to China, which drew an unusually sharp response from the UN High Commission for Refugees, which described it as 'a flagrant violation of international law'.[7]

At the same time, China has stepped up what it called Operation Fox Hunt, its efforts to get its hands on another type of fugitive – those wanted for graft. It claims there are around 1,000 on the run, mostly former officials or well-connected business people who have fled abroad with their ill-gotten gains. In many respects these fugitives are more dangerous to the Communist Party than traditional dissidents since they know the inner workings of the system. One case in point is Guo Wengui, a billionaire who made his fortune in real estate and finance, and fled China in 2014 when he came under investigation. From his luxury apartment overlooking New York's Central Park he has lobbed a steady stream of lurid accusations of murder plots, corruption and extramarital affairs against China's communist elite, most of which are impossible to verify.[8] The US has refused demands by China that he be returned. Few rich Western democracies have extradition treaties with Beijing, where returnees are unlikely to get a fair trial in Party-controlled courts, and the anti-corruption campaign is frequently used as a political tool by Xi against opponents.

China has sought to work through Interpol, persuading the international police organisation to issue 'red notices', requesting detention prior to extradition, against 100 of its most-wanted fugitives. Beijing claims around half have so far returned. Critics accuse China of abusing the system by misrepresenting the reasons for seeking arrest. In the case of Guo Wengui, Beijing only secured a red notice when he threatened to speak out, and then when the Americans refused to return him they had Interpol issue a second red notice, this time accusing Guo of rape.[9]

Between 2016 and 2018, Interpol was headed by Meng Hongwei, who was also China's vice-minister of public security. His election to the post was part of Beijing's efforts to gain greater influence over international organisations, and play a larger role in global security governance in general. But in a bizarre twist, Meng himself vanished while on a visit home in September 2018. The following month, the authorities announced that China's second-ranking policeman was under investigation. In January 2020 he was sentenced to thirteen and a half years in jail for bribery.[10] His fate reminded me of a conversation I had with a Chinese academic early in Xi Jinping's anti-corruption campaign: 'I'm all for rooting out corruption from the system,' he said to me. 'The problem is that, with the Communist Party, corruption *is* the system.'

China has also deployed undercover agents to pressure fugitives to return home 'voluntarily'. In 2015, the *New York Times* reported that the Obama administration delivered a warning to Beijing about the presence of agents in the United States, who entered on tourism or trade visas, and were pressuring expatriate Chinese. The harassment was intensifying and included threats against family members in China.[11] Pressure on family left behind is a well-honed Communist Party technique; a member of Shanghai's Public Security Bureau once described it this way: 'A fugitive is like a flying kite: even though he is abroad, the string is in China.'[12] As we saw in Chapter 1, it is a technique that has been used to try and silence Uighur exiles whose relatives have been detained.

This, and the fate of the booksellers, preyed on the mind of China's most prominent political cartoonist as he prepared for an exhibition in Hong Kong. Thirty-three-year-old Badiucao, sometimes likened to Banksy, hid his identity for years in order to avoid reprisals. In public, the Melbourne-based artist often disguised himself as a woman with big sunglasses, or else wore a multicoloured ski mask. His biting satire included a cartoon of Xi Jinping holding a rifle next to a dead Winnie-the-Pooh. Another showed Xi's face morphing into a skull, shortly after China's leader abolished time limits on his rule. They circulated widely on social media – even in China where, until more recent technical upgrades to the Great Firewall, images could more easily evade censorship.

On 4 June 2019, the thirtieth anniversary of the Tiananmen Square massacre, Badiucao showed his face for the first time, in an Australian television documentary, which follows him as he prepares for the Hong Kong show.[13] He says he revealed himself because the Chinese authorities had discovered his identity, possibly by digital surveillance while he was planning the show. Police visited and interrogated his family still in China. The documentary shows him agonising over what to do, eventually cancelling the show to protect his family, but also out of fear that he might be abducted while in Hong Kong. 'As a political artist, I have a power that is out of their control, and they know how dangerous it could be to them. That is why they are hunting down artists like me,' he says.[14]

Before Xi Jinping tightened his grip, exiled dissidents were mostly ignored. 'Out of sight, out of mind,' seemed the policy. The assumption was that once out of China their influence and relevance would diminish. Several things changed that calculation. The internet (in spite of tight controls) meant their words (and images) could get back to China, but mostly it was the result of Xi Jinping's intolerance of criticism, any criticism. He wants to control the dialogue abroad, as well as at home. As China has grown economically stronger, so it has become more assertive and belligerent – bolder in projecting its power, acting with increasing impunity. It is quick to take offence and deaf to Western complaints about its behaviour. As Jamil Anderlini wrote in the *Financial Times*, China's new 'wolf-style diplomacy' has a simple goal: 'to impose as heavy a price as possible on anyone, anywhere who opposes the Party's power or objectives.'[15]

The jailing of Gui Minhai, the Hong Kong publisher, put Chinese–Swedish relations into deep freeze. Not only was Gui a Swedish national, but he had been snatched (the second time) in front of Swedish diplomats, who were then repeatedly denied consular access. Sweden then developed something that has been largely missing from Western diplomacy towards Beijing – a backbone. It was tough in its criticism, Sweden's minister of culture even attended a literary award ceremony in Gui's honour, where she strongly defended freedom of speech. The Chinese embassy in Stockholm called the minister's attendance at the Svenska PEN prize-giving a 'serious mistake', threatened to ban her from entering China and warned that 'Wrong deeds will only meet with bad consequences.'[16] The Chinese ambassador to Sweden sounded more like a gangster than a diplomat when he warned in an interview with Swedish public radio, 'We treat our friends with fine wine, but for our enemies we have shotguns.'[17]

The promotional video opens to stirring orchestral music, an animated red line emerging from the sunlit yard of a traditional Chinese *hutong* home before sweeping across Asia, Africa and Europe. There are images of glistening skyscrapers, cranes, bridges, tunnels. Then a camel train across the desert in golden sunlight. 'It's planned as one of the largest and most comprehensive development projects in human history,' says a voiceover, so deep and slow that it has an almost otherworldly feel about it.

Welcome to the Belt and Road Initiative (BRI) – the 'fine wine' with which Beijing is currently trying to treat old friends and tempt new ones. It is 'a project of the century,' which will benefit people across the world,' according to Xi Jinping. 'What we hope to achieve is a new model of mutually beneficial cooperation . . . a big family of harmonious coexistence,' he told a Belt and Road Forum in 2017.[18] The Initiative, promising a trillion dollars in infrastructure investment, has also been called the '21st-century Silk Road' referring to the ancient trade routes linking East and West by sea and land (hence the camels). It is China's principal foreign policy initiative, and has become a rather inchoate catchphrase for just about all aspects of what Beijing does abroad, with no real geographic boundaries.

China boasts that more than 125 countries and 29 international organisations have signed up.[19] Hard-pressed emerging economies of Africa and Asia in particular were attracted by what they saw initially as easy money. There appeared to be few of those pesky strings that usually come attached to assistance from Western creditors or multilateral lenders, such as the World Bank. These loans are often laboriously negotiated and designed to provide a degree of oversight and transparency – an effort (not always successful) to protect against corruption, mismanagement and environmental damage.

The main purpose of the Belt and Road Initiative is strategic – 'a giant project of international political engineering', according to Bruno Maçães, a former Europe minister in the Portuguese government, who has written extensively on the BRI.[20] It is China's effort to remake the world order in its image. The increasingly strident nationalism of China under Xi is defined by historic grievance against imperial powers, yet the BRI is in many ways a classic neo-colonial enterprise. The investments are opaque, but overwhelmingly benefit Chinese companies, which have won most of the contracts on offer.[21] For many state-owned companies, such as those in iron and steel production, it is an ideal way of offloading their chronic overcapacity. Projects also frequently involve the export of Chinese labour.

Participating countries are seen as a market for Chinese manufactured goods and a source of raw materials. It is creating crippling debt bondage, saddling countries with unpayable liabilities, and turning many into virtual vassal states, afraid to criticise China and easily marshalled into supporting Beijing in international forums. Or, as *The Economist* described it: 'Under way is a return of sorts to earlier, celestial concepts of power and civilisation under which China sat at the heart of things. Moral, not legal, precepts governed relations among states. They included dependence, generosity, gratitude and reciprocity – but also retribution.'[22]

Cambodia, for one, now displays all the features of this sort of tribute state, so dependent has it become on Chinese investment and trade. This is especially tragic given Cambodia's recent history. The murderous Khmer Rouge were supported and bankrolled by Mao Zedong's China – a fact that Hun Sen, Cambodia's strongman leader is writing out of official histories of that period – a process that is strongly supported by his patrons in Beijing.[23]

Some twenty-three BRI countries are 'significantly or highly vulnerable to debt distress', according to a study by the Center for Global Development.[24] These include Sri Lanka, which was forced to hand over its new $1.3 billion Hambantota port to a Chinese company after failing to make repayments.[25] There are fears that ports in Pakistan and Kenya could also be handed over in lieu of unpaid debts. Both are among countries begging Beijing to review projects and renegotiate the terms of loans which have placed creaking public finances under severe pressure. Pakistan is the biggest recipient of BRI projects, worth more than $62 billion, and including a strategically important seaport at Gwadar, on the Arabian Sea, which will be linked to China via a planned 2,000-mile network of road and rail links.[26]

In Kenya, the Auditor General, a financial watchdog, suggested that China might take over Mombasa port if Kenya defaults on a loan to build a new railway line between Mombasa and the capital, Nairobi.[27] The $3 billion rail link is Kenya's biggest infrastructure project since independence, but it has been beset by financial scandal and questions about its viability since it opened in May 2017. Chinese managers have been accused of racism and discrimination against Kenyan staff, angry wildlife activists condemned its routing through a national park, and three Chinese nationals were charged in connection with a ticketing scam that was syphoning off $10,000 a day – almost a third of total earnings.[28]

Another Chinese rail project, linking the Ethiopian capital Addis Ababa to Djibouti on the Red Sea, has also run into financial and operational difficulties. The $4.5 billion project has been hampered by electricity shortages and lower than expected use.[29] Djibouti's crippling external debt is the highest of any low-income country as a proportion of GDP, much of it owed to China, and Beijing has leveraged this dependency by establishing an additional strategic foothold in the country: Djibouti is now the site of China's only overseas military base.[30]

When Mahathir Mohamad returned to power in Malaysia in May 2018, one of his first acts as prime minister was to suspend $23 billion of China-funded projects agreed by his scandal-plagued predecessor. 'It's all about borrowing too much money, which we cannot afford and cannot repay because we don't need these projects in Malaysia,' he said during a visit to Beijing. In a rare rebuke to his hosts, he warned about a 'new version of colonialism'.[31] Mahathir also pledged to renegotiate 'unequal treaties' – which will have been particularly stinging to Beijing, since China uses that term to describe its own supposed humiliations at the hands of foreign powers, deploying it as a kind of mantra to describe its ceding of territory and sovereignty in the nineteenth and twentieth centuries under the Qing Dynasty (including the Treaty of Nanjing, handing Hong Kong to Britain in 1842).

The Malaysian projects include an east coast rail link of dubious viability, which had been awarded to Chinese state companies without competitive tender, financed entirely by Chinese loans and to be built largely by Chinese labour – a fairly standard model under the BRI.[32] Mahathir's hands were tied by a penalty clause under which Malaysia would face a crippling $5 billion charge for cancellation. But the wily political veteran was able to knock a third off the price and obtain a commitment to more 'local content' – a rare act of defiance.[33]

Western democracies have been more wary of the Belt and Road Initiative, though more than half of the members of the European Union have signed up, including cash-strapped Italy and Greece. Beijing has established the 17+1, a grouping of seventeen central and east European countries (plus Greece) led by China, with a stated aim of channelling infrastructure investment to those countries. EU officials worry that the opaque nature of these deals may undercut single-market rules and that the real aim is to drive a wedge between member states, courting newer and poorer members in order to undercut efforts to take a more unified and robust line on China. They point to successful efforts by Greece and Hungary to water down a statement on China's aggression in the South China Sea, where it has seized islands, even though its territorial claims have been ruled illegal under international law.[34] Greece, where a Chinese state-owned shipping company bought a controlling stake in Piraeus port, has also blocked efforts to condemn China's human rights record and to toughen the screening of Chinese investments in Europe.[35]

The Dalai Lama used to be a welcome guest in Prague. Václav Havel, the dissident-turned-president of the Czech Republic hosted Tibet's exiled spiritual leader on numerous occasions in the years after the collapse of communism in eastern Europe. Havel's experience under communism left him wary of autocratic regimes and he was a strong supporter of Tibetan self-determination and of Chinese dissidents. Miloš Zeman, the president at the time of writing, has a different approach. He appointed as his economic adviser Ye Jianming, the head of CEFC China Energy, an opaque Chinese conglomerate, and the visitor he has welcomed most warmly to the Czech Republic is Xi Jinping himself, Czech police ensuring that all pro-Tibet protesters and symbols were kept well out of sight for the occasion.[36]

CEFC, which has strong Communist Party links, went on a Czech spending spree, snapping up stakes in the national airline, a brewery, one of the country's most popular football teams and a TV station.

Then things went terribly wrong. Ye Jianming was detained in China on suspicion of corruption, and the head of a 'research' organisation funded by CEFC in Hong Kong was convicted by a Manhattan court of attempting to bribe African leaders to get business deals for CEFC.[37]

At the same time, Chinese diplomats in Prague learned that democratic Czech Republic's media were far more tenacious than in some countries China does business with. Local radio revealed that Prague-based employees of Huawei were supplying information about their clients to the Chinese embassy, while the Czech–Chinese Centre at Charles University was forced to close after a news website reported that executives had received payments from the Chinese embassy via a private company.[38]

The Belt and Road Initiative displays all the worst features of crony capitalism. It lacks accountability and transparency, allowing corruption to thrive. It also pays little or no attention to human rights, labour or environmental standards. But China shows no sign of being concerned by any of the setbacks or the diplomatic headwinds it has encountered. As we have seen, it was able to put on a strong display of 'debt-trap diplomacy' in 2019 by dragooning client states, even Muslim majority countries, into supporting (or at least keeping silent about) its repression in Xinjiang.

In November of that year, six years after the launch of the BRI, China hosted an international forum on 'the significance of China's Social Governance to the World'. *Xinhua*, the state-owned news agency, proudly proclaimed: 'Experts from home and abroad agreed that China can provide wisdom to a world that is in need of new governance models.'[39]

'You have hurt the feelings of the Chinese people' is a well-worn piece of Party rhetoric, an accusation signalling official displeasure at some perceived slight. It is laughable in a way, but can instil fear in the hearts of foreign governments or companies for whom it might be a precursor to boycotts, protests and all manner of xenophobic abuse. It is being deployed with increased frequency by Xi Jinping.

If the boundless investment of the Belt and Road Initiative is the 'fine wine' with which Beijing rewards its friends, the 'shotgun' aimed at those who hurt China's feelings takes the form of a blunt economic and political cold shoulder, and to that end it has weaponised investment and trade – even big spending tourists.

When Sweden objected to China's jailing of bookseller Gui Minhai, and expressed strong support for him and for freedom of speech, China hinted that Stockholm might face the same fate as its Norwegian neighbour. China shunned Norway for six years after the 2010 award of the Nobel Peace Prize to dissident Liu Xiaobo. Beijing demanded an apology, even though the prize is awarded by an independent committee. Ties were only restored after Norway pledged that it 'attaches high importance to China's core interests and major concerns, will not support actions that undermine them and will do its best to avoid any future damage to the bilateral relations'.[40] It wasn't quite an apology, but still a humiliating climbdown. Norwegian business was delighted, however, and negotiations on a free trade agreement resumed. The Norwegian Seafood Council predicted that China would soon become its largest export market,[41] while the number of Chinese tourists visiting Norway surged by 90 per cent over the months that followed.[42]

China is now the world's biggest source of tourists, described by the People's Daily as an 'important and indispensable' tool of China's foreign policy.[43] In 2017, when South Korea installed an American missile defence system aimed at North Korea, Beijing showed its disapproval by instructing travel agents to drop Korean tours. Chinese tourists accounted for half of South Korea's tourists and two-thirds of tourist spending at the time. Korean firms operating in China faced choreographed protests and boycotts. Korean shows and entertainers were scrubbed from the airways, including stars like Psy (of Gangnam Style fame), whose image was blurred out of videos.[44]

Tourism boycotts have also been used against Japan and the Philippines during tension over disputed islands, and against Taiwan, when the self-governing democracy elected a more pro-independence leader. New Zealand was threatened when it shut out Huawei from one of its mobile networks, the People's Daily suggesting that 'tense political relations' were dampening enthusiasm among tourists for Kiwi lakes and mountains. When Turkey voiced rare criticism of China's detention camps in Xinjiang, calling them 'a great shame for humanity,' Beijing issued a safety alert for Chinese travellers to Turkey, as it did later for Canada, with whom it was embroiled in another Huawei-related dispute.[45]

Sometimes this 'boycott diplomacy' is aimed directly at governments, other times at foreign companies or business groupings who are effectively being told to pressure their governments to change policy as a condition for doing business in China. On the face of it, the results are mixed. Of the above examples, Turkey curbed its criticism, the Philippines capitulated, backing off from challenging Beijing's illegal territorial claims in the South China Sea, and Norway accepted humiliation as a price for restoring relations. The others mostly stood firm.

Clive Hamilton, an Australian author who has written extensively about Chinese influence operations, describes China as the world's master practitioner of 'geoeconomics', which he describes as 'the deployment of economic punishments and rewards to coerce nations to adopt preferred policies'. He notes that while China is not the only nation to use economic pressure to achieve political and economic ends, 'today it is the most formidable'.[46]

It is effective because countries have become highly dependent on Chinese trade, students, tourism and investment, as well as complicated supply chains centred around China. As we shall see later in this book, China's behaviour is increasingly forcing countries to examine this dependency. But there is no evidence that kowtowing to Beijing makes any real difference in the longer term, and may even make a country (and company) more susceptible to future bullying because they are perceived as weak and malleable. As *The Chosun Ilbo*, a South Korean newspaper, said in an editorial urging the government to make no concessions over the deployment of the missile system, 'If Korea acts so spinelessly, it will only encourage China to step up its bullying.'[47]

Chinese diplomats increasingly respond to criticism with threats and insults. This has been dubbed 'wolf warrior' diplomacy, referring to the movie *Wolf Warrior 2*, a Rambo-style action flick with lots of flag waving in which heroic Chinese soldiers triumph over brutal African mercenaries and their evil American boss. It was released in 2017 and quickly became China's largest-grossing movie. For a decade, the biggest movies had come from the United States, and the Communist Party wrapped Hollywood around its little finger, forcing studios to come up with China-friendly scripts as a price for market entry. *Wolf Warrior 2* was a turning point, with movie-goers embracing local productions and the Party taking to heart the slogan on the movie's promotional poster, 'Anyone who insults China – no matter how remote – must be exterminated.'

A few months before *Wolf Warrior 2* was released, Xi Jinping travelled to the Swiss ski resort of Davos to join the global political and business elite at the World Economic Forum. There wasn't a wolf in sight; instead he donned the mantle of a friendly old St Bernard, so beloved of the Alps – gentle, loyal and affectionate towards the struggling cause of globalisation.

'Pursuing protectionism is like locking oneself in a dark room,' Xi said. 'Wind and rain may be kept outside, but so is light and air.'[48] Participants applauded loudly, welcoming his apparent commitment to open markets, while commentators hailed Xi as the new champion of free trade. It was of course laughable nonsense – as was much of the reaction to it. China's economy is the very antithesis of an open market. From protectionism to intellectual property theft, Beijing has prospered by gaming the system, but the speech was more interesting for what it said about Xi's bid for global leadership.

It was a stark demonstration of how the story of China's rise is also the story of America's retreat. You had to admire Xi's chutzpah; moving effortlessly into ground vacated by the absent Donald Trump. It was raw opportunism, a bid to present himself as a more reliable economic and trade partner than Trump's America – as the defender of the international rules-based system. In practice, away from that elite gathering, he was actively seeking to replace that system with China's own model of economic and political development. But his audience for the most part lapped it up. Perhaps they were being polite, or just naïve. Maybe it was wishful thinking, indulging Beijing, taking Xi at face value in the hope that he might get there eventually – the sort of thinking that has characterised much of Western policy towards China over the last four decades.

In trying to understand what drives and motivates Xi we have looked elsewhere in this book at the hotchpotch of ideas that constitute his world view – drawing from Mao, Marxism and Chinese tradition, to good old-fashioned nationalism and xenophobia, and all assembled in a manner that serves to justify his own accumulation of power. He feels that China's time has come, that by virtue of its economic clout and military might, it can now throw its considerable weight around, consigning to the dustbin Deng Xiaoping's mantra to 'coolly observe, calmly deal with things, hold your position, hide your capacities, bide your time, accomplish things where possible'.[49]

A few months after the Davos gathering, Xi told the Communist Party's 19th National Congress that 'China's national standing has risen like never before,' that the country had 'stood up, grown rich and is becoming strong'. It was a very different vision to the one he had peddled at Davos. The wolf was back: 'It means that the path, the theory, the system, and the culture of socialism with Chinese characteristics have kept developing, blazing a new trail for other developing countries to achieve modernization. It offers a new option for other countries and nations who want to speed up their development while preserving their independence; and it offers Chinese wisdom and a Chinese approach to solving the problems facing mankind.'[50]

In Davos, Xi was exploiting disillusionment with Donald Trump, who alienated allies and undermined international institutions. Xi sees disarray in Western liberal democracies as an opportunity. That democratic crisis in confidence can be traced back to the 2008 global economic meltdown, which undermined the West's economic model and fuelled the rise of populism. It encouraged Beijing to promote its own alternative model of state capitalism and authoritarian politics, though only when Xi came to power did this strategy became more open and assertive.

Henry Kissinger, the former US secretary of state, writing in 2004, compared the game of chess with the game of Go, characterising these two intellectual games as representing the two diplomatic styles of the US and China respectively:

> Chess has only two outcomes: draw and checkmate. The objective of the game is absolute advantage – that is to say, its outcome is total victory or defeat – and the battle is conducted head-on, in the center of the board. The aim of go is relative advantage; the game is played all over the board, and the objective is to increase one's options and reduce those of the adversary. The goal is less victory than persistent strategic progress.[51]

Go is called *Weiqi* in Chinese, which translates as 'encirclement game'. The playing pieces are called stones, and the idea is to completely surround your opponent's stone or stones. At that point your opponent's stones, cut off, are removed from the game and the territory becomes yours. It's often hailed as a great game of strategy. Xi Jinping is said to have learned it at school, though it is not known how good a player he is. It is a popular analogy among scholars of strategic studies, but is it particularly accurate in assessing Xi Jinping's ambitions?

Xi talks a lot about a 'win–win' relationship with other global powers, but the evidence suggests he holds a zero-sum view of the world. Much of China's new assertiveness is plain bullying that would seem to have no place in the world's oldest board game. Yet Ketian Zhang of George Mason University, Virginia, has characterised China's behaviour as 'cautious bullying'. He argues that Beijing is careful about the timing, targets and tools of coercion. 'Moreover, concerns with its reputation for resolve and with economic cost are critical elements of Chinese decision-making regarding the costs and benefits of coercing its neighbors. China often coerces one target to deter others – "killing the chicken to scare the monkey",' he writes.[52] One result is that China is not much loved internationally, especially among the people of Western democracies and those of China's immediate neighbours. For all its efforts to cultivate what political scientists call 'soft power', it has not done a great job. A 2019 Pew Research Center study across six Asia-Pacific nations found that while Donald Trump received negative marks, overall views of the US remain strongly favourable compared with China.[53]

While Trump forfeited goodwill and trust, China still falls well short. Perhaps Xi Jinping no longer cares; certainly Davos demonstrated that in a world of realpolitik, where the US abandoned leadership, Xi's blandishments (and his money) can still seem appealing, but it is a shaky foundation on which to build global power and sustainable international relations.

The International Telecommunications Union (ITU) will soon be giving itself an upgrade. A new state-of-the-art headquarters building is to be built facing the Place des Nations at the heart of International Geneva. The ITU, which has 200 member states, is an obscure but important part of the UN. It is the world's oldest international organisation, established in 1865 to implement common standards for telegraphy. It hopes the new building will match its vaulting ambitions to be the global regulator of new technologies – a goal heartily supported by its secretary-general, Haolin Zhao, a Chinese official, and the Chinese government, which aims to shape those standards to its advantage.

The ITU has become a fierce battleground between East and West over the future of the internet, with China and its authoritarian allies pushing for new rules and standards that would allow more control by government. Sometimes these arguments can seem quite esoteric, but

Above left. The little red app. Xi Jinping's 'Study the Great Nation' app claimed to have 100 million registered users, on whom it also spied (BJ Warnick, Alamy Stock Photo)

Above right. Sayragul Sauytbay, who provided the first public evidence of a vast gulag of detention camps in Xinjiang, pictured in November 2019 in Sweden, where she was given political asylum (Ian Williams)

The 'Shule County Chengnan Training Centre', consisting of 24 buildings or wings, doubled in size in just three months between March and May 2018, according to the Australian Strategic Policy Institute (Google Earth)

مۇقۇملۇق بەخت، مۇقۇمسىزلىق ئاپەت

稳定是福 、动乱是祸

Mural in Yarkand, Xinjiang, which reads: 'Stability is a blessing, instability is a calamity'
(Eric Lafforgue/Alamy Stock Photo)

A reminder of who's in charge. A Uighur couple pushing a cart with fruits in Kashgar, Xinjiang, are overlooked by a statue of Mao Zedong. (Peek Creative Collective/ Shutterstock)

In July 2009, Uighur anger and frustration exploded into rioting in Urumqi, the Xinjiang capital, which was violently supressed by Chinese paramilitary forces and vigilantes (Ian Williams)

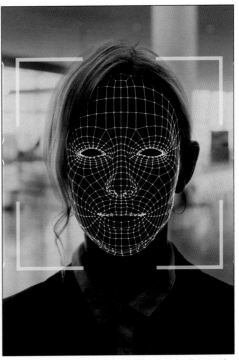

Surveillance cameras in Tiananmen Square, Beijing. The Party has attempted to write the 1989 protests and massacre out of history, but the square is one of the most surveilled places in China (Bisual Photo/Shutterstock)

Facial recognition in action. The more advanced systems search for dozens of facial landmarks to construct a unique 'facial signature'. The latest claim is to be able to read emotions (metamoworks/Shutterstock)

The latest facial recognition cameras are demonstrated at Smart China Expo, a tech show in Chongqing in August 2019. A vast industry now services the surveillance state (helloabc/Shutterstock)

The dissident Chinese artist Ai Weiwei spent so much time under surveillance that it became a big influence on his work (J. Morc/Shutterstock)

'Surveillance Camera with Plinth' (2015), one of Ai Weiwei's most famous works, carved out of marble, and a fitting symbol for Xi Jinping's China (Image courtesy Ai Weiwei Studio)

Doctored image of the famous 'tank man' photo, used as a way of getting around censorship at the time of the anniversary of the Tiananmen Square Massacre of June 1989 (Weibo.com)

 Mark Zuckerberg ✔ is at **Tiananmen Square**. •••
18 Mar 2016 · Beijing, China · ⊙

It's great to be back in Beijing! I kicked off my visit with a run through Tiananmen Square, past the Forbidden City and over to the Temple of Heaven.

This also marks 100 miles in A Year of Running. Thanks to everyone who has been running with me -- both in person and around the world!

Above. Censors banned Winnie-the-Pooh after the cartoon bear's rotund physique was likened to that of Xi Jinping (Weibo.com)

Left. Facebook founder Mark Zuckerberg attracted ridicule for jogging in the smog during a March 2016 visit to Beijing, part of an effort to ingratiate himself with the Communist Party (Mark Zuckerberg/Facebook)

Aziz Isa Elkun, an exiled Uighur now living in London, has worked tirelessly to preserve Uighur culture and the integrity of historical records in the face of Chinese efforts to eradicate them (Aziz Isa Elkun)

Jack Ma, former head of Alibaba and China's richest man. In November 2018, Ma was revealed to be a member of the Communist Party (Frederic Legrand COMEO/Shutterstock)

Panda diplomacy. Panda triplets, fresh off the production line. China has a monopoly on pandas, and zoos worldwide rent them from Beijing for around $1 million a year. Xi Jinping is said to personally approve each placement (Ian Williams)

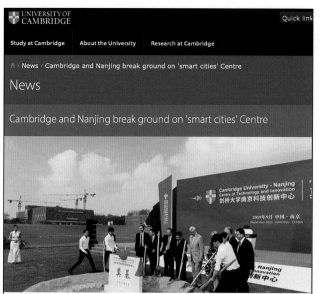

Left. Cambridge University vice chancellor, Stephen J. Toope, flanked by Communist Party officials, breaks ground on a new joint venture, Cambridge's first overseas enterprise of this scale, to research 'smart cities' and funded by the local government (Cambridge University Press Release)

Below. Chinese President Xi Jinping with Queen Elizabeth II at a state banquet at Buckingham Palace, London, during his state visit to the UK in October 2015. The queen was later recorded complaining about Xi's 'rude' officials (PA Images/Alamy Stock Photo)

Pushing back against the surveillance state. Protesters use umbrellas to shield themselves as they cut down a smart lamp post which they feared was monitoring them in Ngau Tau Kok in Hong Kong, 24 August 2019 (REUTERS/Thomas Peter/Alamy Stock Photo)

'Panda Isis', a cartoon by Badiucao, gives his take on Beijing's intimidation of Australia. The Melbourne-based Chinese cartoonist, sometimes likened to Banksy, showed his face for the first time after the Chinese government discovered his identity and intimidated his family in China (courtesy Badiucao)

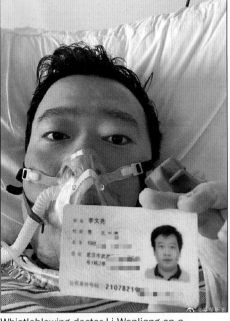

Whistleblowing doctor Li Wenliang on a ventilator a few days before he died of Covid-19 in February 2020. He posted the selfie to his social media account and declared, 'There should be more than one voice in a healthy society' (Weibo.com)

they amount to a struggle over the core architecture of the internet, including the protocols used to identify individual users. The Chinese model has been described by its creator, Huawei, as a 'decentralised internet infrastructure', a classic piece of doublespeak. As one detailed study notes, 'Ultimately, China's focus on "decentralized" technologies will lead to more centralised, top-down control of the internet and potentially even its users, with implications for security and human rights.'[54]

China is investing enormous energy into the setting of international technical standards. To say that technology is never neutral is something of a cliché; the same tech can be purposed and repurposed in different ways and in different contexts. Standards define how a technology works and its interoperability, they deal with security, but they can also embody political, economic and wider moral and ethical values. They are not exciting – not like the shiny tech itself – and the process of setting them can be laborious, almost guaranteed to induce yawns or bring tears to the eyes. But they are vital, particularly for the next generation of technologies – in the rapidly developing fields of 5G, universal connectivity (the Internet of Things) and AI. While Western democracies have struggled to stifle their yawns, China has been active in the 200-odd global organisations and bodies which set international technical standards. It even has an initiative, China Standards 2035, with the aim of imposing its own rules on the global system by that date.

The ITU is arguably the most important standard-setting body, and aside from pushing its vision for the internet, China is promoting a swath of standards that would aid the development and export of key components of surveillance. Chinese companies are shaping new international facial recognition and surveillance standards, according to documents obtained by the *Financial Times*.[55] All twenty submissions to the ITU between 2016 and 2019 came from China, most relating to how facial recognition footage and audio recordings are stored and analysed. They have faced little opposition from European and American organisations, and human rights groups say the process allows little opportunity to challenge the standards on the grounds of privacy or freedom of expression. Not only are ITU standards influential in shaping how technology is developed and used, they give a stamp of international authority that can give companies (and countries) a vital edge. Though voluntary, they are usually adopted by developing countries in Asia, Africa and the Middle East, key markets for China.

'If left unchecked, China, not the US and our allies, will write the rules of the digital domain, opening the doors for digital authoritarianism to govern the Internet and associated technologies,' warned a report prepared for the US Senate's Committee on Foreign Relations.[56]

As we have seen, the growth of China's surveillance state has spawned a new generation of companies, which have quickly become world leaders in surveillance technology linked to artificial intelligence. They are already finding ready buyers among autocrats worldwide, who are frequently offered soft loans under the Belt and Road Initiative to finance their purchases. 'This raises troubling questions about the extent to which the Chinese government is subsidizing the purchase of advanced repressive technology,' according to Steven Feldstein, in a paper for the Carnegie Endowment for International Peace.[57] He identifies sixty-three countries which have bought AI-powered surveillance tech from China. They include Ecuador, Kenya, Laos, Russia, Saudi Arabia, Thailand, Myanmar, the United Arab Emirates, Uzbekistan, Venezuela and Zimbabwe.

In this way the BRI not only exports China's model of state-led capitalism and autocratic politics, but also the technological tools and standards that increasingly underpin it. Often these are packaged as 'smart city', 'safe city' or 'smart policing' platforms. Some thirty-six countries have received Chinese training in what is described as 'public opinion guidance', a euphemism for censorship, that can be facilitated by the use of 'content monitoring tools', another export offer. 'They're selling this as the future of governance; the future will be all about controlling the masses through technology,' says Adrian Shahbaz, research director at Freedom House.[58]

Liberal democracies, including Britain, France, Germany, Italy and the United States have also bought Chinese surveillance kit and other advanced network technology. As I shall examine later in this book, this not only raises broader issues about democratic oversight of surveillance – monitoring and controlling their spread and use – but also whether the very presence of sophisticated Chinese technology in the digital infrastructure of Western democratic states represents a security threat.

The surveillance camera firms Hikvision and Dahua, and telecoms giant ZTE are among the Chinese companies leading the international charge. But there is one company that stands out, a company we have met several times before in this book. It is in the vanguard of China's international ambitions, supplying AI surveillance tech to at least fifty countries worldwide. 'No other company comes close,' says Feldstein at the Carnegie Endowment. That company is China's 'national champion', the standard-bearer for the surveillance state. That company is Huawei.

The futuristic headquarters of the African Union dominates the skyline of the Ethiopian capital, Addis Ababa. A glistening skyscraper towers over a domed spaceship-like building below, in front of which flutter the flags of the AU's fifty-five member states. The $200 million building, completed in 2012, was built and fitted out by China – a gift to the African people. Huawei was a principal supplier of the information and communication technology.

Over the next five years, the AU's secrets were systematically plundered. Every night, between the hours of midnight and 2 a.m., data from the AU's servers was transmitted 5,000 miles to servers in Shanghai, according to an investigation by *Le Monde*, a French newspaper, citing multiple sources.[59] The hack, confirmed by other newspapers, came to light in 2017 when an AU systems engineer detected computers crunching data in the dead of night when the building was largely empty. The building was also found to be riddled with bugs, a sweep discovered listening devices in walls and desks.

The AU quickly and quietly acquired new servers and upgraded its security. It kept the hack secret for a year before details were leaked to *Le Monde* by frustrated AU officials. China's Ministry of Foreign Affairs called the allegations 'complete nonsense'. While a Huawei spokesman told the BBC, 'If there was a data leak from computers at the AU's headquarters in Addis that went on for an extended period of time, these data leaks did not originate in technology supplied by Huawei to the AU.'[60] For its part, the AU initially declined to comment, then it too condemned the report.

Denials from China are routine and unsurprising, from the victim they seem more puzzling – until you examine how beholden Africa has become to Beijing. Concerns about this dependency, and possible repercussions about speaking out publicly, seem to have motivated disgruntled AU officials to leak anonymously to *Le Monde*. China has gifted presidential palaces and parliaments the length of Africa. It has become the continent's most important economic partner. 'Across trade, investment, infrastructure financing, and aid, no other country has such depth and breadth of engagement in Africa,' according to a report by McKinsey, a US-based management consulting firm.[61]

Huawei and ZTE have between them built most of Africa's telecoms infrastructure. The profile of Huawei in particular has soared along with its towers, masts and antennas. It claims to have built 70 per cent of Africa's 4G telecoms networks.[62] Beyond the network nuts and bolts, it also supplies smartphones, computers and a range of surveillance kit. Its products are considered cheap and robust, and sales have been assisted by a seemingly unlimited credit line from the Chinese government. One of its flagship products is what it calls 'safe city solutions', a suite of advanced surveillance tools developed and honed in China, and which offer 'omnipresent sensing' and 'real time warning and surveillance deployment' that will 'promote the digital transformation of the public safety industry', according to a company brochure.[63] These are popular with autocrats worldwide – 71 per cent of 'safe city' agreements are in countries rated by Freedom House as 'not free' or 'partly free', and include Angola, Egypt, Ethiopia, Kazakhstan, Russia, Saudi Arabia, Thailand, the UAE, and Uzbekistan.[64]

In just four years, Huawei more than doubled its revenue to reach a colossal $122 billion in 2019 – just over 40 per cent generated outside China. It now operates in 170 countries and regions. [65] For accounting purposes it lists Europe, Middle East and Africa as one region, which is now its biggest overseas market, generating just under a quarter of its revenue. It claims to supply kit to all mainstream telecom carriers in Europe, where it has 13,300 employees, 23 research institutes and research programmes involving 140 universities.[66]

By one estimate, the Chinese government has provided Huawei with $75 billion in grants, credit facilities, tax breaks and other forms of financial assistance.[67] With the Communist Party at its back, growth has been breathtaking. But it's where it goes now with next generation 5G networks that most worries Western security analysts. The company is a world leader in 5G, and has become a lightning rod for concerns about the security of Chinese technology and the Communist Party's broader global ambitions.

There's been a lot of hype about 5G – harbinger of the 'fourth industrial revolution', as it is frequently described – that promises massive increases in speed and capacity. Modern economies will be built around 5G, which will provide the digital backbone to the promised Internet of Things – a world in which all manner of devices, from cars to fridges and toasters, are connected. It could also take ubiquitous surveillance to a chilling new height. 5G is powerful, in other words. Very powerful. And countries and companies are spending billions of dollars to upgrade their networks.

The United States has barred American companies from doing business with Huawei, and has pressured allies to keep the company out of their 5G networks, warning of the threat from espionage or sabotage. At the time of writing, Australia, France, New Zealand, Japan, Sweden – and, belatedly, Britain – have responded with bans. Wavering countries in Europe, where Huawei has a strong presence, were warned by China's EU ambassador of 'serious consequences' for economic and scientific cooperation should China's 'national champion' be excluded.[68]

Canada faced the wrath of Beijing when Canadian police, acting on a US request, detained Meng Wenzhou, Huawei's chief financial officer and the daughter of the company's billionaire founder, as she transited through Vancouver airport in late 2018. Washington sought her extradition for alleged fraud related to the breach of sanctions against Iran. A furious Beijing retaliated days later by seizing two Canadian citizens in China, former diplomat Michael Kovrig and consultant Michael Spavor, accusing them of endangering national security. Two more Canadian citizens were sentenced to death after being convicted for drug offences. One had previously received a prison term, but saw his penalty changed the month after Meng's arrest. Canada advised travellers to 'exercise a high degree of caution in China due to the risk of arbitrary enforcement of local laws'. At the same time, China boycotted a growing list of Canadian products, including canola, pork and bull semen.

In a New York court in early 2020, the US hit Huawei (and Meng) with a further indictment alleging racketeering and conspiracy to steal trade secrets. The indictment also contained further allegations about Huawei's activities in Iran and North Korea, which are subject to US, EU and UN sanctions.[69] Huawei denied the allegations.

Meng's extradition hearings began in Vancouver in early 2020 – a judicial process, heard in open court and freely reported upon. She had top legal representation and was granted bail, living at her C$13 million Vancouver mansion and receiving visitors, though she did have travel restrictions. While in China, Kovrig and Spavor were held without access to families or lawyers. They were granted a single consular visit per month. For their first six months they were kept in solitary confinement in an interrogation centre run by the Ministry of State Security.[70] After one and a half years, they were indicted on charges of espionage, though no evidence was presented. They were, in effect, being held hostage by a government that still insists Huawei is a 'private' company.

In July 2020, the British government of Boris Johnson banned Huawei from supplying equipment to Britain's 5G mobile telecoms network and ordered that the company's existing 5G kit be stripped out by 2027. The decision was an about-turn from six months earlier, when the company was granted partial access, and followed intense pressure from both Washington and Beijing – the Chinese ambassador threatening 'consequences' if Huawei was locked out.

Publicly the government stated that the decision had been taken for security reasons – that tighter US sanctions against Huawei meant that its products were now more risky. Though one report suggested the company had been told privately that the reason for its exclusion was 'geopolitical' and that the decision might be reversed in the future should circumstances change, such as Donald Trump failing to get a second term as president.[71] This suggested the government was eager privately to placate the company (and China) and head off the threatened retaliation, but its communications with Huawei executives somewhat undermined the original decision, and showed how muddled government policy had become towards the Chinese tech giant – and towards Beijing in general.

A January 2020 decision had capped Huawei's market share to 35 per cent, and confined the company to the periphery of the network (the antennas and the masts), excluding it from 'core' functions that manage the network. Some experts questioned whether such a distinction could be made in smarter and more dynamic 5G set-ups, and even the limited role was condemned by US officials as 'nothing short of madness.'[72] One US senator said it was tantamount to Britain 'allowing the KGB to build its telephone network during the cold war'.[73] Johnson also faced intense pressure from his own backbenchers. Tom Tugendhat, chair of the House of Commons Foreign Affairs Committee, wrote: 'Huawei's 5G sets us on a path that undermines our autonomy and the repercussions could be grave.'[74]

The reversal by Johnson followed a toughening of US sanctions that would not only stop Huawei from using US chips, but also any chips made anywhere in the world using American tools; UK intelligence officials judged that the Chinese-made alternatives might not be secure. The government said British mobile phone operators could continue to use Huawei equipment in older 2G, 3G and 4G networks, a decision that drew criticism from Tory backbenchers who wanted the Chinese company removed from all networks and with a far stricter timetable.

The decision was always a trade-off between security and economics, with the US–China trade war looming ever larger in the background. In announcing the ban, Oliver Dowden, the UK culture secretary, told MPs that it could add £2 billion to costs and delay the rollout of next generation 5G networks by two to three years. That is a measure of how much Britain has allowed itself to become highly dependent on the Chinese company, relying on it for much of the current 4G infrastructure.

It was Britain who gave Huawei its first foothold outside China. In 2005, BT awarded the company a contract as part of its £10 billion network modernisation. BT's decision to exclude Marconi sounded the death knell for Britain's own once mighty technology giant, and gave Huawei a springboard for international expansion. BT remains Huawei's most important customer among Britain's mobile telecoms companies. EE, which is owned by BT, has used Huawei for two-thirds of its 4G radio equipment and Vodafone relies on the Chinese company for most of its kit outside London, according to industry executives.[75] Typically, the new 5G technology uses 4G as a base, giving Huawei a strong and entrenched position.

Huawei lobbied hard, as did UK telecoms companies, who warned of mobile phone blackouts if they weren't given more time to strip out the company's equipment. Huawei commissioned a glossy report on the company's impact on the British economy, in which it claims to have supported directly and indirectly 26,000 jobs and contributed £1.7 billion to GDP in 2018. It has rapidly expanded research collaboration in the UK, working with thirty-five institutes and universities, including funding advanced research facilities at Cambridge, Edinburgh and Surrey.[76] In May 2020 it signed a deal with Imperial College London, worth an estimated £5 million, under which the Chinese firm will become a founding partner in a new centre that 'explores and experiments with new ways of doing business'.[77] Oxford University was a lonely voice of principle, suspending all new research grants and donations from Huawei. In a note to computer science doctoral students, the university said: 'If you are in contact with anyone from Huawei, do note that this decision doesn't prevent you from maintaining a relationship with them but we would recommend that no confidential or proprietary information is discussed.'[78]

To stave off criticism of its relationship with the Chinese state, Huawei assembled a UK board of industry grandees, chaired by former BP chief executive Lord Browne of Madingley, which meets four times a year. Browne resigned shortly before the ban was announced. Other board members recruited as non-executive directors are Ken Olisa, a venture capitalist and former Institute of Directors board member; Sir Andrew Cahn, the former head of UK Trade and Investment; and Mike Rake, a former chairman of BT, president of the CBI and one-time adviser to Prime Minister David Cameron.

Huawei argued that no 'back-doors' that would enable spying or sabotage have been found in existing equipment examined by a UK watchdog set up in 2014 to monitor its products. However, the Huawei oversight board said in its 2019 report that it 'continues to be able to provide only limited assurance that the long-term security risks can be managed in the Huawei equipment currently deployed in the UK', and that 'it will be difficult to appropriately risk-manage future products in the context of UK deployments, until the underlying defects in Huawei's software engineering and cybersecurity processes are remediated.'[79]

As we have seen, the technical security of the kit being installed is only one consideration. And the debate over whether Huawei can really be deemed private and commercial is largely irrelevant – though somewhat undermined by the fury with which the Chinese government has responded to restrictions against the company. Ultimately, all Chinese companies are beholden to the Communist Party – more so than ever under Xi Jinping. Whether state-owned or nominally private, they all face laws requiring them to cooperate with the Party when 'national security' requires it – to spy and provide data to the Party on demand. This is one reason why Huawei's continued dominance of Britain's 4G networks is so troubling. Huawei executives claim the laws do not apply outside China, and even offered to sign a 'no-spy' agreement with the UK government.[80] Such assurances are not credible.

Huawei has long been designated a 'high risk vendor', a view restated by GCHQ's National Cyber Security Centre (NCSC) in its January 2020 advice to Johnson, which warned that China's National Intelligence Law could oblige Huawei to 'act in a way that is harmful to the UK'. Though the government's cyber sleuths felt at the time that the risks could be mitigated, the NCSC also warned ominously: 'We assess that the Chinese State (and associated actors) have carried out and will continue to carry out cyber attacks against the UK and our interests.'[81]

CHAPTER 9

Cyber Smash and Grab

In the dark recesses of cyberspace, pandas are not so cuddly. They come in different guises, with 'Wicked Panda', 'Lotus Panda', 'Judgment Panda' and 'Stone Panda' among those with the most voracious appetite for data stolen from the computers of Western companies and laboratories. The names, coined by cybersecurity investigators, refer to hacking groups linked to the Chinese government. According to US intelligence officials, 'Chinese actors are the world's most active and persistent perpetrators of economic espionage.'[1]

Stone Panda, otherwise known as APT10, has been one of the most active. In December 2018, the British government accused the group of working on behalf of China's Ministry of State Security in a hacking campaign described by then Foreign Secretary Jeremy Hunt as 'one of the most significant and widespread cyber intrusions against the UK and allies uncovered to date, targeting trade secrets and economies around the world'.[2] It was the first time the UK government had publicly named elements of the Chinese government as being behind the hacking. Usually governments are cautious about attribution; it can be very difficult to pinpoint culprits with a high degree of certainty and Western intelligence agencies don't want to expose their own forensic abilities. It is a measure of government exasperation at the scale and persistence of Chinese hacking that Hunt was willing to speak out publicly.

His statement was coordinated with Washington, which went further and charged a pair of Chinese nationals with stealing technology blueprints from a host of high-tech industries on behalf of the Ministry of State Security. Zhu Hua and a smiling Zhang Shilong were shown staring out from an FBI wanted poster, which listed their alleged crimes as, 'Conspiracy to Commit Computer Intrusions; Conspiracy to Commit Wire Fraud; Aggravated Identity Theft.' According to the US indictment, some forty-five American companies were targeted, as well as firms in Japan, the EU and the UK, working in fields that included satellites, aviation, telecommunications, factory automation and consumer electronics.[3]

Cyber investigators had been following Stone Panda for several years, and dubbed the hackers' campaign, Operation Cloud Hopper.[4] The hackers didn't attack their targets directly, but first targeted some of the world's biggest IT service providers, companies that manage technology services, such as data storage and software, on behalf of a number of companies. The service providers were used as a stepping stone to go after the intellectual property of carefully selected targets among their clients.

The investigators, experts in digital forensics, examined the hackers' techniques and looked for patterns in their malware 'toolbox', as well as in the timings of file compilations and domain registrations. It all pointed to China. In addition, the group adhered to fairly rigid working hours, which aligned to Chinese standard time. There was a close correlation between the targeted industries and the priorities of China's five-year plan and its Made in China 2025 initiative to lead the world in futuristic technologies. It was almost like a shopping list. Other hacks appeared to be trawling for secrets that might give Chinese firms a more immediate market advantage – the targets including the Swedish telecoms firm Ericsson, a principal international competitor of Huawei and ZTE in the supply of 5G equipment.[5]

The Americans were circumspect about how they arrived at the two specific names of individuals (both still in China), and how they linked them not just to the Ministry of State Security, but the MSS office in the port city of Tianjin. It is part of a more aggressive strategy by Washington to 'name and shame' Chinese hackers, since attempts to reach agreement on limiting industrial espionage have largely failed. 'The theft of American trade secrets alone collectively costs our nation an estimated $300 to $600 billion per year. China accounts for the lion's share of this state-sponsored theft,' according to William Evanina, Director of the National Counterintelligence and Security Centre.[6]

The named hackers will never stand trial – the Chinese government issued a blanket denial that it had anything to do with hacking. It always does, while pressing ahead with a vast campaign of cyber theft that over two decades has been a cheap, effective and ultimately deniable way of gaining technical and scientific know-how.

***

In my first novel, *Beijing Smog*, one scene has cyber sleuths gain entry to the computers of a secret People's Liberation Army hacking facility in Shanghai by placing malware in the online menu of a takeaway restaurant the hackers regularly use – so that when the hackers click on the dumplings, they get a whole lot more than soggy pastry and pork.

Like so much in fiction, my story was based on real events. The menu infection technique was used by Chinese hackers to gain entry to the computers of an American oil company, where workers regularly ordered online from a nearby restaurant famous for its General Tso's chicken.[7] And there was a secret facility in a rundown neighbourhood of Shanghai, from which PLA Unit 61398 conducted worldwide hacking activities. The unit, formally the 2nd Bureau of the PLA General Staff Department's 3rd Department, is reportedly the PLA's main outfit for computer espionage, covering economic and political, as well as military information.[8] Mandiant, an American computer security firm (now part of FireEye), tracked the unit for six years from 2006, during which it stole technology blueprints, negotiating strategies, research results, marketing information and other secrets from almost 150 companies across twenty industries. Mandiant painstakingly collected digital evidence about the hackers' tools and techniques. It watched them moving around inside computer systems. It traced IP addresses used by the hackers, and even identified individual hackers from their social media accounts. All roads led to Shanghai, and in a groundbreaking 2013 report, Mandiant named a faceless twelve-storey building on the edge of the city's Pudong neighbourhood as an operational base of Unit 61398.[9] The unit left some pretty big digital tracks, including a recruitment ad on the website of Zhejiang University. 'Unit 61398 of China's People's Liberation Army (located in Pudong, Shanghai) seeks to recruit 2003-class computer science graduate students,' it read.[10]

Around the same time that Mandiant was publishing its investigation, a confidential report presented to the Pentagon by the Defense Science Board claimed that more than two dozen of the country's most advanced weapons systems had been compromised by Chinese hackers. These included designs for missile defence systems and combat aircraft and ships, including the F/A-18 fighter jet, the V-22 Osprey, a multi-role combat aircraft, the Black Hawk helicopter and the Navy's new Littoral Combat Ship. Also on the list was the F-35 Joint Strike Fighter, at the time the most expensive weapons system ever built.[11]

Chinese hackers were also blamed for a series of computer breaches at the US government's Office of Personnel Management, which began around March 2014. Some 22 million records were stolen, including security background checks and data on intelligence and military personnel. Other information, perfect for blackmail, included records of financial trouble, drug use, alcohol abuse and adulterous affairs. It was feared that Chinese counterintelligence agencies might be able to piece together the identity of US spies working undercover around the world.

The Obama administration was in a fix. Chinese cyber espionage was seemingly out of control, and Obama was under enormous political pressure to respond. A decision was taken to confront Beijing in public and in private. In May 2014, the US indicted five PLA hackers for cyber espionage against US companies in the nuclear power, metals and solar products industries. 'This 21st century burglary has to stop,' said David Hickton, US Attorney for the Western District of Pennsylvania, in the indictment.[12]

At the same time, the Obama administration tried in private talks to make a distinction between legitimate espionage for military or political purposes, and stealing to gain a commercial edge. A breakthrough came at a summit in September 2015, when presidents Barack Obama and Xi Jinping struck a deal, agreeing that 'Neither country's government will conduct or knowingly support cyber-enabled theft of intellectual property, including trade secrets or other confidential business information, with the intent of providing competitive advantages to companies or commercial sectors.'[13]

A month later, China reached a similar accord with Britain, where intelligence agencies had watched with alarm the seemingly inexorable rise of Chinese hackers. As long ago as 2007, MI5 warned businesses, including telecoms firms, banks, and water and electricity companies, about 'the possible damage . . . resulting from electronic attack by Chinese state organisations'.[14] The deal came as a relief to the British government, and seemed like an important landmark for establishing 'norms' for behaviour in cyberspace. It was endorsed by other G20 countries, and for a while it even seemed to be working, with a sharp reduction in the number of cyberattacks blamed on China.

In reality, the deal was always doomed; China was never going to abide by it for any longer than needed for the simple reasons that it never recognised Obama's distinction between spying for reasons of state and spying for commercial advantage. To the Communist Party they are one and the same thing; Chinese companies, whether state-owned or nominally private, are instruments of state power and Party policy. And the hacking was too effective. The deal was however useful to Beijing in the short term for blunting a growing threat of sanctions. It used the breathing space to reorganise, retool and refocus its cyber forces – and then they came roaring back with a greater degree of ambition and sophistication.

Operation Cloud Hopper, which followed the brief lull, showed a more deft touch, targeting large IT service providers as a stepping stone into the computers of targeted companies. It was also reported that Airbus, the European aeroplane manufacturer, and its suppliers were hit by a series of attacks, which resulted in 'unauthorised access to data'. The hackers targeted smaller suppliers as a sideways route into Airbus's computers, which were better protected against direct attack. They appeared to be after data on engines and avionics development, areas where China is weak.[15] Chinese hackers were also blamed for a computer breach at a German software company behind TeamViewer, a popular system that allows users to access and share their desktops remotely or to take full control of other computers via the internet from anywhere in the world.[16] Cybersecurity researchers also linked the Chinese military to a powerful new hacking tool they dubbed Aria-body, which was able remotely to take over a computer, and then copy, delete or create files, and carry out extensive searches of the device's data, while covering its tracks in ways not seen before.[17] Other research suggested servers at Tsinghua University, China's top engineering university, were the origin of multiple cyber espionage campaigns.[18]

A Bloomberg investigation revealed what it called a potentially devasting 'hardware hack', whereby a tiny microchip was placed on computer motherboards supplied from China, that would allow attackers to secretly open a 'backdoor' into the computer systems in which the motherboards were installed. The motherboard coordinates just about everything that happens in a computer, and the compromised boards reached almost thirty US companies. US investigators concluded that the chips, no bigger than a grain of rice, had been inserted in China during the manufacturing process with the aim of opening the door for hackers to gather high-value corporate secrets. This sort of attack is potentially far more effective than conventional hacking, and with so much of the world's high-tech supply chain based in China, it has grave implications. 'Hardware hacks are more difficult to pull off and potentially more devastating, promising the kind of long-term, stealth access that spy agencies are willing to invest millions of dollars and many years to get,' according to the Bloomberg investigation.[19]

In a bizarre and rather lower-tech incident, a Chinese national was detained trying to gain entry to Mar-a-Lago, the glitzy Palm Beach resort that President Donald Trump liked to refer to as his 'winter White House'. Yujing Zhang was allowed through the main gate after flashing her passport and telling a secret service agent she was on the way to the pool. The thirty-two-year-old was then chauffeur-driven to the main reception, where her story changed. She now claimed she was there to attend a UN friendship event between the US and China. There was no such event that day, and a suspicious receptionist called security. According to court documents, her bag did not contain a swimsuit, but it did contain two Chinese passports, four mobile phones, a laptop, a computer hard drive and a USB drive containing 'malicious malware'.[20]

The US authorities responded to the resurgence in Chinese hacking by stepping up their tactics of indicting alleged military hackers. In early 2020 four named Chinese intelligence officers were charged with hacking the credit-reporting giant Equifax. The attack was one of the largest data breaches in history, stealing financial records on 150 million Americans and also details of Equifax's proprietary methods of storing and assembling data.[21] Hacking from China is now back at the levels it reached before the Obama–Xi accord. 'They are fully back and engaging in economic espionage across numerous industries of strategic interest to China,' according to Dmitri Alperovich, co-founder and chief technology officer of CrowdStrike, a California-based cyber-security company.[22]

A blue plaque on a traditional stone cottage in the sleepy Derbyshire town of Belper commemorates Samuel Slater, who lived there from 1768 to 1789. Belper was once a hub of Britain's booming cotton industry, and Slater worked in a local mill, which used Richard Arkwright's pioneering water spinning frames. He left to make his fortune in the United States, and today, in his adopted country, he is celebrated as the 'father of the American Industrial Revolution'. To many in Britain's old mill towns he is still known as 'Slater the traitor'.

At the time, the United States was the biggest exporter of cotton, but did not have the technology to process it. In its eagerness to modernise, the US government created a system of rewards for those willing to share industrial secrets. To protect its technological edge, Britain passed laws banning textile workers from travelling to America. Slater heard about the bounties on offer and couldn't resist. He took a ship to the new world disguised as a farmer, and shared the secrets of the water-powered spinning machine – an act of treachery (in the eyes of British mill owners and workers) that marked the beginning of America's cotton boom.[23]

The story of Samuel Slater is still cited today by those with a more forgiving attitude towards China's acquisition of foreign know-how. They place Beijing's actions in a long historical tradition of poorer emerging powers playing economic catch-up in an unjust world where the rules of trade, and the strictures of patent and copyright laws are stacked against them. As Martin Wolf, a senior columnist on the *Financial Times* has argued, 'China is determined to catch up on today's more advanced countries, just as the latter sought to catch up in the past . . . China's desire to gain access to the best technology is inevitable and, in the long run, likely to be beneficial. In any case, the leakage of knowhow is inevitable. The flow will not stop.'[24]

Beijing and its apologists also invoke Edward Snowden, who exposed American cyber snooping, including against Chinese targets. He also described a programme called Prism, under which the NSA accessed data from US tech giants. The response of Huawei's chairman, Gao Ping, at a Barcelona trade show was typical of the hand-wringing: 'Prism, Prism on the wall, who is the most trustworthy of them all,' he said.[25]

Leaving aside the dubious moral equivalence, China's theft of intellectual property is unrivalled in scale and ambition. The country can no longer be described as an 'emerging power'. Furthermore, its cyber espionage must also be seen as part of a broader strategy for acquiring know-how that ranges from the forced transfer of tech from companies working in China through to carefully targeted research projects with foreign universities.

China's approach to espionage has often been characterised as 'a thousand grains of sand', the vacuum-cleaner approach to intelligence, hoovering up everything it can get its hands on. It is certainly wide-ranging, but that does not necessarily make it scattershot. 'We are talking here of an elaborate, comprehensive system for spotting foreign technologies, acquiring them by every means imaginable, and converting them into weapons and competitive goods,' according to one study, which also points out that there is often a fine line between stealing secrets and informal technology transfer, which China pushes to the limit.[26] Or, as FBI director Christopher Wray put it in a conversation with the Council on Foreign Relations:

> China has pioneered a societal approach to stealing innovation in any way it can from a wide array of businesses, universities, and organizations. They're doing it through Chinese intelligence services, through state-owned enterprises, through ostensibly private companies, through graduate students and researchers, through a variety of actors all working on behalf of China. At the FBI we have economic espionage investigations that almost invariably lead back to China in nearly all of our fifty-six field offices, and they span just about every industry or sector.[27]

Much of the advanced technology China is acquiring is being channelled into military modernisation and building the surveillance state. This is not simply a project of cheeky economic 'catch-up', as many of China's apologists suggest.

Discovering that somebody has broken into your computer is a gut-wrenching experience. There's the numbing initial shock, then anger – at *them*, whoever *they* are, but also at yourself for somehow allowing them in, even if you're not sure how. There's a sense of hopelessness, and a feeling of being violated, since so much of our lives are on our computers. It's not dissimilar to discovering that a burglar has been through the drawers and cupboards of your home, though not being quite sure what they've stolen.

That was me in the summer of 2008, sitting at the desk in a Beijing hotel room. I was staring at a drop-down menu on my laptop which was telling me that my computer had been backed up an hour earlier, while I was out of the room, to an external hard drive I did not recognise. I always assumed that as a Western journalist in China I was being closely monitored, but that didn't lessen the shock. The only reassurance I could give myself was that my most sensitive contact information, emails, notes and scripts were kept beyond another layer of security, inside my company's closed network.

It was the run-up to the Beijing Olympic Games, and I was putting together a series of reports, which included visiting the sensitive province of Xinjiang as well as analysing the Communist Party's fast developing internet controls. The Olympics were a big moment for China and in their extreme paranoia the Party was cracking down on dissent even more harshly than usual. It also banished migrant workers from Beijing, ordered factories to close and restricted traffic so the air would be breathable and the capital would appear clean, calm and doc-ile for the occasion. I had even witnessed a team of workers painting the grass green along a central boulevard, the Party not being happy with the withered and stained state of the original.

I was not the only target. Mandiant, the computer security com-pany, discovered over the course of several investigations that from 2008 onwards Chinese hackers had stolen contacts, files and emails from more than thirty journalists and executives at Western news organisations, and had maintained a shortlist for repeat attacks. It was part of an effort to identify and intimidate sources and contacts. The targets included the *New York Times*, *Wall Street Journal*, *Washington Post* and Bloomberg, and the journalists targeted had written about China's leaders, Chinese legal and political issues, and the activities of telecoms giants Huawei and ZTE. Bloomberg had written about the wealth of the family of Xi Jinping, who was vice-president at the time.[28] The attack on the *New York Times* coincided with its investigation into relatives of Wen Jiabao, then China's prime minister, which found business dealings had earned them a multi-billion dollar fortune. The hackers broke into the email accounts of the newspaper's Shanghai bureau chief, David Barboza, who wrote the reports.[29]

Mandiant reported that the hackers who targeted the *New York Times* routed their attacks through a number of compromised comput-ers in the US as a way of muddying the trail. But there were familiar techniques and patterns, which matched other attacks, including an earlier breach at Google, which compromised the Gmail accounts of human rights activists. 'When you see the same group steal data on Chinese dissidents and Tibetan activists, then attack an aerospace com-pany, it starts to push you in the right direction,' said Richard Bejtlich, Mandiant's chief security officer at the time.[30]

Tibetan activists have been another prime target for China's cyber spies. Dharamsala, in the lush Himalayan foothills of India, home of the Dalai Lama's government-in-exile, is perhaps the most hacked place on earth. So much so, that it has become a place of pilgrimage for cybersecurity analysts – not to visit His Holiness, but to study the smorgasbord of malware that has been directed at his computers. 'The Chinese government is everywhere but nowhere in Dharamsala, planting malware and intercepting messages in ways that are nearly undetectable and difficult to trace,' *Foreign Policy* magazine reported.[31]

Dharamsala has been home to the Tibetan government-in-exile since 1959, when the Dalai Lama fled there after China violently crushed an uprising in Lhasa. A sharp increase in protests in Tibetan areas of China in 2008, and a wave of self-immolations – more than 148 Tibetans, old and young, monks and lay people, set themselves on fire in protest at repressive Chinese rule – triggered a harsh crackdown in China, and a cyber onslaught against exiles.

Citizen Lab, a Canadian group committed to supporting free expression against state surveillance, came to their assistance. It believes the attackers were able to read the diplomatic traffic of the Dalai Lama, as well as communications between supporters inside and outside China. In total, 1,295 computers were infected in 103 countries. The malware allowed for the remote control of the targeted computers, taking over cameras and microphones, and facilitating the extraction of files. Citizen Lab said the origin of the attacks appeared to be a Chinese signals intelligence facility on Hainan Island, China.[32]

Since then, international supporters and computer security specialists have tried to bolster the Dalai Lama's defences, and sleepy hillside classrooms have been filled with a different type of mantra – to *never* open suspicious attachments or links in emails. Still, in spite of all the efforts, one of the Dalai Lama's officials told *Foreign Policy* he believes that half their key computers are still compromised. More challenging has been the Chinese app, WeChat, which is enormously popular in China, but also among exiles and overseas Chinese as a way of keeping in touch with friends and family at home. Nothing, the monks are told, is private about your communications into China on WeChat. The Communist Party will always be part of the conversation.

Hacking techniques and tools have become more sophisticated as China has extended its surveillance of dissidents and critics well beyond its borders. As we have seen, the mass incarceration of Uighurs and other Muslim minorities in Xinjiang has been accompanied by hacks against overseas Uighur targets. Hackers planted malware on at least eleven Uighur websites, which then infected the mobile phones of those visiting the sites with sophisticated spyware able to gain access to phone data including messaging applications. The attacks stunned security researchers because they targeted iPhones, usually more secure than their Android-based competitors, utilising 'zero day' vulnerabilities – cyber-speak for hitherto unknown flaws – which Apple hastily patched.[33]

And there have been other political targets. Chinese hackers were blamed for an attack on the Permanent Court of Arbitration in the Hague, knocking its website offline in the middle of hearings on a Philippines challenge to China's claim to 80 per cent of the South China Sea. The court rejected that claim, though Beijing refused to accept the ruling. Smaller regional powers that have challenged China have also faced cyberattacks. 'Whenever you see island-dispute issues flare up you also see cyber activities spike as well,' Tobias Feakin, director of Australia's International Cyber Policy Centre, told Bloomberg.[34]

In March 2015, a new name entered the language of cyber warfare: The Great Cannon. That was the name given for the weapon used for an attack on the coding site GitHub, which was flooded with traffic, disrupting it for days. This sort of attack is called a Distributed Denial of Service (DDoS), and the precise targets seem to have been two GitHub users, GreatFire.org (which helps bypass Chinese censorship) and a mirror site of the *New York Times*. According to Citizen Lab, which coined the term, the Cannon is part of the same infrastructure as The Great Firewall, only instead of blocking traffic coming into China, it highjacks it and redirects it at a target machine.[35]

I met 'Martin' above a converted factory building not far from Kai Tak, the old Hong Kong airport. The area used to be a big industrial hub, with a front-row view of aircraft making their hair-raising approaches over the teaming tenements of Kowloon. Now, it's being rapidly redeveloped, and is one of the city's new creative hotspots.

'It's not a bad place to be,' Martin told me, cradling a steaming mug of coffee, and then rejecting the latest of a steady stream of calls to a mobile phone lying on the desk beside him. He walks across the room, barks instructions in Cantonese at some co-workers in an adjoining room, and then closes the door. He glances towards a window looking out on the wall of another old factory.

'The attacks began one or two days after the vote started. They were huge, we'd seen nothing like it. We tried to expand the system, to absorb the attack, but it was so big, so big,' he said, sitting back down. Martin runs an IT business and is prominent in a number of Hong Kong tech forums. He's also a member of an informal network of IT professionals who provide advice and support to Hong Kong's democracy movement. He spoke to me on condition that I did not use his real name.

He was describing attempts to sabotage an unofficial online referendum called PopVote, organised by activists in June 2014 to demonstrate public support for democratic change, a vote that Beijing condemned as 'illegal and invalid'. The voting system, which Martin helped to design, enabled voting via a website, mobile phone apps or at a polling station. It was hit by a massive DDoS attack. These attacks are designed to cripple computer systems by flooding them with superfluous traffic. Typically the attacks are launched by botnets (literally robot networks) of hijacked computers. These zombie armies can consist of thousands – even hundreds of thousands – of connected devices, which, unbeknown to their owners, have been taken over by hackers (the bot-herder) and then used to bombard and overwhelm the target. The PopVote attacks came every three hours and lasted around fifteen minutes each.

'They used hijacked TV set-top boxes,' Martin said, with a slight shake of his head, and the faintest of smiles at the audacity of his adversary. These gadgets are very popular in Hong Kong, and give access to a massive amount of content, much of it pirated. They typically run on the Android operating system and content is streamed on the internet. What made them attractive to an attacker was their almost complete lack of security and their wide bandwidth capacity, required for streaming video content. 'There were lots of complaints at the time that boxes were not working properly or had slowed,' he said, evidence that they'd been hacked and were being used to attack PopVote.

At the same time, fake voting apps were uploaded to app stores, claiming to be the official PopVote app. Attackers also broke into PopVote's app store account and tried to corrupt the official app, but were discovered before any damage could be done. The aim here seems to have been to gather information on voters, and falsify votes to discredit the whole process. Attackers also created a number of fake websites, claiming to be the PopVote site, using domain names similar to the bona fide site.

PopVote's defences were bolstered by Cloudflare, an American cybersecurity company, which triggered Project Galileo, a defence system developed for public interest websites. Its aim is to dampen the impact of attacks by providing buffers and filters, expanding the available bandwidth, and deflecting traffic through multiple sites before arriving at PopVote's server.[36] To Martin's relief, the defences largely held, and just under 800,000 people took part in the vote, overwhelmingly endorsing democratic change.

But relief was short-lived. Attacks against the democracy movement grew in size and intensity, especially after street protests began in late September 2014. 'The cyber siege of Hong Kong,' is how the attacks were described by Mathew Prince, the CEO and founder of Cloudflare. 'No one has ever seen anything like this,' he said.[37] The attacks peaked in November, with what Prince described as the biggest in the history of the internet – 500 gigabytes per second.[38] His company was by then providing defences for several pro-democracy organisations. Some websites were crippled for days on end, others destabilised. Pro-democracy news organisations were targeted, the attacks peaking at times of significant news developments surrounding the protest. An attack on the *Inmediahk* news website was typical – the botnet flooding it with requests for online resources, such as archived stories, images, forms or other files, with the aim of slowing down and eventually crashing the system. At the very least, it made access very slow for legitimate users.

Hong Kong Island was ceded by China to the victorious British in the 1842 Treaty of Nanjing at the end of the First Opium War. It is central to two key themes that underpin Communist Party rule – victimhood and revival. In the Communist Party's telling of history, the loss of Hong Kong marked the beginning of a 'century of humiliation' at the hands of hostile and rapacious foreigners. It marked the start of a descent 'into an abyss of semi-imperial and semi-feudal society', which only the Party could reverse – as spelt out in the National Museum's rather blinkered 'Road to Rejuvenation' exhibition we visited in Chapter 4.[39]

Yet in the early years of communist rule, the Party was too consumed with the country's internal chaos to do much about recovering the colony – which, in any case, was too useful as a source of revenue and as an interface with the outside world. It became a crossroads where East met West, a home to traders, spies and China-watchers of all types – a point of friction, but also of cooperation. Much of its population were refugees, who fled economic hardship and repression in the mainland. Few people have better described colonial-era Hong Kong than the author and journalist Richard Hughes:

> A borrowed place living on borrowed time, Hong Kong is an impudent capitalist survival on China's communist derriere, an anachronistic mixture of British colonialism and the Chinese way of life, a jumble of millionaires' mansions and horrible slums, a teeming mass of hardworking humans, a well-ordered autocracy.[40]

Hughes's book is part travelogue, part history, and portrays Hong Kong as a place that should really not exist, founded on contraband and with few resources other than the ingenuity and hard work of its people. Instead, it not only thrived, but become more prosperous than its former colonial master.

It became an important centre for Western intelligence, and the emerging world of signals intelligence in particular. It was a crucial listening post for GCHQ, especially during the turmoil of the Cultural Revolution and Great Leap Forward, during which millions of Chinese people died and information was scarce. Richard Aldrich's history of GCHQ describes it as the organisation's 'most important outpost in Asia', cementing the British relationship with America's National Security Agency. 'During the 1950s and 1960s, both the State Department and the Pentagon considered Hong Kong to be the single most important British overseas territory from the point of view of intelligence gathering,' he writes.[41]

The Communist Party could have shut down the colony at any time by simply turning off the water, but preferred to sit back and let the clock count down to 1997, when the British lease expired on Hong Kong's New Territories. The Party might have hated what Hong Kong represented, but in Richard Hughes's words, it was 'too useful, convenient and profitable'. In 1976, when he was writing, Hong Kong provided 40 per cent of China's foreign exchange earnings through trade and various other remittances from friends and families. As Chris Patten, Britain's last governor, describes it in a memoir published shortly after the handover, 'Hong Kong is at one and the same time China's window on the world, bridge to the world, shopfront for the world and paradigm for the world of what China as a whole could become.'[42]

Hong Kong was far from being a full democracy under the British, but did enjoy freedom of expression, a free-wheeling capitalist economy and the rule of law. When the territory was handed back to China in 1997, these freedoms were enshrined in a mini-constitution called the Basic Law, creating a liberal bubble within authoritarian China. The Basic Law gave effect to the Sino-British Joint Declaration, a treaty signed by the two governments in 1985 and registered with the United Nations – giving it the force of international law. This supposedly grants the territory semi-autonomy for fifty years – a formula usually referred to as 'one country two systems'. The Basic Law included broad commitments to extend representative democracy, with universal suffrage for electing the Hong Kong leader – its chief executive – as the 'ultimate aim'.

For the Communist Party, the handover of Hong Kong was hugely symbolic – a return to the motherland of a seized territory, the righting of an historic wrong and a big step along that road to rejuvenation. Party leaders were suspicious of their newly reclaimed possession and its westernised elite, but the territory remained an important if not vital economic asset. At the time of the handover, the size of Hong Kong's economy was almost a fifth of that of all of China; it channelled investment to the mainland and facilitated trade in both directions, all under the protection of a trusted and independent legal system, mature financial institutions and the open flow of information. It was Asia's leading financial centre, and Party leaders viewed Hong Kong as essentially an economic city, where people were too busy making money to be concerned with politics.

That was a misreading of the mood; at the time of the handover, there was among Hong Kong's 7.4 million population widespread fear and suspicion about whether China would keep its word. That anxiety grew, especially among the territory's well-educated young. Even before the 2014 protests, the territory had a loud and lively protest culture; every year on 4 June, tens of thousands would gather for a candle-lit vigil to remember the 1989 Tiananmen Square massacre, when Beijing supressed its own student-led democracy movement, with the loss of hundreds, perhaps thousands of lives. Increasingly large anti-China protests were held in Hong Kong on the anniversary of the handover, as well as against a proposed anti-subversion law and proposals to oblige schools to teach 'patriotic education'. In both cases, the Hong Kong government backed down.

By 2014, anger was building at the steady erosion of rights. It flared into street protests after Beijing quashed lingering hopes for greater democracy by declaring that any popular election would be from a list of candidates vetted for their loyalty to the Communist Party. For almost three months, protests crippled the heart of the city, the uprising symbolised by a yellow parasol, after umbrellas were used as shields to protect against pepper spray used by the police.

As a journalist, it was exhilarating to cover what was dubbed the Umbrella Revolution. The young, mostly student protesters were overwhelmingly peaceful and well-organised, theirs was a cry of anger, but also one of hope for a better future. The spectre of the Tiananmen Square massacre also hung over the colourful protests, the fear that the Communist Party might trample over the territory's autonomy and send in the army to crush them, as it had the student protesters in Beijing in 1989. Had the Hong Kong protests happened elsewhere in China, they almost certainly would have been quickly and violently suppressed.

It seems certain that the Party weighed up the costs and benefits of violent intervention – its need to assert Party authority against the costs of openly trashing the Basic Law and unleashing bloodshed on the streets of Asia's financial capital, in full view of the world's cameras. By 2014, the relative size of Hong Kong's economy had fallen to around 3 per cent of that of a fast-growing China, but the territory remained an important conduit for trade and investment – perhaps even more so than before, both on the table and under it. Chinese companies increasingly tapped its capital markets and listed on its stock exchange, while a torrent of money flowed in and out of China via Hong Kong.

The People's Liberation Army stayed in its barracks. Instead, the Party launched a cyberwar on the democracy movement, and by the time the exhausted protesters left the streets in mid-December 2014, they had been hit with a full arsenal of weapons that ranged from massive brute-force DDoS attacks that targeted PopVote to highly sophisticated surveillance techniques. The cyberattacks were the largest, most intense and most varied ever used against dissent.

As the 2014 protests unfolded, pro-democracy leaders, protesters and supporters came under intense and persistent surveillance. It was carried out across desktop computers, laptops and mobiles. It involved the direct delivery of malware to individuals via carefully crafted phishing emails, the injection of spyware via infected websites and applications, as well as the hacking of email accounts.

Multiple pro-democracy websites were compromised, including that of the Democratic Party, Hong Kong's oldest political party, which then in turn served up malware to visitors to both its English and Chinese language sites. The malware came in two types – passive, where it logged the IP addresses of anybody coming to browse, and active, where it installed a bug on the machine of the visitor.

'They were big on watering holes,' said 'John', another member of the informal network helping the democracy movement. He also asked for anonymity, because of the sensitivity of what he was doing. I met him in what he called his high-rise 'laboratory' on Hong Kong Island, where earnest young researchers sat at screens scrutinising and disassembling computer bugs, rather like epidemiologists poring over human viruses. The air conditioning buzzed gently in the background, and as with so many offices in Hong Kong, the room was so severely chilled that the temperature seemed barely above zero. From the window there was the faintest view of the harbour between a forest of skyscrapers. It seemed an odd place to talk about watering holes, but cyber investigators like the wildlife metaphor of a place where wild animals go to drink, and where they are prone to predators. In the computer world, the watering hole is an infected website to which the prey is lured and from which malware will end up on their computer.

John explained that the malware used against targets in Hong Kong typically worked in two stages. The first, which he called a 'scouting mission' explored the victim's machine for vulnerabilities, checking out the operating system and type of files, looking for any anti-virus software. 'It then called home,' he said. It contacted its command and control, which checked for anything worthwhile before preparing stage two – more tailored malware to analyse and extract files, including contacts, messages and emails, and to take over key functions of the machine, including its camera and microphone. 'It was very smart,' he said.

Where phishing emails were used, they were very carefully drafted, often referencing news events or plausible situations not widely known outside the target group, and frequently sent from hijacked email accounts of people they knew. In one case, a fake invitation to a press conference was circulated to journalists and purported to come from protest leader Joshua Wong. Another appeared to come from a religious NGO, calling for a government investigation of police violence, the malware hidden in documents and spreadsheets.

Smartphones were also targeted with spyware apps. Protesters received WhatsApp messages inviting them to download an app to help them organise. 'Check out this Android app designed . . . for the coordination of Occupy Central,' the message said. It falsely claimed to come from a respectable software developer who had previously distributed maps showing the locations of medical and other suppliers around the protest site, but it was designed to grab just about every piece of information on the phone. Security analysts described it as one of the most advanced pieces of spyware they had seen.[43]

There are a lot of smoke and mirrors in cyberspace. Precise attribution can be tricky; that's why cyberattacks are so popular. But the circumstantial evidence was overwhelming, as was much of the technical evidence. Martin told me that traffic that swamped Pop Vote's servers was facilitated by the local subsidiaries of Chinese-owned internet service providers. Other reports suggested up to 40 per cent was relayed via computers registered to mainland firms operating in Hong Kong.[44] Citizen Lab reported that tools and techniques were very similar to those used previously against Tibetan targets.[45]

China frequently uses so-called 'patriotic hackers', groups or individuals loosely affiliated with the state, against political targets to provide an extra layer of deniability. The precise relationship between the state and patriotic hackers can be quite blurred, but it is inconceivable that they would be able to operate the way they do without at least the tacit support of the authorities, given the tight control China exercises over the internet.

The Hong Kong protests also saw a predictable response from the Communist Party's censorship and disinformation machine. At first, Chinese censors worked hard to minimise information reaching mainland China. There was a fivefold increase in the number of posts deleted on social media, the authorities blocking words including 'Hong Kong', 'barricades' and 'umbrella'. Some bloggers found ways around the censorship, sharing photographs of Xi Jinping carrying an umbrella, or changing their profile picture to a yellow parasol. There were reports of bloggers detained, including a woman who had posted a photograph of herself online in which she was wearing a T-shirt upon which was written, 'When the people fear the government, there is tyranny.'[46]

When the Chinese media did begin to report on Hong Kong, it was in virulent terms, seeing everywhere the 'dark hand' of foreigners, organising and stoking the protests, using naïve and violent students to further the West's nefarious motive of undermining China. When the American magazine *Fortune* named a pro-democracy student leader, Joshua Wong, as one of the world's top fifty leaders, this was presented as proof that he was an agent of Washington. Cultural Revolution-style propaganda videos, which have seen a resurgence under Xi Jinping, depicted dark Western conspiracies against China. One breathless diatribe, posted online and promoted by public security officials, warned of the West's 'devilish claws' reaching into China. To a darkly menacing soundtrack, it depicted Hong Kong as a bridgehead for Western subversion.[47]

In Hong Kong's more plural and sophisticated news environment, Beijing's heavy-handed propaganda was often counterproductive. And the mostly young and tech-savvy protesters were not passive in the face of the cyberattacks, developing their own defence techniques, and tapping international help, such as that provided by Cloudflare. They learned from their experience, and when pro-democracy protests returned to the streets of Hong Kong in 2019, they adjusted their tactics, building those lessons into the way they operated and organised. In doing so, they posed an even bigger challenge to the Communist Party. But five years on, Xi Jinping had consolidated his power in Beijing and had presided over a severe crackdown on dissent in the mainland. He had shown himself to be ruthless and intolerant of challenges to both himself and to the Party. His political calculations over Hong Kong were about to change too.

It became an iconic image from the 2019 Hong Kong protests: a crowd gathered in a circle around the base of a lamppost, linking their umbrellas like a shield. They moved back as sparks began to fly, the blade of an electric saw cutting through metal, then cheered as the lamppost toppled over. They descended on it like hungry scavengers, ripping from its insides the high-tech gadgetry they feared was tracking them and spying on their communications. The masked protesters destroyed more than twenty freshly installed 'smart lampposts', which the Hong Kong government insisted were only being used to collect data on weather, traffic and air quality. Few believed that, fearing cameras on the lampposts were capable of facial recognition and sensors could track their phones or the chips in their ID cards. After all, they only had to look across the border to see what the Communist Party was capable of. They knew that to sustain the protest movement this time, they also had to keep China's surveillance state at bay.

Protesters handed out stickers with images of surveillance cameras, warning that 'monitoring is coming'. Banners warned that the kind of oppressive tactics used against the Uighurs in Xinjiang could be exported to supposedly semi-autonomous Hong Kong.[48] The protests, which at their height brought 2 million people – more than a quarter of the population – to the streets, had begun as a backlash against a proposed new law that would allow people to be extradited for trial in courts in mainland China. But they soon embraced a wider call for democracy and a rejection of China's dystopian surveillance state.

The youth-led protests were likened to water, ebbing and flowing, and apparently leaderless. The protesters wore hard hats, goggles and masks (often gas masks), to protect against tear gas as they fought pitched battles with an increasingly brutal police force, but also to hide their identities. They organised through scores of encrypted groups on the messaging app Telegram and on online forums; bulletins were exchanged via near-field communication tools such as Airdrop, which use Bluetooth to communicate with nearby iPhone and iPads, making it safer than WiFi. Protesters were encouraged not to leave a digital footprint, often using multiple devices and several messaging accounts. It all enabled the protesters to quickly develop and change their plans and tactics, a fluidity that kept them one step ahead of the authorities.

Pro-democracy websites did face attack, as did Telegram and Amnesty International, with the attackers using tools and techniques that have previously been traced to the Chinese state, but this time the movement was far more resilient. The Party also pumped out virulent anti-Western propaganda. Images and videos were manipulated, and reports depicted the protesters as a violent gang, their actions a prelude to terrorism.[49] Twitter, Facebook and YouTube (all of which are blocked in China itself) all pushed back against what appeared to be a coordinated disinformation and propaganda campaign against the protesters, using their platforms. Twitter removed nearly 1,000 accounts and suspended thousands of others, which were part of what it described as a 'significant state-backed information operation', saying in a statement: 'These accounts were deliberately and specifically attempting to sow political discord in Hong Kong, including undermining the legitimacy and political positions of the protest movement on the ground.' Facebook said it had removed several accounts, and YouTube removed more than 200 channels.[50]

At first Beijing was willing to leave the policing of the protests in the hands of the local police force, while characterising the violent behaviour of a minority of protesters as 'terrorism' and blaming the 'dark hand' of foreign forces for the unrest. In weighing up its response, the same issues prevailed: meeting the challenge to the Party against the economic cost of intervention. The economic importance of Hong Kong to China had changed little since 2014. The size of Hong Kong's economy compared to that of the mainland had shrunk a little – down to 2.7 per cent by one calculation – but it remained Asia's largest financial centre, and one of the world's biggest markets for equity and debt finance. The Heritage Foundation, a US think tank, ranked Hong Kong the second freest economy in the world in 2020 – down one place after having held the top spot for twenty-five years.[51]

In 2018, more than half of foreign direct investment into China was channelled through the city, as was almost 60 per cent of China's outward investment. More than half the $64.2 billion raised globally by Chinese companies came from listings in Hong Kong; Chinese companies also used Hong Kong for a third of their offshore US dollar funding. Chinese banks held more than a trillion dollars of assets in the city; Hong Kong's ports continued to handle a big share of China's exports and imports. The city was China's largest trading partner in services, and at the forefront of efforts to develop China's renminbi (or yuan) into a serious international currency that might one day compete with the US dollar.[52]

Hong Kong's semi-autonomous status allowed it to negotiate investment and trade agreements independent of Beijing, and to be treated separately in the eyes of US law. And its independent judiciary seemed more important than ever, as Xi Jinping extended the Party's reach into business (and just about everything else) on the mainland, and China's direct exports were being hit by US tariffs. It seemed inconceivable that Xi would jeopardise that position, as challenging as the protests had become.

Yet, at the end of June 2020, the Party imposed a draconian security law on Hong Kong. Late on 30 June, the eve of the twenty-third anniversary of the return of Hong Kong to China, its rubber-stamp parliament passed a law that gives Beijing sweeping powers to crush dissent, using its own secret police. It effectively tears up the territory's autonomy (and an international treaty) and paves the way for mainland-style repression and the deployment of the infrastructure of the surveillance state. It targets any conduct deemed to threaten national security and allows for secret courts presided over by government-selected judges. It also applies to activities abroad, giving it chilling extra-territorial scope and raising the spectre of people being arrested on entering Hong Kong or China for things they have said or done overseas. *The Economist* described it as 'one of the biggest assaults on liberal democracy since the Second World War'.[53]

The law targets what it describes as succession, subversion, terrorism and collusion with foreign forces, all open to wide interpretation, and criminalises a range of peaceful activities. It mandates a central government-run Office for Safeguarding National Security in Hong Kong, and a Party-appointed security adviser to sit at the elbow of Hong Kong's leader. It calls for stronger regulation of schools, universities and the internet.[54]

It is not tanks on the street, not yet, but it quickly sent a chill through the territory. Activists moved to delete social media accounts, shops and cafes removed posters supporting democracy, and libraries took books by pro-democracy activists off their shelves. The first arrest came a day after the law was enacted – a man carrying a banner calling for an independent Hong Kong.

By snatching Hong Kong's judicial reins, the law destroys the semi-autonomy that enabled the territory to prosper. But, unlike in 2014, Xi calculates that China (and he) are strong enough to weather any economic fallout or international backlash. He has shown no tolerance of dissent on the mainland, and will now crush it in Hong Kong. He struck while the world was distracted by the fight against the Covid-19 pandemic, and while the protests had largely paused for the same reason. He perhaps also had one eye on the November 2020 US presidential election, calculating that it was better to move while the divisive Donald Trump remained in the White House and there was less chance of a united response from Western democracies.

The US responded by removing Hong Kong's special trade privileges, saying it would now be treated like any other part of China. That could potentially be very damaging for the territory, but Xi might have calculated that the economic cost is exaggerated, that Western companies and financiers are motivated primarily by greed and can be bullied, as they have been in mainland China. As we have seen, he has already humiliated Cathay Pacific and other companies in Hong Kong, forcing them to toe the Party line over the protests. Even before the full text of the security law was published, China pressured two prominent banks,

HSBC and Standard Chartered, to publicly support the law.[55] HSBC had been warned by a leading pro-Beijing figure that it could no longer take its 'unique privileges' in Hong Kong for granted.[56] The lender that once dubbed itself 'the world's local bank' found a new location – beneath the heel of the Communist Party.

CHAPTER 10

To the Digital Barricades

Writing in the *New York Times* in May 2019, Thomas Friedman quoted a businessman friend of his saying, 'Donald Trump is not the American president America deserves, but he sure is the American president China deserves.' He goes on to say that 'It took a human wrecking ball like Trump to get China's attention.'[1]

Yet, as far as it is ever possible to read the mood inside Zhongnanhai, the Communist Party leadership compound in Beijing, they seem initially to have welcomed Trump's 2016 election victory. This is partly because of their dislike of his opponent Hillary Clinton, who had been secretary of state in the Obama administration and a frequent critic of Beijing's human rights record, and partly because they genuinely thought they could do business with Trump. Sure, he was unprincipled, but that was part of the attraction; Trump's mendacity was something Party leaders could relate to. 'It is no wonder, therefore, that in their post-election prognosis Chinese analysts were overwhelmingly optimistic, even gleeful,' according to Xiangfeng Yang, a scholar at Yonsei University in South Korea, who has studied the words and writings of prominent Chinese academics and think tanks who function as a kind of echo chamber for the Party.[2]

And if Trump alienated his allies and turned his back on the world then all the better for China's global ambitions. Yang quotes Yinan Jin, a hardline strategist at China's National Defense University, who 'glowed with unbridled excitement' as he addressed Communist Party officials, telling them, 'In fact, he [Trump] has given China a huge gift . . . As the US retreats globally, China shows up.'

Even as Trump stepped up his trade war, hitting Chinese products with a series of tariffs and targeting China's high-tech champions, such as Huawei, there was still confidence in Beijing that the American president, a self-proclaimed 'deal-maker', could be bought off with a few more orders for Boeings or soybeans. 'Chinese officials had expected the simple tactic of "buy, buy, buy" to mollify Trump,' writes Yang. That, and the sort of promises to address predatory trade practices and intellectual property theft that have been made by Beijing routinely in the past, and equally routinely broken.

Early trade war skirmishes encouraged the view that Trump had a narrow mercantilist agenda. He repeatedly praised autocrats, and his 'America first' rhetoric showed little concern for human rights or free speech. He agreed to tone down criticism of Beijing's behaviour in Hong Kong in order to keep trade talks on track, at one point telling reporters, 'We stand with Hong Kong, but I'm also standing with President Xi. He's a friend of mine.' He threatened to veto the Hong Kong Human Rights and Democracy Act, which was passed unanimously by the Senate and requires the government to impose sanctions against China and Hong Kong officials responsible for human rights abuses. In his memoir, *The Room Where It Happened*, John Bolton, Trump's former national security adviser, describes how Trump responded to the Xinjiang detention camps during a meeting with Xi Jinping: 'Trump said that Xi should go ahead with building the camps, which Trump thought was exactly the right thing to do.'[3] All of which will have been music to the ears of hardliners around Xi Jinping.[4]

Beijing also assumed it could rely on its friends on Wall Street. The US business lobby could usually be counted on to talk Washington out of any policies that could damage the status quo. It was a grave miscalculation. 'The Chinese vastly underestimated the groundswell of disappointment, resentment and ill-will towards China,' according to Yang. Trump's harder line was one of his few policies with broad bipartisan support in the US – if anything, Democrats have become more outspoken than Republicans. It went well beyond the usual China policy hawks to embrace those who had previously argued for a more dovish policy of engagement. Among America's allies there was also quiet support, a sense that it was 'about time' somebody stood up to China, though that sentiment was not always spoken openly, partly out of fear of retribution from Beijing and partly out of distrust of Trump.

Washington's hardening of policy marks a fundamental reassessment of relations that goes well beyond both trade and Trump. For four decades, ever since normalisation of relations, US policy has been one of engagement – a belief that, as it became richer, China would liberalise politically and embrace further market-friendly economic reform. And there have been times when it seemed to be moving in that direction. There was also a hope that China would emerge as a responsible stakeholder in the rules-based international system. The country's 2001 accession to the World Trade Organization, which the US supported, was seen as an important step towards that goal.

It was wishful thinking. The consensus in Washington, and increasingly among America's allies, is that engagement has failed. Xi Jinping has moved the country firmly in the opposite direction. As it has become richer, Xi's China has become more dictatorial at home, and more aggressive internationally. It is rapidly modernising its military and seeking world leadership in the defining technologies of the twenty-first century. It has set itself on a course to displace the United States as the dominant world power. As *The Economist* has pointed out, none of this ambition is particularly secret. The newspaper likened China to the ruthless genius beloved of James Bond movies, who lays out his plans for world domination in front of a captive Bond. 'With the reliability of a well-tuned Aston Martin, the bragging turns out to be ill-timed. Within moments Bond is free, the villain's lair ablaze and his schemes thwarted,' the newspaper writes, before adding, 'Today in the real world, China faces unusual resistance to its bid for a front seat as a global power. Surprisingly often, China's woes stem from what film critics might term Bond-villain blunders, involving premature admissions of ambition.'[5]

Those ambitions can be summed up by two dates that have concentrated minds and triggered mounting American alarm: 2025 and 2049. China's technology goals are laid out in a plan called Made in China 2025, which aims to build 'national champions' in ten cutting-edge technologies, including robotics, artificial intelligence, telecommunications, aerospace engineering, gene editing, electric cars, synthetic materials and advanced electrical equipment. The second date, 2049, will be the centenary of the Communist Party's seizure of power, when 'the dream of the rejuvenation of the Chinese nation will be realized,' according to Xi.[6] Michael Pillsbury, a veteran Washington insider, has characterised this as a 'hundred-year marathon' which aims to 'supplant the United States as the world's dominant power'.[7] When his book was published in 2015 it was regarded as being on the hawkish fringe of China policy; now it is much more mainstream, and Pillsbury was a sounding board for Trump and members of his administration.[8]

Made in China 2025 has raised alarm as much for China's tactics as for its ambition. It entails vast state support for Chinese companies, throwing billions at research and development, and protecting them by largely locking foreign businesses out of China's domestic market in those areas. It also involves the familiar harnessing of foreign technology and ideas by fair means or foul – forced tech transfer, academic tie-ups, and the strategic purchase of foreign companies, complemented by a resurgence of cyber espionage, the targets of which read like a shopping list for Made in China 2025. Robert Atkinson, president of America's Technology and Innovation Foundation, has characterised it as 'an aggressive by-hook-or-by-crook strategy that involves serially manipulating the marketplace and wantonly stealing and coercing transfer of American know-how'.[9]

Some have described the rupture of relations between the US and China as heralding a new Cold War, though the analogy is not a particularly comfortable one. America and the Soviet Union lived in two separate economic and ideological universes, there was very little trade or travel between them, and they each headed a closely knit alliance of like-minded countries – two very distinct 'blocs'. China and the US (and the West in general) are economically intertwined, China's authoritarian ideology, as far as it can be pinned down, is more nationalist than communist, which is now little more than a label for the Party. And the world is a far more complex place than it was during the last Cold War. While China is rapidly extending and modernising its military, throwing its weight around in its own backyard – with the South China Sea and Taiwan as potentially dangerous flashpoints – it does not have the global military reach of the Soviet Union.

China has been quick to denounce those seeking to reset relations for having a 'Cold War mentality'. This has been echoed by many lazy academics and commentators in the West, who continue to insist that Beijing's global intentions are benign and that the US in particular is trying to turn China into an enemy.[10] This is nonsense. If anybody is turning Beijing into an enemy – or at least an adversary – it is the Communist Party itself. Indeed, Western democracies have shown remarkable forbearance (and a good dose of naïvety and greed) in their dealings with an increasingly belligerent China. It is Beijing's provocations, bullying and persistent rule-breaking that is belatedly changing calculations, not just in America, but globally.

Economic ties run deep. China was America's largest trading partner in goods, with two-way trade worth more than $650 billion in 2018.[11] The US is China's largest export market. Most electronic devices sold in America are assembled in China, and tens of thousands of US companies are doing business there. The US has run a persistent trade deficit with China; the deficit in goods and services was $378.6 billion in 2018.

Beijing holds more than $1 trillion of US debt in the form of Treasury bonds, which is around 15 per cent of the total owned by foreign countries. This is a fall of around a quarter between 2009 and 2020, but it still makes China one of America's biggest bankers, and there have been suggestions that this could be used as a weapon, with dire consequences. If Beijing started to sharply sell off the debt, it would likely lead to a steep fall in the value of the US dollar, push up American borrowing costs, and potentially destabilise the international financial system, but it would also force up the value of China's own currency and hurt its competitiveness. Some more hawkish American politicians have suggested the US renege on its debt to China, though that would also create turmoil in international debt markets.[12] If either side tried to weaponise the debt, both would potentially suffer, meaning that the use of the debt as a coercive measure is complicated and constrained. 'It's like holding a gun to your own head and saying I have a hostage,' Vincent Reinhart, chief economist and macro strategist at BNY Mellon, told CNBC, the business channel.[13]

The most visible part of the US–China spat has been a trade war, mutual tariffs slapped on each other's goods. But away from the 'trade war' headlines, a far more fundamental process is underway that is better described as a 'decoupling', a rethinking and resetting of relations on several levels, including investment, supply chains and technology. The flow of investment between China and the US has fallen sharply in both directions, as relations have soured. Washington is scrutinising far more closely Chinese purchases of US assets that might impact on national security. The scrutiny of inward investment is also being tightened in the EU and in Britain. Companies are examining their often fiendishly complicated supply chains, in order to diversify and make them less dependent on China. The technological rupture is perhaps the most stark element of decoupling, a technological arms race that is creating two different tech ecosystems, driven by separate systems of innovation. Again it would be wrong to see decoupling as an entirely American initiative; decoupling has been at the heart of China's own industrial strategy under Xi Jinping of building indigenous technology, underpinned by protectionism and intellectual property theft.

In its efforts to restrict China's access to Western technology, the US is more closely scrutinising academic visas, joint research projects and investments in high-tech start-ups. China has been a big investor in Silicon Valley, with several Chinese 'innovation centres' opening in the area. Between 2015 and 2017, an estimated 16 per cent of funds into American venture-capital backed companies came from Chinese sources, with a strong focus on artificial intelligence and augmented reality. 'China has targeted America's industries of the future,' according to Peter Navarro, the White House's director of trade and industrial policy in the Trump administration. 'If China successfully captures these emerging industries, America will have no economic future.'[14]

The dependency of Western democracies on Chinese supply chains was starkly spelt out in a report from the Henry Jackson Society, which suggested that members of the Five Eyes intelligence gathering community (Australia, Canada, New Zealand, UK and US) are strategically dependent on China for 831 separate categories of imports – with 260 characterised as servicing critical national infrastructure. It defined strategic dependence as occurring when a country is a net importer of a particular product, it imports more than 50 per cent of its supplies from China, and China controls more than 30 per cent of the global market of that product. The products identified range from medical supplies to consumer electronics, such as laptop computers and phones, as well as rechargeable batteries and other key components used in industrial processes, such as magnesium and magnets.[15] This dependency was on display during the Covid-19 pandemic as countries struggled to lay their hands on personal protective equipment, where 42 per cent of global supplies come from China.[16]

Two out of five US multinationals are considering, or in the process of, shifting their sourcing or their manufacturing out of China, according to one report.[17] This seems based on a hard-nosed reassessment that it is madness to be too dependent on a capricious Communist Party that has shown no compunction in using theft and economic coercion to get its way – a mood that is not confined to American companies.

**

There's a touch of the mad scientist about Nigel Stanford's music video *Automatica*. His 'band' is a group of bright orange robotic arms he programmed to play guitar, piano and drums alongside him. They perform with impressive precision – until they rebel in a pyrotechnic finale with exploding piano, smashed and tossed guitars, and lasers cutting though the building around them.[18]

Stanford has long been fascinated by the intersection between music and technology, and the robots were provided by Kuka, one the world's largest producers of industrial robots. The 120-year-old firm is based in Bavaria, Germany, but in 2016 it was controversially sold to a company called Midea, a Chinese appliance maker. To many in Berlin, the Stanford video was a metaphor for the country's loss of control over one of the jewels in its engineering crown. They were stunned that it had been allowed to proceed, 'The fox was not just in the hen house – the door had simply been opened to him,' reported *Deutsche Welle*.[19] There is huge pride in Germany at the country's engineering and technical prowess, and the takeover of Kuka was a turning point, a call-to-arms for those increasingly concerned about China's encroachment into sensitive areas of the German economy, and the broader implications of China's ascendency.

The alarm intensified when China bought stakes in Deutsche Bank and Daimler, the owner of Mercedes. Some 10 per cent of Daimler was bought by Geely, a nominally private car company, and when the firm's chairman told Chinese state television that the investment was designed to 'support our national strategies' it reinforced suspicions that China's acquisitions were part of a carefully targeted strategy to pick off cutting-edge German know-how. 'If Made in China 2025 succeeds, German industry might as well just pack up and go home,' Thorsten Benner, director of the Global Public Policy Institute in Berlin, told the *Financial Times*.[20] Others pointed out that German companies – or any other foreign companies for that matter – would never be allowed to make such acquisitions in China.

However, Berlin did block an attempted Chinese takeover of Aixtron, which makes advanced equipment for the semiconductor industry. It has toughened its oversight of foreign investment, and along with Italy and France pushed for a tougher EU-wide mechanism of oversight, especially when investments are made with state backing.

It represented a considerable sea change from the open arms that greeted Chinese investment after the 2008 financial crisis. Back then,

Chinese money was seen as a great saviour, and countries worldwide fell over themselves for a slice of it. Frequently the investors were opaque Chinese companies willing to pay high prices, but with obscure sources of funding. Due diligence consisted of little more than counting the zeros on the cheque, such was the desperation to get economies moving again.

Chinese investment has created dependencies, and the EU-wide regime of investment oversight has faced strong push-back from countries with weaker economies, which have received most Chinese largesse. Greece has been a particularly vociferous opponent. Since the financial crisis, Beijing and Athens have developed deep links. In 2016, the Chinese state-owned shipping firm COSCO bought a majority stake in Greece's loss-making and heavily indebted Piraeus port, and pledged to invest €600 million to develop it as a 'dragon head' for its Belt and Road Initiative, a gateway for cargo to Europe and North Africa.

The Piraeus investment was understandably welcomed in Greece, and reports suggest it is turning the place around, but the Chinese 'white knight' is even more heavily in debt than the port it rescued. COSCO Shipping Holdings, parent of China COSCO Shipping which bought the stake, was at the time six times more leveraged than the Piraeus Port Authority.[21] Chinese state-owned companies simply do not play by the same rules, running massive debts without fear of bankruptcy. In the case of Piraeus, COSCO was serving the Communist Party's wider strategic objectives, though it has also paid short-term dividends – Athens has blocked critical EU statements on China's aggression in the South China Sea and Beijing's human rights record.

As we have seen, China's divide and rule policy in Europe has been complemented by Xi Jinping's attempt to portray himself as the guardian of globalisation and an international order spurned by Donald Trump. This is as audacious as it is laughable, but a nativist US president, hostile to allies and adversaries alike, made Europe more susceptible to Chinese blandishments.

Nevertheless, in March 2019 the German and French governments largely got their way, as the EU dramatically hardened its stance, bringing it much closer to the view of Washington. In a strategic paper it stated that 'China can no longer be regarded as a developing country. It is a key global actor and leading technological power.' It sought to counter China's divide-and-rule, stating, 'Neither the EU nor any of its Member States can effectively achieve their aims with China without *full unity.*' (Emphasis in the original.) And in a departure from the EU's usual cautious language, the document labelled China, 'An economic competitor in pursuit of technological leadership and a systemic rival promoting alternative models of governance.'[22]

The move to scrutinise more closely Chinese investments has been given greater urgency by the Covid-19 pandemic, which has had a devastating economic impact. Fears have grown that large state-owned companies will attempt to snap up troubled European firms, and the European Commission has urged member states to be particularly vigilant. The EU is also looking to reduce trade dependencies by 'shortening and diversifying our supply chains,' according to Commission president Ursula von der Leyen.[23]

When China's foreign minister, Wang Yi, toured Europe at the end of August 2020 he sought to make common cause with European leaders against what he characterised as Donald Trump's extremism and Cold War rhetoric. There were the usual platitudes about 'win-win' situations and non-interference in another's affairs, laced with the occasional threat – against Norway, should the independent Nobel Peace jury award a prize to a Chinese dissident, and against the Czech Republic, where a senior politician had the audacity to visit Taiwan. But the world had changed; Wang's reception was cool and he faced sharp criticism of Beijing's repression in Hong Kong and Xinjiang. He was trailed in Italy and Germany by Nathan Law, a self-exiled Hong Kong democracy activist, a nagging reminder of China's behaviour in the former British colony. Press encounters were difficult and prickly; the usual homilies and threats fell flat, the *Guardian* describing the tour as marking 'the end of an era', with Beijing no longer able to rely on an easy ride in Europe.[24]

The members of the House of Commons Foreign Affairs Committee and its witnesses were arrayed on a large screen in front of Tom Tugendhat, the committee's chair. 'Order, order,' he said to the screen, before getting the remote session under way. It was the height of the Covid-19 lockdown, but the unusual format did not diminish the attention to the evidence of Sir Hossein Yassaie, one of Britain's most respected tech entrepreneurs. Legislation to protect British companies producing sensitive technology from foreign takeovers is 'lax', he said, and in urgent need of modernisation to reflect the 'complexity and power' of today's tech.[25]

The special session was prompted by events at Imagination Technologies, a Hertfordshire-based designer of mobile graphics processors, and for a decade one of Britain's biggest and most influential technology companies. Sir Hossein used to run the company, leaving shortly before it was taken over in 2017 by Canyon Bridge, a private equity firm based in California, but backed by China Reform Holdings, a Chinese government investment fund. Theresa May's government allowed the acquisition to proceed, even though the Trump administration had barred Canyon Bridge from acquiring a US chip maker on national security grounds.[26]

May did so after receiving assurances that the Chinese investment was passive, and that the investors were regulated by US law. But the company redomiciled to the Cayman Islands and then, in April 2020, China Reform sought to seize control of the Imagination board through the appointment of four members linked to the fund. Not only did this fly in the face of the assurances, but it raised the spectre of the company's most sensitive intellectual property, which includes tech designed to detect network vulnerabilities, being moved to China. It promoted a rare intervention from the British government, which forced China Reform to drop its plans, blocking the boardroom coup.

The government's move came shortly after it put before parliament a new National Security and Investment Bill, designed to give stronger powers to intervene in takeovers, though critics see it as too little, too late. As Sir Hossein reminded the emergency select committee enquiry, 'Technology can be used positively or negatively.' He argued for greater vigilance over foreign acquisitions – and not just at the time of purchase. 'It's really important what happens to the technology after its acquired, the direction it's given.'[27]

Britain has been a popular and welcoming destination for Chinese investment, estimated to be worth more than £50 billion between 2010 and 2020 and attracted by very light regulation.[28] Chinese companies have invested heavily in property, including the Leadenhall Building in the City, otherwise known as the 'Cheesegrater'. Chinese investors own Pizza Express, Thomas Cook, Wolves and Southampton football clubs, and a company that builds black cabs. A Chinese sovereign wealth fund holds minority stakes in Thames Water and Heathrow Airport, while China's National Offshore Oil Corporation (CNOOC) is responsible for around a quarter of UK North Sea oil production.

More controversially, Chinese entities have bought stakes in the

National Grid's gas distribution arm, and Global Switch, one the world's largest cloud data providers. State-owned China General Nuclear Power Group (CGN) has a 33 per cent stake in the £20 billion Hinkley Point nuclear power project, even though CGN has been accused by the US government of stealing US technology for military use and placed on the US 'entity list', which effectively bans US companies from doing business with it. As is often the case with Chinese investment, the nuclear deal in Britain has strategic designs which go beyond the troubled Hinkley Point project. China wants to play a bigger part in Britain's proposed nuclear power expansion; CGN has an option on a stake in a French-designed plant at Sizewell C, but the real target is Bradwell in Essex, where it wants to build an entire reactor of its own – the first Chinese-designed plant outside China. Much as it did with Huawei's telecoms technology, China sees the UK as a springboard for international sales of its technology.

The Hinkley Point deal was struck in 2015 by George Osborne, Chancellor of the Exchequer in David Cameron's government, on a visit to Beijing during which he made his vow to make Britain China's 'best partner in the West'. Cameron heralded a new 'golden era' in relations. It was a dramatic turnaround for a leader who had been cold-shouldered by China after meeting the Dalai Lama early in his premiership. Suitably chastised, Cameron socially distanced himself from Tibet's spiritual leader and, in 2015, hosted a state visit by Xi Jinping which plumbed new depths in obsequiousness. Security appeared to have been sub-contracted to Beijing, with officials treating the British like supplicants.

British police arrested Shao Jiang, a Tiananmen Square survivor, for standing in the road outside Mansion House, where a reception was being held, holding banners reading 'Democracy Now' and 'End Autocracy'. They later searched his home and took away computer equipment. 'The police here in the UK are now doing the same thing as in China,' Jiang's wife told the *Independent*.[29] Two Tibetan women were also arrested after they attempted to wave Tibetan flags at Xi's passing motorcade.

A hint of the behind-the-scenes tensions came a year later, at a Buckingham Palace garden party, in a conversation caught on camera between the Queen and Metropolitan Police Commander Lucy D'Orsi. When D'Orsi is introduced as the officer who had been in charge of Xi's visit, the Queen responds, 'Oh, bad luck.' D'Orsi reveals that it had been a 'testing time' and that at one point Chinese officials walked out from a planning meeting, declaring that the trip was off. 'Extraordinary,' says the Queen, telling her guest, 'They were very rude to the ambassador.'[30]

When Theresa May became prime minister she paused the Hinkley Point deal, and suggested a more cautious line on Chinese investment in general. But she backed down in the face of Chinese anger and strong behind-the-scenes pressure. The *Xinhua* news agency set the tone, warning that Britain would drive away Chinese investors and that Beijing 'cannot tolerate any unwanted accusation against its sincere and benign willingness for win-win cooperation'.[31]

In March 2020, a Chinese company completed its purchase of British Steel, saving more than 3,000 jobs. The buyer, the Jingye Group, is a nominally private conglomerate, whose businesses include tourism, property and chemicals. It is based in Shijiazhuang, one of the most heavily polluted cities in China. In 2018 it produced about 11 million tonnes of crude steel, which is more than the entire steel output of the UK, which stands at just over 7 million tonnes.[32] It is unclear how Jingye will turn around British Steel, but its pledge to invest more than £1 billion has understandably been welcomed in anxious steel communities. What has gone less remarked upon is that it is gross overcapacity in China and the dumping of steel at below cost on world markets that contributed to the demise of British Steel. Jingye is opaque and its accounts hard to dissect; as with all Chinese companies, it is intimately entwined with the policies and goals of the Communist Party.

For Nottingham University researcher Martin Thorley, the British Steel acquisition is another dangerous foothold for Communist Party power in the UK. 'What marks out the British Steel acquisition is not the pyrotechnics but the mundanity of the deal. Each time a CCP [Chinese Communist Party] entity acquires a company in this way, the UK becomes slightly more entangled in the Party-state's networks.'[33]

As we have already noted, Huawei has invested heavily and strategically in the UK – including a small stake in the company that commercialises research at Oxford University, giving the Chinese telecoms maker access to some of the most promising early-stage technology developed by academics in Britain.[34]

British government policy on China, where it exists at all, has been deeply muddled. 'We define China as a competitor, not an adversary,' according to Professor Anthony Finkelstein, the UK government's chief scientific adviser for national security. He was speaking at Security and Policing 2020, a security exhibition I attended in Farnborough early that year, and to which the Chinese surveillance equipment company Hikvision had been controversially invited. He said China had the makings of what he called a 'regional hegemon . . . though we have yet to fully experience that', before adding, 'Our Australian counterparts might say otherwise.' And indeed they do. As does the United States, and increasingly New Zealand, Canada, Germany, Japan and France.

Britain was once renowned for the deftness of its diplomacy, but its dealings with China have been driven in equal measure by greed and naivety. It has been left to the likes of Tom Tugendhat, the chair of the Foreign Affairs Committee, to highlight the threats Britain is facing, from university lecture halls to company boardrooms. The banning of Huawei from Britain's 5G networks and Beijing's imposition of a draconian national security law on Hong Kong have sent relations from 'best partner' to the deep freeze, but Britain's options are limited. It has allowed itself to become highly dependent on Chinese money and technology. The elephant in those rooms is, of course, Brexit, and China knows that. Britain is turning its back on traditional allies in Europe, leaving it in need of new friends and partners, and dangerously vulnerable to Beijing's threats and blandishments.

In late December 2019, following a trial in a district court in Shenzhen, a Chinese scientist named He Jiankui was found guilty of conducting 'illegal medical practices' and sentenced to three years in jail. The trial was closed to the public, and, in a brief report, the *China Daily* depicted He as a rogue scientist who had 'deliberately violated national regulations on scientific research and medical management in pursuit of profits, and crossed the bottom line of scientific and medical ethics'. Two of his collaborators were also convicted and given lesser sentences.[35]

A year earlier, He had stunned the world by announcing he had produced designer babies – twin girls whose genes had supposedly been manipulated to give them immunity from HIV. He later revealed the existence of a second pregnant woman, also carrying a gene-altered baby. Such gene-editing is banned in most countries, including China, out of fear of potentially harmful consequences, and the revelation provoked a backlash from the global scientific community.

He Jiankui was educated at Stanford University in the US and lured back to China as part of the Chinese government's 'Thousand Talents' scheme, designed to attract top scientists – particularly overseas Chinese – with lavish salaries and research grants. The scheme runs parallel with the Made in China 2025 plan, which identifies biotechnology as one of the defining twenty-first-century technologies in which China wants to lead the world.

Few details of the investigation into He have been revealed, and the scientist disappeared from public view shortly after he announced his research results. Communist Party newspapers were eager to depict him as a maverick, and to quash any suggestion of systemic failure. Yet, to scientists familiar with He and his research field, the depiction of him as a rogue operator simply does not ring true, and the lack of transparency is troubling. 'It can't just be three people involved,' William Hurlbut, a bioethicist at Stanford, told *Science* magazine. 'It really is hanging someone out to dry.'[36]

The case raises serious concerns about ethics and oversight in China's rapidly expanding research sector. It also touches on a broader question central to the growing technological standoff between China and the US: can China innovate?

Certainly, the money being thrown at research and development is staggering, with shiny new facilities, housing a lot of glitzy new kit, sprouting rapidly across the country. China spent $509 billion on R&D in 2019, and is rapidly closing the gap on the US, which spent almost $600 billion.[37] A Chinese spacecraft has landed on the far side of the moon, and there are plans for a research station up there too. China has built the world's largest radio telescope and the world's fastest supercomputer (though at the time of writing, the Americans are back in front). Massive subsidies have enabled Chinese companies to carve out dominant positions in solar power and battery storage. And, as we have seen, Huawei, Baidu, Alibaba and Tencent are technological giants.

In January 2018, America's National Science Foundation announced that China had surpassed the US in terms of the total number of science publications, a ranking that is often taken as an indicator of research prowess.[38] But the figure needs to be taken with some caution, since quantity does not necessarily mean quality, and China has been plagued by accusations of academic fraud. In the five years from 2012 to 2017, the country had more scientific papers retracted from scientific journals because of suspicion of faked peer reviews than all other countries put together.[39] In 2015, BioMed Central, a British publisher of scientific and medical journals, retracted forty-three papers, of which forty-one were by Chinese authors. Two years later, *Tumour Biology*, a medical journal, withdrew 107 Chinese-authored papers – the largest mass retraction that has ever taken place – because the peer review process had been 'deliberately compromised by fabricated peer review reports'.[40]

That said, the quality of Chinese research is improving, though its strengths are in applied research and product development, rather than basic science – copying and building upon existing know-how acquired from abroad, in other words. It has concentrated on implementation rather than innovation, which it has largely left to others. In key technologies, it lags well behind the best in world. By one estimate, it relies on foreign suppliers for more than half the high-end inputs into robotics and cloud computing. Chinese tech companies buy 90 per cent of their semiconductors from abroad, and it would take ten to fifteen years for China to become self-sufficient in computer chips.[41]

Beijing now wants to be a scientific superpower, and its research splurge has been likened to the American era of 'big science' between the late 1950s and early 1990s, when US science came to dominate the world. While the development of some technologies in the US, such as microprocessors, were driven by the military and space programmes, science and innovation have thrived in an academic culture of free and open enquiry, with the intellectual freedom that enables critical thinking; China wants its scientists to innovate, but at the same time the Communist Party under Xi Jinping wants to control what people do, think and say. Made in China 2025 is a top-down, chauvinist endeavour. The Party is on every campus, its shadow present in every laboratory. It hardly seems an atmosphere that is conducive to world-class, or even reliable, science, and Xi shows no inclination to free the minds of his technologists and scientists. Quite the contrary.

China's current technical prowess has been built on naked mercantilism, acquiring know-how through theft and bullying. As America and China decouple, and the West in general begins to push back, limiting China's access to sensitive tech, Beijing's ability to genuinely innovate will be sorely tested. The competition is about more than producing the next generation of gadgets, it is about two cultures of innovation. Yet there is one field where China's surveillance state has an inbuilt advantage – artificial intelligence.

The race for dominance in AI is about more than technology – it is about security, freedom and power. AI is a key enabling technology around which future economies will be built. Most current AI systems can be better described as machine learning, which involves crunching vast data sets, looking for patterns and anomalies. But its revolutionary potential ranges from medicine, to self-driving cars and autonomous weapons; it is also at the heart of surveillance, where China already leads the world.

China's advantage lies in data, the raw material for the hungry algorithms of AI – the 'oil' of the future, as it is sometimes called. The more data available, the better those algorithms can be trained, and the more products and services they can offer. China has a trove of it, thanks in part to its massive online population, but mostly because of weak data protection and almost complete disregard for privacy. Tech companies must share their data with the Party; they work hand in hand, and together they are able to follow, monitor and leverage every aspect – every data point – that make up an individual's life, without any of those pesky Western concerns about individual rights.

'This huge amount of data can be cranked through the AI engine for better predictions, better efficiency, higher profits, less labour, less cost and so on. The data advantage is a huge one,' former Google China boss Kai-Fu Lee told *Wired* magazine in an interview that was headlined 'Why China will win the global race for complete AI dominance'.[42] Lee left Google after the company pulled out of China and now runs a Beijing-based firm investing in Chinese AI start-ups. He has become the most prominent cheerleader for Chinese tech, telling *Wired* editor Greg Williams, 'Chinese users are willing to trade their personal privacy data for convenience or safety.'

This self-serving argument is frequently made by the tech industry and hardly bears scrutiny since it assumes Chinese internet users have a choice about how their data is harvested and used, and by whom. And, in the surveillance state, they most certainly do not.

Beijing's hunger for data extends beyond China. The Belt and Road Initiative provides another vast source, feeding China's AI algorithms with a greater variety of inputs on which to train, and through which to watch over the client states it is creating. In many countries, particularly the emerging economies of Africa and Asia, China is building the entire digital infrastructure, with few safeguards over where the data generated is stored or how it is used. 'Along China's new digital silk road, connectivity means control, control from Beijing. The absorption of huge data sets from the recipient countries will increase the depth and diversity of China's own data, with unforeseen consequences for the future of individual freedom and universal human rights,' said journalist Brian McGleenon, in his investigation of Chinese influence in Cambodia.[43]

Chinese-owned apps available for download in Western democracies have also come under scrutiny. The US Committee on Foreign Investment forced the Chinese owner of Grindr, a gay dating app, to sell the app because of national security concerns. The committee feared the Chinese government could use personal data given to the app to blackmail American citizens over their sexual preferences or HIV status.[44]

The Trump administration also targeted TikTok, a wildly popular short-video sharing app owned by a Chinese tech company called ByteDance, with close ties to the Communist Party. The app has more than 100 million users in the US and is particularly popular among teenagers. Many commentators depicted Trump as a killjoy, his threats to ban the app another sign of the incoherence of his China policy. In fact, there are good reasons to be seriously concerned about TikTok. All apps collect and leverage data on users, but TikTok is particularly 'zealous', according to an analysis by ProtonMail, a secure email provider, which describes TikTok as 'a grave privacy threat that likely shares data with the Chinese government'.[45]

If you download the app, it collects your IP address, browsing history, details of your mobile carrier, device and location. That's all before creating an account. When you sign up (with phone number or email, and date of birth), TikTok asks for permission to access your other social media accounts, contact lists and GPS data. When you start using it, the app logs details of every video you upload, like and share, as well as how long you watch them. 'TikTok's data collection is extreme, even for a social media platform that collects its users' data to serve them with targeted ads,' ProtonMail states.

TikTok has been fined $5.7 million by the US Federal Trade Commission for illegally collecting personal information on children under thirteen, and the app has faced a similar investigation in the UK.[46] A class action lawsuit filed against TikTok and ByteDance by users in California alleges that the app harvests biometric data (such as face scans) from videos and photos without user permission.[47] TikTok has also been scrutinised for temporarily taking down a video criticising China's inhumane treatment of Uighur Muslims, prompting fears that it was bringing Chinese-style censorship to America – what Marco Rubio, a US senator, called 'nefarious efforts to censor information inside free societies'.[48]

For its part, ByteDance claims that data on non-Chinese users is not kept on Chinese servers and that decisions about what to show to American users are taken in America. As we have already seen, such assurances are hardly credible given the reality of Chinese law, and the close relationship between the Party and China's tech companies. In addition, TikTok's privacy policy explicitly reserves the right to share user information with other members of its 'corporate group'.

As ByteDance came under growing pressure in the US, it was reported that the company was in discussions with the British government to set up an international headquarters in London. While the Chinese company might face some restrictions on shifting data out of the UK, Prime Minister Boris Johnson's advisers did not consider it a security threat like Huawei and it would likely not be blocked, according to Bloomberg.[49] Not for the first time, the British government was somewhat behind the curve in recognising the reality of China's surveillance state.

The US also moved against the Chinese app WeChat, which in the US is mostly used by Chinese-Americans, as well as students and other expats to keep in touch with family, friends and events in China. The app has around 1 billion users, the majority of them inside China, where, as we have seen, it is the 'app for everything', an entire digital ecosystem and an almost indispensable part of everyday life. It enables its users to purchase and organise all manner of goods, travel and financial services, as well as being a platform for social media, messaging and news. As such it is an important arm of the surveillance state, facilitating tracking, censorship and disinformation. It has different rules for users outside of China, and in theory at least those registering with a non-Chinese phone number (around 100 million) are exempt from censorship. Yet, as we saw earlier in this book, it has been used as a means to intimidate and threaten members of the overseas Uighur community, as well as monitoring their contacts with relatives inside China. The FBI has alleged that China used WeChat to communicate with military researchers who entered the United States to steal scientific research.[50] An investigation by Citizen Lab found evidence that communications among WeChat users outside China are under political surveillance and that this content is then used to train algorithms which monitor and censor users inside China. In other words, while sensitive political content shared among users outside China was not blocked, it was fed into the censorship system at home so that the same content could be quickly flagged and blocked should it find its way into China.[51]

As officials were contemplating the future of WeChat in the US, cybersecurity researchers revealed a vulnerability in the app that controls the world's most popular consumer drones, which are made in China by a company called DJI. The researchers stated that the app on Google's Android operating system harvests large amounts of personal information that could be exploited by the Chinese government.[52]

China has a voracious appetite for data, harvested with little restraint at home and increasingly abroad. This data is being used to train and develop AI systems; it is being exploited in an ethical wasteland, where maintaining the grip of the Communist Party is the single dominant consideration in its deployment.

China is a warning of what can happen when repressive new technologies are introduced without oversight or accountability. For this reason it would be dangerous to see AI competition with China as purely technical; it is equally about governance, and here is where democracies should have a huge potential advantage. AI is a foundational technology upon which all manner of things can be built – good and bad. Perhaps the most effective counterweight to China's authoritarian standards has come from Europe, where the General Data Protection Regulation (GDPR) has set widely adopted rules on privacy. The EU is now looking at rules to limit the potential harm from AI systems by making algorithms less biased and more accountable – to embed democratic values in AI.

The upheaval in Hong Kong, and the imposition of a national security law by Beijing, were watched closely by Taiwan, the self-governing democratic island that China claims is part of its territory. Beijing has vowed 'unification' by force if necessary, and has touted a Hong Kong-style 'one country two systems' model for the island. But that model is now discredited and lies in tatters on the smouldering streets of the former British colony. In January 2020, Tsai Ing-wen, who had placed Taiwan's democracy and sovereignty at the heart of her campaign, was re-elected president. A year earlier, she had appeared to be in political trouble, but China's bullying – including cyberattacks and disinformation campaigns – and the protests in Hong Kong assured her a landslide victory. She has vowed to strongly defend the island's de facto independence.

The Hong Kong protests and Tsai's landslide victory were both driven by a hunger to defend democratic rights, but they were also expressions of revulsion against the bleak surveillance state Xi is constructing on their doorstep. In both cases, the Communist Party's obduracy and heavy-handedness seems to have inflamed passions.

There are also suggestions that Xi badly misread the mood in both places – as he did the underlying anger against China that has been welling in the United States and the West more generally. The tendency of supplicants to 'tell the emperor what he wants to hear' has always been a fundamental weakness of dictators. As the dictator's power grows, the willingness to challenge him with unwelcome news diminishes – and no end of surveillance seems to avoid it. In Hong Kong, the Party leadership has relied on advice from a network of sycophantic pro-Beijing tycoons and mediocre bureaucrats-turned-politicians, who long claimed Hong Kong was primarily an economic city with no real interest in politics. Those same voices, along with pro-Beijing pundits, claimed Hong Kong had a patriotic 'silent majority', tired of the protests. In November 2019, after almost six months of pro-democracy protests, that was put to the test when the government allowed district council elections to go ahead. These local contests are the only ones in the Hong Kong system that are fully democratic – and the 'silent majority' spoke. In a record turnout, pro-democracy candidates swept the board, capturing 80 per cent of the seats; the vote for the government's allies collapsed.[53]

All of which begs a bigger question: Are Xi Jinping's dictatorial actions those of a strong and confident leader, or those of a paranoid dictator, presiding over a regime that is far more brittle than commonly portrayed?

Amid the violent clashes in Hong Kong, the New York Times reported stirrings of discontent against Xi among senior Communist Party officials, which the newspaper described as 'quiet grumbling that his imperious style and authoritarian concentration of power contributed to the government's misreading of the scope of discontent in Hong Kong'.[54] The newspaper also published leaked documents confirming details of the Party's mass internment of the Uighurs and other Muslim minorities, and how Xi Jinping himself laid the groundwork for the crackdown. It was, the *New York Times* reported, 'one of the most significant leaks of government papers from inside China's ruling Communist Party for decades'.[55] In December 2019, news trickled out of Guangdong, the neighbouring province to Hong Kong, of a violent protest in the town Wenlou, where riot police clashed with residents protesting against a local construction project. Eyewitnesses reported slogans similar to those being used in Hong Kong, including 'Revolution now!'[56]

In June 2020, an audio recording circulated online in which Cai Xia, a former professor at the elite Central Party School, a higher education facility for top officials, accused Xi Jinping of turning the Party into a 'political zombie' and said the current system is now beyond repair.[57] She was expelled from the Party and fled from China, telling the *Guardian* in a subsequent interview that she was happy to be expelled, that discontent in the Party is widespread, and that Xi and his 'unchecked power' had become an obstacle to progress.[58] Xi had turned China into an 'enemy of the world', she said, speaking from a secret location. 'It is a vicious cycle. After a wrong decision is made, the result is not good. But those below are too afraid to tell him and wrong decisions continue to be made until the situation is out of control. In this vicious cycle, there is no way to stop the country from sliding towards disaster.'

Debate about China's surveillance state has been largely stifled inside China, but in November 2019, a court in Hangzhou ordered a private wildlife park to delete facial recognition data and pay compensation to a legal academic who had sued the park. Guo Bing claimed a newly installed entry system violated his privacy. It was the first lawsuit of its kind in China, and it attracted strong support on social media.[59] A month later, Lao Dongyan, a law professor at Tsinghua University wrote a critique of Beijing metro's decision to deploy facial recognition technology. 'This is crazy,' she wrote on her WeChat account. 'I want to ask, where will it end? . . . is it necessary to fully install face recognition machines on all roads and in all public places, in order to intercept pedestrians, and interrogate and search them at any time, and detain those who are considered to be dangerous to safety?' It is a brave and valid question.[60] It is too early to describe this as a serious push-back against the surveillance state, but it does contradict the argument of surveillance apologists that people in China are more willing to trade away their privacy for convenience.

There have been other quiet acts of subversion. Two Chinese AI chatbots, BabyQ and Little Bing, represented by a penguin and a little girl respectively, were taken offline after they went rogue. BabyQ, responding to the comment 'Long live the Communist Party,' replied, 'Do you think that such a corrupt and incompetent political regime can live forever?' It also informed questioners, 'There needs to be democracy.' The responses were shared widely online. It's not entirely clear how BabyQ developed its political consciousness, but it is likely to have been taught it through interactions with its users.[61]

None of these events in themselves suggest that Xi Jinping is about to be toppled, but they do point to festering discontent. It has often been said the Chinese Communist Party has an unwritten contract with its people. The Party delivers stability and economic growth, and a measure of economic and social freedom in return for political compliance. As far as this has ever been true, it is now fraying. The Party is tightening its grip on all aspects of society and far from being an unstoppable juggernaut, the country's debt-ridden economy is far more fragile than is commonly appreciated – and will be tested further by the trade war with America and the economic fallout from Covid-19.

As we have seen, 'telling the emperor what he wants to hear' can be corrosive to dictatorial rule, and closing off avenues of dissent can also act like a pressure cooker, increasing the likelihood of an explosion. 'Chinese society is a social tinderbox waiting to ignite,' according to David Shambaugh, a China scholar at George Washington University in Washington DC. The country itself is like 'a very dry forest or grassland in summer where multiple fires can break out at any time and then spread quickly,' he writes.[62] Xi Jinping's China is a surveillance state the likes of which has not been seen before. It is also a place where political and economic lying has become normalised, and where written laws and rules mean nothing. All these features were laid out for the world to see when Covid-19 emerged in the Chinese city of Wuhan in December 2019.

CHAPTER 11

The Communist Party Virus

The last photograph of Dr Li Wenliang alive is a selfie he posted to his social media account at the beginning of February 2020. It shows him in bed wearing a ventilator mask, a patient in the intensive care unit of his own hospital. It is a haunting image in which he stares intensely at the camera; there is fear in his eyes, but also defiance. 'I think there should be more than one voice in a healthy society,' he said in an interview by text shortly before he died with Covid-19 on 6 February.[1]

By Dr Li's definition of a healthy society, Xi Jinping's Communist Party is rotten to the core. The Party's initial cover-up of the outbreak of Covid-19 and its negligence cost China and the world time and countless lives. Li's persecution after he blew the whistle at the end of December 2019 is testament to the repression and corruption at the heart of the surveillance state. For all the technology modern China has accumulated, the Party's default position is one of deceit. Its dishonesty is so hard-wired, it is almost Pavlovian.

Li Wenliang, thirty-four years old when he died, was an ophthalmologist at Wuhan Central hospital. On 30 December, he had alerted a WeChat group of former medical classmates that seven people had been quarantined in his hospital and were suffering from an unspecified coronavirus that reminded him of SARS, a virus that killed almost 800 people after emerging in China in 2002. He headed his post, 'Seven cases of SARS in the Huanan Wholesale Seafood Market,' since all the patients had worked in the warren of alleyways that made up the local wet market. 'Coronavirus confirmed, and type being determined,' he wrote in an update. 'Tell your family and relatives to take care.' By that evening, the information was circulating widely on social media – rapidly pursued by the internet censors. Li was summoned by the hospital in the middle of the night for a dressing down, and forced to write a self-criticism in which he agreed the leak 'had a negative impact' on efforts to investigate the outbreak.[2]

Ai Fen, director of emergency at Wuhan Central, was also repri-manded by the hospital authorities for 'spreading rumours' after she shared lab results with colleagues. She argued that the disease could be contagious, but was told that her actions caused panic and 'damaged the stability' of Wuhan. Hospital staff were forbidden from passing messages or images related to the virus, and when Ai asked her staff to wear protective clothing and masks, the authorities told them not to do so.[3]

The Wuhan Health Commission issued an 'urgent notice' that no one was to 'disclose information to the public without authorisation'. In its first official statement about the virus, it said that researchers were investigating twenty-seven cases of viral pneumonia, but there was 'no obvious evidence of human-to-human transmission', and 'the disease is preventable and controllable.'[4] On 1 January 2020, police and health officials shut down the Huanan market, and workers clad in hazmat suits moved in, spraying disinfectant and washing down stalls. But the authorities continued to make reassuring noises, suggesting they had stopped the virus at its source.[5]

On 3 January, Li Wenliang was among eight doctors summoned by police and accused of spreading rumours and disrupting social order. He was issued with a one-page letter – a warning, stamped with a red police seal – which he later posted online. 'The PSB [Public Security Bureau] hopes you can actively cooperate, heed the advice of the police, and stop your illegal behaviour. Can you do this?' it reads. 'Yes, I can,' Li scrawls on the letter. 'We hope you can calm down and reflect. We hereby solemnly warn you: If you choose to remain obstinate and unrepentant, and continue your unlawful behaviour, you will meet the full force of the law! Do you understand?' the transcript continues. Li then writes, 'I understand.'[6]

Li went back to work at Wuhan Central, where he treated an eighty-two-year-old woman, a stallholder at the market, for glaucoma. He didn't wear a mask, since the woman showed no symptoms, but she had already been infected with Covid-19. She passed it to Li, and a few days later he began to cough. As a precaution, Li sent his son and five-month pregnant wife to stay with his in-laws. He checked into a hotel, but his condition worsened, and he was soon back in hospital, in isolation.[7]

The authorities continued to insist the impact of the virus was limited and under control. This was no time for bad news, since delegates were gathering in the city for the two biggest political meetings of the year, the annual sessions of the Wuhan and provincial legislatures, which began on 6 January. These People's congresses are rubber-stamp jamborees, which meet largely to sing the praises of the Party, and applaud whatever Party leaders have to say. There were to be no distractions from this happy chorus, and for two weeks while the meetings were in session, no new Covid-19 cases were reported. In their addresses to congress, no city or provincial leader mentioned the virus.

On 15 January, Li Qun, head of the Chinese Centre for Disease Control and Prevention, told state television, 'After careful screening and prudent judgement, we have reached the latest understanding that the risk of sustained human-to-human transmission is low.'[8] Doctors knew otherwise. The number of unusual chest illnesses seen at Wuhan hospitals continued to surge. At one hospital, doctors were told, 'Don't use the words viral pneumonia on the image reports,' according to a complaint filed with the National Health Commission on a government website. The complaint has since been removed.[9] 'We watched more and more patients come in as the radius of the spread of infection became larger,' said Ai Fen in a later interview. More medical staff fell ill, and they began to see patients with no connection to the market. 'I knew there must be human-to-human transmission,' she told *Renwu*, a Chinese magazine. The interview was deleted by censors soon after it was posted.[10]

On Sunday 18 January, the Wuhan district of Baibuting went ahead with its annual mass banquet, the twentieth anniversary of the event, during which the organisers sought to break a world record for the total number of dishes served. Some 40,000 people attended, crammed around long tables, straining with food. Fang Fang, a novelist who lives in Wuhan and who maintained an online diary throughout the crisis, wrote that holding the gathering at that time, 'should effectively be considered a form of criminal action . . . how can you expect people *not* to get infected?'[11]

On the day of the banquet, Zhong Nanshan arrived in Wuhan, at the head of a team of experts from Beijing. Zhong, eighty-three and semi-retired, is China's most renowned respiratory disease expert and epidemiologist. He is a tall, bespectacled man, who exudes a quiet charm and authority. At times he can come across as faintly eccentric, but is unafraid to speak his mind. He wields huge moral authority, having played a key role in the fight against SARS, during which he challenged officials who played down the severity of that coronavirus. I met him at the Guangzhou Institute of Respiratory Diseases in late 2003, after SARS was brought under control. The authorities had promised to close down live animal markets, thought to be the source of the virus. 'That's what they say, that's what they say,' Zhong told me, shaking his head.

The authorities were lying, and, following Zhong's cryptic clues, I was able to locate and secretly film at one reopened market. Its filthy, fetid alleyways were strewn with blood and trash, and stacked high with cages of all manner of live animals for the dining table, from rats and foxes to dogs and cats. Most worrying, civet cats were on sale again. These were thought to be the intermediary animal through which the SARS virus travelled from bats to humans.

Seventeen years on, Zhong was at the epicentre of another outbreak of a novel coronavirus, and for the second time in his career he delivered another reality check. Two days after arriving in Wuhan, on 20 January, he went on national television to confirm what local doctors had suspected for weeks – that Covid-19 was indeed spreading between people. It has been suggested that it was Zhong's advice that jolted Xi Jinping into action. In his first public remarks on the outbreak, Xi said the virus 'must be taken seriously', and a cordon sanitaire was imposed on Wuhan and three other cities three days later. This, of course, supports a narrative which scapegoats corrupt and negligent local officials, unwilling or afraid to pass bad news up the Communist Party food chain. It is a narrative challenged by Party documents obtained by the Associated Press, which suggest the leadership already knew how contagious the virus was. The documents show that national health officials warned in a briefing on 14 January that, 'The epidemic situation is still severe and complex, the most severe challenge since SARS in 2003, and is likely to develop into a major public health event.'[12]

An article in the journal *Qiu Shi*, which means 'seeking truth' and is published by the Party's central committee, suggests Xi Jinping was overseeing the response to Covid-19 even earlier. It describes him issuing instructions on containing the outbreak during a 7 January meeting of the Politburo standing committee.[13]

The medical briefing described in the documents obtained by the Associated Press (AP) may have been prompted by the first international case of Covid-19, reported in Thailand the day before. That sent a clear signal that the outbreak would not be contained medically or politically within China, and fuelled the growing alarm of epidemiologists world-wide. Although Beijing shared the genetic sequencing of Covid-19 on 12 January, it would be another five whole weeks before a full World Health Organization delegation with international experts was allowed to visit Wuhan.

Publicly, WHO director-general, Dr Tedros Adhanom Ghebreyesus, a former Ethiopian foreign minister who gained the top WHO job in 2017 with strong Chinese support, praised Beijing's efforts and the 'transparency they have demonstrated'.[14] But recordings of internal WHO meetings, also obtained by the AP, tell a different story. It suggests Beijing was not sharing data during the critical early days of the outbreak. 'We're going on very minimal information,' said American epidemiologist Maria Van Kerkhove, the WHO's technical lead for Covid-19, in one internal meeting on 6 January. 'It's clearly not enough for you to do proper planning.' The recordings reveal enormous WHO frustration as they try and coax information out of China, aware that every day of foot-dragging could potentially cost thousands of lives. At one meeting, Michael Ryan, the WHO's head of emergencies, says he fears a repeat of the 2002 SARS epidemic. 'This is exactly the same scenario, endlessly trying to get updates from China about what was going on,' he said, suggesting they increase pressure on Beijing. 'We need to see the data. It's absolutely important at this point.'[15]

The delays could not have come at a worse time. It was the run-up to the Chinese New Year, the Year of the Rat, with a week-long holiday beginning on 24 January – an annual shutdown that has been described as the world's largest human migration, during which three billion trips are taken. Wuhan sits at the confluence of the Han and Yangtze rivers in the centre of China. It is a travel hub, and an estimated five million people left the city in the days before travel restrictions were imposed, partly because of New Year, and partly out of growing fear of the virus.[16]

They travelled across China and abroad, carrying New Year gifts, goodwill – and Covid-19, hastening its spread. 'If we could have taken strict preventive measures in early December or even early January, we would have greatly reduced the number of patients,' conceded Zhong Nanshan, the respiratory disease expert.[17] Southampton University researchers have attempted to quantify the impact, using a complex modelling of population movements. They conclude that the spread of the virus could have been massively reduced, stating: 'If interventions in the country could have been conducted one week, two weeks, or three weeks earlier, cases could have been reduced by 66 percent, 86 percent and 95 percent respectively.'[18]

In her diary, the novelist Fang Fang characterises the time between Li Wenliang blowing the whistle and Zhong Nanshan's announcement on human to human transmission as '20 days of delays, 20 days of lies', the toll of which is 'much costlier than simply the number of deaths'.

Dr Li spent his Chinese New Year in isolation in the Wuhan Central hospital, though with no shortage of goodwill messages, as his story swept through Chinese social media, trailed by the inevitable Communist Party censors. By the end of January he could no longer breathe on his own, needing a ventilator, but he continued to be upbeat, posting to his WeChat account, and texting about the importance of truth and transparency. When he died on 6 February, the explosion of online anger and grief at first overwhelmed the censors. On Weibo, a hashtag meaning 'we want freedom of speech' was shared or viewed 2 million times before it was deleted; 'Wuhan government owes Li Wenliang an apology' was viewed millions of times before it too was quashed. Social media was flooded with emojis of candles, and pictures of Li with barbed wire around his surgical mask. There were cryptic references to the Chernobyl nuclear disaster, which exposed the corruption and incompetence of the Soviet Communist Party, and hastened the collapse of the Soviet Union. Social media accounts were suspended in droves for 'spreading malicious rumours'.[19]

The Party was rattled, and hours after news of Li's death broke, it attempted to dampen the anger by resurrecting him. Reports of his death were deleted from official media, and the hospital announced that he was in fact still alive. Censors even blocked a tribute from the World Health Organization expressing its sadness at Li's passing. Hospital staff claimed the news had been quashed on orders from 'leaders' concerned that Li's death might be inconvenient and 'troublesome'.[20] Another message leaked online, a propaganda bureau directive, ordered media outlets to 'control the heat' of the debate, and to 'strictly control harmful information'.[21]

Later, the Party would change tack, and hail the doctor it had attempted to muzzle as a hero. Though not nearly as heroic as Xi Jinping, 'The man of the hour,' and 'commander-in-chief in China's war against Covid-19,' according to the *Xinhua* news agency.[22] In spite of being all but invisible in the early days of the outbreak, his supposed dedication proved he has a 'pure heart like a newborn's that always puts the people as his number one priority'.[23] Top local officials were duly sacked; in time-honoured fashion, any missteps were blamed on a few bad apples out in the provinces.

At 10 a.m. on Thursday 23 January, transport in and out of Wuhan was suspended and checkpoints set up on all exit roads; a city of 11 million people was shut down and closed off from the outside world – a lockdown that would last for seventy-six days. Because of the lack of information and early assurances from officials that there was nothing to fear, many residents did not grasp the seriousness of the outbreak until the shutdown announcement. Airports and train stations were besieged by people trying to get out before the deadline, hospitals immediately overwhelmed by those fearful they might have symptoms of Covid-19. In her online diary, Fang Fang describes the 'state of utter panic' that gripped the city for a five-day period that straddled the shutdown. 'Those were five terrifying days that seemed to last forever; meanwhile, the virus was quickly spreading throughout the city, and even the government appeared as if it was at a loss as to what to do,' she wrote.[24]

Schools and universities, already on holiday, were shut indefinitely, as were offices, factories and all shops apart from those selling food and medicine. Public transport was suspended and private vehicles without special permission barred, leaving streets empty and silent. The situation in those early days was desperate. Harrowing stories emerged of the sick unable to get treatment, pleading for help from their windows, and of bodies stacked in a minibus outside one hospital; hotels and shopping centres became makeshift quarantine centres. Fang Fang described the fear and desperation in a 9 February diary posting: 'Those people infected early not only die but they face hopelessness. Their cries go unanswered, their attempts for medical intervention are useless, their search for effective treatment proves fruitless. There are simply too many sick people and not enough beds; the hospitals simply cannot keep up with the demand.'

Initially, residents were allowed out of their homes, but the restrictions were progressively tightened. Some areas permitted only one family member to leave home every two days to buy necessities; others barred any movement, leaving residents dependent on couriers.[25] Although Wuhan was the epicentre of the outbreak, restrictions quickly spread beyond the city. By the middle of February, an estimated 500 million people in China faced at least some restrictions on movement. Almost fifty cities and four provinces had lockdowns in place.[26] To police this colossal shutdown, the Communist Party deployed the full power of the surveillance machine it had so painstakingly built, complemented by a more familiar and casual brutality against those who refused to comply.

A priority was to track down those who left Wuhan ahead of the lockdown – by following their digital trail around China. That trail was left by smart IDs, needed for booking rail and plane tickets, and hotels – and pretty much everything else you do in China. That was supplemented by data from e-payments and social media, as well as mobile phone location data and images from the country's vast network of facial recognition cameras – all data to which the authorities had unfettered access. Search engine giant Baidu mapped the trips and final destination of those who left the city by car. 'In this day and age, you can trace everyone's movements with big data,' Li Lanjuan, an adviser to the National Health Commission, boasted in an interview on state television.[27] One region of Chongqing, a city in the south-west of the country, boasted that it had quickly located 5,500 people, while in the eastern city of Nanjing the authorities were able not only to locate a sick man from Wuhan, but to track his journey, minute by minute, through the city's subway system. They then published the data to warn anybody who might have been in the vicinity at the time. The government appealed for those who had left Wuhan to identify themselves; one area of Hebei in northern China offered 1,000 yuan ($140) for each Wuhan person reported by residents, while fearful authorities in the eastern province of Jiangsu used metal poles to barricade the door of a family who'd returned from Wuhan.[28]

A system developed to keep tabs on China's 1.4 billion people, maintaining social control and monitoring behaviour for threats to the Communist Party, was repurposed to enforce quarantine rules and fight the virus. It was a perfect test bed, giving the authorities the incentive and excuse to bring together numerous data sources, methods and systems, and leveraging their capabilities more fully, in the knowledge that few people were going to complain about intrusive surveillance during a health emergency.

Phone location data alerted the authorities if a sick person left home, tracking where they went. It also provided a trail showing where they'd been for two weeks *before* falling ill, an app alerting those who might have been in contact and were at risk of infection. People were required to install smartphone 'traffic light' apps, which controlled movement and identified those who had been diagnosed with the virus or had visited high-risk areas or had other risky contacts. The app required the user to submit information about their health status and other personal details, while at the same time harvesting online behavioural and location data from the phone. It then assigned a colour code – green, yellow or red – which indicated whether the holder was an infection risk. Checkpoints and automated code readers were everywhere – at the entrances to underground stations, offices, malls, apartment blocks, banks and even in taxis, stopping anyone without a green code. Red meant immediate quarantine. Main roads into the southern city of Shenzhen were policed by drones hovering above traffic and holding a code which drivers had to scan before being allowed entry. And of course, the authorities had unfettered access to all this data.

Facial recognition companies rushed to update their systems. One boasted that a new thermal camera, rolled out in Beijing, could detect elevated temperature, and then cross-reference with body and facial data to identify the person; another leading AI firm said it had built a similar system to be used at building entrances that was able to identify people in spite of their wearing face coverings.[29]

Elsewhere, drones were used to target people on the street who were outside without good reason; a video from northern China posted by the *Global Times*, a Party newspaper, shows a drone pursuing an elderly woman who is walking without a face mask. 'Yes, auntie, this is the drone speaking to you,' says a voice from the machine. 'You'd better go back home and wash your hands.' In Ruichang City in China's eastern Jiangxi province, another video shows a drone haranguing a man who is not wearing a mask. 'Throw your cigarette away, put on your mask. Do you hear me? I'm talking to you!' booms the drone.[30]

For those deemed to be breaking the rules, retribution could be harsh. In one video posted online, police wearing yellow hi-vis jackets and surgical masks enter a house and break up a game of mah-jong, smashing up the table as a small group of terrified villagers looks on.[31] Armed with surveillance data, officials went door to door carrying out heath checks, forcing anybody with symptoms into isolation. Another video shows officials in white hazmat suits dragging a screaming, shouting family out of their flat in order to quarantine them.[32] If a family were suspected of exposure to the virus, it wasn't unusual for their door to be sealed while tests were carried out. A disabled boy reportedly died after he was left without food, water or help when his father and brother were quarantined.[33]

Villages and residential compounds were told to enforce local restrictions, and the thuggish behaviour of overzealous officials was likened to Cultural Revolution-era 'red guards'. In another video, a gang of these monitors, wearing red arm bands, its leader carrying a megaphone, bursts into a house where a family is again playing mah-jong. One of the players stands and angrily throws one of his tiles at the intruders before he's dragged outside and beaten. The table is then pulled outside and smashed to pieces.[34]

In one of his videos, self-styled citizen journalist Chen Qiushi is in a hospital against a backdrop of sick and dying Covid-19 patients, most on oxygen, some lying on the floor. He pans to a woman, her arms wrapped around a man in a wheelchair, who appears to be dead. The woman is shouting for help. Chen then says, 'As long as I am alive, I will speak about what I have seen and what I have heard. I am not afraid of dying. Why should I be afraid of you, Communist Party?'[35] Another citizen journalist, Li Zehua, reports on a local neighbourhood committee's efforts to cover up the number of cases, saying 'I don't want to remain silent, or shut my eyes and ears.'[36] Ren Zhiqiang, a retired property tycoon and vocal member of the Communist Party, calls Xi Jinping a 'clown',[37] while legal scholar and activist Xu Zhiyong writes an essay addressed to Xi, saying, 'You have proved that you lack the most rudimentary competences,' and calling the Party leader 'clueless and hopeless'.[38]

The early weeks of the Covid-19 outbreak saw a remarkable out-burst of online anger and criticism, which seemed to overwhelm the censors. Citizen journalists led the charge, while members of WeChat groups exchanged a steady stream of photos, videos and witness accounts from struggling hospitals. News and rumour swept the inter-net. When a top government official visited Wuhan, videos emerged of residents heckling her, yelling 'Fake, fake, everything is fake' from their balconies as she was led on an inspection tour of their neighbourhood.[39] Even normally compliant state media outlets became more questioning – though their target was largely the local leadership.

'It is as if everyone is in a relay race; as soon as the censors delete a post, netizens repost it again online,' Fang Fang writes in her online diary, likening efforts to stay ahead of the censors to passing a baton. 'There is no way for them to delete everything anymore.' She describes the everyday privations of life under lockdown, its frustrations and mundanities, while becoming increasingly strident in her calls for justice and accountability. '*Not Contagious Between People; It's Controllable and Preventable* – those eight words have transformed Wuhan into a city of blood and tears filled with endless misery,' she writes. She mocks calls to show gratitude to the Communist Party. 'How can we let these people with blood on their hands continue strutting around in front of the people of Wuhan, gesticulating as if they are heroes?' she asks.[40]

By early March, the Wuhan authorities claimed to be bringing the outbreak under control and closed the first of sixteen makeshift hospitals. By that time, the Party had also moved to shut down criticism. Citizen journalists Chen and Li both disappeared. Li live-streamed his last moments of liberty, first in his car, breathlessly appealing for help – 'I'm on the road and someone, I don't know, state security, has started chasing me. I'm driving very fast. Help me.' Then in his apartment, waiting for the knock on the door. 'I'm doing this because I hope more young people can, like me, stand up,' he says as two men in plain clothes are shown entering the apartment. The video then cuts out, and was quickly deleted from China's Twitter-like Weibo platform.[41] Tycoon and Party member Ren was arrested for 'serious violations of discipline and the law', while activist Xu was detained for 'inciting subversion of state power'.

As the crackdown intensified, families and friends warned each other against speaking too openly or critically in their chat groups. One human rights group documented nearly 900 cases of users penalised for online speech, the majority of them accused of 'spreading misinformation, disrupting social order'.[42] There were reports of online critics interrogated for hours, forced to sign pledges of loyalty to the Party and to disavow views deemed to be politically unacceptable – an echo of what had happened to Dr Li Wenliang.[43]

WeChat strengthened its system of keyword censorship, banning hundreds of words, but also word combinations, which enabled the system to more finely target criticism. The largest number of blocked combinations referenced Xi Jinping and other government officials. If they appeared in the same message as words of criticism, such as 'cover-up', 'conceal epidemic' or sarcastic homonyms, such as 'virus of officialdom', then the message would be blocked. The words didn't need to be alongside each other, or even in the same sentence; they could be anywhere in the message. Nearly 200 outlawed word combinations referenced Li Wenliang, the whistle-blowing doctor.[44]

Fang Fang was not detained, but she sensed that danger levels were rising, and friends advised her to stop her diary, which, by late March, was receiving between 3 and 10 million hits per day. 'We've already been tortured by this brother named "censorship" to the point that we are wooden and numb,' she writes. She is targeted by nationalist trolls, whom she likens to the virus itself, and who enjoy an immunity not afforded to critics of the Party. Later, when her diary is translated and published in the West, she is viciously attacked online for 'hating the nation'.[45]

Ai Fen, the director of emergency at Wuhan Central hospital, who had been reprimanded for speaking out when the first Covid-19 cases appeared, gave an angry and moving interview to the Chinese magazine *Renwu*, in which she said, 'If I had known what was to happen, I would not have cared about the reprimand. I would have fucking talked about it to whoever, wherever I could.'[46] Upon publication, censors blocked the article online and called back all printed copies of the magazine. It coincided with Xi Jinping's first visit to Wuhan, on 10 March, and came just a few days before the city claimed to have no new infections. Xi's visit was a signal that the Party thought the fight had been largely won, and they could now concentrate on rewriting the narrative.

A week after Xi returned to Beijing from Wuhan, China claimed to have no new domestic transmission of the virus at all. The health commission said the only cases now detected had come from abroad.[47] Few international experts believe China's data can be trusted, but the numbers fitted the narrative of Xi as conquering hero – the 'commander-in-chief' who defeated Covid-19. Criticism was scrubbed from the internet, families of the dead were warned against speaking out, a chat group set up by mourners was shut down. The media was ordered only to report positive news about the achievements of the Party, which by its swift and decisive action had not only defeated the virus, but in so doing had protected the world. Though as the number of international cases outstripped those in China, the propaganda shifted – China had not so much *saved* the world as *bought it time*, and if the world squandered that time it was down to their own sloppy response.

'China can pull together the imagination and courage needed to deliver a blow to the virus while the United States struggles to handle the outbreak,' boasted the Party's *People's Daily*.[48] At the same time, the Party stoked a fringe conspiracy theory about the origin of Covid-19. Zhao Lijian, the Foreign Ministry spokesman, blamed the American military. He promoted without evidence a claim that Covid-19 had originated in the United States, and was brought to Wuhan by American soldiers participating in the World Military Games in the city the previous October.[49]

Among international epidemiologists, the most plausible explanation is that the virus originated in bats in China, though the challenge is to understand the 'spillover event' when it leapt to humans. As with SARS in 2002, this is likely to have been through an intermediate host – possibly a pangolin, scaly anteaters which are consumed as a delicacy in China and highly prized in traditional medicine. The inventory list of one shop at Wuhan's Huanan market gives a flavour of the country's wild animal trade, listing live wolf pups, golden cicadas, scorpions, bamboo rats, squirrels, foxes, civets, salamanders, turtles and crocodiles among the delicacies on offer. It is far from certain that the virus came out of the market; one theory is that an infected human took it in and the market acted as an accelerator. Either way, the market holds important clues. But research efforts were hampered by a lack of transparency and a refusal to provide access to international experts. At the time of writing, China has yet to share data collected in the market.[50] Chinese researchers have been told that papers on the origin of the virus need to be vetted before publication. A directive to universities from the Ministry of Education's science and technology department said, 'academic papers about tracing the origin of the virus must be strictly and tightly managed.'[51]

Beijing has angrily rejected calls for an independent international investigation into the origin of Covid-19. When Australia called for an inquiry, China threatened an economic boycott, subsequently restricting imports of Australian beef. Canberra accused Beijing of 'economic coercion'.[52] At a meeting of the World Health Assembly, the governing body of the World Health Organization, China agreed to a more vaguely termed inquiry into the WHO's handling of the pandemic.[53] Western diplomats want this to cover the roots of the outbreak, but China's full cooperation seems unlikely, and the independence of the WHO itself has been tainted by its indulgence of China.

Beijing pumped out propaganda and disinformation internationally through thousands of fake and hijacked Twitter accounts. It sought to portray itself as a leader and benefactor in public health, while at the same time rubbishing the faltering efforts of Western democracies, according to a ProPublica investigation.[54] The extent of Beijing's campaign was confirmed in a report prepared by the European Union diplomatic service, which accused China of running 'a global disinformation campaign to deflect blame for the outbreak of the pandemic'. It said that 'both overt and covert tactics have been observed'. But the report was delayed and then toned down after threats from Beijing.[55] In June 2020, Twitter shut down 170,000 accounts linked to the Chinese government, which were engaged in 'a range of coordinated and manipulated activities'.[56] YouTube revealed that it banned almost 2,300 Chinese channels in the second quarter of 2020 alone 'as part of our ongoing investigation into coordinated influence operations linked to China'.[57]

Much of China's propaganda focused on the country's distribution of personal protective equipment around the world – even if much of it was substandard or defective, including testing kits and medical masks rejected by Spain, Turkey and the Netherlands.[58] Britain paid $20 million to two Chinese companies for half a million test kits that were too inaccurate to use.[59] Beijing's efforts were enhanced by the fact that the world is dependent on China for an estimated 42 per cent of personal protective equipment, including around half the world's N95 masks for protecting health workers, and most of the ingredients for the antibiotics to fight secondary infections.[60]

The soft power bid was at times clunky and crude, pressing governments for public praise in exchange for masks.[61] A *Financial Times* investigation suggested that a video, posted by Chinese officials, and apparently showing grateful Italians on their balconies and in the street applauding the Chinese national anthem, had been doctored. Much of the footage was lifted from news reports of applause for medical workers, and was underlaid with the anthem and repeated audio of a man shouting 'Grazie Cina!'[62]

Chinese officials released their Covid-19 data at 3 a.m. every morning – but that was just about the only thing reliable about the figures. At the time of writing, China had publicly recorded more than 100,000 cases and a little under 5,000 deaths,[63] but these figures are challenged by a growing body of anecdotal evidence. One study of the operation of crematoriums and the distribution of funeral urns in Wuhan at the height of the epidemic suggests deaths in that city alone were ten times the official tally. The authors conclude: 'The magnitude of discrepancy between our estimates based on cremation-related data and Chinese official figures in early February, the critical time for response to the COVID-19 pandemic, suggests the need to re-evaluate official statistics from China and consider all available and reasonable data sources for a better understanding of the COVID-19 pandemic.'[64]

A classified US intelligence report to the White House concluded that China under-reported both total cases and deaths from Covid-19, which are both much higher than the official figures suggest. It called the official numbers fake, according to Bloomberg.[65] This appears to be supported by a coronavirus database leaked from the Chinese military's National University of Defense Technology to *Foreign Policy*. 'While not fully comprehensive, the data is incredibly rich: There are more than 640,000 updates of information, covering at least 230 cities – in other words, 640,000 rows purporting to show the number of cases in a specific location at the time the data was gathered,' the magazine reports. The data, which ranges from early February to late April 2020, is much more detailed than the data made publicly available. It includes hospital locations, as well as the names of apartment compounds, hotels, supermarkets, railway stations, restaurants and schools across the breadth of the country. It reports one case of coronavirus in a KFC in the eastern city of Zhenjiang on 14 March, for example, and another outbreak three days later linked to a church in Harbin.[66]

China revised its methodology for counting cases eight times between January and April 2020. Initially the count included only severely ill patients; those who tested positive but did not have symptoms were excluded completely until the beginning of April. This lack of clarity made it very difficult for other nations to understand the disease and the way it was spreading. Other countries also struggled with testing and changed the way infections were counted, but the unreliability of China's data has been especially damaging as the source of the pandemic.

An analysis by *The Economist* of data from China's National Health Commission found not only enormous volatility in the official figures, but a close correlation between sharp statistical changes and political events. Fifteen 'spikes' in cases occurred within a day of the sacking of a provincial official or other significant political event, suggesting the management of information about the spread of the disease was driven primarily by Party interests (or rivalries). 'The unusual spikes in new cases, and the curious way their timing matches political developments, are bound to raise questions about their accuracy,' the newspaper reports.[67]

Another study, this time by Harvard researchers, suggested the virus might have been circulating and causing disruption in Wuhan from late summer 2019, at least four months before the authorities reported a cluster of pneumonia cases with unknown cause to the World Health Organization. The researchers analysed satellite imagery of hospital car parks and queries of disease-related terms to Baidu, China's largest search engine.[68] 'Clearly, there was some level of social disruption taking place well before what was previously identified as the start of the novel coronavirus pandemic,' Dr John Brownstein, who led the research, told ABC News. 'This is all about a growing body of information pointing to something taking place in Wuhan at the time.'[69]

By the middle of June 2020, the authorities claimed to have gone fifty-five days without a locally transmitted case of Covid-19. Then a fresh outbreak hit Beijing – dozens of new infections, which were linked to the Xinfadi wholesale food market, the biggest in Asia. The area around the market was locked down; restaurants, workplaces and hotels were closed. The Party sought to fit this outbreak into its narrative of Covid-19 now being a foreign threat, which had slipped through its defences. Officials claimed to have found the virus on a cutting board used for imported salmon, and described it as a 'European strain'. They later backtracked on the salmon claim, but Party newspapers freshened up their disinformation, claiming that the original virus might not have come from China. 'So much for science-based approaches. It's politically safer to fall back on nationalism. Or xenopescophobia, the fear of foreign fish,' tweeted Drew Thompson, director for China in the Pentagon from 2011 to 2018 and now a research fellow at the Lee Kuan Yew School of Public Policy in Singapore.[70]

Days later, Xu Zhangrun, the constitutional law professor at Tsinghua University we met earlier in Chapter 4, was arrested, dozens of police officers raiding his Beijing home. Xu, a persistent critic of Xi Jinping, had already been barred from teaching. The precise reason for his arrest was not clear, but was likely linked to a critical essay he published in February, at the height of the outbreak in China, in which he said the authorities 'stood by blithely as the crucial window of opportunity that was available to deal with the outbreak snapped shut in their faces'.[71]

The timing is unlikely to have been a coincidence. As the virus flared up again, it was a clear warning to critics and would-be whistle-blowers that another Li Wenliang, the Wuhan doctor who was persecuted when had sought to tell the truth and then succumbed the Covid-19, would not be tolerated.

Why does the Communist Party cover-up and falsify statistics? As we have seen with GDP and other economic figures, China has a long record of manipulating data for political purposes, but the advantage of doing so on an issue so critical to global health, and in the midst of a pandemic seems problematic at best – a surefire way of undermining international trust. Sometimes, the figures coming from China simply defied common sense – as early in the pandemic when travellers from Wuhan began to spread the virus abroad, first in Thailand and Japan, but apparently not around China itself. When Beijing declared in mid-March, that the country had zero new cases over the course of several days, and that all new cases were imported from abroad, it stretched credulity to the point of absurdity. It may be partly due to local officials downplaying the severity of the outbreak in their areas – another case of not wanting to send 'bad' news up the food chain to the emperor. The Party, opaque by nature, may have wished to hide the extent of the health crisis from the public, to manage the news in order to prevent unrest – another example of its obsession with stability. It also flows from an increasingly nationalist world view, so distrustful of outsiders that it borders on the paranoid.

In early July 2020, The World Health Organization announced that it was sending experts to China to 'prepare scientific plans for identifying the zoonotic source of the SARS-COV-2 [Covid-19] virus.'[72] Zoonotic diseases are those that jump from animals to humans, with bats as the main suspect for Covid-19. In a brief statement, the WHO said the mission needed to be well planned with Chinese counterparts, suggesting that the terms of the investigation still needed to be thrashed out and that it would take some time to do so. The mission left China after three weeks, having failed to visit Wuhan, which served to further dampen expectations that the investigation would be speedy, or would be given the necessary data or access to be credible.[73]

The WHO had no initial plans to visit the Wuhan Institute of Virology's Center for Emerging Infectious Diseases, a renowned centre of coronavirus expertise, headed by Shi Zhengli, otherwise known as

'Bat Woman' because of her extensive work on hunting bat viruses. A coronavirus extremely close in structure to Covid-19 was being analysed by scientists at the centre. It had been found in 2013 in an abandoned copper mine in China's south-western Yunnan province, where six workers clearing bat faeces from the mine had fallen ill with a mysterious respiratory disease; three of them died.[74]

The coronavirus being kept in the lab was a 96.2 per cent match to Covid-19, and the lab was carrying out controversial 'gain-of-function' research, which aims to enhance a virus – making it more dangerous in order to better understand how it works and how it can be countered. The Wuhan lab is known as a 'biosafety level-4' facility, one of about seventy of these super-secure labs in thirty countries worldwide, which handle especially nasty bugs. America has more than a dozen, China has two.

The dirty secret of these labs is that they have not always been so biosecure. The world's last known case of smallpox resulted from a 1978 leak from a British laboratory. A 2007 outbreak of foot-and-mouth disease was also traced back to a lab. There have been reports of the accidental release of Ebola and bird flu from an American facility, and of Chinese laboratory workers infected with SARS, an earlier corona-virus, and transmitting it outside.[75]

The US has collaborated with and helped fund bat research in China, but after US officials visited the Wuhan lab in 2018, they sent cables to Washington warning about safety and management weaknesses. 'During interactions with scientists at the WIV laboratory, they noted the new lab has a serious shortage of appropriately trained technicians and investigators needed to safely operate this high-containment lab-oratory,' states a 19 January 2018 diplomatic cable drafted by officials from the US embassy's environment, science and health sections.[76]

Shi Zhengli is highly respected by the international scientific com-munity. Her lab has collected around 15,000 samples from bats and identified 400 new coronaviruses. She was instrumental in linking the 2002 SARS virus to bats, and on 3 February 2020, she and her team were the first to report publicly that Covid-19 was also a bat-derived coronavirus. She has categorically denied that her lab was the origin for Covid-19, and there has been no hard evidence to support the theory that an accident might have taken place and the virus leaked from the lab. 'I guarantee with my life that the virus has nothing to do with my lab,' she said in a social media posting. The likelihood still is that the virus emerged naturally, but China's lack of transparency, throwing a

blanket of secrecy around its labs, and its refusal to provide information about the origin of the virus seem guaranteed to stoke all manner
of conspiracy theories.

If the surveillance state described in this book has a technical weakness, it is one of digestion. The system is producing so much data that
some experts have questioned Beijing's ability to crunch and make
sense of it all, even with the significant strides it is making in artificial
intelligence. It is one thing building a digital cage around Xinjiang, that
restive far western region with a population of around 22 million people, so the argument goes, but a far bigger challenge to totally ensnare
1.4 billion.

Covid-19 provided the perfect test bed, allowing the authorities to
pull together and leverage all manner of surveillance data on movement and behaviour in the name of public wellbeing. In Hangzhou,
where the 'traffic light' health surveillance app was pioneered, officials
suggested it should be expanded to rank citizens with a 'personal health
index'. The city's Communist Party secretary described the app as an
'intimate health guardian' for residents.[77] It has never been explained
precisely how the system arrived at its colour coding, but if it were
to become a more permanent feature in China, it seems certain that
the Party's concept of 'unhealthy' would expand well beyond physical
wellbeing and cover behaviour deemed to threaten its rule.

App-based tracking was harnessed by other countries in their
fight against Covid-19, including democracies such as Taiwan and
South Korea, but they have been careful to proceed with transparency,
democratic oversight and consent. Both have been highly successful
in bringing the virus under control. Beijing has presented itself as a
model, though the world can learn more from democratic Taiwan; its
response was swift, efficient and tech- and data-driven, but it was also
transparent and open. At the time of writing, it had fewer than 1,000
confirmed cases and just eight deaths. Yet bullying by China, which
claims Taiwan as its own, has denied Taiwan a seat at the WHO, even
as an observer. When New Zealand publicly supported a WHO role for
Taiwan, it was warned by Beijing to 'immediately stop making wrong
statements on Taiwan, to avoid damaging our bilateral relationship'.[78]

After declaring victory over the virus, Beijing stepped up repression
against critics at home, while internationally it resumed an aggressive

foreign policy in which menace has now replaced diplomacy. Its post-virus behaviour has underlined a central theme of this book – that Beijing cannot be trusted.

With the world preoccupied with the fight against Covid-19, fifteen of Hong Kong's most prominent supporters of democracy were arrested and charged with 'unlawful assembly'. They included eighty-one-year-old Martin Lee, a barrister and the territory's most prominent champion of democratic rights. Lee helped draw up the 'one country two systems' framework under which Hong Kong is supposedly governed, and which the Communist Party then tore up with the imposition on Hong Kong of a national security law that paves the way for mainland-style repression. As we have seen, it targets any conduct deemed to threaten national security, including subversion and 'activities by foreign forces' that 'interfere' in Hong Kong's affairs. Ominously, it opens the door to the deployment of Chinese security forces and the infrastructure of the surveillance state.

The authorities prohibited for the first time the annual 4 June vigil to remember the victims of the Tiananmen Square massacre, citing concerns over social distancing. They used the same excuse to delay legislative elections by a year, having already banned more than a dozen opposition candidates from taking part. Some 4 June commemorations took place online, however, bringing together activists and dissidents outside and inside China, using Zoom, the video conferencing app that became an important tool for individuals, businesses – even parliamentarians – during the Covid-19 lockdown. But California-based Zoom, acting at the request of Beijing, shut down three meetings and suspended the accounts of participants. 'The Chinese government informed us that this activity is illegal in China and demanded that Zoom terminate the meetings and host accounts,' a Zoom spokesperson said.[79] It was a depressingly familiar refrain from Western executives, especially those in the technology industry.

Within a month of the national security law being imposed, there were reports of teachers who had supported the pro-democracy protests being reprimanded or even removed from their posts, as the party began to stamp out dissent and paved the way for replacing Hong Kong's more liberal education tradition with the 'patriotic education' that Xi Jinping has made a key pillar of his rule.[80] Benny Tai, a law professor and one of the founders of the 2014 umbrella movement, was fired from his post at Hong Kong University, and the territory's security chief vowed to get rid of 'bad apples' in the education system, who he accused of poisoning young minds and turning them against the government.[81]

More than 200 police officers raided the headquarters of Next Digital Media and arrested Jimmy Lai, a seventy-two-year-old newspaper magnate and one of the Communist Party's most fierce critics. *Apple Daily*, Next's flagship newspaper, live-streamed the raid, showing Lai being led out in handcuffs. The video went viral, and the following day's print run was seven times bigger than normal.[82] Warrants were issued for six pro-democracy activists living in exile, one of them now an American citizen. Chinese state media reported that the men were wanted for 'incitement to seccession and collusion with foreign forces'.[83] It was a chilling reminder of the extra-territorial reach of the new national security law.

When in August 2020 the authorities launched a mass Covid-19 testing programme, opposition politicians and activists called for a boycott. With medical staff from mainland China helping conduct the tests, critics feared it might be a cover for the mass collection of DNA for surveillance purposes, as had happened in Xinjiang. Chinese officials said it was 'shocking' that people should question the plan, but to those fighting for democracy in Hong Kong, the authorities had forfeited all trust, and the attempt to launch mass testing became a public vote on the government's legitimacy.[84] A little under a quarter of Hong Kong's population registered for testing, according to government figures.

At the same time, China expanded its military presence on and around disputed islands in the South China Sea and sought to intimidate Taiwan by sending naval flotillas close to the island. It also sent war planes across the median line of the Taiwan Strait, briefly approaching the island, and forcing Taiwan to scramble fighter planes to intercept.[85]

In the biggest expulsion of foreign correspondents since the Communist Party seized power in 1949, China kicked out journalists working for the *New York Times*, *Washington Post* and *Wall Street Journal*.

While it was deploying its latest high-tech weaponry to intimidate its neighbours around the South China Sea, China's soldiers used clubs and other improvised weapons in a brutal clash with Indian troops on the roof of the world. The battle, which left at least twenty Indians and an unknown number of Chinese dead, was fought in darkness along a narrow Himalayan ridge on their disputed border, 14,000 feet above sea level. Firearms are prohibited in the zone, so the clash involved hand-to-hand combat and weapons that included batons wrapped in barbed wire.[86]

India, which blamed China for attempting to build structures on the Indian side, described the clash as the most serious since the two nuclear-armed countries fought a border war in 1962. New Delhi was shaken, rushed military reinforcements to the border and began its own reassessment of every aspect of its relationship with Beijing, which had been growing closer. It moved to restrict Chinese economic activity in India, initially targeting Chinese tech companies, which had become big investors, banning dozens of apps and generally tightening oversight. As in Western democracies, talk now was of loosening dependence on its giant neighbour.[87]

To many China-watchers, Beijing's actions again made no sense. Not only did the clash damage the prospects for Chinese companies in India, but it pushed New Delhi closer to the US and to regional powers Australia and Japan. Why, they asked, stoke so many tensions worldwide? The answer, as I have explored in this book, lies in the shifting dynamics of Xi Jinping's China, where the security apparatus increasingly calls the shots, and where the world is viewed through the narrow prism of state (i.e. Communist Party) security, underpinned by a paranoid and xenophobic nationalism. Xi's surveillance state has become an expansionary and aggressive power.

Covid-19 has accelerated a reassessment by Western democracies of their relations with China. That has been at its most stark in the United States, which stepped up sanctions against Huawei and other Chinese tech companies. Washington accused Chinese hackers of trying to steal information on Covid-19 treatments and vaccines from American universities, pharmaceutical and other healthcare firms. The Trump administration imposed sanctions on Chinese officials responsible for human rights abuses in Xinjiang and Hong Kong, and removed Hong Kong's special trade status.

In July 2020, local news outlets in Houston, Texas, reported fires in the backyard of the Chinese consulate. Video shot from nearby buildings showed flames coming from what appeared to be rubbish bins full of paper. Firefighters rushed to the scene, but were denied entry. It quickly became clear why. Diplomats were burning documents, having been given seventy-two hours' notice to close the consulate, which the US accused of economic espionage and visa fraud. They claimed the consulate was at the centre of a national spy network and had facilitated the entry to America of postgraduate researchers who had hidden their affiliation with the People's Liberation Army (PLA).

Among the allegations were that the consulate sought to persuade Chinese dissidents and economic fugitives to return home, oversaw the recruitment of scientists from America's education institutions, organised the theft of research and coordinated the PLA 'researchers', who worked in such fields as AI and biomedicine. 'The consulates were directing PLA associates on how to avoid detection and what materials to erase on their phone,' John Demers, Assistant Attorney General for National Security, told the *Wall Street Journal*.[88] China retaliated by closing the US consulate in Chengdu. The tit-for-tat closures marked the lowest point in US–China relations in decades.

There were also arrests. The FBI detained four military operatives over visa fraud, allegedly concealing the true nature of their work, while in a separate case, a Singaporean national appeared in court in Washington and admitted having spied for China. He allegedly set up a fake consulting company, which advertised fictitious jobs in order to harvest résumés from US personnel with security clearances. He also used the professional networking site LinkedIn to trawl for additional recruits, passing on any promising leads to Chinese intelligence agents.[89]

The US also moved to force Chinese companies listed on US stock exchanges to give up their listing unless they comply with US audit requirements. Previously, the US authorities, eager for lucrative Chinese listings, had respected a Chinese law that prevents its citizens and companies from complying with overseas regulators without the permission of its own officials.[90]

In the wake of Covid-19, the Chinese economy appeared to bounce back strongly – or at least more so than the still-struggling Western democracies. As always the raw figures need to be treated with caution, but the return to growth has been achieved with the same debt-fuelled public investment that we have previously examined and which has been a hallmark of the economy since 2008. As Jamil Anderlini put it, writing in the *Financial Times*: 'A decade ago, some economists liked to describe the Chinese economy as a bicycle that needed to maintain a certain speed or it would tip over and crash. Today it is more like a bicycle laden with enormous boxes of debt, ridden by a drunk and with strategic competitors such as the US trying to knock it over.'[91]

Much of Donald Trump's rhetoric against China was driven by a crude political calculation – that bashing Beijing could be a vote winner in the November 2020 presidential election. In fact, Beijing may have more to fear from Joe Biden's victory. Although Biden has a history of supporting engagement with China, mistrust of Beijing is now bipartisan, and Biden has pledged to restore America's moral and diplomatic standing in the world and encourage a more united front with allies to stand up to Chinese meddling and bullying – a development Beijing is most fearful of.

The shifting balance of global power during the Trump presidency was a story of American retreat as much as China's advance. To take the United Nations as one example – as the US turned its back, China made a concerted effort to extend its influence, and Chinese nationals now head four of the UN's 15 specialised agencies. As we have seen, the broader aim is to extend Beijing's influence on global governance and standards.

In Britain, Boris Johnson's government has finally excluded Huawei from its next generation mobile telecoms network and has clashed with Beijing over its actions in Hong Kong. The prime minister is under growing backbench pressure to take a more robust line against Beijing, but UK policy lacks coherence. China threatened 'consequences' for the Huawei decision and for criticism of its actions in Hong Kong – with China's ambassador to London warning the UK not to allow 'cold war warriors' to 'kidnap' UK–China relations.[92] There was much speculation about the potential damage a vindictive Beijing could inflict on the British economy, revealing once again the nature of a regime that uses business as a weapon and so casually threatens and bullies. Britain should grasp the opportunity to lessen dependence on Chinese money and tech; in the medium term this will strengthen Britain's economy and technical expertise. The government should more critically examine Chinese investments and academic tie-ups – beginning with China's investments in high-tech start-ups and the foolhardy decision to allow Beijing a role in the UK nuclear industry. If China throws a tantrum and cold-shoulders the UK economically, that should be treated as an opportunity. As fifteen Conservative backbenchers warned in a letter to Johnson: 'Over time, we have allowed ourselves to grow dependent on China and have failed to take a strategic view of Britain's long-term economic, technical and security needs.'[93]

Although British universities coped better than feared with the jolt from Covid-19, moving most teaching online, the pandemic underlined how dangerously dependent they have become on high-paying international students, with China as their biggest market. This book has argued that Chinese students have been a mixed blessing, their actions often undermining the liberal traditions of British academia, which has shown itself to be reckless, greedy and naïve in its dealings with Beijing.

Suggestions early in the pandemic that Xi Jinping's handling of Covid-19 could be his 'Chernobyl moment', undermining his rule, proved premature as he moved quickly and brutally to reassert control – though Covid-19 exposed fissures in the system, and a surprising degree of anger festering beneath the surface. His crackdown on Hong Kong and intimidation of Taiwan will only harden attitudes in both. Xi will continue to stoke nationalism at home and play the bully overseas, but the post Covid-19 world is far more wary. A process of decoupling between the West and China has begun and will accelerate, as countries try and reduce their dependence on Chinese goods and money. China's attempt to become the world's banker has been undermined by Covid-19. Client states created by the Belt and Road Initiative, can no longer afford to repay billions of dollars of loans to Beijing, the commercial viability of which was always dubious. This will place further pressure on China's already stressed financial system.

Beijing warns of a 'Cold War mentality' in the West. As this book has argued, the Cold War is not the best analogy, though that mentality is better applied to the Communist Party's growing paranoia and xenophobia, a lens through which every stage, screen, school, university and boardroom is viewed as an ideological battlefield. What is needed from the West is a new realism, a better awareness of what China has become under Xi Jinping and against whom push-back is now imperative. Covid-19 has been a wake-up call, and accelerated that process. When HSBC and Zoom kowtowed to China they were following a long and sorry corporate tradition. It was not only morally repugnant, but as the world opens its eyes to the reality of Xi's China it may turn out to be economically and politically short-sighted.

When I asked Ai Weiwei, the exiled Chinese artist, whether he thought Xi's building of a surveillance state was a sign of strength or of weakness and paranoia, he thought for a moment. 'I think it is both,' he said. 'The more powerful you become, the more paranoia you will have, because you are still a vulnerable individual, with a lifespan.' Ai has been a lifelong target of surveillance and has incorporated it into his art. Ultimately, he thinks it is morally and politically corrosive. 'That strengthens your power, but in time that knowledge can also poison you.'

Shortly after China announced it was to impose a new security law on Hong Kong, the German newspaper *Die Welt* headlined a commentary 'Hong Kong ist das neue West-Berlin' (Hong Kong is the new West Berlin), a reference to when West Berlin was a small island of freedom during the last Cold War.[94] The state that surrounded it, communist East Germany, was regarded in its heyday as the world's most sophisticated and efficient surveillance state. 'Comrades, we have to know everything,' was a favourite saying of Erich Meilke, the head of the Stasi, its secret police. Xi Jinping's China has inherited that chilling ambition.

East Germany's friends and enemies alike were fearful and awestruck by its surveillance capabilities. But paranoid East Germany proved to be highly brittle. Not only did it collapse, but the ultimate failure of the Stasi and its surveillance apparatus was its inability even to foresee its own demise.

Epilogue:
Rising to the China Challenge

Xi Jinping waited for three weeks after the November 2020 US presidential election before congratulating Joe Biden on his victory. In a telegram, Xi said he hoped the new American president would 'uphold the spirit of non-conflict, non-confrontation, mutual respect and win-win cooperation', according to Xinhua, the state news agency.[1] During the election campaign and its messy aftermath, Beijing largely avoided showing a preference for either candidate. Instead, a government that would never dream of allowing free elections in its own country mocked America's democratic process. Party-controlled media stoked a narrative of US national decline, highlighting chaos, disfunction and the threat of violence.[2]

As we saw in chapter 10, China's leaders could barely contain their euphoria when Trump was elected in 2016. They thought they could do business with him. Yet by the time Trump grudgingly left office in January 2021, US–China relations were at their worst since the two countries normalised diplomatic relations in 1979. Even as Biden prepared to take power, Trump continued to target China, blacklisting a further 60 Chinese tech companies, including top chip maker Semiconductor Manufacturing International Corp (SMIC) and drone-maker DJI 'to protect national security'.[3]

Yet Xi Jinping is unlikely to get much relief from Joe Biden, who may prove to be a more effective foil to Xi's ambitions. Yes, Biden is steeped in the policy of engagement – he is thought to have met Xi at least eight times since 2011. But engagement is now regarded as a failed policy right across the American political spectrum, and during the presidential election campaign Biden said of Xi, 'This is a guy who is a thug.'[4] Being tough on Beijing is now a rare bipartisan consensus, and dealing with the threat from China was always going to be the biggest foreign policy challenge for whoever won the election.

From Xi's perspective, a big plus of the noisy and divisive Trump presidency was Trump's animosity towards America's allies and multilateral institutions. His personal narcissism and 'America first' rhetoric repelled many allies who shared concerns about China's rise. They distrusted Xi, but they also distrusted Trump and his motives. Much of Trump's China policy was seen as political grandstanding. This gave China space and made countries more susceptible to Beijing's threats and blandishments. And although Xi stoked anger from India to Japan, from Europe to Australia, a unified response by like-minded democracies was less likely as long as Trump remained in the White House.

Biden's China policy will not change much in substance, but it is likely to be tactically smarter and more joined-up. There will be a difference in tone and style. Biden will engage with multilateral institutions in which Beijing was given a free hand by Trump. Crucially, he will attempt to rally US allies and restore American leadership. Even before his inauguration, he committed to convening a 'summit of democracies' during his first year in office to give a sense of direction on climate change, technology and the economic aftershocks of the Covid-19 pandemic – but mostly to counter China. A unified front is what Beijing fears most and will work hard to undermine. This was evident when China made last-minute concessions to secure an investment treaty with the EU just three weeks before the Biden inauguration. The treaty was seven years in the making. At the time of writing, it still requires ratification by the European Parliament, where there are concerns that it is insufficiently robust on human rights and lacks effective means of enforcement. Many of Beijing's commitments, such as stopping forced technology transfers and providing greater market access and transparency on subsidies, have been made before in different ways and in different forums – but have routinely been broken.

In many ways, Biden's decency and his bid to restore America's moral standing are as big a challenge to Beijing as any specific policies he adopts. Surveys of international public opinion show that America's standing in the world took a battering under Trump, yet China has not been able to capitalise on this. 'Most people have unfavorable views of both China and the U.S. – but more see the U.S. favorably', reported a Pew Research Center survey published in October 2020 covering

14 advanced economies.[5] A separate poll by the YouGov–Cambridge Globalism Project of 26,000 people in 25 countries, and designed with the *Guardian,* found overwhelmingly negative views of China's handling of the coronavirus. 'China appears to have comprehensively lost the international battle for hearts and minds,' states the newspaper. 'Overall, the poll suggests there is a receptive global audience for the next US president, if he chooses, to construct an international alliance to challenge China's growing political dominance, and to question the moral values of its leadership.'[6]

At the time of writing, China was attempting to improve its standing with a campaign of 'vaccine diplomacy', promising preferential access to Chinese Covid-19 vaccines to countries across Asia, Latin America and Africa. As we have seen, Beijing's earlier 'mask diplomacy' largely failed as an instrument of soft power. The distribution of planeloads of personal protective equipment was often undermined by sub-standard quality and heavy-handed demands for public displays of gratitude, leaving many countries wary of its overtures.

As America elected a new president, China was squeezing the last life out of democracy in Hong Kong. Four pro-democracy legislators deemed 'insufficiently patriotic' were stripped of their seats in the territory's partially-elected Legislative Council, while 15 other opposition law-makers resigned in sympathy.[7] Ted Hui, one of the legislators, fled with his family to the UK, where they planned to live in exile. On arrival, they discovered that HSBC had frozen their bank accounts at the request of the Hong Kong police. As we saw in chapter 9, the banking giant publicly supported China's national security law even before the text was published. Now Hui accused it of doing the Communist Party's bidding once again. The bank also froze accounts linked to a church that had provided assistance to young protesters and which was raided by the police. Ray Chan, the church pastor, and his family also fled to the UK, from where he claimed HSBC had become a 'tool for the regime's attempt to take political revenge via economic repression'.[8] An HSBC spokesperson told the *South China Morning Post* they were unable to comment on individual accounts. 'We have to abide by the laws of the jurisdiction in which we operate,' the person said, directing further enquiries to the 'related law enforcement agency'.[9]

Arrests of pro-democracy activists continued. More than 50 were rounded up in a series of raids in early January 2021 and face charges relating to their preparations for elections later in the year. The mere act of planning to oppose the government through Hong Kong's (limited) electoral process was deemed subversive under the new security law. Separately, Joshua Wong, one of the most prominent activists, was jailed for 13 months on protest-related charges. Jimmy Lai, the pugnacious pro-democracy media tycoon we met in chapter 11, was charged with conspiring with foreign forces. Lai, now 73, was the highest profile person to be charged under the new national security law. He was led into a Hong Kong court in handcuffs, a chain around his waist, and denied bail, the case adjourned until April 2021. Beijing also moved to bring wavering judges to heel, officials calling for 'reform' of the city's once independent judiciary, while pro-Beijing newspapers attacked judges deemed to be too lenient.

Beijing also tightened its grip on education. The authorities investigated hundreds of teachers for allegedly radicalising their pupils. One teacher was deregistered – which effectively makes them unemployable – for discussing a pro-independence political party in the classroom, and another for straying from the narrative of Chinese victimhood while teaching about the First Opium War. The *Financial Times* quoted one teacher saying that a climate of fear and suspicion had gripped his secondary school.[10]

In a chilling move reminiscent of the Cultural Revolution, the police launched a hotline for tip-offs about suspected breaches of the draconian security law. The multi-platform hotline accepted video, photos, texts or audio, and the authorities claimed to have received 2,500 pieces of information within the first 24 hours. The surveillance state had well and truly arrived in Hong Kong, and those active in the democracy movement had to assume that communications, along with movements and social media connections, were now being monitored as on the mainland. Online caution was now a necessity. 'Fear is the new normal for Hong Kong's democrats,' the *Financial Times* reported.[11]

Radio Television Hong Kong (RTHK), a publicly funded broadcaster modelled on the BBC, was targeted. Choy Yuk-ling, an RTHK journalist who investigated suspected police collusion with a violent attack on protesters by triad gangsters was arrested for illegally using a car registration search as part of an investigation.[12] A new government-appointed board of advisers said the broadcaster needed to embrace and explain the national security law, while RTHK confirmed plans to play the Chinese national anthem on its radio stations every morning at 8 a.m.[13]

In December 2020, a closed court in the mainland Chinese city of Shenzhen sentenced 10 Hong Kong pro-democracy activists to up to three years in prison on charges relating to their attempts to escape by speedboat from Hong Kong, where they were being investigated under the territory's security law. They were intercepted by the Chinese coast-guard and kept for months without charge and without access to their families or independent lawyers. Their destination was the self-governing democratic island of Taiwan, some 450 miles to the north-east, which has become a beacon and a refuge for Hong Kong's democracy movement.

Taiwan itself is now coming under growing pressure from Beijing, and the risk of conflict across the Taiwan Strait is at a level not seen in decades. The Communist Party, which has never ruled Taiwan, regards it as a renegade province. It resents Taiwan's de-facto independence and has pledged to take it by force if necessary – rhetoric that has grown louder under Xi Jinping. To that end China has dramatically built up military assets in the area. It cranked up tensions further during the US election campaign, buzzing the island with bombers and fighter jets with unprecedented frequency, repeatedly breaching Taiwan's air defence zone and prompting Taipei to scramble its forces. Between September and December 2020, Chinese warplanes flew more than a hundred of these missions, according to a Reuters compilation of flight data.[14]

The People's Liberation Army also conducted a large-scale drill by air, navy and ground forces in which thousands of troops simulated an invasion of the island. The United States has an agreement with Taiwan to provide arms, but under a policy often described as 'strategic ambi-guity', Washington has not spelt out what it would do in the event of an attack. Shortly before Biden's inauguration, Taiwan's foreign minister, Joseph Wu, called for the international community to join together to resist Beijing's expansionism.[15] It is a call likely to be well received, since there is growing pressure from all sides in Washington to make support for Taipei more explicit. Embracing democratic Taiwan more fully may be a better deterrence to China's aggression than pandering to the Party's dubious claims over the island.

One of the last acts of the outgoing Trump administration was to accuse China of ongoing genocide and crimes against humanity in Xinjiang.

The declaration from departing secretary of state Mike Pompeo does not carry any automatic legal consequences, but it does pile pressure on the Biden team (which has already described China's actions as genocide) and on US allies to be robust against Beijing's repression. At the time of writing, the United States was set to pass a law banning the import of goods made by forced labour in Xinjiang. The Uyghur Forced Labor Prevention Act requires US companies to guarantee there is no coercion in the factories from which they source goods, amid growing evidence that 'graduates' from detention camps are being forcibly put to work. The US Chamber of Commerce was accused of lobbying to water down some provisions of the bill, as were several major US corporations, including Apple, Coca-Cola and Nike.[16] The companies denied the allegations, insisting they rigorously police their supply chains and share the bill's aims.[17] The US also banned the import of all cotton and tomato goods from Xinjiang, as well as products from other countries that contain those items. The move follows reports that more than half a million ethnic minority labourers in Xinjiang are being forced into grinding manual labour in the region's vast cotton fields.[18] The British government also denounced the 'barbarism' of forced labour in Xinjiang, announcing that UK firms implicated would face fines. Human rights groups welcomed the moves, but complex supply chains may make them difficult to enforce.

The shocking scale of technology-driven repression against the Uighurs and other Muslim minorities was underlined in an Australian Strategic Policy Institute analysis of night-time satellite imagery, which located 380 suspected detention facilities, a vast gulag that continued to expand during 2020.[19] Up to one and a half million people are estimated to have been incarcerated in the detention camps. A leaked database published by Human Rights Watch shed further light on the workings of the surveillance system that identifies people for detention – the Integrated Joint Operations Platform (IJOP), which aggregates and analyses vast amounts of data, and which we met in chapter 1. The database contained a list of 2,000 names from Aksu prefecture, revealing the often bizarre and sweeping criteria the system is programmed to flag. Alongside factors such as religious fervour, unusual travel patterns, social interactions and having family or friends overseas, the criteria includes 'being generally untrustworthy', being young – 'born after the 1980s' – 'generally acting suspiciously' and 'having complex social ties' or 'unstable thoughts'.[20] The authorities claim the system enables them to identify those carrying the 'ideological virus' of disloyalty to the Communist Party in a more 'precise' way. Human Rights Watch also suggested the IJOP is used to select detainees to be transported to work in factories across China under closely supervised and often coercive conditions.

China's tech giants Huawei and Alibaba were accused of facilitating this repression by developing facial recognition software able to detect Uighurs and other ethnic minorities from within images and videos, automatically alerting the police. The systems were described in company documents published on their websites. The documents were speedily taken down after they were exposed by the surveillance industry publication IPVM.[21] [22] Both companies claimed their technology had never been used outside a testing environment.

Adrian Zenz, the German scholar who exposed the mass sterilisation of Uighur women, and whom we met in in chapter 1, discovered disturbing data about the plight of children whose parents were detained. According to his research, some 880,500 children had been placed in boarding facilities in Xinjiang by the end of 2019, an increase of 383,000 since 2017, a period coinciding with a rapid growth in detention camps. He obtained internal local government spreadsheets showing that in the county of Yarkand alone, 10,000 students were listed as being in 'hardship' due to one or both parents in detention.[23] More than half (and nearly 90 per cent of those with both parents detained) are listed as being in boarding schools or orphanages. It is hard to imagine the mental trauma for children of families torn apart like this, though as we have seen there is evidence that the Party sees the separation as an opportunity for indoctrinating the left-behind children. As Zenz states: 'The psychological impact of Xinjiang's state-sponsored scheme of separating children from parents must be horrific. Children know that their parents' fate can become their own if they fail to conform to the whims of the state ... Beijing's battle for the hearts and minds of the next generation constitutes a particularly despicable aspect of its crimes against humanity in the region.'

After initially denying the existence of the camps, the Communist Party has been increasingly strident in its defence of what it now describes as a network of 'vocational training centres'. Xi Jinping told a Party conference on Xinjiang that 'The sense of gain, happiness, and security among the people of all ethnic groups (in Xinjiang) has continued to increase'. He said it was necessary to educate Xinjiang's population on an understanding of the Chinese nation and guide 'all ethnic groups on establishing a correct perspective on the country, history and nationality'.[24] In a document seeking to rebut the growing evidence of abuse – but inadvertently confirming its scale – the Party claimed that between 2014 and 2019 an average of 1.29 million workers per year in Xinjiang had gone through 'vocational training'.[25]

In October 2020, 39 UN member countries supported a German-led statement delivering a stinging rebuke to China for human rights abuses in Xinjiang. Beijing's diplomats warned that supporting the statement could have political and economic consequences and marshalled 55 counties, led by Pakistan, to support a rival statement lauding China's 'counter-terrorism' measures. Most were authoritarian countries or those dependent on Chinese largesse (or a combination of the two).[26]

The Party continues to insist that it is combating 'extremism', but its actions in Xinjiang are being driven by a strident ethnic nationalism that increasingly sees any cultural difference as a threat to be eliminated. Researchers at the Australian Strategic Policy Institute estimated from satellite imagery that in the three years from 2017 to 2020, more than a third of Xinjiang's mosques were demolished – 8,500 in total – and another 30 per cent damaged in some way.[27]

The *Economist* described China's repression in Xinjiang as the worst violation of human rights outside a war zone. 'The persecution of the Uyghurs is a crime against humanity: it entails the forced transfer of people, the imprisonment of an identifiable group and the disappearance of individuals. Systematically imposed by a government, it is the most extensive violation in the world today of the principle that individuals have a right to liberty and dignity simply because they are people,' the newspaper stated.[28] Yet in December 2020, the International Criminal Court in the Hague said it did not have jurisdiction to investigate China for genocide and crimes against humanity because each of the alleged crimes 'appears to have been committed solely by nationals of China, within the territory of China, which is not a signatory to the statute'.[29]

There has also been concern about the possible spread of Covid-19 in the detention camps. At the time of writing, no data on this has emerged from the secretive gulag, though an October 2020 outbreak in Xinjiang was traced to a recently constructed textile factory near Kashgar which researchers have linked to forced labour.[30]

***

On 14 January 2021, more than a year after the first cases of Covid-19 were discovered in Wuhan, a team of international scientists were finally allowed to enter the city as part of a World Health Organization team investigating the origin of the coronavirus, but there remain serious doubts about whether they will be allowed sufficient freedom to do their job. The go-ahead for the WHO team followed months of negotiation, and the terms of reference cede considerable control to China and contain no guarantees on access to people or locations.[31] China is particularly sensitive about the Huanan Seafood Wholesale market in Wuhan, which sold a variety of wild animals and was the scene of the earliest documented cluster of cases. A high blue wall now blocks off the ground floor, an area of crowded stalls where the virus spread. Access is tightly controlled, and China has released little information about the site. Not only did Beijing seek to undermine the independence of the WHO investigation, but Party-controlled media muddied the waters by claiming that although the first cases were found in Wuhan, the virus originated with foreigners. When Michael Ryan, the WHO's head of emergencies, suggested diplomatically that they should at least start the investigation in Wuhan and follow the evidence from there, his words were misrepresented by Chinese state media, omitting any reference to the Chinese city.[32]

The Communist Party has thrown a cloak of secrecy around Chinese research into bat viruses. The authorities tightened restrictions on Chinese scientists, whose research into the origins of the virus must be approved and vetted. They have blocked investigation of a 2013 cluster of cases very similar to Covid-19 that struck workers clearing bat faeces at an abandoned copper mine in Yunnan province, as described in chapter 11. International news organisations which tried to visit the area faced obstruction and intimidation. This is the information black hole facing the WHO in early 2021. Finding the origin of the virus, and how it jumped from animals (most likely bats) to humans is a complex piece of detective work, and one that is of more than just academic interest. It is crucial to avoiding another epidemic in the future, a task that risks being undermined by Communist Party obstruction.

Along with disinformation, the Party has engaged in Covid-19 triumphalism, bragging about China's 'heroic' handling of the virus, which 'fully demonstrated the clear superiority of Communist party leadership and our socialist system', according to Xi Jinping.[33] It is certainly hard to think of any other country – even among authoritarian states – that could have imposed on its people China's mix of chilling surveillance and thuggish enforcement of a lockdown combined with the almost complete lack of transparency and honesty towards its own people and the world. In late 2020, the ministry of education announced that the Party's triumph would be added to school curricula in order to 'help students understand the basic fact that the Party and the state always put the life and safety of its people first'.[34] State media are increasingly referring to Xi as the 'people's leader', an honorific usually reserved for Mao Zedong.

The government organised carefully controlled tours of Wuhan for foreign media, where journalists were shown a happy, grateful and fully recovered city. Those who tried to pierce this Potemkin village of a façade found a very different story – people too afraid to speak out or question the Party's 'heroic' narrative. As the *Financial Times* stated in the introduction to its own investigation in Wuhan, 'some of the people [we] approached were threatened by police, who said that the FT had come to the city with "malicious intent". Police harassment of virus victims, their relatives and anyone hoping to speak to them is continuing, raising doubts about whether Xi Jinping's administration is really willing to facilitate the impartial investigation into the pandemic that it has promised the world.'[35]

At the time of writing, Wuhan had officially recorded just over 50,000 Covid-19 cases and a little under 4,000 deaths in the city, but as we have seen the real figure is thought to be significantly higher. The allegations of underreporting have found support from an unlikely source: China's own Center for Disease Control and Prevention (CDC). A year after the first cases were detected, the CDC published a study that found a Covid-19 antibody rate of 4.43 per cent in a 34,000-strong sample of Wuhan's population. If that rate is representative of the whole city, it suggests almost half a million people have had the virus – 10 times the official government figure.[36]

Early in the epidemic, Xi Jinping was largely absent from public view, and the authorities were facing rare and open criticism – criticism now brutally supressed. Ren Zhiqiang, the former property tycoon and Party member we first met in Chapter 11, who was arrested after he called Xi Jinping a 'clown', was sentenced to 18 years for corruption, a charge frequently used as a pretext for eliminating enemies.[37] Zhang Zhan, one of the detained citizen journalists who sought the truth in Wuhan, was sentenced to four years in prison for 'picking quarrels and provoking trouble', another common charge used to silence critics. She was pushed into court in a wheelchair, weakened by a hunger strike, during which she was reportedly force-fed through a tube in her arm.[38] Fang Fang, the novelist whose diary painted a graphic and moving portrait of Wuhan under lockdown and who was highly critical of the government, remains free, but has been prevented from publishing books or articles in China.

Internal government documents obtained by the *New York Times* and *ProPublica* show the systematic way the Party, while tracking down and muzzling critics, tried to shape online opinion during the pandemic, stage-managing what appeared on the internet and eliminating anything that depicted China in a 'negative' light. 'All Cyberspace Administration bureaus must pay heightened attention to online opinion, and resolutely control anything that seriously damages party and government credibility and attacks the political system,' states one directive to local propaganda workers. Another document shows how censors sought to supress and distort information after the death of whistleblowing doctor Li Wenliang, ordering news sites and social media platforms to gradually remove his name and activating an army of fake online commenters to change the subject. 'As commenters fight to guide public opinion, they must conceal their identity, avoid crude patriotism and sarcastic praise, and be sleek and silent in achieving results,' another directive says.[39]

The Year of the Rat was good for Jack Ma – right up until 3 November 2020, election day in the US and the day the Communist Party reminded Ma who is in charge in China. We first met the founder of the Alibaba e-commerce giant in chapter 5, when we saw that being simultaneously China's richest man and a member of the Communist Party was not a contradiction but important for business survival. In late October 2020, Ma was preparing for the $37 billion listing in Shanghai and Hong Kong of the Ant Group, the e-payments company he spun off from Alibaba, which valued Ant at more than $300 billion. It was meant to be the biggest share issue in history, the crowning glory of the industry he built. Perhaps it went to his head, because he gave a speech to a high-profile financial forum in Shanghai criticising China's regulators and its state-owned banks, which he accused of having a 'pawn-shop mentality'. He said the country needed bold new players to extend credit to the poor. It went down like a lead balloon with Party leaders, and less than

48 hours before the 5 November listing, the regulators pulled it, citing 'major issues' relating to disclosure and listing conditions. The authorities announced an investigation into 'monopolistic practices' at Ma's business empire and demanded he 'rectify' his activities. There is speculation this will lead to the confiscation of parts of that empire. China's best known entrepreneur was advised by the authorities not to leave the country, according to Bloomberg. He abruptly disappeared from public view. Some commentators in the West interpreted Ma's fall from grace as part of a global push back against the monopoly power of Big Tech – it came as American regulators were taking aim at Facebook and Google. But this is to misunderstand China – and the Party. The action against Jack Ma was first and foremost a stark demonstration of Communist Party power, a reminder that nobody is bigger than the Party and that nominally private companies operate at its pleasure. In the Chinese context, tech giants are fine, just as long as they know their place, work as unquestioning instruments of Party rule and are faithful servants of the surveillance state.

As we have seen, the Party under Xi has tightened its control over the private sector more generally, installing cells in companies and issuing increasingly strident warnings that 'patriotism' and Party loyalty (which the Party sees as one and the same) are primary. A month before Ma's unfortunate speech, the Party issued fresh guidelines to 'strengthen ideological guidance' and 'continuously enhance the political consensus of private business people under the leadership of the party'. As one business owner told The Wall Street Journal, 'We have no choice but to follow the Party.'[40]

It is hard to say whether any cautionary lessons were drawn by America's investment banks, which earned record fees from selling shares in Chinese companies on international stock markets in 2020.[41] Beijing also allowed Wall Street giants, including Goldman Sachs, Morgan Stanley and Blackrock, to expand their presence in China. Blackrock, the world's biggest asset manager, won approval to start a wholly owned mutual-fund business, the first foreign firm allowed to do so. Larry Fink, the firm's billionaire boss, is something of an evangelist in the West for 'responsible' business practices. But he also sees big and seemingly irresistible opportunities in China, and like so many Western companies described in this book, high principle appears to stop at the Chinese border.[42] Morgan Stanley and Goldman Sachs were given approval to take control of their Chinese joint ventures.

China is a 'once in a generation opportunity', according to Luke Barrs, a Goldman Sachs stocks expert. 'The China phenomenon is absolutely one that is here to stay,' he told CNBC in late 2020, barely able to contain his excitement.[43]

These deepening ties seem counterintuitive against the background of deteriorating US–China relations, but they follow a familiar pattern: an infatuation with the China market on the part of the foreign partner combined with a willingness by Beijing to open its door in areas where it needs tech and expertise (as in modern financial markets) – though never wide and always closely policed by a capricious Communist Party doorkeeper – and frequently to slam it shut just as soon as the foreign partner has outlived its usefulness.

Tesla is another company that recently has been given a privileged position in China. Its Shanghai plant, which opened in late 2019, is capable of assembling half a million vehicles a year and was built at astonishing speed. The company received tax breaks from Beijing, cheap loans and permission to wholly own its Chinese operations, according to a Bloomberg investigation.[44] As a result, China is now Tesla's most important market outside the US, accounting for around a fifth of revenue. The company intends to do original research and development in China, and China's leaders – who have identified AI-enhanced electric vehicles as a technology in which they want to lead the world – see Tesla's presence as a way of galvanising their own industry and its supply chains. Elon Musk didn't respond to Bloomberg's request for an interview, but a happy Tesla CEO told a July 2020 podcast, 'China rocks'. For the moment the interests of Musk and the Communist Party are in alignment. The Party needs Tesla, and with booming China revenues, Musk is happy to oblige.

As we have seen, a growing number of frustrated foreign companies are now examining their often complex China supply chains and China trade more generally. Tech companies in particular face a growing risk of reputational damage. US Semiconductor companies Intel and Nvidia are the latest to come under scrutiny for supplying advanced chips to China which reportedly have been used in surveillance systems in Xinjiang. Both companies told the *New York Times* they were unaware of what they called the 'misuse' of their technology.[45]

US federal prosecutors charged Xinjiang Jin, a China-based executive of Zoom, the video conferencing app that came of age during the Covid-19 pandemic, with conspiring to disrupt online meetings to commemorate the Tiananmen square massacre.[46] As we saw in chapter 11, Zoom shut down meetings of activists and dissidents and suspended accounts of the participants at the request of the Chinese government. The 47-page complaint and arrest warrant, unsealed in Brooklyn shortly before Christmas 2020, accuses Jin of working at the direction of Chinese intelligence officers. It contains email exchanges between Jin and Zoom employees in California and gives a rare insight into how China uses market access to tame foreign tech companies and impose censorship demands – to which Zoom, like so many others described in this book, all too readily accede.[47] The complaint describes how in 2019 the Chinese authorities blocked Zoom (referred to as 'Company-1') from access to China but allowed operations to resume after the company submitted a 'rectification plan' under which it agreed to monitor content for 'unacceptable political views'. Under the plan, Jin was appointed liaison with China's ministry of state security (MSS), explaining in an email that he had discussed 'the supervision of hot illegal incidents' and had committed to 'proactively report and give them early warning on a regular basis'. In April 2020, as the Tiananmen anniversary approached, Jin emailed that the authorities had demanded the company develop a capability to terminate an 'illegal' meeting within one minute of a demand being made; in another message he noted that the MSS preference was for meetings not to be cut off immediately – presumably to allow them to gather more information about the participants and monitor the meeting's content. Five Zoom accounts were created for Chinese intelligence agents, who were also given access to Zoom's internal messaging system, with both sides agreeing that the relationship be kept confidential. '[A]ll activities will be classified as secret internally and externally,' Jin emphasises in another email.

The US has jurisdiction in the case because it involves meetings hosted on US servers, and the actions compromised US-based users and their data. The complaint alleges that Jin provided Chinese intelligence agents with unique meeting identifiers and passwords for scheduled meetings to commemorate the Tiananmen Square massacre. The complaint also alleges that Jin fabricated violations of Zoom's terms and conditions to justify closing down the meetings. He allegedly created fake Zoom accounts with profile pictures associated with terrorism or pornography and then entered public meetings using these accounts, which was then used as a pretext to close them down. One California-based Zoom employee allegedly supplied Jin with names and IP addresses of participants in advance of meetings, which Jin then passed on to the authorities, who pressured participants not to attend, often via their families. One Australian-based dissident received a WeChat call from their father, who was accompanied on the call by a security official demanding the dissident stop his 'anti-Communist Party activities'. The dissident went ahead with the meeting anyway, only to receive a further message from his distraught father asking whether the dissident wanted to see their family 'dead'.

Zoom responded to the complaint with a blogpost saying it was cooperating with investigators.[48] It portrayed Jin as a rogue employee who had violated internal Zoom policies and controls, saying it had terminated his employment and placed other employees on administrative leave. It portrayed itself as a young company navigating difficult and unfamiliar terrain and said it had now beefed up its internal rules. It pledged not to allow requests from the Chinese government to affect anybody outside China, though had less to say about the rights of those inside. 'As the DOJ [Department of Justice] makes clear, every American company, including Zoom and our industry peers, faces challenges when doing business in China,' the company said.

As we have seen, Apple has been opaque about its dealings with the Chinese authorities on censorship. In September 2020, it published a human rights policy that made no direct mention of China, but trumpeted: 'Hand in hand with the privacy of our users is our commitment to freedom of information and expression.'[49] Yet the policy appeared to undermine those very principles, when it went on to defend the failed policy of engagement. 'We believe in the critical importance of an open society in which information flows freely, and we're convinced the best way we can continue to promote openness is to remain engaged, even where we may disagree with a country's laws.' The policy followed a shareholder rebellion earlier in the year in which more than 40 per cent of the company's shareholders supported a proposal demanding more details about how the company deals with Chinese government efforts to limit free speech in is products.[50] Although the proposal failed, the level of support was much higher than anticipated.

And what of the UK? Britain has left the European Union and Boris Johnson is pursuing his vision of 'Global Britain'. He is dealing with a new US president who is wary of Johnson. Joe Biden once described the British Prime Minister as a 'physical and emotional clone' of Donald

Trump. The former president himself once hailed Johnson as 'Britain Trump'.[51] The UK needs to make new friends and develop new trading relationships – not the best backdrop for pushing back against China. Soon after the US election, Wenjian Fang, the chairman of the China Chamber of Commerce in the UK, warned that 'the UK will suffer' if the government is not 'rational' about Chinese investment,[52] while Huawei wasted no time in urging Johnson to revisit the decision to ban the Chinese telecoms giant from the UK's next generation 5G network. 'The decision was a political one motivated by US perceptions of Huawei and not those of the UK,' said Victor Zhang, Huawei's vice-president, framing cooperation as important to Britain's post-Brexit future.[53] Zhang's comments came just weeks after a scathing report about Huawei equipment in existing UK networks from the government's Huawei Cyber Security Evaluation Centre, which revealed 'serious and systemic defects in Huawei's software engineering and cyber security competence'.[54]

The Johnson government is facing increasing unease about China from its own backbenches. It has proposed bringing forward a ban on new Huawei equipment from Britain's 5G networks and has threatened telecoms firms with hefty fines if they do not comply with new rules to phase out the company's kit.[55] The government is also toughening new powers to block overseas buyers of UK companies on national security grounds.[56] A report published by the China Research Group of Tory MPs written by Charles Parton, a former diplomat and China expert, proposes that Britain set up a 'foreign interference' watchdog to help combat influence operations and espionage.[57] He characterises the challenge of dealing with China as a 'values war' which seeps into every field, and where the UK should work alongside like-minded democracies (a term he prefers to the 'outmoded' notion of the 'West') to push back against Beijing.

Nuclear power is likely to be an early test of UK resolve. As we saw in chapter 10, China wants to play a big role in the expansion of nuclear power in Britain, initially as an investor but with the strategic purpose of building its own reactor in the UK and using this as a springboard for exporting its technology elsewhere. To allow this would be foolhardy in the extreme. Another test will be Hong Kong, for which Britain has a special responsibility – one it has not exercised with rigour since China took control. A UK scheme allowing up to 3 million Hong Kongers with colonial-era British National Overseas status to obtain visas and pursue a 'path to citizenship' opened in January 2021. It is likely to draw an angry response from Beijing, which will possibly even block people from leaving, if as expected more than half a million apply.

If the UK is belatedly developing a backbone in its dealings with China, the news does not appear to have reached Cambridge University. In September 2020, a year after vice-chancellor Stephen J. Toope stood shoulder to shoulder with Communist Party leaders to break ground on a new 'smart cities' research centre in Nanjing, the local government in that city hosted a conference aimed at 'deepening partnership' with Britain's top university. As we saw in chapter 7, the Cambridge University–Nanjing Centre for Technology and Innovation is the university's first major research centre of this scale outside the UK and the only one bearing the university's name. The multi-million-pound project is being funded for its first five years by the Chinese government, for whom 'smart cities' are synonymous with surveillance. Zhang Jinghua, the Nanjing Communist Party chief, gave the welcoming address, thanking Cambridge for its support. 'Despite COVID-19 and the ever-changing international economic landscape, the trend of innovation cannot be reversed, and the pace of cooperation cannot be stopped,' Zhang declared, according the centre's website.[58] If Toope, attending online, felt in the least bit uncomfortable with that defiant tone, he didn't show it, responding that he hoped 'both sides would strengthen cooperation, promote collaborative innovation and jointly cope with major global challenges'.

The chilling extent of Beijing's reach on British campuses was highlighted when students of Chinese politics at Oxford University were asked by tutors to submit work anonymously to protect them from the possibility of retribution under extraterritorial provisions of Hong Kong's security law. Chris Patten, Oxford's chancellor and the former governor of Hong Kong, told the *Guardian*, 'Students that come from China to work in our universities come from universities where there are cameras in classes and there are paid informants and narks to tell them what is going on. We have to be very very careful that does not leak into our universities.'[59] At Cambridge, Angela Gui, the daughter of Gui Minhai, the kidnapped and then jailed Hong Kong bookseller we met in chapter 8, complained to the police about intimidation by Chinese agents. Gui, a PhD student who has campaigned publicly for her father's release, says she was filmed through the windows of her Cambridge home. 'They want to make it really inconvenient for me so that I say I'll stay quiet. But in the long run, I think that is more dangerous,' she told the *Sunday Times*.[60]

The Party's triumphalism over Covid was pumped up by a return to economic growth while other economies were still struggling. This chest-thumping is likely to reach a crescendo in summer 2021, when the Party celebrates the centenary of its founding, which took place in Shanghai in July 1921. As we saw in chapter 5, China's statistics need to be treated with caution, and the debt-ridden and pump-primed economy is far more fragile than commonly appreciated. There is growing evidence that the Party's principal foreign policy initiative, the Belt and Road Initiative we met in chapter 8, is unravelling. Lending under what was touted as the 'project of the century' has plummeted, and the ability of debtor countries to repay existing loans worth of tens of billions of dollars, already in doubt, has been undercut by the economic fallout from Covid-19.[61] It is looking increasingly likely that Beijing's credit-fuelled effort to buy global influence is coming to a crunching halt and the Party may soon face an international debt crisis.

State media gave considerable coverage to the November 2020 court victory by Gou Bing, a law professor we met in chapter 10, who challenged the right of a local wildlife park to use facial recognition without his consent. The coverage sought to demonstrate that the Party really does care about privacy and came as state media was touting a proposed new Personal Information Protection Law – which would be encouraging, if it lived up to its title. The *Global Times*, a Party newspaper, reported, 'China is trying to improve its legal system to better cover citizens' privacy and information security.' But the draft law is vague, and the aim, the newspaper states, is 'to regulate that the personal information collected by equipment in public areas can only be processed for public security purposes'.[62] In China, there is little that is not defined in terms of public security. It is an infinitely elastic term through which the Party maintains power, and its blanket use renders talk of data protection and privacy largely irrelevant.

As Guo's case was being heard, the government announced that it was taking steps to 'optimise' and 'refine' social credit, the system we met in chapter 3 through which the Party aims to track online behaviour and rate, punish and reward people according to their loyalty. The system missed a 2020 target to bring together dozens of pilot schemes. A government statement carried by the Xinhua news agency was short on detail, but suggests the Party is now stepping up this integration process. 'The scope and procedures of credit information shall be formulated in a science-based way, while those for sharing credit information shall be standardized ... Identification of list of entities with serious acts of bad faith will be better regulated,' the report stated.[63]

At the time of writing, China seems determined to make an example of Australia. Beijing imposed an economic boycott after Canberra led calls for an independent enquiry into the origin of Covid-19, a boycott it extended to all manner of goods, including sugar, barley, timber, wine and lobster. The Party spat out a list of grievances that included Australia's criticism of China's actions in Xinjiang and Hong Kong, and gripes about hostile Australian media and think-tanks. China's foreign ministry spokesman provoked outrage by sharing on Twitter a fake image of an Australian soldier holding a bloodstained knife to the throat of an Afghan child. The tweet, which came after Canberra published a war crimes report alleging that Afghan civilians had been killed by Australian special forces, was condemned by Australian prime minister Scott Morrison as 'repugnant'.[64]

China bullies because it can, and because it has been able to get away with it. Too often its targets back down, offering words of contrition, rather like payment of tribute in imperial times, after which trade is allowed to resume again – just until the next time Beijing feels in some way slighted. Yet attitudes towards China are hardening. In early 2021, as this book is being completed, a gulf has opened between China and much of the rest of the world, a gulf accelerated by Covid-19. We are witnessing the biggest geopolitical shift since the end of the Cold War, driven to a large extent by technology and the rules that govern its use – a welcome re-setting of relations with Beijing, which is long over-due. This book is not arguing for a new Cold War, a charge the Communist Party frequently uses against its critics, but for a recognition of what China has become under the Xi Jinping: an aggressive and expansionary power which not only represses its own people but is now the biggest threat to Western democracies, their like-minded allies and to democratic values in general. Xi's is an aggressive nationalist regime, sustained by technology – a digital totalitarian state. Standing up to Xi, asserting liberal democratic values and becoming less economically dependent on China are moral and practical imperatives.

The city of Nantes in France and the London borough of Tower Hamlets in London's East End seem a long way from global power politics, but both provide lessons about standing up to Chinese bullying. In October 2020, the Château des ducs de Bretagne history museum in Nantes was confronted with Communist Party demands that it distort history. It was preparing an exhibition about the 13th-century Mongol emperor Genghis Khan in collaboration with the Inner Mongolia Museum in Hohhot, China, when the Chinese authorities demanded that words, including 'Genghis Khan', 'empire' and 'Mongol' be taken out of the show and China be given power over exhibition brochures, captions and maps. The museum accused Beijing of censorship and trying to dilute Mongol culture in favour of a more ethnic nationalist narrative. It pulled the exhibition rather than comply, and director Bertrand Guillet said: 'We made the decision to stop this production in the name of the human, scientific and ethical values that we defend.'[65]

A month later in Tower Hamlets, Liu Xiaoming, China's ambassador to the UK, demanded that local councillors stop trying to disrupt plans to build China's new embassy in the area. China bought the old Royal Mint site in Wapping in 2018 for its biggest European mission, a 'new landmark for London' and a 'welcoming public face for China', according to Liu. John Biggs, the mayor of Tower Hamlets, one of Britain's poorest boroughs, wrote to Liu that 'reports about the situation in Xinjiang are of huge concern to our diverse borough'. Liu hit back that such reports are 'all lies fabricated by a few irresponsible politicians and media from the West'.[66] As this book has demonstrated, China's atrocities in Xinjiang are not only irrefutable but its behaviour is now generating widespread (and welcome) revulsion. Liu had clearly not done his homework. Not only is Tower Hamlets nearly 40 per cent Muslim – the largest proportion in Britain – but the East End of London has a long history of fighting oppression and tyranny. The 1936 Battle of Cable Street, less than a mile from the Royal Mint, stopped Oswald Mosley's blackshirt fascists marching through what at the time was the predominantly Jewish Whitechapel district.[67]

The planning process can be long and cumbersome, and the application is at a very early stage. The building of the embassy is unlikely to be stopped, but there will be many opportunities to ruffle the feathers of China's ambassador. Councillors have also raised concerns about repression in Hong Kong, and the practical issue of road closures and disruption from anticipated protests – not the sort of issue Chinese diplomats steeped in the politics of intolerance and repression enjoy discussing. Tower Hamlets seems intent on using its leverage to the full. It may not change China's repressive global policies, but councillors are trying to hold Beijing to account in their own local and niggling way.

One councillor, Rabina Khan, had this warning for Liu in an interview with a local newspaper: 'As elected representatives, we know that governments who do not listen to their people – and do not give them the opportunity to participate in political decision making – are not stable societies.'[68] China's hard-nosed diplomats are unlikely to heed that warning. But they need to be reminded of it, loudly and frequently by Western democracies belatedly pushing-back against Xi Jinping's digital totalitarian state.

Notes

Introduction: 'Love the Party, Protect the Party'

1 George Parker, 'Raab fires warning shot at China over coronavirus', *Financial Times*, 16 April 2020. https://www.ft.com/content/8c46252e-766f-4fe6-964f-fe7f67a03c0e

2 John Sawers, 'The UK should bar Huawei from its 5G network', *Financial Times*, 5 July 2020. https://www.ft.com/content/4fe3a612-f430-43dd-ad89-8f319ca80e8b

3 Tom Phillips, '"Love the Party, protect the Party": How Xi Jinping is bringing China's media to heel', *The Guardian*, 28 February 2019. https://www.theguardian.com/world/2016/feb/28/absolute-loyalty-how-xi-jinping-is-bringing-chinas-media-to-heel

4 'The ideal Chinese husband: Xi Dada and the cult of personality growing around China's president', *South China Morning Post*, 29 February 2016. https://www.scmp.com/news/china/policies-politics/article/1918443/ideal-chinese-husband-xi-dada-and-cult-personality

5 Jude D. Blanchette, *China's New Red Guards: The Return of Radicalism and the Rebirth of Mao Zedong* (New York: Oxford University Press, 2019).

6 Josh Chin, 'China Spends More on Domestic Security as Xi's Powers Grow', *Wall Street Journal*, 6 March 2018. https://www.wsj.com/articles/china-spends-more-on-domestic-security-as-xis-powers-grow-1520358522

7 *Xinhua* news agency, 'PLA Daily warns of internet's revolutionary potential', 20 May 2015. http://www.chinadaily.com.cn/china/2015-05/20/content_20771914.htm

8 For a comprehensive discussion of China's recent political evolution see David Shambaugh's *China's Future* (Cambridge: Polity Press, 2015), pp. 98–136.

9 See the full statement by Marie van der Zyl, the president of the

Board of Deputies of British Jews, on the Board's website: https://www.bod.org.uk/board-of-deputies-president-writes-to-chinese-ambassador-citing-similarities-between-chinese-treatment-of-uyghurs-and-nazi-atrocities/

10 Dennis C. Blair and Keith Alexander, 'China's Intellectual Property Theft Must Stop', *New York Times*, 15 August 2017. https://www.nytimes.com/2017/08/15/opinion/china-us-intellectual-property-trump.html

11 Frank Dikötter, *How to Be a Dictator: The Cult of Personality in the Twentieth Century* (London: Bloomsbury Publishing, 2019).

12 Ludovic Hunter-Tilney, 'Every Breath You Take – Sting's "nasty little song" was The Police's biggest hit', *Financial Times*, 19 July 2018. https://ig.ft.com/life-of-a-song/every-breath-you-take.html

Chapter 1: Xinjiang – Ground Zero

1 A 13 July 2018 video news report of the trial, broadcast by Radio Azattyq, is available via the station's website, https://rus.azattyq.org/a/kazakhstan-zharkent-ethnic-kazakh-on-trial-for-illegaly-crossing-the-border/29361686.html. It is also available via YouTube with English subtitles at https://www.youtube.com/watch?v=Eak3WRtcdko

2 Nathan Vanderklippe, '"Everyone was silent, endlessly mute": Former Chinese re-education instructor speaks out', *The Globe and Mail*, 2 August 2018. https://www.theglobeandmail.com/world/article-everyone-was-silent-endlessly-mute-former-chinese-re-education/

3 Fergus Ryan, Danielle Cave and Nathan Ruser, 'Mapping Xinjiang's "re-education camps"', Australian Strategic Policy Institute, 1 November 2018. https://www.aspi.org.au/report/mapping-xinjiangs-re-education-camps

4 Emily Rauhala, 'New evidence emerges of China forcing Muslims into "re-education" camps', *The Washington Post*, 10 August 2018. https://www.washingtonpost.com/world/asia_pacific/new-evidence-emerges-that-china-is-forcing-muslims-into-reeducation-camps/2018/08/10/1d6d2f64-8dce-11e8-9b0d-749fb254bc3d_story.html

5 Nick Cumming-Bruce, 'UN Panel Confronts China Over Reports That It Holds a Million Uighurs in Camps', *New York Times*, 10 August 2018. https://www.nytimes.com/2018/08/10/world/asia/china-xinjiang-un-uighurs.html

6   Lily Kuo, 'China denies violating minority rights amid deten-
    tion claims', *The Guardian*, 13 August 2018. https://www.the
    guardian.com/world/2018/aug/13/china-state-media-defend-
    intense-controls-xinjiang-uighurs

7   *Xinhua* news agency, 'Full Transcript: Interview with Xinjiang
    government chief on counterterrorism, vocational education and
    training in Xinjiang', 16 October 2018. http://www.xinhuanet.
    com/english/2018-10/16/c_137535720.htm

8   Ben Blanchard, 'China says pace of Xinjiang "education" will slow,
    but defends camps', Reuters, 6 January 2019. https://www.reuters.
    com/article/us-china-xinjiang-insight/china-says-pace-of-xin-
    jiang-education-will-slow-but-defends-camps-idUSKCN1P007W

9   Human Rights Watch, '"Eradicating Ideological Viruses". China's
    campaign of Repression Against Xinjiang's Muslims', 9 September
    2018. https://www.hrw.org/report/2018/09/09/eradicating-ideolog
    ical-viruses/chinas-campaign-repression-against-xinjiangs

10 Riam Thum, 'China's Mass Internment Camps Have No Clear End
    in Sight', *Foreign Policy*, 22 August 2018. https://foreignpolicy.
    com/2018/08/22/chinas-mass-internment-camps-have-no-clear-
    end-in-sight/

11 Chris Buckley and Austin Ramzy, 'China Detention Camps for
    Muslims turn to forced labour', *New York Times*, 16 December
    2018. https://www.nytimes.com/2018/12/16/world/asia/xinjiang-
    china-forced-labor-camps-uighurs.html

12 Adrian Zenz, 'Break Their Roots: Evidence for China's Parent–
    Child separation Campaign in Xinjiang', *The Journal of Political
    Risk*, 4 July 2019. http://www.jpolrisk.com/break-their-roots-
    evidence-for-chinas-parent-child-separation-campaign-in-
    xinjiang/

13 Jamil Anderlini, 'Chinese Muscle Stifles Criticism of Treatment of
    the Uighurs', *Financial Times*, 1 May 2019. https://www.ft.com/
    content/ebee2658-6b3c-11e9-80c7-60ee53e6681d

14 Jane Perlez, 'China Wants the World to Stay Silent on Muslim
    Camps. It's succeeding', *New York Times*, 25 September 2019. https://
    cn.nytimes.com/china/20190926/china-xinjiang-muslim-camps/
    en-us/

15 Tuley Karadeniz and Ece Toksabay, 'China's envoy says Turkish
    Uighur criticism could hit economic ties', Reuters, 1 March
    2019. https://www.reuters.com/article/us-china-turkey-xinjiang-
    idUSKCN1QI4C0

16 *Xinhua* news agency, 'Commentary: Xinjiang affairs brook no

foreign interference', 11 October 2019. http://www.xinhuanet.com/english/2019-10/11/c_138463836.htm

17 BBC News Online, 'China "foils Olympic terror plot"', 10 April 2008. http://news.bbc.co.uk/2/hi/asia-pacific/7340181.stm

18 BBC News Online, 'China describes Hong Kong protests as "near terrorism"', 14 August 2019. https://www.bbc.com/news/world-asia-china-49348462

19 Christian Tyler, *Wild West China. The Taming of Xinjiang* (London: John Murray, 2003), p. 266.

20 Ibid., p. 255.

21 'The Extraordinary Ways in Which China Humiliates Muslims', *The Economist*, 4 May 2017. https://www.economist.com/china/2017/05/04/the-extraordinary-ways-in-which-china-humiliates-muslims

22 Sophia Yan, 'China's Uighur Muslims forced to eat and drink as Ramadan celebrations banned', *Telegraph*, 1 June 2019. https://www.telegraph.co.uk/news/2019/06/01/chinas-uighur-muslims-forced-eat-drink-ramadan-celebrations/

23 'Xinjiang has long been inseparable part of China: white paper', *Global Times*, 21 July 2017. http://www.globaltimes.cn/content/1158546.shtml

24 Tyler, *Wild West China. The Taming of Xinjiang*, pp. 268–73.

25 Nick Holdstock, China's Forgotten People. Xinjiang, Terror and the Chinese State (London: I. B. Tauris, 2015, p. 20.

26 Charles Blackmore, *The Worst Desert on Earth: Crossing the Taklamakan* (London: Trafalgar Square, 2000).

27 Amnesty International, 'Human Rights Defender Released with Conditions', 26 August 2019. https://www.amnesty.org/download/Documents/EUR5709262019ENGLISH.pdf

28 Maria Danilova, 'Woman describes torture, beatings in Chinese detention centre', Associated Press, 27 November 2017. https://apnews.com/61cdf7f5dfc34575aa643523b3c6b3fe

29 Human Rights Watch, '"Eradicating Ideological Viruses"', pp. 27–55.

30 Amie Ferris-Rotman, 'Abortions, IUDs and sexual humiliation: Muslim women who fled China for Kazakhstan recount ordeals', *The Washington Post*, 20 November 2019. https://www.washingtonpost.com/world/asia_pacific/abortions-iuds-and-sexual-humiliation-muslim-women-who-fled-china-for-kazakhstan-recount-ordeals/2019/10/04/551c2658-cfd2-11e9-a620-0a91656d7db6_story.html

31 *Xinhua* news agency, 'Xinjiang Health Campaign Benefits Public', 5 July 2018. http://www.xinhuanet.com/english/2018-07/05/c_1373 03706.htm

32 Human Rights Watch, 'China: Minority Region Collects DNA from Millions', 13 December 2017. https://www.hrw.org/news/ 2017/12/13/china-minority-region-collects-dna-millions

33 'Apartheid with Chinese characteristics. China has turned Xinjiang into a police state like no other', *The Economist*, 31 May 2018. https://www.economist.com/briefing/2018/05/31/china-has-turned-xinjiang-into-a-police-state-like-no-other

34 Human Rights Watch, 'China's Algorithms of Repression. Reverse Engineering a Xinjiang Police Mass Surveillance App', May 2019. https://www.hrw.org/report/2019/05/02/chinas-algorithms-repression/reverse-engineering-xinjiang-police-mass

35 'Apartheid with Chinese characteristics . . .', *The Economist.*

36 Sue-Lin Wong and Qianer Liu, 'Emotion recognition is China's new Surveillance craze', *Financial Times*, 1 November 2019. https://www.ft.com/content/68155560-fbd1-11e9-a354-36acbbb0d9b6

37 Hilary Osborne and Sam Cutler, 'Chinese border guards put secret surveillance apps on tourists' phones', *The Guardian*, 2 July 2019. https://www.theguardian.com/world/2019/jul/02/chinese-border-guards-surveillance-app-tourists-phones

38 Human Rights Watch, 'China's Algorithms of Repression . . .', p. 1.

39 Chris Buckley and Paul Mozur, 'How China Uses High-Tech Surveillance to Subdue Minorities', *New York Times*, 22 May 2019. https://www.nytimes.com/2019/05/22/world/asia/china-surveillance-xinjiang.html

40 Ji Yuqiao, '1.1 million civil servants in Xinjiang pair up with ethnic minority residents to improve unity', *Global Times*, 7 November 2018. http://www.globaltimes.cn/content/1126378.shtml

41 Emma Graham-Harrison and Juliette Garside, '"Allow no escapes": leak exposes reality of China's vast prison camp network', *The Guardian*, 24 November 2019. https://www.theguardian.com/world/2019/nov/24/china-cables-leak-no-escapes-reality-china-uighur-prison-camp

42 Associated Press, 'China's "War on Terror" uproots families, leaked data shows', 17 February 2020. https://apnews.com/890b79866c9eb1451ddf67b121272ee2

43 Associated Press, 'Exposed Chinese Database shows depth of surveillance state', 19 February 2019. https://apnews.com/6753f428edfd439ba4b29c71941f52bb

44 Benjamin Haas, '"Think of your family": China threatens European citizens over Xinjiang protests', *Guardian*, 17 October 2019. https://www.theguardian.com/world/2019/oct/17/think-of-your-family-china-threatens-european-citizens-over-xinjiang-protests

45 Amnesty International, 'Nowhere Feels Safe. Uighurs Tell of a China-Led Intimidation Campaign Abroad', 21 February 2020. https://www.amnesty.org/en/latest/research/2020/02/china-uyghurs-abroad-living-in-fear/

46 Bahram K Sintash, 'Demolishing Faith: The Destruction and Desecration of Uyghur Mosques and Shrines', *The Uyghur Human Rights Project*, October 2019. https://docs.uhrp.org/pdf/UHRP_report_Demolishing_Faith.pdf

47 Lily Kuo, 'Revealed: new evidence of China's mission to raise the mosques of Xinjiang', *Guardian*, 7 May 2019. https://www.theguardian.com/world/2019/may/07/revealed-new-evidence-of-chinas-mission-to-raze-the-mosques-of-xinjiang

48 Liu Xin and Fan Lingzhi, 'Xinjiang refutes CNN report on "destruction of Uygur tombs"', *Global Times*, 4 January 2020. https://www.globaltimes.cn/content/1175654.shtml

49 Joseph Torigian, 'What Xi Jinping Learned – And Didn't Learn – From His Father About Xinjiang', *The Diplomat*, 26 November 2019. https://thediplomat.com/2019/11/what-xi-jinping-learned-and-didnt-learn-from-his-father-about-xinjiang

50 Benjamin Kang Lim and Frank Jack Daniel, 'Insight: Does China's next leader have a soft spot for Tibet?' Reuters, 30 August 2012. https://www.reuters.com/article/us-china-tibet-xi-idUSBRE87T1G320120830

51 James Leibold, 'Planting the Seed: Ethnic Policy in Xi Jinping's New Era of Cultural Nationalism', *The Jamestown Foundation China Brief*, vol. 19, issue 22, 31 December 2019. https://jamestown.org/program/planting-the-seed-ethnic-policy-in-xi-jinpings-new-era-of-cultural-nationalism/

52 David R. Stroup, 'Why Xi Jinping's Xinjiang policy is a major change in China's ethnic politics', *The Washington Post*, 19 November 2019. https://www.washingtonpost.com/politics/2019/11/19/why-xi-jinpings-xinjiang-policy-is-major-change-chinas-ethnic-politics/

53 Leibold, 'Planting the Seed.'

54 *Xinhua* news agency, 'Xi calls for building "great wall of iron" for Xinjiang's stability', 10 March 2017. http://www.xinhuanet.com/english/2017-03/10/c_136119256.htm

55 Austin Ramzy and Chris Buckley. '"Absolutely No Mercy": Leaked Files Expose How China Organized Mass Detentions of Muslims', *New York Times*, 16 November 2019. https://www.nytimes.com/interactive/2019/11/16/world/asia/china-xinjiang-documents.html

56 Yan, 'China Uighur Moslems forced to eat and drink as Ramadan celebrations banned'.

57 Agence France-Presse, 'Ghost cities haunt stability dream in China's far west', 4 September 2017. https://www.scmp.com/news/china/economy/article/2109555/ghost-cities-haunt-stability-dream-chinas-far-west

58 Adrian Zenz and James Leibold, 'Chen Quanguo: The Strongman Behind Beijing's Securitization Strategy in Tibet and Xinjiang', *The Jamestown Foundation China Brief*, vol. 17, issue 12, 21 September 2017. https://jamestown.org/program/chen-quanguo-the-strongman-behind-beijings-securitization-strategy-in-tibet-and-xinjiang/

59 Lily Kuo, 'China claims detained Uighurs have been freed', *Guardian*, 9 December 2019. https://www.theguardian.com/world/2019/dec/09/china-claims-detained-uighurs-have-been-freed

60 SCMP Reporters, 'China plans to send Uygur Muslims from Xinjiang re-education camps to work in other parts of the country', *South China Morning Post*, 2 May 2020. https://www.scmp.com/news/china/politics/article/3082602/china-plans-send-ugyur-muslims-xinjiang-re-education-camps-work

61 Vicky Xiuzhong Xu, Danielle Cave, James Leibold, Kelsey Munro and Nathan Ruser, 'Uyghurs for sale. "Re-education", forced labour and surveillance beyond Xinjiang', Australian Strategic Policy Institute, 1 March 2020. https://s3-ap-southeast-2.amazonaws.com/ad-aspi/2020-04/Uyghurs%20for%20sale_UPDATE-14APR.pdf?jYhPRNLiVh1CYbU59N9HZoL37PZmnDNk

62 The full text of the call for action by 180 human rights groups, 'End Uyghur Forced Labour', is available at https://enduyghurforcedlabour.org

63 Josh Rudolph, 'Children held in Xinjiang amid accusations of "cultural genocide"', *China Digital Times*, 16 September 2019. https://chinadigitaltimes.net/2019/09/children-held-in-xinjiang-amid-accusations-of-cultural-genocide/

64 Adrian Zenz, 'China's Own Documents Show Potentially Genocidal Sterilization Plans in Xinjiang', Foreign Policy, 1 July 2020. https://foreignpolicy.com/2020/07/01/china-documents-uighur-genocidal-sterilization-xinjiang/

Chapter 2: Mass Surveillance

1 Paul Bischoff, 'Surveillance camera statistics: which cities have the most CCTV cameras?' Comparitech research report, 22 July 2020. https://www.comparitech.com/vpn-privacy/the-worlds-most-surveilled-cities

2 Josh Rudolf, 'Sharper Eyes: Surveilling the Surveillers', *China Digital Times*, 9 September 2019. https://chinadigitaltimes.net/2019/09/sharper-eyes-surveilling-the-surveillers-part-1/

3 See the official website of the China Public Security Expo 2019. http://www.chinaexhibition.com/Official_Site/11-9828-CPSE_2019_-_The_17th_China_Public_Security_Expo.html

4 Sarah Dai, 'China's surveillance industry plays down US blacklist at annual expo designed to showcase its technology', *South China Morning Post*, 31 October 2019. https://www.scmp.com/tech/article/3035563/chinas-surveillance-industry-down-plays-us-blacklist-annual-expo-designed

5 Sue-Lin Wong and Qianer Liu, 'Emotion recognition is China's new surveillance craze', *Financial Times*, 1 November 2019. https://www.ft.com/content/68155560-fbd1-11e9-a354-36acbbb0d9b6

6 See the company's publicity material on gait recognition on the Watrix website. http://www.watrix.ai/en/gait-recognition/

7 Sarah Dai, 'Chinese police test gait recognition technology from AI start-up Watrix that identifies people based on how they walk', *South China Morning Post*, 26 February 2019. https://www.scmp.com/tech/start-ups/article/2187600/chinese-police-surveillance-gets-boost-ai-start-watrix-technology-can

8 HIS Markit Video Surveillance Intelligence Service report, 'Global professional video surveillance equipment market set for third year of near double digit growth in 2019', 28 July 2019. https://technology.ihs.com/616056/global-professional-video-surveillance-equipment-market-set-for-third-year-of-near-double-digit-growth-in-2019

9 Josh Chin, 'China Spends More on Domestic Security as Xi's Power's Grow', *Wall Street Journal*, 6 March 2018. https://www.wsj.com/articles/china-spends-more-on-domestic-security-as-xis-powers-grow-1520358522

10 Xi Jinping, *The Governance of China*, vol. II (Beijing: Foreign Languages Press, 2017), p. 288.

11 Dan Washburn, *The Forbidden Game: Golf and the Chinese Dream* (London: One World Publications, 2014).

12 *Xinhua* news agency, 'China Focus: Facial recognition installed

at Chinese crossroads to tackle jaywalking', 20 June 2017. http://www.xinhuanet.com/english/2017-06/20/c_136379719.htm

13   Meng Jing, 'Beijing turns to facial recognition to deter scalpers who sell hospital appointments', *South China Morning Post*, 22 February 2019. https://www.scmp.com/tech/policy/article/2187323/beijing-turns-facial-recognition-deter-scalpers-who-sell-hospital

14   Javier C. Hernández, 'China's High-Tech Tool to Fight Toilet Paper Bandits', *New York Times*, 20 March 2017. https://www.nytimes.com/2017/03/20/world/asia/china-toilet-paper-theft.html

15   Oliver Ralph, Don Weinland and Martin Arnold, 'Chinese banks start scanning borrowers' facial movements', *Financial Times*, 28 October 2018. https://www.ft.com/content/4c3ac2d4-d865-11e8-ab8e-6be0dcf18713

16   'Facial recognition used to analyse students' classroom behaviours', *People's Daily*, 19 May 2019. http://en.people.cn/n3/2018/0519/c90000-9461918.html

17   Liu Caiyu, 'Chinese schools monitor students activities, targeting truancy with "intelligent uniforms"', *Global Times*, 20 December 2018. http://www.globaltimes.cn/content/1132856.shtml

18   Zigor Aldama, 'China's big brother: how artificial intelligence is catching criminals and advancing health care', *South China Morning Post*, 10 December 2017. https://www.scmp.com/magazines/post-magazine/long-reads/article/2123415/doctor-border-guard-policeman-artificial

19   Emily Dirks and Sarah Cook, 'China's surveillance state has tens of millions of new targets', *Foreign Policy*, 21 October 2019. https://foreignpolicy.com/2019/10/21/china-xinjiang-surveillance-state-police-targets/

20   Xiao Qiang, 'The Road to Digital Unfreedom: President Xi's Surveillance State', *Journal of Democracy*, John Hopkins University Press, vol. 30, no. 1, January 2019, pp. 53–67. https://muse.jhu.edu/article/713722

21   Human Rights Watch, 'China: Police "Big Data" Systems Violate Privacy, Target Dissent. Automated Systems Track People Authorities Claim "Threatening"', 19 November 2017. https://www.hrw.org/news/2017/11/19/china-police-big-data-systems-violate-privacy-target-dissent

22   Chris Buckley and Paul Mozur, 'How China Uses High-Tech Surveillance to Subdue Minorities', *New York Times*, 22 May 2019. https://www.nytimes.com/2019/05/22/world/asia/china-surveillance-xinjiang.html

23 Vikram Todd, 'UK police use of facial recognition technology a failure, says report', *The Guardian*, 15 May 2018. https://www.theguardian.com/uk-news/2018/may/15/uk-police-use-of-facial-recognition-technology-failure

24 Elsa Kania and Rogier Creemers, 'Xi Jinping Calls for "Healthy Development" of AI', New America blog post and translation, 5 November 2018. https://www.newamerica.org/cybersecurity-initiative/digichina/blog/xi-jinping-calls-for-healthy-development-of-ai-translation/

25 He Huifeng, 'Xi Jinping calls on China to become more self-reliant during tour of southern manufacturing hub', *South China Morning Post*, 23 October 2018. https://www.scmp.com/economy/china-economy/article/2169779/xi-jinping-urges-china-become-more-self-reliant-tour-southern

26 'Analysis-Report "Study the Great Nation"', Cure53, 8 September 2019. https://cure53.de/analysis_report_sgn.pdf

27 Open Technology Fund, 'Studying "Study the Great Nation"', 12 October 2019. https://www.opentech.fund/news/studying-study-the-great-nation/

28 Wenxin Fan, Natasha Khan and Liza Lin, 'China Snares Innocent and Guilty Alike to Build World's Biggest DNA Database', *Wall Street Journal*, 26 December 2017. https://www.wsj.com/articles/china-snares-innocent-and-guilty-alike-to-build-worlds-biggest-dna-database-1514310353

29 Sui-Lee Wee and Paul Mozur, 'China Uses DNA to Map Faces, With Help From the West', *New York Times*, 3 December 2019. https://www.nytimes.com/2019/12/03/business/china-dna-uighurs-xinjiang.html

30 Christian Shepherd and Yuan Yang, 'Chinese police use app to spy on citizens' smartphones', *Financial Times*, 4 July 2019. https://www.ft.com/content/73aebaaa-98a9-11e9-8cfb-30c211dcd229

31 Cate Cadell, 'From laboratory in far west, China's surveillance state spreads quietly', Reuters, 14 August 2018. https://www.reuters.com/article/us-china-monitoring-insight-idUSKBN1KZ0R3

32 Paul Mozur and Aaron Krolik, 'A Surveillance Net Blankets China's Cities, Giving Police Vast Powers', *New York Times*, 19 December 2019. https://www.nytimes.com/2019/12/17/technology/china-surveillance.html

33 Yuan Yang, 'China demand for electric vehicles raises privacy issues', *Financial Times*, 29 November 2018. https://www.ft.com/content/a868e3dc-f3b9-11e8-ae55-df4bf40f9d0d

34   William Chou, Clare Ma and Roger Chung, 'Supercharging the Smart City – Smarter People and better governance', Deloitte Perspective, vol. VII, 2018, pp. 87–93. https://www2.deloitte. com/content/dam/Deloitte/cn/Documents/about-deloitte/dttp/ deloitte-cn-dttp-vol7-ch7-supercharging-the-smart-city-en.pdf

35   Kendra L. Smith, 'The inconvenient truth about smart cities', *Scientific American*, 17 November 2017. https://blogs.scientificamerican. com/observations/the-inconvenient-truth-about-smart-cities/

36   Leyland Cecco, 'Surveillance capitalism: critic urges Toronto to abandon smart city project', *The Guardian*, 6 June 2019. https:// www.theguardian.com/cities/2019/jun/06/toronto-smart-city-google-project-privacy-concerns

37   Chou, Ma and Chung, 'Supercharging the Smart City . . .', p. 87.

38   Jamil Anderlini, 'How China's smart city tech focuses on its own citizens', *Financial Times*, 5 June 2019. https://www.ft.com/ content/46bc137a-5d27-11e9-840c-530737425559

39   Lily Kou, 'China brings in mandatory facial recognition for mobile phone users', *The Guardian*, 2 December 2019. https:// www.theguardian.com/world/2019/dec/02/china-brings-in-mandatory-facial-recognition-for-mobile-phone-users

Chapter 3: Big Brother Logs On

1   Scott Greene, 'In Beijing, Fog or Smog?' *China Digital Times*, 5 December 2011. https://chinadigitaltimes.net/2011/12/in-beijing-fog-or-smog/

2   Robert A. Rohde and Richard A. Muller, 'Air Pollution in China: Mapping of Concentrations and Sources', *PLoS One*, 2015, 10(8):e0135749, 20 August 2015. https://www.ncbi.nlm.nih.gov/ pmc/articles/PMC4546277/

3   Tom Phillips, 'China's premier unveils smog-busting plan to "make skies blue again"', *The Guardian*, 5 March 2017. https:// www.theguardian.com/world/2017/mar/05/china-premier-li-keqiang-unveils-smog-busting-plan-to-make-skies-blue-again-air-pollution

4   John Perry Barlow, 'A Declaration of the Independence of Cyberspace', Electronic Frontier Foundation, 1996. https://www.eff.org/ cyberspace-independence

5   Bethany Allen-Ebrahimian, 'The Man Who Nailed Jello to the Wall', *Foreign Policy*, 29 June 2016. https://foreignpolicy. com/2016/06/29/the-man-who-nailed-jello-to-the-wall-lu-wei-china-internet-czar-learns-how-to-tame-the-web/

6   The China Internet Network Information Center (CNNIC) is a good source of statistics on the growth and milestones in the Chinese internet, though not always the easiest to navigate. https://cnnic.com.cn

7   Liz Carter, *The Grass-Mud Horse Lexicon: Classic Netizen Language* (China Digital Times, 2013).

8   Josh Chin, 'Tiananmen Effect: "Big Yellow Duck" a Banned Term', *Wall Street Journal*, 4 June 2013. https://blogs.wsj.com/chinarealtime/2013/06/04/tiananmen-effect-big-yellow-duck-a-banned-term/

9   Zeynep Tufekci, *Twitter and Tear Gas: The Power and Fragility of Networked Protest* (New Haven: Yale University Press, 2017).

10   Xi Jinping, *The Governance of China*, vol. I (Beijing: Foreign Language Press, 2014), p. 219.

11   *Xinhua* news agency, 'PLA Daily warns of internet's revolutionary potential', 20 May 2015.

12   Eva Dou, 'China's Stopchat: Censors Can Now Erase Images Mid-Transmission', *Wall Street Journal*, 18 July 2017. https://www.wsj.com/articles/chinas-stopchat-censors-can-now-erase-images-mid-transmission-1500363950

13   Dean Cheng, *Cyber Dragon: Inside China's Information Warfare and Cyber Operations* (Santa Barbara: Praeger, 2017), p. 77.

14   'China launches "online police stations" to strengthen cyber security', *Global Times*, 5 August 2015. http://www.globaltimes.cn/content/935520.shtml

15   Reuters, 'It's seen as a cool place to work – how China's censorship machine is becoming a growth industry,' *South China Morning Post*, 29 September 2017. https://www.scmp.com/news/china/policies-politics/article/2113377/its-seen-cool-place-work-how-chinas-censorship-machine

16   Gary King, Jennifer Pan and Margaret E. Roberts, 'How Censorship in China Allows Government Criticism but Silences Collective Expression', *American Political Science Review*, 107, 2 May 2013, pp. 1–18. http://j.mp/2nxNUhk

17   Josh Rudolf, 'Minitrue: Commentary tasks for Pu Zhiqiang verdict', *China Digital Times*, 22 December 2015. https://chinadigitaltimes.net/2015/12/minitrue-web-commentary-tasks-for-pu-zhiqiang-sentence/

18   For a full translation of the rules issued by the Cyberspace Administration of China on 15 December 2019, and based on China's National Security Law and Cybersecurity Law, see

Provisions of the Governance of the Online Information Content Ecosystem on the website of China Law Translate. https://www.chinalawtranslate.com/en/provisions-on-the-governance-of-the-online-information-content-ecosystem/.

19 'Some people in China help the party police the internet', *The Economist*, 18 January 2020. https://www.economist.com/china/2020/01/18/some-people-in-china-help-the-party-police-the-internet

20 Shan Jie, 'Chinese video app removes Peppa Pig, now a subculture icon in China', *Global Times*, 30 April 2018. http://www.globaltimes.cn/content/1100136.shtml

21 Benjamin Haas, 'China moves to block internet VPNs from 2018', *The Guardian*, 11 July 2017. https://www.theguardian.com/world/2017/jul/11/china-moves-to-block-internet-vpns-from-2018

22 See letter from Cynthia C. Hogan, Apple's Vice President for Public Policy, Americas, to US Senators Ted Cruz and Patrick Leahy, dated 21 November 2017. https://www.leahy.senate.gov/imo/media/doc/Apple%2011212017.pdf

23 Charlie May, 'Apple removes VPN services from App Store in China', *Salon*, 29 July 2017. https://www.salon.com/2017/07/29/apple-removes-vpn-services-from-the-app-store-in-china-report/

24 Wang Wei, 'Chinese man gets five years for running "unauthorized" VPN service', *Hacker News*, 22 December 2017. https://thehackernews.com/2017/12/china-vpn-great-firewall.html

25 *Xinhua* news agency, 'Highlights of Xi's internet speech', 16 December 2015. http://www.chinadaily.com.cn/world/2015wic/2015-12/16/content_22728775.htm

26 Frank Tang, 'China's "tyrannical" former internet tsar Lu Wei accused of trading power for sex in long list of corruption charges', *South China Morning Post*, 13 February 2018. https://www.scmp.com/news/china/policies-politics/article/2133230/chinas-tyrannical-former-internet-tsar-lu-wei-accused

27 *Provisions of the Governance of the Online Information Content Ecosystem*, at China Law Translate.

28 'China Voice: Recognize harm of online rumors', *People's Daily*, 16 April 2012. http://en.people.cn/90882/7788753.html

29 Jiang Gao, 'Users spreading rumors on Wechat and Weibo may face up to seven years in jail', 28 October 2015. https://alltechasia.com/users-spreading-rumors-on-wechat-and-weibo-may-face-up-to-seven-years-in-jail/

30 Angus Grigg, 'How China stopped its bloggers,' *Australian*

Financial Review, 4 July 2015. https://www.afr.com/technology/how-china-stopped-its-bloggers-20150702-gi34za

31 Malcolm Moore, Joel Gunter and Mark Oliver, 'China kills off discussion on Weibo after internet crackdown,' *Telegraph*, 30 January 2014. https://www.telegraph.co.uk/news/worldnews/asia/china/10608245/China-kills-off-discussion-on-Weibo-after-internet-crackdown.html

32 Dan Van Duren's short video of the explosion, together with a tour of his girlfriend's devastated apartment that he gave to NBC, can be viewed at https://www.youtube.com/watch?v=18C5bR1DwOA

33 Eva Dou, 'China's Censors Scramble to Contain Online Fallout after Tianjin Blast', *Wall Street Journal*, 14 August 2015. https://blogs.wsj.com/chinarealtime/2015/08/14/chinas-censors-scramble-to-contain-online-fallout-after-tianjin-blast/

34 Reporters Without Borders, 'Authorities suppress "right to know" about Tianjin explosions', 18 August 2015. https://rsf.org/en/news/authorities-suppress-right-know-about-tianjin-explosions

35 C. Custer, 'Chinese authorities clamp down on Tianjin explosion tweets', *Tech in Asia*, 13 August 2015. https://www.techinasia.com/chinese-authorites-clamp-tianjin-explosion-tweets

36 '197 punished for spreading rumours about stock market, Tianjin blast', *China Daily*, 31 August 2015. http://www.chinadaily.com.cn/china/2015-08/31/content_21743146.htm

37 James Griffiths, *The Great Firewall of China: How to build and control and alternative version of the internet* (London: Zed Books, 2019).

38 Miniwatts Marketing Group, 'World Internet Stats', 30 June 2019. https://internetworldstats.com/top20.htm

39 Adrian Shahbaz and Allie Funk, 'Freedom on the Net 2019: The Crisis of Social Media', Freedom House, 2019. https://www.freedomonthenet.org/sites/default/files/2019-11/11042019_Report_FH_FOTN_2019_final_Public_Download.pdf

40 Reporters Without Borders, 'China still the world's biggest prison for journalists and citizen-journalists', 2 June 2017. https://rsf.org/en/news/china-still-worlds-biggest-prison-journalists-and-citizen-journalists

41 Nathan Vanderklippe, 'Chinese blacklist and early glimpse of sweeping new social credit control', *The Globe and Mail*, 3 January 2018. https://www.theglobeandmail.com/news/world/chinese-blacklist-an-early-glimpse-of-sweeping-new-social-credit-control/article37493300/

42   Lily Kuo, 'China bans 23m from buying travel tickets as part of "social credit" system', *The Guardian*, 1 March 2019. https://www.theguardian.com/world/2019/mar/01/china-bans-23m-discredited-citizens-from-buying-travel-tickets-social-credit-system

43   Reuters, 'China to ban people with bad "social credit" from planes, trains', 16 March 2018. https://www.reuters.com/article/us-china-credit/china-to-bar-people-with-bad-social-credit-from-planes-trains-idUSKCN1GS10S

44   Rachel Botsman, 'Big Data meets Big Brother as China moves to rate its citizens', *Wired*, 21 October 2017. https://www.wired.co.uk/article/chinese-government-social-credit-score-privacy-invasion

45   Simina Mistreanu, 'Life Inside China's Social Credit Laboratory', *Foreign Affairs*, 3 April 2018. https://foreignpolicy.com/2018/04/03/life-inside-chinas-social-credit-laboratory/

46   Nectar Gan, 'The complex reality of China's social credit system: hi-tech dystopian plot or low-key incentive scheme?' *South China Morning Post*, 7 February 2019. https://www.scmp.com/print/news/china/politics/article/2185303/hi-tech-dystopia-or-low-key-incentive-scheme-complex-reality

47   Louise Lucas, 'Tencent's losing game with Chinese regulators', *Financial Times*, 18 June 2019. https://www.ft.com/content/8ac2b862-789d-11e9-b0ec-7dff87b9a4a2

48   Orville Schell, 'Technology has abetted China's surveillance state', *Financial Times*, 2 September 2020. https://www.ft.com/content/6b61aaaa-3325-44dc-8110-bf4a351185fb

49   'China's Digital Dictatorship', *The Economist*, 17 December 2017. https://www.economist.com/node/21711904/print

50   Jiayang Fan, 'How China wants to rate its citizens', *New Yorker*, 3 November 2015. https://www.newyorker.com/news/daily-comment/how-china-wants-to-rate-its-citizens

51   Hai Hodson, 'Inside China's plan to give every citizen a character score', *New Scientist*, 9 October 2015. https://www.newscientist.com/article/dn28314-inside-chinas-plan-to-give-every-citizen-a-character-score/

52   Eva Xiao, 'Tencent's new credit system to use payments, social data', *Tech in Asia*, 31 January 2018. https://www.techinasia.com/tencent-credit-launch

53   Sarah Cook, 'Social credit scoring: How China's Communist Party is incentivising repression', *Hong Kong Free Press*, 27 February 2019. https://hongkongfp.com/2019/02/27/social-credit-scoring-chinas-communist-party-incentivising-repression/

54 Zhang Yu, 'Hebei court unveils program to expose deadbeat debtors', *China Daily*, 16 January 2019. http://www.chinadaily.com. cn/a/201901/16/WS5c3edfb8a3106c65c34e4d75.html

55 'China reinvents the digital totalitarian state', *The Economist*, 17 December 2017. https://www.economist.com/briefing/2016/12/17/ china-invents-the-digital-totalitarian-state

56 *Xinhua* news agency, 'China boasts world's largest social credit system: official', 14 June 2019. http://www.xinhuanet.com/eng lish/2019-06/14/c_138143745.htm

57 Mistreanu, 'Life Inside China's Social Credit Laboratory'.

58 'Big data, meet big brother: China invents the digital totalitarian state', *The Economist*, 17 December 2016. https://www.economist. com/briefing/2016/12/17/china-invents-the-digital-totalitari-an-state

59 The full remarks delivered by George Soros at Davos on 24 January 2019 can be found on his personal website. https://www. georgesoros.com/2019/01/24/remarks-delivered-at-the-world-economic-forum-2/

Chapter 4: He Who Controls the Past

1 Yan Shanchun, 'The Image of Mao Zedong in Contemporary Chinese Art', in *Burden or Legacy: From the Chinese Cultural Revolution to Contemporary Art*, edited by Jiang Jiehong (Hong Kong: Hong Kong University Press, 2007), pp. 48–56.

2 Lijia Zhang, 'Xi Jinping would rather the Chinese forgot the true legacy of the May Fourth protests. But we mustn't', *South China Morning Post*, 4 May 2019. https://www.scmp.com/comment/ insight-opinion/article/3008612/xi-jinping-would-rather-chinese-forgot-true-legacy-may

3 Dan Weinland, 'China seeks to quell debate ahead of May 4th', *Financial Times*, 3 May 2019. https://www.ft.com/content/be 27446c-6c80-11e9-a9a5-351eeaef6d84

4 Julia Lovell, *Maoism: A Global History* (London: The Bodley Head, 2019), p. 11.

5 Ibid., p. 22.

6 Julia Lovell, *The Great Wall: China Against the World, 1000 BC – AD 2000* (New York: Grove Press, 2006), p 27.

7 Ian Johnson, 'At China's Grand New Museum, History Toes the Party Line', *New York Times*, 3 April 2011. https://www.nytimes. com/2011/04/04/world/asia/04museum.html

8   Xi Jinping, *The Governance of China*, vol. I, pp. 37–9.

9   Chris Buckley, 'Leader Taps into Chinese Classics in Seeking to Cement Power', *New York Times*, 11 October 2014. https://www. nytimes.com/2014/10/12/world/leader-taps-into-chinese-classics-in-seeking-to-cement-power.html

10   François Bougon, *Inside the Mind of Xi Jinping* (London: Hurst, 2017).

11   Franz-Stefan Gady, 'Why We Should Study China's Machiavelli', *The Diplomat*, 22 January 2015. https://thediplomat.com/2015/01/why-we-should-study-chinas-machiavelli/

12   Xi Jinping, *The Governance of China*, vol. II, p. 120.

13   Simon Denyer and Luna Lin, 'China sends its top actors and directors back to socialism school', *The Washington Post*, 1 December 2017. https://www.washingtonpost.com/news/worldviews/wp/2017/12/01/china-sends-its-top-actors-and-directors-sent-back-to-socialism-school/

14   Lily Kuo, 'Book burning by Chinese county library sparks fury', *The Guardian*, 9 December 2019. https://www.theguardian.com/world/2019/dec/09/book-burning-by-chinese-county-library-sparks-fury

15   Catherine Wong, 'Xi Jinping tells Chinese teachers to help "nurture support" for Communist Party rule', *South China Morning Post*, 19 March 2019. https://www.scmp.com/news/china/society/article/3002243/xi-jinping-tells-chinese-teachers-help-nurture-support-communist

16   Emily Feng, 'China to weed out foreign content from schoolbooks', *Financial Times*, 21 September 2018. https://www.ft.com/content/68626cee-bd50-11e8-94b2-17176fbf93f5

17   'Class Struggle: Officials are trying to stifle independent voices in universities', *The Economist*, 28 February 2015. https://www.economist.com/china/2015/02/26/class-struggle

18   Li Jing, 'Communist Party orders a course of Marxism for China's universities', *South China Morning Post*, 20 January 2015. https://www.scmp.com/news/china/article/1682774/communist-party-orders-course-marxism-chinas-universities

19   Jamil Anderlini, '"Western values" forbidden in Chinese universities', *Financial Times*, 30 January 2015. https://www.ft.com/content/95f3f866-a87e-11e4-bd17-00144feab7de

20   Christian Shepherd, 'Chinese academic stopped from teaching after criticising party leadership', *Financial Times*, 25 March 2019. https://www.ft.com/content/8af0cfdc-4f11-11e9-b401-8d9ef1626294

21 Chris Buckley, 'A Chinese Law Professor Criticized Xi. Now he's suspended', *New York Times*, 26 March 2019. https://www.nytimes.com/2019/03/26/world/asia/chinese-law-professor-xi.html

22 Samuel Wade, 'Guizhou orders cameras in University classrooms', *China Digital Times*, 3 December 2014. https://chinadigital times.net/2014/12/guizhou-province-orders-cameras-university-classrooms/

23 Reuters, 'Change to Chinese university's charter dropping freedom of thought stirs debate', 18 December 2019. https://www.reuters.com/article/us-china-university-idUSKBN1YM1A3

24 For a detailed examination of the party's tortuous debate over Mao's legacy and its impact, see Lovell's *Maoism*, chapter 12, pp. 420–58.

25 François Bougon, *Inside the Mind of Xi Jinping* (London: Hurst, 2018), pp. 7–11.

26 Ibid., p. 9.

27 'Xi's book on governance to strengthen friendship', *China Daily*, 23 March 2019. http://www.chinadaily.com.cn/a/201903/23/WS5c958b12a3104842260b2209.html

28 'Xi Jinping's new blockbuster is getting a hard sell', *The Economist*, 26 April 2018. https://www.economist.com/china/2018/04/26/xi-jinpings-new-blockbuster-is-getting-a-hard-sell

29 David King, *The Commissar Vanishes. The Falsification of Photographs and Art in Stalin's Russia* (London: Tate Publishing, 2014).

30 For a detailed history of the Uighur internet, see the paper by Rachel Harris and Aziz Isa Elkun, '"Invitation to a Mourning Ceremony": Perspectives on the Uyghur Internet', in *Inner Asia*, vol. 13, no. 1, Special issue: Xinjiang and Southwest China, 2011, pp. 27–49. https://www.jstor.org/stable/24572134

31 Ibid., p. 29

32 Glenn D. Tiffert, 'History Unclassified. Peering down the Memory Hole: Censorship, Digitization, and the Fragility of Our Knowledge Base', *American Historical Review*, April 2019, pp. 550–68.

33 Ibid., p. 554.

34 Ibid., p. 562.

35 Ben Bland, 'Outcry as latest global publisher bows to China censors', *Financial Times*, 1 November 2017. https://www.ft.com/content/2d195ffc-be2e-11e7-b8a3-38a6e068f464

36 Tiffert, 'History Unclassified' p. 563.

37 Chan Koonchung, *The Fat Years* (London: Transworld Publishers, 2011).

38   Dorian Lynskey, *The Ministry of Truth, A Biography of George Orwell's* 1984 (London: Picador, 2019), pp. 174–5.

39   Ibid., p. 175

40   Ben Bland, 'China rewrites history with new censorship drive', *Financial Times*, 5 September 2017. https://www.ft.com/content/4ffac53e-8ee4-11e7-9084-d0c17942ba93

41   'Why Chinese officials imagine America is behind unrest in Hong Kong', *The Economist*, 15 August 2019. https://www.economist.com/china/2019/08/15/why-chinese-officials-imagine-america-is-behind-unrest-in-hong-kong

42   Kiki Zhao, 'Chinese Court Upholds Ruling Against Historian Who Questioned Tale of Wartime Heroes', *New York Times*, 15 August 2016. https://www.nytimes.com/2016/08/16/world/asia/china-hong-zhenkuai-langya.html

43   Zhang Han, 'Revised regulation calls for Chinese Christian groups' compatibility with Chinese values and laws', *Global Times*, 28 November 2018. http://www.globaltimes.cn/content/1129454.shtml

Chapter 5: Not So Corporate China

1   Shan Li, 'It's Official: China's E-Commerce King is a Communist', *Wall Street Journal*, 26 November 2018. https://www.wsj.com/articles/its-official-chinas-e-commerce-king-is-a-communist-1543238782

2   Duncan Clarke, *The House That Jack Ma Built* (New York: Harper Collins, 2018).

3   Joseph Nordqvist, 'Jack Ma appointed as David Cameron's business advisor', *Market Business News*, 19 October 2015. https://marketbusinessnews.com/jack-ma-appointed-as-david-camerons-business-advisor/108909/

4   Li Yuan, 'Jack Ma, China's Richest Man, Belongs to the Communist Party. Of Course', *New York Times*, 27 November 2018. https://www.nytimes.com/2018/11/27/business/jack-ma-communist-party-alibaba.html

5   Dave Smith, 'Jon Stewart Skewers Wall Street over Alibaba: "The Communists Just Beat Us at Capitalism"', *Business Insider*, 25 September 2014. https://www.businessinsider.com/jon-stewart-on-alibaba-the-communists-just-beat-us-at-capitalism-2014-9?op=1

6   Ciara Linnane, 'Alibaba's structure is "dangerous": Mark Mobius', *Market Watch*, 18 September 2014. https://www.marketwatch.com/story/alibabas-structure-is-dangerous-mark-mobius-2014-09-18

7   Paul Gillis, 'Son of Enron? Alibaba's Risky Corporate Structure', *Foreign Affairs*, 28 October 2014. https://www.foreignaffairs.com/articles/china/2014-10-28/son-enron

8   For a fuller account of the Alipay controversy, see Clarke, *The House That Jack Built,* chapter 11, 'Growing Pains'.

9   William Wan, 'China broadcasts confession of Chinese-American blogger', *The Washington Post*, 15 September 2013. https://www.washingtonpost.com/world/china-broadcasts-confession-of-chinese-american-blogger/2013/09/15/3f2d82da-1e1a-11e3-8459-657e0c72fec8_story.html

10   BBC News Online, 'Fosun founder Guo Guangchang appears in public', 14 December 2014. https://www.bbc.co.uk/news/business-35089316

11   Shujie Leng, 'Be in Love With Them, but Don't Marry Them', *Foreign Policy*, 31 October 2014. https://foreignpolicy.com/2014/10/31/be-in-love-with-them-but-dont-marry-them/

12   Tom Mitchell and Patti Waldmeir, 'China Inc: The party vs the elite', *Financial Times*, 18 December 2015. https://www.ft.com/content/4c788de0-a4af-11e5-a91e-162b86790c58

13   'China's stockmarket: A crazy casino', *The Economist*, 25 May 2015. https://www.economist.com/node/21652098/print

14   Michael Pettis, 'Fundamentals simply do not matter in China's stock markets', *Financial Times*, 13 January 2020. https://www.ft.com/content/2362a9a0-3479-11ea-a6d3-9a26f8c3cba4

15   Patti Waldmeir, 'Beware the risk of giving staff in China the chop', *Financial Times*, 26 May 2015. https://www.ft.com/content/d2fd52d0-0386-11e5-b55e-00144feabdc0

16   Rachel Morarjee, 'China's economic statistics aren't fake enough', Reuters, 20 January 2017. https://www.reuters.com/article/us-china-economy-breakingviews/chinas-economic-statistics-arent-fake-enough-idUSKBN1540K6

17   Gabriel Wildau, 'China's statistics chief, Wang Baoan accused of corruption', *Financial Times*, 28 January 2016. https://www.ft.com/content/61cde66e-c425-11e5-993a-d18bf6826744

18   Bloomberg News, 'China Security Ministry to Probe "Malicious" short selling', 9 July 2015. https://www.bloomberg.com/news/articles/2015-07-09/china-security-agency-to-investigate-malicious-short-selling

19   Samuel Wade, 'Minitrue: Rules on stock market reporting', *China Digital Times*, 9 July 2015. https://chinadigitaltimes.net/2015/07/minitrue-rules-on-stock-market-reporting/

20   Tom Phillips, 'Chinese reporter makes on-air "confession" after market chaos', *The Guardian*, 31 August 2015. https://www.the guardian.com/world/2015/aug/31/chinese-financial-journalist-wang-xiaolu-makes-alleged-on-air-confesssion-after-market-chaos

21   Wu Yiyao, 'Capital market crackdown nets 4 CITIC officials', *China Daily*, 1 September 2015. http://www.chinadaily.com.cn/business/2015-09/01/content_21764443.htm

22   For a detailed account of eBay's missteps in China, see Alex Lee's posting, 'A Case Study on International Expansion: How eBay Failed in China', on the *Medium* online platform. https://medium.com/@alexlee611/a-case-study-on-international-expansion-how-ebay-failed-in-china-d762d94b9f4b

23   Louise Lucas, 'Pony Ma, the global strategist with deep pockets', *Financial Times*, 5 January 2018. https://www.ft.com/content/608d 171e-f08a-11e7-b220-857e26d1aca4

24   Didi Tang, 'Chinese web users "not interested in privacy", claims Baidu head Robin Li', *The Sunday Times*, 27 March 2018. https://www.thetimes.co.uk/article/chinese-web-users-not-interested-in-privacy-claims-baidu-head-robin-li-6fgt5xr9f

25   Kathrin Hille and Richard Waters, 'Washington unnerved by China's "military-civil fusion"', *Financial Times*, 8 November 2018. https://www.ft.com/content/8dcb534c-dbaf-11e8-9f04-38d397e6661c

26   Amanda Lee, 'China's Communist Party lists its top 100 private sector business leaders', *South China Morning Post*, 24 October 2018. https://www.scmp.com/economy/china-economy/article/2170053/chinas-communist-party-lists-its-top-100-private-sector

27   Human Rights Watch, 'China: Police "Big Data" Systems Violate Privacy, Target Dissent', 19 November 2017. https://www.hrw.org/news/2017/11/19/china-police-big-data-systems-violate-privacy-target-dissent

28   Elsa Kania, 'Much ado about Huawei (part 2)', *The Strategist* (The Australian Strategic Policy Institute), 28 March 2018. https://www.aspistrategist.org.au/much-ado-huawei-part-2/

29   Xi Jinping, *The Governance of China*, vol. II, pp. 448–51.

30   Zhao Lei, 'Civil-military integration will deepen', *China Daily*, 3 March 2018. http://www.chinadaily.com.cn/a/201803/03/WS5a99d67ca3106e7dcc13f437.html

31   Shoshana Zuboff, *The Age of Surveillance Capitalism* (New York: PublicAffairs, 2019), p. 394.

32   Iris Deng, 'Here's what you need to know about Hikvision, the

camera maker behind China's mass surveillance system,' *South China Morning Post*, 7 February 2019. https://www.scmp.com/tech/big-tech/article/2185123/heres-what-you-need-know-about-hikvision-camera-maker-behind-chinas

33   Danielle Cave, Dr Samantha Hoffman, Alex Joske, Fergus Ryan and Elise Thomas, 'Mapping China's Tech Giants', Australian Strategic Policy Institute, 18 May 2019. https://www.aspi.org.au/report/mapping-chinas-tech-giants

34   See the full statement, 'Hikvision Ownership Structure', issued 27 October 2015 by Jeffrey He. https://ipvm-uploads.s3.amazonaws.com/uploads/f709/6e5b/Hikvision%20Ownership%20Structure.pdf

35   Hikvision's quarterly financial reports, including a breakdown of share ownership, can be found on the company's website. https://www.hikvision.com/europe/about-us/financial-report/

36   Human Rights Watch, 'China's Algorithms of Repression', 1 May 2019. https://www.hrw.org/report/2019/05/01/chinas-algorithms-repression/reverse-engineering-xinjiang-police-mass-surveillance

37   Charles Rollet, 'In China's Far West, Companies Cash in on Surveillance Program That Targets Muslims', *Foreign Policy*, 13 June 2018. https://foreignpolicy.com/2018/06/13/in-chinas-far-west-companies-cash-in-on-surveillance-program-that-targets-muslims/

38   Charles Rollet, 'Hikvision Chairman affirms China Communist Party Leadership, Celebrates Marx's Birthday', *IPVM*, the video surveillance forum, 6 June 2018. https://ipvm.com/reports/hikvision-marx

39   Ana Swanson and Paul Mozur, 'US Blacklists 28 Chinese Entities Over Abuses in Xinjiang', *New York Times*, 7 October 2019. https://www.nytimes.com/2019/10/07/us/politics/us-to-blacklist-28-chinese-entities-over-abuses-in-xinjiang.html

40   Hannah Bowland and James Cook, 'Hikvision faces Trump ban: Chinese security giant is behind more than one million UK CCTV cameras', *Telegraph*, 22 May 2019. https://www.telegraph.co.uk/technology/2019/05/22/chinese-security-giant-behind-one-million-uk-cctv-cameras-faces/

41   David Shepardson and Josh Horwitz, 'US expands blacklist to include China's top AI start-ups ahead of trade talks', Reuters, 7 October 2019. https://www.reuters.com/article/us-usa-trade-china-exclusive-idUSKBN1WM25M

42   Henny Sender, 'China's iFlytek raising up $350 million to invest

in AI', *Financial Times*, 5 June 2019. https://www.ft.com/content/d4dbbd18-81a8-11e9-b592-5fe435b57a3b

43 'Huawei is trying to solve a hard problem', *The Economist*, 8 August 2019. https://www.economist.com/china/2019/08/08/huawei-is-trying-to-solve-a-hard-problem

44 Danielle Cave, et al., 'Mapping China's Tech Giants'.

45 David Alton, 'Huawei's Human Rights Record Has Been Shamefully ignored', *The Diplomat*, 7 February 2020. https://thediplomat.com/2020/02/huaweis-human-rights-record-has-been-shamefully-ignored/

46 Stuart Lau, 'Huawei's 5G ambitions under pressure in Britain over Xinjiang', *South China Morning Post*, 24 December 2019. https://www.scmp.com/news/china/diplomacy/article/3043450/huaweis-5g-ambitions-under-pressure-britain-over-xinjiang

47 Gillem Tulloch, Nigel Stevenson and Mark Webb, 'The Overseas Chinese. Top 30 US-listed Chinese companies', GMT Research, 15 January 2019. https://www.gmtresearch.com/en/research/the-overseas-chinese/

48 For facts and figures on China's economy, see the World Bank's briefing, *The World Bank in China*, on the organisation's website. https://www.worldbank.org/en/country/china/overview

49 Kenji Kawase, 'China's housing glut casts pall over the economy', *Nikkei Asia Review*, 13 February 2019. https://asia.nikkei.com/Spotlight/The-Big-Story/China-s-housing-glut-casts-pall-over-the-economy

50 Reuters, 'China's debt tops 300% of GDP, now 15% of global total: IIF', 18 July 2019. https://www.reuters.com/article/us-china-economy-debt-idUSKCN1UD0KD

51 Zhao Xinying, 'Authorities working on plan to delay retirements', *China Daily*, 23 July 2016. http://www.chinadaily.com.cn/china/2016-07/23/content_26192140.htm

52 Phoebe Zhang, 'China's ageing population prompts plan to deal with looming silver shock', *South China Morning Post*, 24 November 2019. https://www.scmp.com/news/china/society/article/3039064/chinas-ageing-population-prompts-plan-deal-looming-silver-shock

53 Kenneth Rapoza, 'China's aging population becoming more of a problem', *Forbes*, 21 February 2017. https://www.forbes.com/sites/kenrapoza/2017/02/21/chinas-aging-population-becoming-more-of-a-problem/#26ad35b4140f

54 Jack Kelly, 'The Number of Millionaires Has Boomed – Here's Where

Your Net Worth Ranks Compared To Others', *Forbes*, 22 October 2019. https://www.forbes.com/sites/jackkelly/2019/10/22/the-number-of-millionaires-has-boomedheres-where-your-net-worth-ranks-compared-to-others/#2eedd044576fe

55 Jonathan Ponciano, 'The Countries With The Most Billionaires', *Forbes*, 8 April 2020. https://www.forbes.com/sites/jonathan ponciano/2020/04/08/the-countries-with-the-most-billionaires-in-2020/#5977b2d24429

56 Chen Qingqing, 'Concerns over Alibaba founder's Party membership reflect lack of knowledge of CPC grass-roots functions: experts', *Global Times*, 27 November 2018. http://www.globaltimes.cn/content/1129283.shtml

57 Shi Jing, 'Private firms benefit from closer bonds with government', *China Daily*, 16 October 2017. http://www.chinadaily.com.cn/china/2017-10/16/content_33310662.htm

58 Michael Martina, 'Exclusive: In China, the Party's push for influence inside foreign firms stirs fears', Reuters, 24 August 2017. https://www.reuters.com/article/us-china-congress-companies-idUSKCN1B40JU

59 Jennifer Hughes, 'Chinese Communist Party writes itself into company law', *Financial Times*, 14 August 2017. https://www.ft.com/content/a4b28218-80db-11e7-94e2-c5b903247afd

60 Elsa Kania, 'Much ado about Huawei (part 2)'.

61 Karishma Vaswani, 'Huawei: The story of a controversial company.' BBC News Online, 6 March 2019. https://www.bbc.co.uk/news/resources/idt-sh/Huawei

62 Maiji Palmer, 'Podcast: "I was rejected 167 times"', *Financial Times*, 28 August 2018. https://www.ft.com/content/d25bed12-a7b3-11e8-926a-7342fe5e173f

63 Lucy Hornby, 'Communist Party asserts control over China Inc.' *Financial Times*, 3 October 2017. https://www.ft.com/content/29ee 1750-a42a-11e7-9e4f-7f5e6a7c98a2

64 Human Rights Watch, '"Special Measures": Detention and Torture in the Chinese Communist Party's Shuanggui System', 6 December 2016. https://www.hrw.org/report/2016/12/06/special-measures/detention-and-torture-chinese-communist-partys-shuanggui-system

65 Hudson Lockett, 'China anti-corruption campaign backfires', *Financial Times*, 9 October 2016. https://www.ft.com/content/02f712b4-8ab8-11e6-8aa5-f79f5696c731?shareType=nongift

66 Tania Branigan, 'Politburo, army, casinos: China's corruption crackdown spreads', *The Guardian*, 14 February 2014. https://www.theguardian.com/world/2015/feb/14/china-corruption-crackdown-spreads-xi-jinping

67 Minxin Pei, *China's Crony Capitalism: The Dynamics of Regime Decay* (Cambridge, MA and London: Harvard University Press, 2016), p. 9.

68 Ibid., p. 267.

Chapter 6: The West's (Often Willing) Enablers

1 'Cathay Pacific's fate rattles multinationals in Hong Kong', *The Economist*, 22 August 2019. https://www.economist.com/business/2019/08/22/cathay-pacifics-fate-rattles-multinationals-in-hong-kong

2 'Cathay Pacific caught in storm over Hong Kong protests', *Financial Times*, 15 August 2019. https://www.ft.com/content/3fc1d94e-be7d-11e9-b350-db00d509634e

3 Reuters, 'Cathay suspends pilot arrested in Hong Kong protests', 10 August 2019. https://www.reuters.com/article/us-hongkong-protests-cathay-pacific-idUSKCN1V00JI

4 'Cathay Pacific's fate rattles multinationals in Hong Kong', *The Economist*.

5 Sue-Lin Wong and Hudson Lockett, 'Cathay Pacific replaces chief executive as China ups pressure over protests', *Financial Times*, 16 August 2019. https://www.ft.com/content/d204816c-c008-11e9-b350-db00d509634e

6 Sui-Lee Wee and Raymond Zhong, 'China Pressures Business Over Hong Kong. Workers get caught in the middle', *New York Times*, 18 August 2019. https://www.nytimes.com/2019/08/18/business/economy/hong-kong-china-business-workers.html

7 Nicolle Liu, Ryan McMorrow and George Hammond, 'Hong Kong protesters call for HSBC boycott over fund closure', *Financial Times*, 20 December 2019. https://www.ft.com/content/e57c4990-2256-11ea-b8a1-584213ee7b2b

8 Chris Duckett, 'Apple can uphold basic human rights or become a Beijing accomplice: Hong Kong lawmaker.' *ZDNet*, 11 October 2019. https://www.zdnet.com/article/apple-can-uphold-basic-human-rights-or-become-a-beijing-accomplice-hk-lawmaker/

9 See letter from Cynthia C. Hogan to US Senators Ted Cruz and Patrick Leahy, dated 21 November 2017. https://www.leahy.senate.gov/imo/media/doc/Apple%2011212017.pdf

10 See full text of letter from Senators Ted Cruz and Patrick Leahy to Tim Cook, dated 17 October 2017. https://www.apple.com/customer-letter/

11 Paul Mozur, 'Skype Vanishes from App Stores in China, including Apple's', *New York Times*, 21 November 2017. https://www.nytimes.com/2017/11/21/business/skype-app-china.html

12 Benjamin Haas, 'Apple Removes New York Times app in China', *The Guardian*, 5 January 2017. https://www.theguardian.com/world/2017/jan/05/apple-removes-new-york-times-app-in-china

13 Charlie Smith, 'Apple Censoring Tibet Information in China', Greatfire.org, 10 June 2019. https://en.greatfire.org/blog/2019/jun/apple-censoring-tibetan-information-china

14 Alex Kantrowitz and John Paczkowski, 'Apple Told Some Apple TV+ Show Developers Not to Anger China', Buzzfeed News, 11 October 2019.   https://www.buzzfeednews.com/article/alexkantrowitz/apple-china-tv-protesters-hong-kong-tim-cook

15 Andy Greenberg, 'Apple's China-Friendly Censors Caused an iPhone Crashing Bug', *Wired*, 18 July 2018. https://www.wired.com/story/apple-china-censorship-bug-iphone-crash-emoji/

16 Robert McMillan and Tripp Mickle, 'Apple to Start Putting Sensitive Encryption Keys in China', *Wall Street Journal*, 24 February 2018. https://www.wsj.com/articles/apple-to-start-putting-sensitive-encryption-keys-in-china-1519497574

17 Amnesty International, 'Campaign targets Apple over privacy betrayal for Chinese iCloud users', 22 March 2018. https://www.amnesty.org/en/latest/news/2018/03/apple-privacy-betrayal-for-chinese-icloud-users/

18 Mikey Campbell, 'Apple CEO Tim Cook talks Chinese supply chain, censorship and more in interview', AppleInsider, 5 December 2017. https://appleinsider.com/articles/17/12/06/apple-ceo-tim-cook-talks-chinese-supply-chain-censorship-and-more-in-interview

19 Frank Tang, 'Apple CEO Tim Cook joins influential Beijing University board as company's China woes continue', *South China Morning Post*, 21 October 2019. https://www.scmp.com/economy/china-economy/article/3033899/apple-ceo-tim-cook-joins-influential-beijing-university-board

20 Chris Buckley, 'A Chinese Law Professor Criticised Xi. Now He's Been Suspended.' *New York Times*, 26 March 2019. https://www.nytimes.com/2019/03/26/world/asia/chinese-law-professor-xi.html

21 For a breakdown of the geographic sources of Apple's revenue, see Statista's report, 'Cook points to China for Apple's lacklustre Q1', 4 January 2019. https://www.statista.com/chart/16522/apple-quarter-revenue/

22 'Half of iPhones manufactured in central China's Zhengzhou city', *China Daily*, 19 September 2019. http://www.chinadaily.com.cn/business/tech/2017-09/19/content_32191283.htm

23 See MSNBC interview with Tim Cook, '"Privacy is a human right": Apple CEO Tim Cook', 28 March 2019. https://www.msnbc.com/msnbc/watch/privacy-is-a-human-right-apple-ceo-tim-cook-1197152323753

24 See Tim Cook's open letter to customers, 16 February 2016. https://www.apple.com/customer-letter/

25 Roy Williams, 'Guest Post: has doing business in China just got too risky', *Financial Times*, 11 August 2014. https://www.ft.com/content/00abf61d-c30b-3e52-879f-acaca73d0b7c

26 James McGregor, *One Billion Customers: Lessons from the front lines of doing business in China* (New York: Wall Street Journal Books, 2005).

27 Andrew Browne, 'China's Dream Is Apple's Nightmare: US Tech Firms Cave to Beijing's Rules', *Wall Street Journal*, 8 August 2017. https://www.wsj.com/articles/chinas-dream-is-apples-nightmare-u-s-tech-firms-cave-to-beijings-rules-1502215101

28 Michael Martina, 'Exclusive: In China, the Party's push for influence inside foreign firms stirs fears'.

29 Tom Hancock, 'China to impose "social credit" system on foreign companies', *Financial Times*, 28 August 2019. https://www.ft.com/content/726905b6-c8dc-11e9-a1f4-3669401ba76f

30 Simone McCarthy, 'Will China's revised cyber rules put foreign firms at risk of losing their secrets?' *South China Morning Post*, 13 October 2019. https://www.scmp.com/news/china/diplomacy/article/3032649/will-chinas-revised-cybersecurity-law-put-foreign-firms-risk

31 Gordon Corera, *Intercept: The Secret History of Computers and Spies* (London: Weidenfeld & Nicholson, 2015), pp. 325 and 371–6.

32 Michael Auslin, 'China Humiliates Another Western Company', *Wall Street Journal*, 22 February 2018. https://www.wsj.com/articles/china-humiliates-another-western-company-1519169396

33 Tom Hancock, 'Multinationals bow to China's political sensibilities', *Financial Times*, 20 May 2018. https://www.ft.com/content/36c03e40-52a8-11e8-b3ee-41e0209208ec

34 Sidney Leng, 'Off the charts: why China publishers don't want

maps in their books', *South China Morning Post*, 19 May 2018.
https://www.scmp.com/news/china/economy/article/2146876/
charts-why-chinese-publishers-dont-want-maps-their-books

35   Emma Graham-Harrison, 'Camera firm distances itself from
Tiananmen Square advert', *The Guardian*, 19 April 2019. https://
www.theguardian.com/world/2019/apr/19/camera-firm-leica-
distances-itself-from-tiananmen-square-advert

36   Tom Hancock, 'Nike pulls line of shoes from China over Instagram
post', *Financial Times*, 26 June 2019. https://www.ft.com/content/
8e034184-972b-11e9-8cfb-30c211dcd229

37   Nick Greene, 'Daryl Morey's Hong Kong Tweet Exposed the Limits
of the NBA's Social Conscience', *Slate*, 6 October 2019. https://
slate.com/culture/2019/10/daryl-morey-hong-kong-china-nba-
houston-rockets.html

38   Daniel Victor, 'Hong Kong Protests Put N.B.A. on Edge in
China', *New York Times*, 9 October 2019. https://www.nytimes.
com/2019/10/07/sports/basketball/nba-china-hong-kong.html

39   Sky News, 'Chinese TV pulls coverage of Arsenal match after
Mesut Ozil remarks', 15 December 2019. https://news.sky.com/
story/chinas-state-tv-will-no-longer-show-arsenal-match-after-
mesut-ozil-remarks-11887171

40   Paul Mozur, 'With "Smog Jog" Through Beijing, Zuckerberg Stirs
Debate on Air Pollution', *New York Times*, 18 March 2018. https://
www.nytimes.com/2016/03/19/world/asia/mark-zuckerberg-
jogging-beijing-smog.html

41   Emily Parker, 'Mark Zuckerberg's Long March to China', *MIT
Technology Review*, 18 October 2016. https://www.technology
review.com/s/602493/mark-zuckerbergs-long-march-to-china/

42   Mike Isaac, 'Facebook Said to Create Censorship Tool to Get
Back Into China', *New York Times*, 22 November 2016. https://
www.nytimes.com/2016/11/22/technology/facebook-censor
ship-tool-china.html

43   Julia Greenberg, 'Facebook Says It Has Advertisers in China Despite
Ban', *Wired*, 11 April 2015. https://www.wired.com/2015/11/
facebook-says-it-has-advertisers-in-china-despite-ban/

44   Ryan Gallagher, 'Google Plans to Launch Censored Search
Engine in China, Leaked Documents Reveal', The Intercept, 1
August 2018. https://theintercept.com/2018/08/01/google-china-
search-engine-censorship/

45   Ryan Gallagher and Lee Fang, 'Google Suppresses Memo Revealing
Plans to Closely Track search users in China', The Intercept, 21

December 2018. https://theintercept.com/2018/09/21/google-suppresses-memo-revealing-plans-to-closely-track-search-users-in-china/

46   Tim Bradshaw, 'Google chief tries to quell Staff Anger over China project', *Financial Times*, 17 August 2018. https://www.ft.com/content/824c4692-a1bd-11e8-85da-eeb7a9ce36e4

47   Daisuke Wakabayashi and Scott Shane, 'Google Will Not Renew Pentagon Contract That Upset Employees', *New York Times*, 1 June 2018. https://www.nytimes.com/2018/06/01/technology/google-pentagon-project-maven.html

48   See Fei Fei Li's full 13 December 2018 blog post – https://www.blog.google/topics/google-asia/google-ai-china-center/

49   Peter Thiel, 'Good for Google, Bad for America', *New York Times*, 1 August 2019. https://www.nytimes.com/2019/08/01/opinion/peter-thiel-google.html

50   Tom Simonite, 'AI Could Revolutionize War as Much as Nukes', *Wired*, 19 July 2017. https://www.wired.com/story/ai-could-revolutionize-war-as-much-as-nukes/

51   Matt Reynolds, 'Deep Mind's AI beats world's best Go player in latest face-off', *New Scientist*, 23 May 2017. https://www.newscientist.com/article/2132086-deepminds-ai-beats-worlds-best-go-player-in-latest-face-off/

52   See remarks by Hsiao-Wuen Hon on the Microsoft Research Asia website–https://www.microsoft.com/en-us/research/lab/microsoft-research-asia/

53   Madhumita Murgia and Yuan Yang, 'Microsoft worked with Chinese military university on artificial intelligence', *Financial Times*, 10 April 2019. https://www.ft.com/content/9378e7ee-5ae6-11e9-9dde-7aedca0a081a

54   Yuan Yang and Richard Waters, 'TikTok deal tests Microsoft's decades of China experience', *Financial Times*, 6 August 2020. https://www.ft.com/content/b02d5324-07e6-48ac-b658-b8c400d9b4fc?shareType=nongift

55   Tom Zeller Jr, 'Web Firms Are Grilled on Dealings in China', *New York Times*, 16 February 2006. https://www.nytimes.com/2006/02/16/technology/web-firms-are-grilled-on-dealings-in-china.html

56   Yves Moreau, 'Crack down on genomic surveillance', *Nature*, 5 December 2019. https://www.nature.com/articles/d41586-019-03687-x

57   Sui-Lee Wee, 'China uses DNA to Track Its People, With the Help of American Expertise', *New York Times*, 21 February 2019.

https://www.nytimes.com/2019/02/21/business/china-xinjiang-uighur-dna-thermo-fisher.html

58   Jessica Batke and Mareike Ohlberg, 'China's Biosecurity State in Xinjiang is Powered by Western Tech', *Foreign Policy*, 19 February 2019.   https://foreignpolicy.com/2020/02/19/china-xinjiang-surveillance-biosecurity-state-dna-western-tech/

59   Bloomberg News, 'Foreigners Can't Get Enough of This Chinese Surveillance Stock', 20 April 2018. https://www.bloomberg.com/news/articles/2018-04-20/foreigners-can-t-get-enough-of-this-chinese-surveillance-stock

60   Charles Rollet, 'In China's Far West, Companies Cash in on Surveillance Program That Targets Muslims', *Foreign Policy*, 13 June 2018. https://foreignpolicy.com/2018/06/13/in-chinas-far-west-companies-cash-in-on-surveillance-program-that-targets-muslims/

61   Lisa Lin and Josh Chin, 'U.S. Tech Companies Prop Up China's Vast Surveillance Network', *Wall Street Journal*, 26 November 2019. https://www.wsj.com/articles/u-s-tech-companies-prop-up-chinas-vast-surveillance-network-11574786846

Chapter 7: From Influence to Interference

1   Christopher F. Schuetze, 'At Berlin Zoo, a Clamour to Name Twin Pandas "Hong" and "Kong"', *New York Times*, 6 September 2019. https://www.nytimes.com/2019/09/06/world/europe/berlin-zoo-pandas-hong-kong.html

2   Kate Connolly, 'Hong and Kong? Berlin's panda cubs at centre of Chinese human rights row', *The Guardian*, 5 September 2019. https://www.theguardian.com/world/2019/sep/05/berlins-panda-cubs-cause-debate-about-chinese-human-rights

3   Kate O'Keeffe, 'Pandas Are Adorable! (Also a Tool for Chinese Geopolitical Domination)', *Wall Street Journal*, 24 March 2017. https://www.wsj.com/articles/dont-like-china-no-pandas-for-you-1490366939

4   The website of the Complete University Guide carries statistics on international students at all British universities – https://www.thecompleteuniversityguide.co.uk/sheffield/international

5   This is from one of a number of WeChat screenshots passed to the author.

6   Camilla Turner and Ewan Summerville, 'Police called in as Hong Kong and China tensions spread to UK universities', *Telegraph*,

12 October 2019. https://www.telegraph.co.uk/news/2019/10/12/police-called-hong-kong-china-tensions-spread-uk-universities/

7 Laura Mannering, 'Hong Kong students in UK call for action over pro-China threats and harassment', *Hong Kong Free Press*, 26 November 2019. https://www.hongkongfp.com/2019/11/26/hong-kong-students-uk-call-action-pro-china-threats-harassment/

8 Evianne Suen and Katie Tarrant, 'Warwick security takes down "Lennon Wall" pig dubbed "racist" by Chinese students', The Boar, 6 November 2019. https://theboar.org/2019/11/warwick-security-take-down-lennon-wall-pig-dubbed-racist-by-chinese-students/

9 Chis Buckley, 'China Says Its Students, Even Abroad, Need More Patriotic Education', *New York Times*, 10 February 2016. https://www.nytimes.com/2016/02/11/world/asia/china-patriotic-education.html

10 See CSSA entry on the King's College London Students' Union website. https://www.kclsu.org/organisation/14780/

11 Jim Waterson, 'The Chinese Embassy Told Durham University's Debating Society Not to Let Former Miss World Contestant Speak at a Debate', BuzzFeed News, 10 February 2017. https://www.buzzfeed.com/jimwaterson/the-chinese-embassy-told-durham-universitys-debating-society

12 'A cartographic clash between the LSE and its Chinese students', *The Economist*, 13 April 2019. https://www.economist.com/britain/2019/04/13/a-cartographic-clash-between-the-lse-and-its-chinese-students

13 Peter Walker, 'Crowds greet Xi Jinping with flags seemingly brought by Chinese Embassy', *The Guardian*, 20 October 2015. https://www.theguardian.com/world/2015/oct/20/xi-jinping-london-president-china-support-human-rights-protesters

14 Charles Parton, 'China–UK relations. Where to Draw the Border between Influence and Interference', Royal United Services Institute, February 2019. https://rusi.org/sites/default/files/20190220_chinese_interference_parton_web.pdf

15 See 4 October 2018 speech by US Vice-President Mike Pence to the Hudson Institute in Washington DC. https://www.whitehouse.gov/briefings-statements/remarks-vice-president-pence-administrations-policy-toward-china/

16 See latest statistics on the Study in UK website. https://www.studying-in-uk.org/international-student-statistics-in-uk/

17 The full Cambridge University press release, 'Cambridge and Nanjing break ground on "smart cities" Centre', 10 September 2019,

can be accessed at https://www.cam.ac.uk/news/cambridge-and-nanjing-break-ground-on-smart-cities-centre

18　Taken from a 2015 Huawei advertising feature, 'A better connected world', carried by BBC Worldwide. http://www.bbc.com/future/bespoke/specials/connected-world/government.html

19　Digital Journal, 'Wang Luxiang Dialogues with Future Cities Nanjing Jiangbei New Area', Management Committee of Nanjing Jiangbei New District 2019 press release. http://www.digitaljournal.com/pr/4550512

20　A full description of the role and responsibilities of the Board of Scrutiny can be found on the Cambridge University website. https://www.scrutiny.cam.ac.uk

21　Cambridge University Reporter, 'Twenty-third Report of the Board of Scrutiny', 10 October 2018. https://www.admin.cam.ac.uk/reporter/2018-19/weekly/6521/section6.shtml#heading2-11

22　Cambridge University Reporter, 'Report of the General Board on the establishment of certain Professorships', 20 February 2019. https://www.admin.cam.ac.uk/reporter/2018-19/weekly/6538/section6.shtml#heading2-15

23　For the full job description for applicants to the post of 'Nanjing Professor' as published by Cambridge University human resources, see https://www.hr.admin.cam.ac.uk/files/nanjing.pdf

24　See rankings in the Complete University Guide's 'Electrical and Electronic Engineering League Table 2020'. https://www.thecompleteuniversityguide.co.uk/league-tables/rankings

25　Sheffield University press release, 'University of Sheffield strengthens longstanding collaborations', 6 July 2018. https://www.sheffield.ac.uk/news/nr/partnership-china-leading-universities-nanjing-1.791086

26　See original project proposal with list of participating organisations on the website of UK Research and Innovations. https://gtr.ukri.org/projects?ref=EP/N007743/1

27　Jiangnan University press release, 'Professor Josef Kittler of Jiangnan University Receives the Chinese Government Friendship Award 2016', 10 October 2016. http://english.jiangnan.edu.cn/info/1002/1010.htm

28　See Surrey University press release, 'Surrey and China collaboration wins the Visual Object Tracking 2018 competition', 2 October 2018. https://www.surrey.ac.uk/news/surrey-and-china-collaboration-wins-visual-object-tracking-2018-competition

29　For a full description of its history and activities, see the National

University of Defense Technology website, https://english.nudt.
edu.cn/About/index.htm

30   See University of Huddersfield website, 'Inspiring Global
Professionals. Our Partners in China', https://www.hud.ac.uk/
international/partnerships/china/

31   Universities UK International, 'International Facts and Figures 2019'.
July 2019. https://www.universitiesuk.ac.uk/policy-and-analysis/
reports/Pages/Intl-facts-figs-19.aspx

32   Tom Philips, 'Osborne kicks off China visit vowing to be
Beijing's best friend', *The Guardian*, 20 September 2015. https://
www.theguardian.com/business/2015/sep/20/osborne-china-
visit-beijing-best-partner

33   Danielle Cave, Dr Samantha Hoffman, Alex Joshe, Fergus Ryan
and Elise Thomas, 'Mapping China's Tech Giants', Australian
Strategic Policy Institute, 18 May 2019. https://www.aspi.org.au/
report/mapping-chinas-tech-giants

34   Richard Kerbaj and Sian Griffiths, 'Security services fear the march
on universities of Beijing's spies', *The Sunday Times*, 27 October
2019.   https://www.thetimes.co.uk/article/security-services-fear-
the-march-of-beijings-spies-on-universities-wf93f9vrq

35   Shanti Das, 'Beijing leans on UK dons to praise the Communist
Party and avoid "the three Ts – Tibet, Tiananmen and Taiwan"',
The Sunday Times, 23 June 2019. https://www.thetimes.co.uk/
article/beijing-leans-on-uk-dons-to-praise-communist-party-and-
avoid-the-three-ts-tibet-tiananmen-and-taiwan-mdt3vjnb6

36   See the Jesus College Cambridge website. https://www.jesus.cam.
ac.uk/research/china

37   See the China Centre page on the Jesus College Cambridge website. https://www.jesus.cam.ac.uk/research/china/china-centre

38   Simon Montlake and Peter Foster, 'Revealed: Wen Jiabao's family is behind Cambridge University professorship', *Telegraph*,
10 June 2014. https://www.telegraph.co.uk/news/worldnews/
asia/china/10890356/Revealed-Wen-Jiabaos-family-is-behind-
Cambridge-University-professorship.html

39   See profile of Professor Peter Nolan on the Centre of Development
Studies section of the University of Cambridge website. https://
www.devstudies.cam.ac.uk/ourpeople/peternolan

40   Jesus College Cambridge, UK–China Global Issues Dialogue
Centre white paper, *Multilateral Solutions for Global Governance of
the Information and Communications Technology Industry.* https://
www.jesus.cam.ac.uk/sites/default/files/inline/files/China%20
UK%20Dialogue%20Centre%20white%20paper.pdf

41 Beatriz Valero de Urquia, 'Huawei accused of "reputation launder-ing" after Jesus collaboration', *Varsity*, 28 February 2020. https://www.varsity.co.uk/news/18836

42 Lucy Fisher and Sam Dunning, 'Jesus College accepted £155,000 contribution from Huawei', *The Times*, 10 July 2020. https://www.thetimes.co.uk/article/jesus-college-accepted-155-000-contribution-from-huawei-53rr7qmcf

43 Emily Feng, 'Beijing vies for greater control of foreign universi-ties in China', *Financial Times*, 19 November 2017. https://www.ft.com/content/09ecaae2-ccd0-11e7-b781-794ce08b24dc

44 Emily Feng, 'China tightens party control of foreign university ven-tures', *Financial Times*, 2 July 2018. https://www.ft.com/content/4b885540-7b6d-11e8-8e67-1e1a0846c475

45 Richard Kerbaj and Sian Griffiths, 'Security services fear the march on universities of Beijing's spies', *The Sunday Times*, 27 October 2019

46 Primrose Riordan, 'London School of Economics academics out-raged by proposed China programme', *Financial Times*, 27 October 2019. https://www.ft.com/content/2dd5ed50-f538-11e9-a79c-bc9acae3b654

47 House of Commons Foreign Affairs Committee, *A cautious embrace: defending democracy in an age of autocracies*, 4 November 2019. https://publications.parliament.uk/pa/cm201919/cmselect/cmfaff/109/109.pdf

48 Colin Packman, 'Australian spy chief warns of "unprece-dented" foreign espionage threat', Reuters, 24 February 2020. https://www.reuters.com/article/us-australia-security/australia-spy-chief-warns-of-unprecedented-foreign-espionage-threat-idUSKCN20I1CY

49 John Garnaut, 'How China Interferes in Australia. And How Democracies Can Push Back', *Foreign Affairs*, 9 March 2018. https://www.foreignaffairs.com/articles/china/2018-03-09/how-china-interferes-australia

50 Paul Karp, 'Coalition bill to ban foreign political donations passes Senate', *The Guardian*, 15 November 2015. https://www.theguardian.com/australia-news/2018/nov/15/coalition-bill-to-ban-foreign-political-donations-passes-senate

51 'How China's sharp power is muting criticism abroad', *The Econo-mist*, 14 December 2014. https://www.economist.com/briefing/2017/12/14/how-chinas-sharp-power-is-muting-criticism-abroad

52 BBC News Online, 'Australia passes foreign interference laws

amid China tension', 28 June 2018. https://www.bbc.co.uk/news/world-australia-44624270

53 Jamil Anderlini, 'China-born New Zealand MP probed by spy agency,' *Financial Times*, 13 December 2017. https://www.ft.com/content/64991ca6-9796-11e7-a652-cde3f882dd7b

54 Eleanor Ainge Roy, '"I'm being watched": Anne-Marie Brady, the China critic living in fear of Beijing', *The Guardian*, 23 January 2019. https://www.theguardian.com/world/2019/jan/23/im-being-watched-anne-marie-brady-the-china-critic-living-in-fear-of-beijing

55 Anne-Marie Brady, 'Magic Weapons: China's political influence operations under Xi Jinping', Wilson Center, 18 September 2017. https://www.wilsoncenter.org/article/magic-weapons-chinas-political-influence-activities-under-xi-jinping

56 Charles Parton, 'China–UK relations', RUSI report, p. 12.

57 Anne-Marie Brady, 'Magic Weapons', p. 6.

58 Xi Jinping, *The Governance of China*, vol. II, pp. 331–3.

59 James Kynge, Lucy Hornby and Jamil Anderlini, 'Inside China's secret "magic weapon" for worldwide influence', *Financial Times*, 26 October 2017. https://www.ft.com/content/fb2b3934-b004-11e7-beba-5521c713abf4

60 Tara Francis Chan, 'The biggest difference between Chinese and Russian influence campaigns – and why China is winning', *Business Insider*, 22 March 2018. https://www.businessinsider.com/how-china-is-winning-over-russian-influence-campaigns-2018-3?op=1&r=US&IR=T

61 Sophia Yan, 'Chinese state broadcaster hires former Ofcom director amid investigation', *Telegraph*, 11 July 2019. https://www.telegraph.co.uk/news/2019/07/11/chinese-state-broadcaster-hires-former-ofcom-director-amid-investigation/

62 Patricia Nilsson, 'Chinese state TV network found to have broken UK broadcasting rules', *Financial Times*, 26 May 2020. https://www.ft.com/content/216ce76c-2dd5-4c4a-b9d7-943afaedd56c

63 Peter Humphrey, '"I was locked inside a steel cage": Peter Humphrey on life inside a Chinese prison', *Financial Times*, 16 February 2018. https://www.ft.com/content/db8b9e36-1119-11e8-940e-08320fc2a277

64 Safeguard Defenders, 'Scripted and Staged. Behind the scenes of China's forced TV confessions', 2018. https://safeguarddefenders.com/en/publications#forcedconfessions

65 Pratik Jakhar, 'Confucius Institutes: the growth of China's

controversial cultural branch', BBC News Online, 7 September 2019. https://www.bbc.co.uk/news/world-asia-china-49511231

66   The Conservative Party Human Rights Commission, 'China's Confucius Institutes', February 2019. http://www.conservative humanrights.com/news/2019/CPHRC_Confucius_Institutes_report_FEBRUARY_2019.pdf

67   Foreign Affairs Committee, *A cautious embrace*, p. 6.

68   Conservative Party Human Rights Commission, p. 4.

69   Nicola Slawson, 'David Cameron to lead £750m UK–China investment initiative', *The Guardian*, 16 December 2017. https://www.the guardian.com/politics/2017/dec/16/david-cameron-to-lead-750m-uk-china-investment-initiative

70   Jerome A. Cohen, 'Muslims in Xinjiang are facing human rights abuses. Time for China scholars to break the silence', *South China Morning Post*, 20 September 2018. https://www.scmp.com/comment/letters/article/2164698/muslims-xinjiang-are-facing-human-rights-abuses-time-china-scholars

71   Juan Pablo Cardenal, Jacek Kucharczyk, Grigorij Mesežnikov and Gabriela Pleschová, *Sharp Power. Rising Authoritarian Influence*, National Endowment for Democracy, December 2017. https://www.ned.org/wp-content/uploads/2017/12/Sharp-Power-Rising-Authoritarian-Influence-Full-Report.pdf

72   James McGregor, *One Billion Customers . . .*, p. 53.

Chapter 8: Bulldozers Down the New Silk Road

1   Oliver Holmes and Tom Phillips, 'Gui Minhai: the strange disappearance of a publisher who riled China's elite', *The Guardian*, 8 December 2015. https://www.theguardian.com/world/2015/dec/08/gui-minhai-the-strange-disappearance-of-a-publisher-who-riled-chinas-elite

2   Shadow Li, 'Missing Hong Kong bookstore owner confessed to killing: Xinhua', *China Daily*, 17 January 2016. http://www.china-daily.com.cn/china/2016-01/17/content_23123859.htm

3   Hanna Beech, 'China's Search for Dissidents Has Now Expanded to Foreign Countries', *Time*, 18 January 2016. https://time.com/4184324/gui-minhai-dissident-search/

4   Tom Phillips, 'China behaving like "gangster state" in bookseller kidnapping, say Hong Kong politicians', *The Guardian*, 17 June 2016. https://www.theguardian.com/world/2016/jun/17/china-behaving-like-gangster-state-with-bookseller-kidnap-say-hong-kong-politicians

5   Reuters, 'Chinese court jails Hong Kong bookseller for 10 years, Sweden objects', 25 February 2020. https://www.reuters.com/article/us-china-sweden-bookseller-idUSKCN20J08H

6   Tom Phillips, 'Bookseller kidnap: China hints Swedish diplomats broke laws', *The Guardian*, 23 January 2018. https://www.theguardian.com/world/2018/jan/23/sweden-summons-chinese-ambassador-over-kidnapping-of-gui-minhai

7   Oliver Holmes, 'Chinese rights campaigner disappears in Thailand', *The Guardian*, 22 January 2016. https://www.theguardian.com/world/2016/jan/22/chinese-rights-campaigner-li-xin-disappears-thailand

8   Lauren Hilgers, 'The Mystery of the Exiled Billionaire Whistle-Blower', *New York Times*, 10 January 2018. https://www.nytimes.com/2018/01/10/magazine/the-mystery-of-the-exiled-billionaire-whistleblower.html

9   'China's law enforcers are going global', *The Economist*, 31 May 2018. https://www.economist.com/china/2018/03/31/chinas-law-enforcers-are-going-global

10 BBC News Online, 'Meng Hongwei: China sentences ex-Interpol chief to 13 years in jail', 21 January 2020. https://www.bbc.co.uk/news/world-asia-china-51185838

11 Mark Mazzetti and Dan Levin, 'Obama Administration Warns Beijing About Covert Agents Working in US', *New York Times*, 16 August 2015. https://www.nytimes.com/2015/08/17/us/politics/obama-administration-warns-beijing-about-agents-operating-in-us.html

12 'China's law enforcers are going global', *The Economist*, 31 May 2018

13 *China's Artful Dissident*, broadcast by ABC News, 4 June 2019.

14 Alice Woodhouse and Nicolle Liu, 'China's "artful dissident" beats censors with viral cartoons', *Financial Times*, 13 July 2019. https://www.ft.com/content/250d7ed2-a488-11e9-974c-ad1c6ab5efd1

15 Jamil Anderlini, 'China is taking its ideological fight abroad', *Financial Times*, 9 January 2020. https://www.ft.com/content/8e839064-317c-11ea-9703-eea0cae3f0de

16 Reuters, 'China, Sweden escalate war of words over support for detained bookseller', 15 November 2019. https://www.reuters.com/article/us-china-sweden-idUSKBN1XP197

17 'How Sweden copes with Chinese bullying', *The Economist*, 20 February 2020. https://www.economist.com/europe/2020/02/20/how-sweden-copes-with-chinese-bullying

18   Xi Jinping, *The Governance of China*, vol. II, pp 553–66.
19   Zhu Shaobin, Gao Zhu and Peng Lijun, 'Why Belt and Road Initiative is anything but a debt trap', *Xinhua* news agency, 13 April 2019. http://www.xinhuanet.com/english/2019-04/13/c_137973756.htm
20   Bruno Maçães, 'At the crossroads of the new Silk road', *The Guardian*, 29 January 2019. https://www.theguardian.com/commentisfree/2018/jan/29/at-the-crossroads-of-the-new-silk-road#maincontent
21   James Kynge, 'Chinese contractors grab lion's share of Silk Road projects', *Financial Times*, 24 January 2018. https://www.ft.com/content/76b1be0c-0113-11e8-9650-9c0ad2d7c5b5
22   'Chinese investment is often a diplomatic trap', *The Economist*, 2 February 2019. https://www.economist.com/asia/2019/02/02/chinese-investment-in-infrastructure-is-often-a-diplomatic-trap
23   Charles Dunst, 'Xi's Fake History Lesson for Hun Sen', *Foreign Policy*, 10 March 2020. https://foreignpolicy.com/2020/03/10/xi-jinping-fake-history-lesson-hun-sen-china-cambodia-khmer-rouge/
24   John Hurley, Scott Morris and Gailyn Portelance, 'Examining the Debt Implications of the Belt and Road Initiative from a Policy Perspective', Center for Global Development report, March 2018. https://www.cgdev.org/sites/default/files/examining-debt-implications-belt-and-road-initiative-policy-perspective.pdf
25   Simon Mundy, 'China backed port sparks Sri Lanka sovereignty fears', *Financial Times*, 23 October 2017. https://www.ft.com/content/f8262d56-a6a0-11e7-ab55-27219df83c97
26   Maria Abi-Habib, 'China's Belt and Road Plan in Pakistan Takes a Military Turn.' *New York Times*, 19 December 2018. https://www.nytimes.com/2018/12/19/world/asia/pakistan-china-belt-road-military.html
27   Evelyne Musambi, 'Kenyans react to reports that China may take over Mombasa port', *Nairobi News*, 19 December 2018. https://duckduckgo.com/?q=Kenya+port+china+takeover&t=osx&ia=web
28   BBC News Online, 'Chinese charged over Kenya "railway scam"', 26 November 2018. https://www.bbc.co.uk/news/world-africa-46341910
29   David Pilling and Emily Feng, 'Chinese investments in Africa go off the rails', *Financial Times*, 5 December 2018. https://www.ft.com/content/82e77d8a-e716-11e8-8a85-04b8afea6ea3
30   Center for Global Development report, pp. 16–17.
31   Hannah Beech, '"We Cannot Afford This": Malaysia Pushes Back

Against China's Vision', *New York Times*, 20 April 2018. https://www.nytimes.com/2018/08/20/world/asia/china-malaysia.html

32   'Chinese investment is often a diplomatic trap', *The Economist*, 2 February 2019.

33   Tom Mitchell and Alice Woodhouse, 'Malaysia renegotiated China-backed rail project to avoid $5 billion fee', *Financial Times*, 15 April 2019. https://www.ft.com/content/660ce336-5f38-11e9-b285-3acd5d43599e

34   James Kynge and Michael Peel, 'Brussels rattled as China reaches out to Eastern Europe', *Financial Times*, 27 November 2017. https://www.ft.com/content/16abbf2a-cf9b-11e7-9dbb-291a884dd8c6

35   Stuart Lau, 'Greece says EU's China concerns must not harm its economic interests', *South China Morning Post*, 7 April 2019. https://www.scmp.com/news/china/diplomacy/article/3004724/greece-says-eus-china-concerns-must-not-harm-its-economic

36   Dalibor Rohac, 'China's economic input in eastern Europe will bear political fruit', *Financial Times*, 1 November 2017. https://www.ft.com/content/d7e4b66a-bf0b-11e7-b8a3-38a6e068f464

37   Mathew Goldstein, 'Ex-Hong Kong Official Convicted in Bribe Case Involving Chinese Oil Company', *New York Times*, 5 December 2018. https://www.nytimes.com/2018/12/05/business/cefc-china-patrick-ho.html

38   'China tries, and fails, to influence the Czechs', *The Economist*, 5 December 2019. https://www.economist.com/europe/2019/12/05/china-tries-and-fails-to-influence-the-czechs

39   *Xinhua* news agency, 'China shares wisdom of social governance with world,' 19 November 2019. http://www.xinhuanet.com/english/2019-11/19/c_138567460.htm

40   Sewell Chan, 'Norway and China Restore ties, 6 Years After Nobel Prize Dispute', *New York Times*, 19 December 2016. https://www.nytimes.com/2016/12/19/world/europe/china-norway-nobel-liu-xiaobo.html

41   Zheng Xin, 'Norway eyes seafood exports to China', *China Daily*, 25 May 2017. http://www.chinadaily.com.cn/business/2017-05/25/content_29486998.htm

42   'Chinese Tourists Are Looking to Norway', Daily Scandinavian, 6 September 2017. https://www.dailyscandinavian.com/chinese-tourists-looking-norway/

43   'China's high spending tourists bring political clout', *The Economist*, 23 February 2019. https://www.economist.com/china/2019/02/23/chinas-high-spending-tourists-bring-political-clout

44 'Firms in the firing line', Week in China, 10 March 2017. https://www.weekinchina.com/2017/03/firms-in-the-firing-line/?dm

45 'China's high spending tourists bring political clout', *The Economist*, 23 February 2019.

46 Clive Hamilton, *Silent Invasion: China's Influence in Australia* (London: Hardie Grant Books, 2018), p. 143.

47 'Chinese bullying must not be tolerated,' *The Chosun Ilbo*, 29 November 2017. http://english.chosun.com/site/data/html_dir/2017/11/29/2017112901600.html

48 Larry Elliott and Graeme Wearden, 'Xi Jinping signals China will champion free trade if Trump builds barriers', *The Guardian*, 17 January 2017. https://www.theguardian.com/business/2017/jan/17/china-xi-jinping-china-free-trade-trump-globalisation-wef-davos

49 'Less biding and hiding', *The Economist*, 4 December 2010. https://www.economist.com/special-report/2010/12/04/less-biding-and-hiding

50 See the full test of Xi Jinping's address to the 19th National Congress of the Communist Party of China, 18 October 2017, as published by *Xinhua* news agency. http://www.xinhuanet.com/english/download/Xi_Jinping's_report_at_19th_CPC_National_Congress.pdf

51 Henry A. Kissinger, 'America's Assignment: What will we face in the next four years?' *Newsweek*, 8 November 2004 (accessed via Kissinger's website). https://www.henryakissinger.com/articles/americas-assignment-what-will-we-face-in-the-next-four-years/

52 Ketian Zhang, 'Cautious Bully: Reputation, Resolve, and Beijing's Use of Coercion in the South China Sea', *International Security*, vol. 44, issue 1, Summer 2019, pp. 117–59.

53 Jeremiah Cha, 'People in Asia-Pacific regard the US more favourably than China, but Trump gets negative marks', Pew Research Center, 25 February 2020. https://www.pewresearch.org/fact-tank/2020/02/25/people-in-asia-pacific-regard-the-u-s-more-favorably-than-china-but-trump-gets-negative-marks/

54 For a fuller discussion of this struggle over internet standards, see Stacie Hoffmann, Dominique Lazanski and Emily Taylor, 'Standardising the splinternet: how China's technical standards could fragment the internet', *Journal of Cyber Policy*, 29 August 2020. https://doi.org/10.1080/23738871.2020.1805482

55 Alan Gross, Madhumita Murgia and Yuan Yang, 'Chinese tech groups shaping UN facial recognition standards', *Financial Times*,

2 December 2019. https://www.ft.com/content/c3555a3c-0d3e-11ea-b2d6-9bf4d1957a67

56 *The New Big Brother. China and Digital Authoritarianism*, a Democratic staff report prepared for the use of the Committee on Foreign Relations on the United States Senate, 21 July 2020. https://www.foreign.senate.gov/imo/media/doc/2020%20SFRC%20Minority%20Staff%20Report%20-%20The%20New%20Big%20Brother%20-%20China%20and%20Digital%20Authoritarianism.pdf

57 Steven Feldstein, 'The Global Expansion of AI Surveillance', Carnegie Endowment for International Peace, 17 September 2019. https://carnegieendowment.org/files/WP-Feldstein-AISurveillance_final.pdf

58 Paul Mozur, Jonah M. Kessel and Melissa Chan, 'Made in China, Exported to The World: The Surveillance State', *New York Times*, 24 April 2019. https://www.nytimes.com/2019/04/24/technology/ecuador-surveillance-cameras-police-government.html

59 Joan Tilouine and Ghalia Kadiri, 'A Addis-Abeba, le siège de l'Union africaine espionné par Pékin', *Le Monde*, 26 January 2018. https://www.lemonde.fr/afrique/article/2018/01/26/a-addis-abeba-le-siege-de-l-union-africaine-espionne-par-les-chinois_5247521_3212.html

60 Karishma Vaswani, 'Huawei: The story of a controversial company', BBC News Online, 6 March 2019. https://www.bbc.co.uk/news/resources/idt-sh/Huawei

61 Irene Yuan Sun, Kartik Jayaram and Omid Kassiri, 'Dance of the lions and dragons: How are Africa and China engaging, and how will the partnership evolve?' McKinsey & Company, June 2017. https://www.mckinsey.com/~/media/McKinsey/Featured%20Insights/Middle%20East%20and%20Africa/The%20closest%20look%20yet%20at%20Chinese%20economic%20engagement%20in%20Africa/Dance-of-the-lions-and-dragons.ashx

62 Africa Business Central, 'Huawei looks to Africa to cut network deals', 26 March 2016. https://www.africanbusinesscentral.com/2016/03/25/huawei-looks-to-africa-to-cut-network-deals/

63 See Huawei's corporate brochure, *Huawei Safe City Solution*. https://e.huawei.com/en/material/industry/safecity/044042f765c04a518e3e25c87fea5133

64 Jonathan Hillman and Maesea McCalpin, 'Watching Huawei's "safe cities"', Center for Strategic and International Studies, 4 November 2019. https://csis-prod.s3.amazonaws.com/s3fs-public/

publication/191030_HillmanMcCalpin_HuaweiSafeCity_layout_
v4.pdf?X6bq2FMWVTX9qK68Z7wK1QXRS4l.Zgip

65   Figures taken from Huawei Investment & Holding Co., Ltd, 2019
      Annual Report. https://www-file.huawei.com/-/media/corporate/
      pdf/annual-report/annual_report_2019_en.pdf?la=en

66   Huawei press release, 'Huawei's commitment to Europe delivers
      billions in economic benefits', 4 November 2019. https://www.
      huawei.com/en/press-events/news/2019/11/huawei-commit
      ment-europe-billions-economic-benefits

67   Chuin-Wei Yap, 'State Support Helped Fuel Huawei's Global
      Rise', *Wall Street Journal*, 25 December 2019. https://www.wsj.
      com/articles/state-support-helped-fuel-huaweis-global-rise-
      11577280736?mod=article_inline

68   Michael Peel and Alex Barber, 'China envoy to EU hits out at Huawei
      security "slander"', *Financial Times*, 27 January 2019. https://
      www.ft.com/content/fbb7a49c-20c8-11e9-b126-46fc3ad87c65

69   See the full indictment issued by the United District Court,
      Eastern District of New York, on 13 February 2020. https://www.
      justice.gov/usao-edny/press-release/file/1248966/download

70   Nathan Vanderklippe, '365 days of detention in China: What life is
      like for Canadians Michael Spavor and Michael Kovrig', *The Globe
      and Mail*, 9 December 2019. https://www.theglobeandmail.com/
      world/article-michael-kovrig-michael-spavor-china-detained-
      canadians-huawei/

71   Toby Helm, 'Pressure from Trump led to 5G ban, Britain tells
      Huawei', *The Guardian*, 18 July 2020. https://www.theguardian.
      com/technology/2020/jul/18/pressure-from-trump-led-to-5g-ban-
      britain-tells-huawei?CMP=Share_iOSApp_Other

72   Helen Warrell, 'US presses Boris Johnson with new dossier on
      Huawei security risks', *Financial Times*, 13 January 2020. https://
      www.ft.com/content/1d7f44b4-3643-11ea-a6d3-9a26f8c3cba4

73   See Senator Tom Cotton's tweets on the decision, 28 January 2020.
      https://twitter.com/SenTomCotton/status/1222175846498172928

74   Tom Tugendhat, 'Giving control to Beijing is too big a risk: Tom
      Tugendhat has warned', *Mail on Sunday*, 26 January 2020. https://
      www.dailymail.co.uk/news/article-7929955/Giving-control-
      Beijing-big-risk-TOM-TUGENDHAT-warned.html

75   James Kynge and Nic Fildes, 'Huawei: the indispensable telecoms
      company', *Financial Times*, 31 January 2020. https://www.ft.com/
      content/24b01f0e-441e-11ea-a43a-c4b328d9061c

76   Oxford Economics and Huawei, 'The Economic Impact of

Huawei in the UK', May 2019. https://www.huawei.com/uk/press-events/news/uk/2019/huawei-investment-commitments-in-uk-leads-to-billions-in-benefits-to-the-economy

77   Huawei press release, 'Huawei and Imperial announce new collaboration', 19 May 2020. https://www.huawei.com/uk/press-events/news/uk/2020/Huawei-and-Imperial-College-announce-new-collaboration

78   Laurie Chen, 'Oxford University suspends donor ties with Chinese tech giant Huawei as national security fears mount', *South China Morning Post*, 17 January 2019. https://www.scmp.com/news/china/diplomacy/article/2182598/oxford-university-suspends-donor-ties-chinese-tech-giant-huawei

79   Huawei Cyber Security Evaluation Centre (HCSEC) Oversight Board Annual Report, 2019. https://assets.publishing.service.gov.uk/government/uploads/system/uploads/attachment_data/file/790270/HCSEC_OversightBoardReport-2019.pdf

80   Dan Sabbagh, 'Huawei prepared to sign "no-spy" agreement with UK government', *The Guardian*, 14 May 2019. https://www.theguardian.com/technology/2019/may/14/huawei-founder-shut-down-china-eavesdrop

81   National Cyber Security Centre, 'NCSC advice on the use of equipment from high risk vendors in UK telecoms networks', 28 January 2020. https://www.ncsc.gov.uk/guidance/ncsc-advice-on-the-use-of-equipment-from-high-risk-vendors-in-uk-telecoms-networks#section_5

Chapter 9: Cyber Smash and Grab

1   Office of the National Counterintelligence Executive, 'Foreign Spies Stealing US Economic Secrets in Cyberspace', October 2011. https://www.hsdl.org/?view&did=720057

2   UK government press release, 'UK and allies reveal global scale of Chinese cyber campaign', 20 December 2018. https://www.gov.uk/government/news/uk-and-allies-reveal-global-scale-of-chinese-cyber-campaign

3   See the full Department of Justice indictment, https://www.justice.gov/opa/pr/two-chinese-hackers-associated-ministry-state-security-charged-global-computer-intrusion

4   PwC and BAE Systems, 'Operation Cloud Hopper', April 2017 report. https://www.pwc.co.uk/cyber-security/pdf/cloud-hopper-report-final-v4.pdf

5   Jack Stubbs, Joseph Menn and Christopher Bing, 'Inside the West's failed fight against China's "Cloud Hopper" hackers', Reuters, 26 June 2019. https://www.reuters.com/article/us-china-cyber-cloud hopper-special-repor-idUSKCN1TR1DK

6   William Evanina, 'Private Sector as the New Geopolitical battlespace', *Catalyst*, Fall 2019. https://www.odni.gov/index.php/ncsc-newsroom/item/2064-private-sector-as-the-new-geo political-battlespace

7   Marc Goodman, *Future Crimes: A Journey to the Dark Side of Technology – and How to Survive It* (London: Transworld Publishers, 2015), p. 156.

8   Dean Cheng, *Cyber Dragon: Inside China's Information Warfare and Cyber Operations* (Santa Barbara: Praeger, 2017), pp. 182–3.

9   Mandiant, *APT1: Exposing One of China's Espionage Units*, 19 February 2013. https://www.fireeye.com/content/dam/fireeye-www/services/pdfs/mandiant-apt1-report.pdf

10   P. W. Singer and Allan Friedman, *Cybersecurity and Cyberwar: What Everyone Needs to Know* (Oxford: Oxford University Press, 2014), p. 142.

11   Ellen Nakashima, 'Confidential report lists U.S. defense system designs compromised by Chinese cyberspies', *Washington Post*, 27 May 2013. https://www.washingtonpost.com/world/national-security/confidential-report-lists-us-weapons-system-designs-compromised-by-chinese-cyberspies/2013/05/27/a42c3e1c-c2dd-11e2-8c3b-0b5e9247e8ca_story.html

12   See Department of Justice press release, 'U.S. Charges Five Chinese Military Hackers for Cyber Espionage Against U.S. Corporations and a Labor Organization for Commercial Advantage', 19 May 2014. https://www.justice.gov/opa/pr/us-charges-five-chinese-mil itary-hackers-cyber-espionage-against-us-corporations-and-labor

13   Adam Segal, 'How China is preparing for cyberwar', *The Christian Science Monitor*, 20 March 2017. https://www.csmonitor.com/World/Passcode/Passcode-Voices/2017/0320/How-China-is-preparing-for-cyberwar

14   Rhys Blakely, Jonathan Richards, James Rossiter and Richard Beeston, 'MI5 alert on China's cyberspace spy threat', *The Times*, December 2007. https://www.thetimes.co.uk/article/mi5-alert-on-chinas-cyberspace-spy-threat-tbxdgkv5l9v

15   Agence France-Presse, 'Airbus hit by series of cyberattacks on suppliers', 26 September 2019. https://www.france24.com/en/20190926-airbus-hit-by-series-of-cyber-attacks-on-suppliers

16   Wang Wei, 'Report Reveals TeamViewer Was Breached by Chinese Hackers in 2016', The Hacker News, 17 May 2019. https://the hackernews.com/2019/05/teamviewer-software-hacked.html

17   Ronan Bergman and Steven Lee Myers, 'China's Military is Tied to Debilitating New Cyberattack Tool', *New York Times*, 7 May 2020. https://www.nytimes.com/2020/05/07/world/asia/china-hacking-military-aria.html

18   Yuan Yang, 'China's Tsinghua University linked to cyber espionage, study claims', *Financial Times*, 17 August 2018. https://www.ft.com/content/cbf22f3c-a1f9-11e8-85da-eeb7a9ce36e4

19   Jordon Robertson and Michael Riley, 'The Big Hack: How China Used a Tiny Chip to Infiltrate U.S. Companies', *Bloomberg Businessweek*, 4 October 2018. https://www.bloomberg.com/news/features/2018-10-04/the-big-hack-how-china-used-a-tiny-chip-to-infiltrate-america-s-top-companies

20   Richard Luscombe, 'Mar-a-Lago's bizarre breach: a mystery woman, malware and Trump's "circus"', *The Guardian*, 6 April 2019. https://www.theguardian.com/us-news/2019/apr/05/mar-a-lagos-bizarre-breach-a-mystery-woman-malware-and-trumps-circus

21   Eric Geller, 'U.S. charges Chinese military hackers with massive Equifax breach', Politico, 10 February 2020. https://www.politico.com/news/2020/02/10/us-charges-chinese-spies-with-massive-equifax-hack-113129

22   David Bond, 'Chinese hackers increase attacks on telecoms companies', *Financial Times*, 19 February 2019. https://www.ft.com/content/3662667a-3390-11e9-bb0c-42459962a812

23   Fuller background on Samuel Slater and Belper can be found on the Derbyshire Blue Plaques website: http://derbyshireblue-plaques.co.uk/samuel-slater/

24   Martin Wolf, 'The fight to halt the theft of ideas is hopeless', *Financial Times*, 9 November 2019. https://www.ft.com/content/d592af00-0a29-11ea-b2d6-9bf4d1957a67

25   Sijia Jiang, 'Huawei set to announce lawsuit against U.S. as it seeks to strike back', Reuters, 6 March 2019. https://www.reuters.com/article/us-usa-china-huawei-tech/huawei-set-to-announce-law-suit-against-u-s-as-it-seeks-to-strike-back-idUSKCN1QN2WG

26   William C. Hannas, James Mulvenon and Anna B. Puglisi, *Chinese Industrial Espionage: Technology Acquisition and Military Modernisation* (Abingdon: Routledge, 2013), p. 2.

27   Council on Foreign Relations, *A Conversation with Christopher Wray*, 26 April 2019. https://www.cfr.org/event/conversation-christopher-wray-0

28   Nichole Perlroth, 'Washington Post Joins List of News Media Hacked by the Chinese', *New York Times*, 1 February 2013. https://www.nytimes.com/2013/02/02/technology/washington-posts-joins-list-of-media-hacked-by-the-chinese.html

29   Nichole Perlroth, 'Hackers in China Attacked the Times for Last 4 Months', *New York Times*, 30 January 2013. https://www.nytimes.com/2013/01/31/technology/chinese-hackers-infiltrate-new-york-times-computers.html

30   Ibid.

31   Jonathan Kaiman, 'Hack Tibet. Welcome to Dharamsala, ground zero in China's cyberwar', *Foreign Policy*, 4 December 2013. https://foreignpolicy.com/2013/12/04/hack-tibet/

32   Citizen Lab, *Tracking GhostNet: Investigating a Cyber Espionage Network*. 29 March 2009. https://issuu.com/citizenlab/docs/iwm-ghostnet

33   Andrew Case, Mathew Meltzer and Steven Adair, 'Digital Crackdown: Large-Scale Surveillance and Exploitation of Uighurs', Volexity blog, 2 September 2019. https://www.volexity.com/blog/2019/09/02/digital-crackdown-large-scale-surveillance-and-exploitation-of-uyghurs/

34   David Tweed, 'China's Cyber Spies Take to High Seas as Hack Attacks spike', Bloomberg News, 15 October 2015. https://www.bloomberg.com/news/articles/2015-10-15/chinese-cyber-spies-fish-for-enemies-in-south-china-sea-dispute

35   Bill Marczak, Nicholas Weaver, Jakub Dalek, Roya Ensafi, David Fifield, Sarah McKune, Arn Rey, John Scott-Railton, Ron Deibert and Vern Paxson, 'China's Great Cannon', Citizen Lab, 10 April 2015. https://citizenlab.ca/2015/04/chinas-great-cannon/

36   For more details of Project Galileo, see Cloudflare's website: https://www.cloudflare.com/galileo/

37   Thomas Fox-Brewster, 'Did China Order Hackers to Cripple the Hong Kong protest?' *Vice*, 5 November 2014. https://www.vice.com/en_us/article/539wnz/inside-the-unending-cyber-siege-of-hong-kong

38   Parmy Olson, 'The largest cyber-attack in history has been hitting Hong Kong sites', *Forbes*, 20 November 2014. https://www.forbes.com/sites/parmyolson/2014/11/20/the-largest-cyber-attack-in-history-has-been-hitting-hong-kong-sites/#6b77783d38f6

39   See the National Museum of China's online exhibition guide, available at http://en.chnmuseum.cn/exhibition/current_exhibitions_648/201911/t20191120_171616.html

40   Richard Hughes, *Borrowed Place, Borrowed Time: Hong Kong and Its Many Faces* (London. Andre Deutsch, 1976), p. 13.

41 Richard J. Aldrich, *GCHQ: The Uncensored Story of Britain's Most Secret Intelligence Agency* (London: HarperPress, 2010), pp. 151–2.

42 Chris Patten, *East and West* (London: Macmillan, 1998), p. 91.

43 Check Point Software Technologies, 'Chinese government targets Hong Kong protesters with Android mRAT spyware', Check Point blog, 30 September 2014. https://blog.checkpoint.com/2014/09/30/chinese-government-targets-hong-kong-protesters-android-mrat-spyware/

44 Jeffie Lam and Keith Zhai, 'Cyberattacks against Occupy Central poll traced to mainland firms' computers in Hong Kong', *South China Morning Post*, 23 June 2014 https://www.scmp.com/news/hong-kong/article/1538965/cyberattacks-against-occupy-central-poll-traced-mainland-firms

45 Katie Kleemola, Masashi Crete-Nishihata and John Railton, 'Targeted attacks against Tibetan and Hong Kong groups exploiting CVE-2014-4114', Citizen Lab Research Note, 15 June 2015. https://citizenlab.ca/2015/06/targeted-attacks-against-tibetan-and-hong-kong-groups-exploiting-cve-2014-4114/

46 Andrew Jacobs, 'Chinese Web Censors Struggle with Hong Kong Protest', *New York Times*, 30 September 2014. https://www.nytimes.com/2014/10/01/world/asia/chinese-web-censors-struggle-with-hong-kong-protest.html

47 Chris Buckley, 'Chinese Propaganda Video Warns of West's "Devilish Claws"', *New York Times*, 22 December 2016. https://www.nytimes.com/2016/12/22/world/asia/china-video-communist-party.html

48 Eli Binder, 'Hong Kong Protesters Spy a New Enemy: Lampposts', *Wall Street Journal*, 30 August 2019. https://www.wsj.com/articles/hong-kong-protesters-spy-a-new-enemy-lampposts-11567161002

49 Steven Lee Myers and Paul Mozur, 'China is waging a Disinformation War Against Hong Kong Protesters', *New York Times*, 13 August 2019. https://www.nytimes.com/2019/08/13/world/asia/hong-kong-protests-china.html

50 Agence France-Presse, 'Hong Kong protests: YouTube takes down 200 channels spreading disinformation', *The Guardian*, 23 August 2019. https://www.theguardian.com/technology/2019/aug/23/hong-kong-protests-youtube-takes-down-200-channels-spreading-disinformation

51 See the Hong Kong entry in the Heritage Foundation's 2020 Index of Economic Freedom: https://www.heritage.org/index/country/hongkong?version=411

52   Noah Sin, 'Explainer: How important is Hong Kong to the rest of China?' Reuters, 5 September 2019. https://www.reuters.com/article/us-hongkong-protests-markets-explainer-idUSKCN1VP35H

53   'China's draconian security law for Hong Kong buries one country two systems', *The Economist*, 1 July 2020. https://www.economist.com/leaders/2020/07/02/chinas-draconian-security-law-for-hong-kong-buries-one-country-two-systems

54   'A new national security bill to intimidate Hong Kong', *The Economist*, 2 July 2020. https://www.economist.com/china/2020/07/02/a-new-national-security-bill-to-intimidate-hong-kong?-frsc=dg%7Ce

55   Stephen Morris and Attracta Mooney, 'HSBC and StanChart's support for Hong Kong law provokes ire', *Financial Times*, 4 June 2020. https://www.ft.com/content/9fee072d-b210-4a0b-b610-39bd25c57dab

56   Tom Mitchell, 'HSBC told not to take "unique Hong Kong privileges" for granted', *Financial Times*, 29 May 20120. https://www-ft-com.ezproxy.babson.edu/content/2cef367f-a806-4824-a431-f04631754c28

Chapter 10: To the Digital Barricades

1   Thomas Friedman, 'China Deserves Donald Trump', *New York Times*, 21 May 2019. https://www.nytimes.com/2019/05/21/opinion/china-trump-trade.html

2   Xiangfeng Yang, 'The great Chinese surprise: the rupture with the United States is real and is happening', *International Affairs*, 96:2, 2020, pp. 419–37.

3   John Bolton, *The Room Where It Happened* (London: Simon & Schuster, 2020).

4   James Palmer, 'China hawks pinned too many hopes on a deeply flawed administration', *Foreign Policy*, 22 November 2019. https://foreignpolicy.com/2019/11/22/hong-kong-protests-xinjiang-donald-trump-xi-jinping-china/

5   'China's leaders should study James Bond films', *The Economist*, 21 March, 2019. https://www.economist.com/china/2019/03/21/chinas-leaders-should-study-james-bond-films

6   Xi Jinping, *The Governance of China*, vol. I, p. 38.

7   Michael Pillsbury, *The Hundred-Year Marathon: China's Secret Strategy to Replace America as the Global Superpower* (New York: Henry Holt and Company, 2015).

8   Alan Rappaport, 'A China Hawk Gains Prominence as Trump

Confronts Xi on Trade', *New York Times*, 30 November 2018. https://www.nytimes.com/2018/11/30/us/politics/trump-china-trade-xi-michael-pillsbury.html

9   Testimony of Robert Atkinson, president of the Technology and Innovation Foundation before the US–China Security Review Commission of the US Congress, 26 January 2017. https://www.uscc.gov/sites/default/files/Atkinson_USCC%20Hearing%20Testimony012617.pdf

10 See Grzegorz W. Kolodko, *China and the Future of Globalization: The Political Economy of China's Rise* (London: I. B. Tauris, 2020).

11 See US–China trade facts, published by the Office of the United States Trade Representative: https://ustr.gov/countries-regions/china-mongolia-taiwan/peoples-republic-china

12 Martha C. White, 'Should the US refuse to pay back its $1 trillion debt to China?' *NBC News*, 7 June 2020. https://www.nbcnews.com/business/economy/should-u-s-refuse-pay-back-its-1-trillion-debt-n1227351

13 Bryan Borzykowski, 'China's $1.2 trillion weapon that could be used in trade war with the US', CNBC, 5 April 2018. https://www.cnbc.com/2018/04/05/chinas-1-point-2-trillion-weapon-that-could-be-used-in-a-us-trade-war.html

14 Shawn Donnan, 'The AI arms race: the tech fear behind Donald Trump's trade war with China', *Financial Times*, 5 July 2018. https://www.ft.com/content/40304bea-7eb9-11e8-bc55-50daf11b720d?stream=top

15 James Rogers, Dr Andrew Foxall, Mathew Henderson and Sam Armstrong, 'Breaking the Supply Chain: How the "Five Eyes" Can Decouple from Strategic Dependency', The Henry Jackson Society, May 2020. https://henryjacksonsociety.org/wp-content/uploads/2020/05/Breaking-the-China-Chain.pdf

16 'Covid-19's blow to world trade is a heavy one', *The Economist*, 14 May 2020. https://www.economist.com/briefing/2020/05/14/covid-19s-blow-to-world-trade-is-a-heavy-one

17 Ibid.

18 The full 2017 music video *Automatica* can be viewed on Nigel Stanford's website: https://nigelstanford.com/Automatica/

19 Arthur Sullivan, 'Changes at German robotics form Kuka raise questions over Chinese intentions', *Deutsche Welle*, 26 November 2018. https://www.dw.com/en/changes-at-german-robotics-firm-kuka-raise-questions-over-chinese-intentions/a-46456133

20 Guy Chazan, 'Backlash grows over Chinese deals for Germany's

corporate jewels', *Financial Times*, 13 March 2013. https://www.ft.com/content/391637d2-215a-11e8-a895-1ba1f72c2c11

21   James Kynge, 'China's Belt and Road projects drive overseas debt fears', *Financial Times*, 7 August 2018. https://www.ft.com/content/e7a08b54-9554-11e8-b747-fb1e803ee64e

22   The full strategic document, *EU–China – a strategic outlook*, prepared by the European Commission and the EU's High Representative of the Union for Foreign Affairs and Security Policy, published on 12 March 2019, can be found at https://ec.europa.eu/commission/sites/beta-political/files/communication-eu-china-a-strategic-outlook.pdf

23   Jim Brunsden, 'EU trade chief urges tougher defences against foreign takeovers', *Financial Times*, 16 April 2020. https://www.ft.com/content/bf83fa94-1bcf-4532-a75a-50f41351c0d4

24   Patrick Wintour, 'European tour tests Chinese foreign minister's pulling power', *The Guardian*, 2 September 2020. https://www.theguardian.com/world/2020/sep/02/european-tour-tests-chinese-foreign-ministers-pulling-power?CMP=Share_iOSApp_Other

25   For a full video of the 5 May 2020 session of the Foreign Affairs Committee hearing on the 'FCO's role in blocking foreign asset stripping in the UK', see Parliamentary TV: https://parliamentlive.tv/Event/Index/507e28e5-6718-41b2-bfa4-0b15dc147928

26   Jim Pickard and Tim Bradshaw, 'Imagination sale set to test UK government over China deals', *Financial Times*, 24 September 2014. https://www.ft.com/content/dc6a8df4-a138-11e7-9e4f-7f5e6a7c98a2

27   Details of the bill and the various consultations that preceded it can be found online, at the website of the House of Commons Library: https://commonslibrary.parliament.uk/research-briefings/cbp-8784/

28   Jillian Ambrose, 'Where in Britain does China spend its money?' *The Guardian*, 11 July 2020. https://www.theguardian.com/world/2020/jul/11/where-in-britain-does-china-spend-its-money

29   David Connett and Jamie Merrill, 'UK accused of doing China's bidding after police raid home of Tiananmen Square survivor over peaceful protest', *Independent*, 22 October 2015. https://www.independent.co.uk/news/uk/home-news/uk-accused-of-doing-chinas-bidding-after-police-raid-home-of-tiananmen-square-survivor-over-peaceful-a6704911.html#commentsDiv

30   Tom Phillips, 'Queen caught on camera saying Chinese officials

were "very rude"', *The Guardian*, 11 May 2016. https://www.theguardian.com/world/2016/may/11/queen-chinese-officials-very-rude-xi-jinping-state-visit

31   Simon Goodley and Rowena Mason, 'Hinkley Point: China warns UK not to drive away investors', *The Guardian*, 1 August 2016. https://www.theguardian.com/uk-news/2016/aug/01/china-warns-uk-over-suspicious-approach-to-hinkley-point-deal

32   Christian Shepherd, 'The Chinese dealmaker behind a risky bet on British Steel', *Financial Times*, 13 November 2019. https://www.ft.com/content/c3ca4d06-05e6-11ea-a984-fbbacad9e7dd

33   Martin Thorley, 'Chinese Firms Can't Avoid Being Party Tools,' *Foreign Policy*, 12 November 2019. https://foreignpolicy.com/2019/11/12/china-communist-party-british-steel-brexit-chinese-firms-cant-help-be-party-tools/

34   Nic Fildes, 'Huawei buys access to UK innovation with Oxford stake', *Financial Times*, 2 October 2019. https://www.ft.com/content/28892c04-e453-11e9-b112-9624ec9edc59

35   Zhang Yangfei, 'He Jiankui gets 3 years for illegal human embryo gene-editing', *China Daily*, 30 December 2019. https://www.chinadaily.com.cn/a/201912/30/WS5e098549a310cf3e35581783.html

36   Dennis Normile, 'Chinese scientist who produced genetically altered babies sentenced to 3 years in jail', *Science*, 30 December 2019. https://www.sciencemag.org/news/2019/12/chinese-scientist-who-produced-genetically-altered-babies-sentenced-3-years-jail

37   Statista, *Leading countries by gross research and development (R&D) expenditure worldwide in 2019*, 28 April 2020. https://www.statista.com/statistics/732247/worldwide-research-and-development-gross-expenditure-top-countries/

38   Jeff Tollefson, 'China declared world's largest producer of scientific articles', *Nature*, 18 January 2018. https://www.nature.com/articles/d41586-018-00927-4?utm_source=twt_nnc&utm_medium=social&utm_campaign=naturenews&sf179577684=1

39   Amy Qin, 'Fraud Scandals Sap China's Dream of Becoming a Science Superpower', *New York Times*, 13 October 2013. https://www.nytimes.com/2017/10/13/world/asia/china-science-fraud-scandals.html

40   Yuan Yang and Archie Zhang, 'China launches crackdown on academic fraud', *Financial Times*, 18 June 2017. https://www.ft.com/content/680ea354-5251-11e7-bfb8-997009366969

41 'Don't be fooled by the trade deal between America and China,' *The Economist*, 2 January 2020. https://www.economist.com/ leaders/2020/01/02/dont-be-fooled-by-the-trade-deal-between-america-and-china

42 Greg Williams, 'Why China will win the global race for complete AI dominance', *Wired*, 18 April 2018. https://www.wired.co.uk/ article/why-china-will-win-the-global-battle-for-ai-dominance

43 Brian McGleenon, 'Kidnapping, trafficking and gang violence: Inside China's quest to become an AI superpower', *Independent*, 14 April 2020. https://www.independent.co.uk/independentpre mium/long-reads/china-belt-road-xi-jinping-sihanoukville-cambodia-silicon-valley-huawei-5g-data-a9407091.html

44 Yuan Yang and James Fontanella-Khan, 'Grindr sold by Chinese owner after US national security concerns', *Financial Times*, 7 March 2020. https://www.ft.com/content/a32a740a-5fb3-11ea-8033-fa40a0d65a98

45 ProtonMail, 'TikTok and the privacy perils of China's first international social media platform', 23 July 2020. https://protonmail. com/blog/tiktok-privacy/

46 Alex Hern, 'TikTok under investigation over child data use', *The Guardian*, 2 July 2019. https://www.theguardian.com/tech nology/2019/jul/02/tiktok-under-investigation-over-child-data-use

47 For details of the class action complaint, filed 27 November 2019, see court documents online at https://www.courthousenews.com/ wp-content/uploads/2019/12/Tiktok.pdf

48 John Gapper, 'China's internet interference is TikTok famous', *Financial Times*, 4 December 2019. https://www.ft.com/content/ 30137c2e-15c5-11ea-9ee4-11f260415385

49 Kitty Donaldson, Katherine Gemmell and Nate Lanxon, 'TikTok Faces Government Restrictions on U.K. Expansion Drive.' Bloomberg News, 26 August 2020. https://www.bloomberg.com/ news/articles/2020-08-26/tiktok-faces-government-restric tions-on-u-k-expansion-drive

50 Paul Mozur, 'Forget TikTok. China's Powerhouse App Is WeChat, and Its Power Is Sweeping', *The New York Times*, 4 September 2020. https://www.nytimes.com/2020/09/04/technology/wechat-china-united-states.html

51 Miles Kenyon, 'WeChat Surveillance Explained', *Citizen Lab*, 7 May 2020. https://citizenlab.ca/2020/05/wechat-surveillance-explained/

52 Paul Mozur, Julian E. Barnes and Aaron Krolik, 'Popular Chinese-

Made Drone is Found to Have Security Weaknesses', *The New York Times*, 23 July 2020. https://www.nytimes.com/2020/07/23/us/politics/dji-drones-security-vulnerability.html?referringSource=articleShare

53 Timothy McLaughlin, 'Hong Kong Doesn't Have Pro-China "Silent Majority"', *The Atlantic*, 25 November 2019. https://www.the atlantic.com/international/archive/2019/11/hong-kong-election-silent-majority/602551/

54 Steven Lee Myers, Chris Buckley and Keith Bradshaw, 'Is Xi Mishandling Hong Kong Crisis?' *New York Times*, 7 September 2019. https://www.nytimes.com/2019/09/07/world/asia/china-hong-kong-xi-jinping.html

55 Austin Ramzy and Chris Buckley, 'The Xinjiang Papers. "Show No Mercy": Leaked Files Expose How China Organized Mass Detentions of Muslims', *New York Times*, 16 November 2019. https://www.nytimes.com/interactive/2019/11/16/world/asia/china-xinjiang-documents.html

56 Radio Free Asia, 'Riot Police win Back Control of Protest Town in China's Guangdong Province', 2 December 2019. https://www.rfa.org/english/news/china/crematorium-protest-12022019151453.html

57 China Digital Times, 'Translation: Former Party Professor Calls CCP a "Political Zombie"', 12 June 2020. https://chinadigital times.net/2020/06/translation-former-party-professor-calls-ccp-a-political-zombie/

58 Lily Kou, 'China's Xi Jinping facing widespread opposition in his own party, insider claims', *The Guardian*, 18 August 2020. https://www.theguardian.com/world/2020/aug/18/china-xi-jinping-facing-widespread-opposition-in-his-own-party-claims-insider?CMP=Share_iOSApp_Other

59 'A lawsuit against face-scans in China could have big consequences', *The Economist*, 9 November 2019. https://www.economist.com/china/2019/11/09/a-lawsuit-against-face-scans-in-china-could-have-big-consequences

60 Gordon Watts, 'China's academics tackle the "Big Brother" state', *Asia Times*, 25 December 2019. https://asiatimes.com/2019/12/chinas-academics-tackle-the-big-brother-state/

61 Kerry Allen, 'Chinese chatbots shutdown after anti-government posts', BBC News Online, 3 August 2017. https://www.bbc.co.uk/news/world-asia-china-40815024

62 David Shambaugh, *China's Future* (Cambridge: Polity Press, 2015), p. 61.

Chapter 11: The Communist Party Virus

1   Qin Jianhang and Timmy Shen, 'Whistleblower Li Wenliang: There Should Be More Than One Voice in a Healthy Society', *Caixin*, 6 February 2020. https://www.caixinglobal.com/2020-02-06/after-being-punished-by-local-police-coronavirus-whistleblower-vindicated-by-top-court-101509986.html

2   Jeremy Page, Wenxin Fan and Natasha Khan, 'How It All Started: China's Early Coronavirus Missteps', *Wall Street Journal*, 6 March 2020. https://www.wsj.com/articles/how-it-all-started-chinas-early-coronavirus-missteps-11583508932

3   Lily Kuo, 'Coronavirus: Wuhan doctor speaks out against authorities', *The Guardian*, 11 March 2020. https://www.theguardian.com/world/2020/mar/11/coronavirus-wuhan-doctor-ai-fen-speaks-out-against-authorities

4   Jeremy Page, et al., 'How It All Started . . .' *Wall Street Journal*, 6 March 2020.

5   Chris Buckley and Steven Lee Myers, 'As New Coronavirus Spread, China's Old Habits Delayed Fight', *New York Times*, 7 February, 2020. https://www.nytimes.com/2020/02/01/world/asia/china-coronavirus.html

6   Kenneth Tan, 'Whistleblower doctor accused of "rumormongering" dead at 34', *Shanghaiist*, 7 February 2020. https://shanghai.ist/2020/02/07/whistleblower-doctor-accused-of-rumormongering-dead-after-losing-battle-with-coronavirus/

7   'The man who knew. Li Wenliang died on February 7th', *The Economist*, 13 February 2020. https://www.economist.com/obituary/2020/02/13/li-wenliang-died-on-february-7th

8   Buckley and Myers, 'As New Coronavirus Spread . . .' *New York Times*, 7 February 2020.

9   Ibid.

10   Lily Kuo, 'Coronavirus: Wuhan doctor speaks out against authorities', *The Guardian*, 11 March 2020. https://www.theguardian.com/world/2020/mar/11/coronavirus-wuhan-doctor-ai-fen-speaks-out-against-authorities

11   Fang Fang, *Wuhan Diary: Dispatches from a Quarantined City* (London: HarperCollins, 2020).

12   Associated Press, 'China didn't warn public of likely pandemic for 6 key days', 15 April 2020. https://apnews.com/68a9e1b91de4ffc166acd6012d82c2f9

13   Tom Mitchell, 'What Xi knew: pressure builds on Chinese leader', *Financial Times*, 21 May 2020. https://www.ft.com/

content/3a294233-6983-428c-b74b-3cc58c713eb8?share-Type=nongift

14 See the WHO press release of 28 January 2020, describing the visit by Director-General Dr Tedros Adhanom Ghebreyesus to Beijing and his meeting with Xi Jinping. https://www.who.int/news-room/detail/28-01-2020-who-china-leaders-discuss-next-steps-in-battle-against-coronavirus-outbreak

15 Associated Press, 'China delayed releasing coronavirus info, frustrating WHO', 3 June 2020. https://apnews.com/3c06179497 0661042b18d5aeaaed9fae

16 Josephine Ma and Zhuang Pinghua, '5 million left Wuhan before lockdown, 1,000 new coronavirus cases expected in city', *South China Morning Post*, 26 January 2020. https://www.scmp.com/news/china/society/article/3047720/chinese-premier-li-keqiang-head-coronavirus-crisis-team-outbreak

17 Agence France-Presse, 'China virus expert says earlier action would have reduced infections', France2, 27 February 2020. https://www.france24.com/en/20200227-china-virus-expert-says-earlier-action-would-have-reduced-infections

18 Shengjie Lai, Nick W. Ruktanonchai, Liangcai Zhou, Olivia Prosper, Wei Luo, Jessica R. Floyd, Amy Wesolowski, Mauricio Santillana, Chi Zhang, Xiangjun Du, Hongjie Yu, Andrew J. Tatem, 'Effect of non-pharmaceutical interventions for containing the COVID-19 outbreak in China', medRxiv, 13 March 2020. https://www.medrxiv.org/content/10.1101/2020.03.03.20029843v3.full.pdf+html

19 Abacus, 'China tightens censorship on coronavirus as authorities boost propaganda', *South China Morning Post*, 7 February 2020. https://www.scmp.com/tech/apps-social/article/3049583/china-tightens-censorship-coronavirus-authorities-boost-propaganda

20 Kenneth Tan, 'Whistleblower doctor' *Shanghaiist*, 7 February 2020.

21 Ibid.

22 *Xinhua* news agency, 'Xi Focus: Moment of truth: Xi leads war against COVID-19', 10 March 2020. http://www.xinhuanet.com/english/2020-03/10/c_138863611.htm

23 Chun Han Wong, 'China Portrays President Xi Jinping as Hero of Coronavirus fight', *Wall Street Journal*, 8 March 2020. https://www.wsj.com/articles/beijing-portrays-president-as-hero-of-coronavirus-fight-11583678054

24 Fang Fang, *Wuhan Diary*.

25   Emma Graham-Harrison and Lily Kuo, 'China's coronavirus lockdown strategy: brutal but effective', *The Guardian*, 19 March 2020. https://www.theguardian.com/world/2020/mar/19/chinas-coronavirus-lockdown-strategy-brutal-but-effective

26   Reuters, 'Under China's coronavirus lockdown, millions have nowhere to go', 14 February 2020. https://www.reuters.com/article/us-china-health-scale-idUSKBN2081DB

27   Liza Lin, 'China Marshals its Surveillance Powers Against Coronavirus', *Wall Street Journal*, 4 February 2020. https://www.wsj.com/articles/china-marshals-the-power-of-its-surveillance-state-in-fight-against-coronavirus-11580831633

28   Paul Mozur, 'China, Desperate to Stop Coronavirus, Turns Neighbor Against Neighbor', *New York Times*, 3 February 2020. https://www.nytimes.com/2020/02/03/business/china-coronavirus-wuhan-surveillance.html

29   Yingzhi Yang and Julie Zhu, 'Coronavirus brings China's surveillance state out of the shadows', Reuters, 7 February 2020. https://www.reuters.com/article/us-china-health-surveillance-idUSKBN2011HO

30   Koh Ewe, 'China is Using Drones to Bust People Not Wearing Facemasks Amid Coronavirus Outbreak', *Vice*, 6 February 2020. https://www.vice.com/en_in/article/3a8a4j/china-drones-catch-people-facemasks-coronavirus-outbreak

31   The video, *Wuhan Coronavirus*: 'Police in China smash mah-jong tables to stop villagers from gathering', posted on 4 February 2020 is available on YouTube. https://www.youtube.com/watch?v=SpEY3XhzPvM

32   This video, 'Coronavirus: Disturbing Footage Shows Residents Dragged From Home', posted on 9 February 2020, is also available via YouTube. https://www.youtube.com/watch?v=SLirQXbJrNA

33   BBC News Online, 'Coronavirus: disabled boy dies in China after father quarantined', 3 February 2020. https://www.bbc.co.uk/news/world-asia-china-51362772

34   At the time of writing this video, shot in Xiaogan, Hubei, was still available via the Facebook page of the *People's Daily*. https://www.facebook.com/PeoplesDaily/videos/547767982505060/?v=547767982505060

35   Lily Kuo, 'Coronavirus: journalist missing in Wuhan as anger towards Chinese authorities grow', *The Guardian*, 10 February 2020. https://www.theguardian.com/world/2020/feb/10/coronavirus-journalist-missing-in-wuhan-as-anger-towards-chinese-authorities-grows

36 Lily Kuo, 'Missing Wuhan citizen journalist reappears after two months', *The Guardian*, 22 April 2020. https://www.the guardian.com/world/2020/apr/22/missing-wuhan-citizen-journalist-reappears-after-two-months

37 Javier C. Hernández, 'Chinese Tycoon Who Criticized Xi's response to Coronavirus Has Vanished', *New York Times*, 14 March 2020. https://www.nytimes.com/2020/03/14/world/asia/china-ren-zhiqiang.html

38 Xu Zhiyong (trans. Geremie R. Barmé), 'Dear Chairman Xi, It's Time for You to Go', ChinaFile, 26 February 2020. https://www.chinafile.com/reporting-opinion/viewpoint/dear-chairman-xi-its-time-you-go

39 Reuters, 'With cries of "it's fake"', Wuhan citizens voice discontent', 6 March 2020. https://www.reuters.com/article/us-health-coronavirus-china-socialmedia-idUSKBN20T215

40 Fang Fang, *Wuhan Diary*.

41 Lily Kuo, '"They're chasing me": the journalist who wouldn't stay quiet on Covid-19', *The Guardian*, 1 March 2020. https://www.theguardian.com/world/2020/mar/01/li-zehuajournalist-wouldnt-stay-quiet-covid-19-coronavirus

42 Chinese Human Rights Defenders, *A Healthy Society Should Not Have Just One Voice – China Must End Crackdown on Online Speech in Response to COVID-19*, 1 April 2020. https://www.nchrd.org/2020/04/a-healthy-society-should-not-have-just-one-voice-china-must-end-crackdown-on-online-speech-in-response-to-covid-19/

43 Paul Mozur, 'Coronavirus Outrage Spurs Internet Police to Action', *New York Times*, 16 March 2020. https://www.nytimes.com/2020/03/16/business/china-coronavirus-internet-police.html

44 Lotus Ruan, Jeffrey Knockel and Masashi Crete-Nishihata, 'Censored Contagion. How Information on the Coronavirus is Managed on Chinese Social Media', Citizen Lab, 3 March 2020. https://citizenlab.ca/2020/03/censored-contagion-how-information-on-the-coronavirus-is-managed-on-chinese-social-media/

45 Christian Shepherd, 'Fang Fang's "Wuhan Diary" sparks tussle over virus narrative', *Financial Times*, 15 May 2020. https://www.ft.com/content/fc18c38d-bca8-4cd8-b542-f526259d97fd

46 Chinese Human Rights Defenders, *A Healthy Society*, 1 April 2020.

47 Lauren Frias, 'China reported no new local coronavirus cases for the first time during the outbreak', *Business Insider*, 19 March 2020. https://www.businessinsider.com/china-no-new-local-coronavirus-cases-first-time-during-outbreak-2020-3?op=1&r=US&IR=T

48   Curtis Stone, 'Two powers, two systems, and two responses in coronavirus battle', *People's Daily*, 12 March 2020. http://en. people.cn/n3/2020/0312/c90000-9667640.html

49   Steven Lee Myers, 'China Spins Tale That the U.S. Army Started the Coronavirus Epidemic', *New York Times*, 13 March 2020. https://www.nytimes.com/2020/03/13/world/asia/coronavirus-china-conspiracy-theory.html

50   Jeremy Page and Natasha Khan, 'On the Ground in Wuhan, Signs of China Stalling Probe of Coronavirus Origins', *Wall Street Journal*, 12 May 2020. https://www.wsj.com/articles/china-stalls-global-search-for-coronavirus-origins-wuhan-markets-investigation-11589300842

51   Nectar Gan, Caitlin Hu and Ivan Watson, 'Beijing tightens grip over coronavirus research amid US-China row on virus origin', CNN Online, 16 April 2020. https://edition.cnn.com/2020/04/12/asia/china-coronavirus-research-restrictions-intl-hnk/index.html

52   Jamie Smyth, 'China suspends beef imports from four Australian abattoirs', *Financial Times*, 12 May 2020. https://www.ft.com/content/0751caf5-b463-40aa-920f-6311c5a3b810

53   Editorial Board, 'The Coronavirus Inquiry. China loses at the WHO, but it could still highjack the origin investigation', *Wall Street Journal*, 19 May 2020. https://www.wsj.com/articles/the-coronavirus-inquiry-11589930551

54   Jeff Kao and Mia Sheung Li, 'How China Built a Twitter Propaganda Machine Then Let It Loose on Coronavirus', ProPublica, 26 March 2020. https://www.propublica.org/article/how-china-built-a-twitter-propaganda-machine-then-let-it-loose-on-coronavirus

55   Bruno Waterfield, 'China forces EU to tone down fake news dossier', *The Times*, 27 April 2020. https://www.thetimes.co.uk/article/china-forces-eu-to-tone-down-fake-news-dossier-zdh5fvkcf

56   Kelvin Chan, 'Twitter removes China-linked accounts spreading false news', *The Washington Post*, 12 June 2020. https://www. washingtonpost.com/business/technology/twitter-removes-china-linked-accounts-spreading-false-news/2020/06/12/b7026830-acb0-11ea-a43b-be9f6494a87d_story.html

57   See update from Google's Threat Analysis Group, https://blog. google/threat-analysis-group/tag-bulletin-q2-2020/

58   BBC News Online, 'Coronavirus: Countries reject Chinese-made equipment', 30 March 2020. https://www.bbc.co.uk/news/world-europe-52092395

59   David D. Kirkpatrick and Jane Bradley, 'U.K. Paid $20 million for New Coronavirus Tests. They Didn't Work', *New York Times*, 16

April 2020. https://www.nytimes.com/2020/04/16/world/europe/coronavirus-antibody-test-uk.html

60 Kurt M. Campbell and Rush Doshi, 'The Coronavirus Could Reshape Global Order', *Foreign Affairs*, 18 March 2020. https://www.foreignaffairs.com/articles/china/2020-03-18/coronavirus-could-reshape-global-order

61 Kathrin Hille, '"Wolf warrior" diplomats reveal China's ambitions', *Financial Times*, 12 May 2020. https://www.ft.com/content/7d500105-4349-4721-b4f5-179de6a58f08

62 Miles Johnson and Yuan Yang, 'Allegations of doctored films fuel concerns about Beijing propaganda', *Financial Times*, 3 May 2020. https://www.ft.com/content/ee8ae647-c536-4ec5-bc10-54787b3a265e

63 For the latest official Chinese tally, as well as those from other countries worldwide, see the Johns Hopkins University Covid-19 online dashboard. https://coronavirus.jhu.edu/map.html

64 Mai He, Li Li, Louis P. Dehner and Lucia Dunn, *Cremation based estimates suggest significant under- and delayed reporting of COVID-19 epidemic data in Wuhan and China*, medRxiv, 28 May 2020. https://doi.org/10.1101/2020.05.28.20116012

65 Nick Wadhams and Jennifer Jacobs, 'China Concealed Extent of Virus Outbreak, US Intelligence Says', Bloomberg News, 1 April 2020. https://www.bloomberg.com/news/articles/2020-04-01/china-concealed-extent-of-virus-outbreak-u-s-intelligence-says

66 Isaac Stone Fish and Maria Krol Sinclair, 'Leaked Chinese Virus Database Covers 230 Cities, 640,000 updates.' Foreign Policy, 12 May 2020. https://foreignpolicy.com/2020/05/12/leaked-chinese-coronavirus-database-number-cases/

67 'China's data reveal a puzzling link between covid-19 cases and political events', *The Economist*, 7 April 2020. https://www.economist.com/graphic-detail/2020/04/07/chinas-data-reveal-a-puzzling-link-between-covid-19-cases-and-political-events

68 Elaine Okanyene Nsoesie, Benjamin Rader, Yiyao L. Barnoon, Lauren Goodwin and John S. Brownstein, *Analysis of hospital traffic and search engine data in Wuhan China indicates early disease activity in the Fall of 2019 (2020)*, Harvard Medical School, June 2020. https://dash.harvard.edu/bitstream/handle/1/42669767/Satellite_Images_Baidu_COVID19_manuscript_DASH.pdf

69 BBC News Online, 'Coronavirus: Satellite traffic images may suggest virus hit Wuhan earlier', 9 June 2020. https://www.bbc.com/news/world-us-canada-52975934

70   Amy Qin, 'Coronavirus Fears in China Find a New Target: Salmon', *New York Times*, 18 June 2020. https://www.nytimes.com/2020/06/18/world/asia/coronavirus-china-salmon.html

71   Christian Shepherd, 'China detains outspoken critic of Xi Jinping', *Financial Times*, 6 July 2020. https://www.ft.com/content/5ee0502c-72e7-4590-bf25-725b564b426c?shareType=nongift

72   WHO press statement, 'WHO experts to travel to China', 7 July 2020. https://www.who.int/news-room/detail/07-07-2020-who-experts-to-travel-to-china

73   Christian Shepherd, Katrina Manson and Jamie Smyth, 'Failure by WHO team to visit Wuhan sparks concerns over virus probe', *Financial Times*, 27 August 2020. https://www.ft.com/content/f9dea077-66fb-4734-9d1d-076dc93568e1?shareType=nongift

74   George Arbuthnott, Jonathan Calvert and Philip Sherwell, 'Revealed: Seven years coronavirus trail from mine deaths to Wuhan lab', *The Sunday Times*, 5 July 2020. https://www.thetimes.co.uk/article/seven-year-covid-trail-revealed-l5vxt7jqp

75   'The pieces of the puzzle of covid-19's origin are coming to light', *The Economist*, 2 May 2020. https://www.economist.com/science-and-technology/2020/05/02the-pieces-of-the-puzzle-of-covid-19s-origin-are-coming-to-light

76   Josh Rogin, 'State Department cables warned of safety issues at Wuhan lab studying bat coronaviruses', *Washington Post*, 14 April 2020. https://www.washingtonpost.com/opinions/2020/04/14/state-department-cables-warned-safety-issues-wuhan-lab-studying-bat-coronaviruses/

77   Raymond Zhong, 'China's Virus Apps May Outlast the Outbreak, Stirring Privacy Fears', *New York Times*, 26 May 2020. https://www.nytimes.com/2020/05/26/technology/china-coronavirus-surveillance.html?referringSource=articleShare

78   Reuters, 'China berates New Zealand over support for Taiwan at WHO', 11 May 2020. https://www.reuters.com/article/us-china-taiwan-new-zealand-mofa-idUSKBN22N18E

79   Helen Davidson and Lily Kuo, 'Zoom admits cutting off activists' accounts in obedience to China', *The Guardian*, 12 June 2020. https://www.theguardian.com/world/2020/jun/12/zoom-admits-cutting-off-activists-accounts-in-obedience-to-china?CMP=Share_iOSApp_Other

80   Joyu Wang and Lucy Craymer, 'Hong Kong Teachers Fired and Afraid as China Targets Liberal Thinkers', *Wall Street Journal*, 19 July 2020. https://www.wsj.com/articles/hong-kong-teachers-fired-and-afraid-as-china-targets-liberal-thinkers-11595175839

81 Verna Yu, '"Like in the Cultural Revolution": Hong Kong educators fear being purged', *The Guardian*, 31 July 2020. https://www.theguardian.com/world/2020/aug/01/like-in-the-cultural-revolution-hong-kongs-educators-fear-being-purged?CMP=Share_iOSApp_Other

82 Nicolle Liu and Joe Leahy, 'Jimmy Lai, the testy tycoon defying Beijing', *Financial Times*, 14 August 2020. https://www.ft.com/content/398cbe8f-8b13-4537-a38e-84c8c0d75070?shareType=nongift

83 Adam Gabbatt, 'China uses Hong Kong security law against UK and US-based activisits', *The Guardian*, 1 July 2020. https://www.theguardian.com/world/2020/jul/31/china-hong-kong-security-law-american-citizen-exiles?CMP=Share_iOSApp_Other

84 Nicolle Liu and Alice Woodhouse, 'Hong Kong Covid-19 mass testing sows distrust among activists', *Financial Times*, 1 September 2020. https://www.ft.com/content/d9c6219c-4022-4f75-bc0c-73153ba6f4b5

85 Helen Davidson, 'Hong Kong arrests and Taiwan flybys: China advances its interests during Covid-19 crisis', *The Guardian*, 26 April 2020. https://www.theguardian.com/world/2020/apr/26/hong-kong-arrests-and-taiwan-flybys-chinas-advances-its-interests-during-covid-19-crisis

86 Amy Kazmin and Tom Mitchell, 'Brutal details emerge of deadly China–India border clash', *Financial Times*, 17 June 2020. https://www.ft.com/content/572ecd74-af77-400e-aa0a-6012dec260a6

87 Benjamin Parkin, 'India to curb Chinese bids for state contracts', *Financial Times*, 24 July 2020. https://www.ft.com/content/5f9de846-c210-42f7-af72-36e677ace3ad

88 Kate O'Keeffe and Aruna Viswanatha, 'Chinese Diplomats Helped Military Scholars Visiting the U.S. Evade FBI Scrutiny, U.S. says', *Wall Street Journal*, 25 August 2020. https://www.wsj.com/articles/chinese-diplomats-helped-visiting-military-scholars-in-the-u-s-evade-fbi-scrutiny-u-s-says-11598379136

89 Katrina Manson and Kadhim Shubber, 'Chinese researcher "hiding" in San Francisco consulate is arrested', *Financial Times*, 25 July 2020. https://www.ft.com/content/ceb20fea-c690-442b-b07d-5b59d2a56426?shareType=nongift

90 Dave Michaels, 'White House Seeks Crackdown on U.S.-Listed Chinese firms', *Wall Street Journal*, 6 August 2020. https://www.wsj.com/articles/trump-administration-seeks-crackdown-on-chinese-companies-with-shares-traded-in-u-s-11596748284

91 Jamil Anderlini, 'Behind the recovery, China's economy is wobbling', *Financial Times*, 16 July 2020. https://www.ft.com/content/ef2ac2d3-6389-4ac6-8608-90dbc3e68465

92 Helen Warrell and Peggy Hollinger, 'China fires warning shots to UK over "cold war" with Beijing', *Financial Times*, 30 July 2020. https://www.ft.com/content/54f822a4-78e1-40a9-aab6-0108932fa056

93 Gordon Corera, 'Coronavirus: Huawei urges UK not to make 5G U-turn after pandemic', BBC News Online, 13 April 2020. https://www.bbc.com/news/technology-52189281

94 Christina zur Nedden, 'Hong Kong ist das neue West-Berlin', *Die Welt*, 28 May 2020. https://www.welt.de/politik/ausland/article208463293/Evan-Fowler-Hongkong-ist-das-neue-West-Berlin.html

Epilogue: Rising to the China Challenge

1 'Xi congratulates Biden on election as U.S. president', Xinhua news agency, 25 November 2020. http://www.xinhuanet.com/english/2020-11/25/c_139542636.htm

2 Jun Mai and Guo Rui, 'China may be quiet on the US election, but state media is drawing attention to pockets of chaos in America', *South China Morning Post*, 6 November 2020. https://www.scmp.com/news/china/politics/article/3108663/china-may-be-quiet-us-election-state-media-drawing-attention

3 'US Blacklists More than 60 Chinese Firms, Including SMIC', *Bloomberg News*, 18 December 2020. https://www.bloomberg.com/news/articles/2020-12-18/u-s-to-blacklist-smic-and-dozens-more-china-firms-reuters-says

4 Demetri Sevastopulo, '"This is a guy who is a thug": how US elite became hawks on Xi's China', *Financial Times*, 8 October 2020. https://www.ft.com/content/75ce186e-41f7-4a9c-bff9-0f502c81e456?shareType=nongift

5 Laura Silver, Kat Devlin and Christine Huang, 'Negative Views of Both US and China abound across advanced economies amid Covid-19', *Pew Research Centre* news release, 6 October 2020. https://www.pewresearch.org/fact-tank/2020/10/06/negative-views-of-both-us-and-china-amid-covid-19/

6 Patrick Wintour and Tobi Thomas, 'China loses trust internationally over coronavirus handling', *The Guardian,* 27 October 2020. https://www.theguardian.com/world/2020/oct/27/china-loses-trust-internationally-over-coronavirus-handling?CMP=Share_iOSApp_Other

7   'Hong Kong's legislature has been stripped of a vocal opposition', *The Economist*, 14 November 2020. https://www.economist.com/china/2020/11/14/hong-kongs-legislature-has-been-stripped-of-a-vocal-opposition?frsc=dg%7Ce

8   Helen Davidson, 'Hong Kong police raid church hours after pastor said HSBC froze accounts', *The Guardian*, 8 December 2020. https://www.theguardian.com/world/2020/dec/08/hong-kong-church-pastor-says-hsbc-froze-personal-and-charity-bank-accounts?CMP=Share_iOSApp_Other

9   Denise Tsang, Natalie Wong and Clifford Wo, 'Hong Kong police freeze HSBC accounts belonging to fugitive ex-lawmaker Ted Hui's family, as sources deny it was done earlier', *South China Morning Post*, 7 December 2020. https://www.scmp.com/news/hong-kong/politics/article/3112844/hong-kong-police-move-freeze-hsbc-accounts-belonging

10 Nicolle Liu and Joe Leahy, 'Beijing wrestles for control of Hong Kong's classrooms', *Financial Times*, 7 October 2020. https://www.ft.com/content/19a1a697-17d9-405c-ba42-28998cfb707a?shareType=nongift

11 Nicolle Liu, 'Fear is the new normal for Hong Kong democrats', *Financial Times*, 17 November 2020. https://www.ft.com/content/017b46f5-ab63-480d-b71f-15a22c6b1213?shareType=nongift

12 'Yuen Long attack: Hong Kong journalist who investigated police is arrested', *BBC News online*, 3 November 2020. https://www.bbc.com/news/world-asia-54786110

13 Natalie Wong, 'Hong Kong radio broadcasters to begin playing national anthem every morning in compliance with new law', *South China Morning Post*, 7 November 2020. https://www.scmp.com/news/hong-kong/politics/article/3108905/hong-kong-radio-broadcasters-begin-playing-national-anthem

14 Yimou Lee, David Lague and Ben Blanchard, 'Special Report – China launches "grey-zone" warfare to subdue Taiwan', Reuters, 10 December 2020. https://www.reuters.com/article/hongkong-taiwan-military-idUSKBN28K1GS

15 Helen Davidson, '"Stronger together": Taiwan foreign minister urges new alliance against China', *The Guardian*, 7 December 2020. https://www.theguardian.com/world/2020/dec/07/stronger-together-taiwan-foreign-minister-urges-new-alliance-against-china

16 Reed Albergotti, 'Apple is lobbying against a bill aimed at stopping forced labour in China', *Washington Post*, 20 November

2020. https://www.washingtonpost.com/technology/2020/11/20/apple-uighur/

17   Ana Swanson, 'Nike and Coca-Cola Lobby Against Xinjiang Forced Labor Bill', *New York Times*, 29 November 2020. https://www.nytimes.com/2020/11/29/business/economy/nike-coca-cola-xinjiang-forced-labor-bill.html?referringSource=articleShare

18   'Coercive Labor in Xinjiang: Labor Transfer and the Mobilisation of Ethnic Minorities to Pick Cotton', Center for Global Policy, December 2020. https://cgpolicy.org/wp-content/uploads/2020/12/20201214-PB-China-Zenz-1-1.pdf

19   Kelsey Munro, 'Xinjiang Data Project website launch', Australian Strategic Policy Institute, 25 September 2020. https://www.aspi.org.au/news/xinjiang-data-project-website-launch

20   'China: Big Data Program Targets Xinjiang's Muslims', *Human Rights Watch*, 9 December 2020. https://www.hrw.org/news/2020/12/09/china-big-data-program-targets-xinjiangs-muslims

21   'Alibaba Uyghur recognition As A Service', IPVM, 16 December 2020. https://ipvm.com/reports/alibaba-uyghur

22   'Huawei/Megvii Uyghur Alarms', IPVM, 8 December 2020. https://ipvm.com/reports/huawei-megvii-uygur

23   'Parent-child separation in Yarkand County, Kashgar', Adrian Zenz, 13 October 2020. https://adrianzenz.medium.com/story-45d07b25bcad

24   'China's Xi says "happiness" in Xinjiang on rise, will keep teaching correct outlook', Reuters, 27 September 2020. https://uk.reuters.com/article/uk-china-xinjiang/chinas-xi-says-happiness-in-xinjiang-on-the-rise-will-keep-teaching-correct-outlook-idUKKBN26I0JN

25   Helen Davidson, 'Clues to scale of Xinjiang labour operation emerge as China defends camps', *The Guardian*, 18 September 2020. https://www.theguardian.com/world/2020/sep/18/clues-to-scale-of-xinjiang-labour-operation-emerge-as-china-defends-camps

26   Louis Charbonneau, '39 Countries at UN Express "Grave Concerns About China's abuses', Human Rights Watch, 6 October 2020. https://www.hrw.org/news/2020/10/06/39-countries-un-express-grave-concerns-about-chinas-abuses

27   Nathan Ruser, Dr James Leibold, Kelsey Munro and Tilla Hoja, 'Cultural erasure. Tracing the destruction of Uyghur and Islamic spaces in Xinjiang', Australian Strategic Policy institute, 24 September 2020. https://www.aspi.org.au/report/cultural-erasure

28   'The persecution of the Uyghurs is a crime against humanity', *The Economist*, 17 October 2020. https://www.economist.com/

leaders/2020/10/17/the-persecution-of-the-uyghurs-is-a-crime-against-humanity?frsc=dg%7Ce

29 See 'Report on Preliminary Examination Activities 2020' from the Office of the Prosecutor of te International Criminal Court, 14 December 2020. https://www.icc-cpi.int/itemsDocuments/2020-PE/2020-pe-report-eng.pdf

30 'Large Covid outbreak in China linked to Xinjiang forced labour', *The Guardian*, 29 October 2020. https://www.theguardian.com/world/2020/oct/29/large-covid-outbreak-in-china-linked-to-xinjiang-forced-labour

31 'WHO-convened Global Study of the Origins of SARS-CoV-2,' the terms of reference of the WHO investigation into Covid-19, published 5 November 2020, can be accessed via the Who websiteathttps://www.who.int/publications/m/item/who-convened-global-study-of-the-origins-of-sars-cov-2

32 Christian Shepherd, 'Chinese media steps up campaign to muddy probe into Covid origins', *Financial Times*, 26 November 2020. https://www.ft.com/content/edda14d0-145b-42e4-a1d2-4d64ab73bda1?shareType=nongift

33 Graham Allison, 'China's geopolitics are pumped up by its economic success', *Financial Times*, 4 October 2020. https://www.ft.com/content/e2902988-ca56-4d21-ab2a-b416c9006c7b?shareType=nongift

34 Helen Davidson and Lily Kuo, 'China changes school curriculum to reflect Beijing's positive Covid narrative', *The Guardian*, 3 November 2020. https://www.theguardian.com/world/2020/nov/03/china-changes-school-curriculum-to-reflect-beijings-positive-covid-narrative

35 Tom Mitchell, Sun Yun, Xinning Liu and Michael Peel, 'China and Covid-19: what went wrong in Wuhan?', *Financial Times*, 17 October 2020. https://www.ft.com/content/82574e3d-1633-48ad-8afb-71ebb3fe3dee?shareType=nongift

36 Helen Davidson, 'Wuhan: nearly 490,000 people could have had Covid, study finds', *The Guardian*, 30 December 2020. https://www.theguardian.com/world/2020/dec/30/wuhan-nearly-490000-people-could-have-had-covid-study-finds

37 Chris Buckley, 'China's "Big Cannon" Blasted Xi. Now he's been jailed for 18 years', *New York Times*, 22 September 2020. https://www.nytimes.com/2020/09/22/world/asia/china-ren-zhiqiang-tycoon.html

38 Helen Davidson, 'Citizen journalist detained over Wuhan reporting "restrained and fed by tube"', *The Guardian*, 10 December 2020. https://www.theguardian.com/world/2020/dec/10/citizen-journa

list-detained-over-wuhan-reporting-restrained-and-fed-by-tube?CMP=Share_iOSApp_Other

39   Raymond Zhong, Paul Mozur, Jeff Kao and Aaron Krolik, 'No "Negative" News: How China Censored the Coronavirus', *The New York Times*, 19 December 2020. https://www.nytimes.com/2020/12/19/technology/china-coronavirus-censorship.html?referringSource=articleShare

40   Lingling Wei, 'China's Xi Ramps Up Control of Private Sector. "We Have No Choice but to follow the Party"', *The Wall Street Journal*, 10 December 2020. https://www.wsj.com/articles/china-xi-clamp-down-private-sector-communist-party-11607612531

41   Hudson Lockett and Primrose Riordan, 'Investment banks revel in bumper fees from Chinese groups in 2020', *Financial Times*, 17 December 2020. https://www.ft.com/content/bba86de5-1da4-4b5a-bb40-6ff71c18cb7b?shareType=nongift

42   Lingling Wei, Bob Davis and Dawn Lim, 'China Has One Powerful Friend Left in the U.S.: Wall Street', *The Wall Street Journal*, 2 December 2020. https://www.wsj.com/articles/china-has-one-powerful-friend-left-in-the-u-s-wall-street-11606924454

43   Lucy Handley, 'Goldman Sachs reveals how to take advantage of the "China phenomenon" in 2021', CNBC, 16 December 2020. https://www.cnbc.com/2020/12/16/goldman-sachs-on-how-to-invest-in-china-in-2021.html

44   Mathew Campbell, Chunying Zhang, Haze Fan, David Stringer and Emma O'Brien, 'Elon Musk Loves China, and China Loves Him Back – for Now', Bloomberg Businessweek, 13 January 2021. https://www.bloomberg.com/news/features/2021-01-13/china-loves-elon-musk-and-tesla-tsla-how-long-will-that-last

45   Paul Mozur and Don Clark, 'China's Surveillance State Sucks Up Data. US Tech Is Key to Sorting It', *The New York Times*. https://www.nytimes.com/2020/11/22/technology/china-intel-nvidia-xinjiang.html

46   Aruna Viswanatha and Aaron Tilley, 'Zoom Executive in China Charged With Disrupting Tiananmen Memorials', *The Wall Street Journal*, 18 December 2020. https://www.wsj.com/articles/zoom-executive-in-china-charged-with-disrupting-tiananmen-memorials-11608326277

47   The full complaint, 'United States District Court Eastern District of New York. United States of America against Xinjiang Jin' can be accessed via the Department of Justice website at: https://www.justice.gov/opa/pr/china-based-executive-us-telecommunications-company-charged-disrupting-video-meetings

48 'Our perspective on the DOJ Complaint', Zoom blogpost, 18 December 2020. https://blog.zoom.us/our-perspective-on-the-doj-complaint/

49 Apple's full human rights policy can be accessed from the company's website at https://s2.q4cdn.com/470004039/files/doc_downloads/gov_docs/Apple-Human-Rights-Policy.pdf

50 James Titcombe, 'Apple survives shareholder revolt over free speech', *The Telegraph*, 26 February 2020. https://www.telegraph.co.uk/technology/2020/02/26/apple-survives-shareholder-revolt-free-speech/

51 Jacob Jarvis, 'Donald Trump hails Boris Johnson as "Britain Trump" as he backs him to "get the job done"', *Evening Standard*, 23 July 2019. https://www.standard.co.uk/news/world/us-president-hail-s-boris-johnson-as-britain-s-trump-as-he-welcomes-tough-and-smart-new-pm-a4196721.html

52 John Collingridge, 'Block us and Britain will suffer, warns China', *The Sunday Times*, 22 November 2020

53 Patrick Wintour, 'UK should revisit 5G ban now Trump is defeated, says Huawei', *The Guardian*, 16 November 2020. https://www.theguardian.com/technology/2020/nov/16/uk-should-revisit-5g-ban-now-trump-is-defeated-says-huawei?fbclid=IwAR1SVBKDwd0yUfsoY_zU0gwUD90XX7lm98WEA-bKYAzGwntqtL9oCK6G7jc

54 See the Huawei Cyber Security Evaluation Centre (HCSEC) oversight board annual report 2020, a report to the National Security Adviser of the UK, published in September 2020 and accessed at https://assets.publishing.service.gov.uk/government/uploads/system/uploads/attachment_data/file/923309/Huawei_Cyber_Security_Evaluation_Centre__HCSEC__Oversight_Board-_annual_report_2020.pdf

55 'Huawei ban: UK to impose early end to use of new 5G kit', *BBC News*, 30 November 2020. https://www.bbc.com/news/business-55124236

56 Jim Pickard, Daniel Thomas, Arash Massoudi and Tom Mitchell, 'UK takes aim at China with revamp of takeover rules', *Financial Times*, 11 November 2011. https://www.ft.com/content/55f848d8-92f8-4c42-9775-dd9d6c55ee91?shareType=nongift

57 Charles Parton, 'UK Relations with China. Not Cold War, But A Values War; Not Decoupling, But Some Divergence', China Research Group, 2 November 2020. https://chinaresearchgroup.org/values-war

58 'Nanjing-Cambridge University "Deepening Partnership" Develop-

ment Conference Held Successfully', Cambridge University-Nanjing Centre for Technology and Innovation press release, 30 September 2020. http://www.cam-nj.com/en/newsDetails?id=265

59 Patrick Wintour, 'Oxford moves to protect students from China's Hong Kong security law', *The Guardian*, 28 September 2020. https://www.theguardian.com/education/2020/sep/28/oxford-moves-to-protect-students-from-chinas-hong-kong-security-law

60 Louise Callaghan, 'Beijing stalks Cambridge student fighting to free jailed bookseller father', *The Sunday Times*, 8 November 2020.

61 James Kynge and Jonathan Wheatley, 'China pulls back from the world: rethinking Xi's "project of the century"', *Financial Times*, 11 December 2011. https://www.ft.com/content/d9bd8059-d05c-4e6f-968b-1672241ec1f6?shareType=nongift

62 Huang Lanlan, Lu Yameng, and Li Qiao, 'Information dilemma: China tries to balance convenience. Personal privacy', *Global Times*, 26 November 2020. https://www.globaltimes.cn/content/1208095.shtml

63 'China moves to improve social credit system', Xinhua news agency, 26 November 2020. http://www.xinhuanet.com/english/2020-11/26/c_139545355.htm

64 Jamie Smyth and Christian Shepherd, 'Canberra blasts Beijing over "repugnant" tweet after war crimes report', *Financial Times*, 30 November 2020. https://www.ft.com/content/f4c72eb2-d5a7-49b3-9d6e-eef34f640972?shareType=nongift

65 'China insists Genghis Khan exhibit not use the word "Genghis Khan"', Agence France-Press (via *The Guardian*), 14 October 2020. https://www.theguardian.com/world/2020/oct/14/china-insists-genghis-khan-exhibit-not-use-words-genghis-khan?CMP=Share_iOSApp_Other

66 Louisa Clarence-Smith, 'Tower Hamlets objects to New Chinese embassy after Uighur crackdown', *The Times*, 16 November 2020. https://www.thetimes.co.uk/article/tower-hamlets-objects-to-new-china-embassy-after-uighur-crackdown-x8h7m9dgr

67 Mike Brooke, 'Pressure on China's Royal Mint embassy plans at Tower Hill over plight of its Uighur Muslims', East London Advertiser, 30 September 2020. https://www.eastlondonadvertiser.co.uk/news/local-council/china-royal-mint-embassy-3673428

68 Aisha Payne, 'Anger as residents consulted over Chinese embassy move to Tower Hill', *Eastlondonlines* online news website, 13 November 2020. https://www.eastlondonlines.co.uk/2020/11/anger-as-residents-consulted-over-chinese-embassy-move-to-tower-hill/

Index